Gender Considerations in Online Consumption Behavior and Internet Use

Rebecca English
Queensland University of Technology, Australia

Raechel Johns
University of Canberra, Australia

A volume in the Advances in Human and Social Aspects of Technology (AHSAT) Book Series

Information Science REFERENCE
An Imprint of IGI Global

Published in the United States of America by
Information Science Reference (an imprint of IGI Global)
701 E. Chocolate Avenue
Hershey PA, USA 17033
Tel: 717-533-8845
Fax: 717-533-8661
E-mail: cust@igi-global.com
Web site: http://www.igi-global.com

Library of Congress Cataloging-in-Publication Data

Names: English, Rebecca, 1977- | Johns, Raechel, 1976- editor.
Title: Gender considerations in online consumption behavior and Internet use / Rebecca English and Raechel Johns, editors.
Description: Hershey, PA : Information Science Reference, [2016] | Includes bibliographical references and index.
Identifiers: LCCN 2015050770| ISBN 9781522500100 (hardcover) | ISBN 9781522500117 (ebook)
Subjects: LCSH: Internet and women. | Internet users. | Online social networks. | Women consumers. | Electronic commerce.
Classification: LCC HQ1178 .G44 2016 | DDC 004.67/8082--dc23 LC record available at http://lccn.loc.gov/2015050770

This book is published in the IGI Global book series Advances in Human and Social Aspects of Technology (AHSAT) (ISSN: 2328-1316; eISSN: 2328-1324)

British Cataloguing in Publication Data
A Cataloguing in Publication record for this book is available from the British Library.

All work contributed to this book is new, previously-unpublished material. The views expressed in this book are those of the authors, but not necessarily of the publisher.

For electronic access to this publication, please contact: eresources@igi-global.com.

Advances in Human and Social Aspects of Technology (AHSAT) Book Series

Ashish Dwivedi
The University of Hull, UK

ISSN: 2328-1316
EISSN: 2328-1324

Mission

In recent years, the societal impact of technology has been noted as we become increasingly more connected and are presented with more digital tools and devices. With the popularity of digital devices such as cell phones and tablets, it is crucial to consider the implications of our digital dependence and the presence of technology in our everyday lives.

The **Advances in Human and Social Aspects of Technology (AHSAT) Book Series** seeks to explore the ways in which society and human beings have been affected by technology and how the technological revolution has changed the way we conduct our lives as well as our behavior. The AHSAT book series aims to publish the most cutting-edge research on human behavior and interaction with technology and the ways in which the digital age is changing society.

Coverage

- ICTs and social change
- Activism and ICTs
- Philosophy of technology
- Human Rights and Digitization
- Technology Dependence
- Public Access to ICTs
- Cyber Bullying
- Technology and Freedom of Speech
- Gender and Technology
- Technology Adoption

IGI Global is currently accepting manuscripts for publication within this series. To submit a proposal for a volume in this series, please contact our Acquisition Editors at Acquisitions@igi-global.com or visit: http://www.igi-global.com/publish/.

The Advances in Human and Social Aspects of Technology (AHSAT) Book Series (ISSN 2328-1316) is published by IGI Global, 701 E. Chocolate Avenue, Hershey, PA 17033-1240, USA, www.igi-global.com. This series is composed of titles available for purchase individually; each title is edited to be contextually exclusive from any other title within the series. For pricing and ordering information please visit http://www.igi-global.com/book-series/advances-human-social-aspects-technology/37145. Postmaster: Send all address changes to above address.

Titles in this Series

For a list of additional titles in this series, please visit: www.igi-global.com

Analyzing Digital Discourse and Human Behavior in Modern Virtual Environments
Bobbe Gaines Baggio (American University, USA)
Information Science Reference • copyright 2016 • 320pp • H/C (ISBN: 9781466698994) • US $175.00 (our price)

Overcoming Gender Inequalities through Technology Integration
Joseph Wilson (University of Maiduguri, Nigeria) and Nuhu Diraso Gapsiso (University of Maiduguri, Nigeria)
Information Science Reference • copyright 2016 • 324pp • H/C (ISBN: 9781466697737) • US $185.00 (our price)

Cultural, Behavioral, and Social Considerations in Electronic Collaboration
Ayse Kok (Bogazici University, Turkey) and Hyunkyung Lee (Yonsei University, South Korea)
Business Science Reference • copyright 2016 • 374pp • H/C (ISBN: 9781466695566) • US $205.00 (our price)

Handbook of Research on Cultural and Economic Impacts of the Information Society
P.E. Thomas (Bharathiar University, India) M. Srihari (Bharathiar University, India) and Sandeep Kaur (Bharathiar University, India)
Information Science Reference • copyright 2015 • 618pp • H/C (ISBN: 9781466685987) • US $325.00 (our price)

Human Behavior, Psychology, and Social Interaction in the Digital Era
Anabela Mesquita (CICE – ISCAP/Polytechnic of Porto, Portugal & Algoritmi Centre, Minho University, Portugal) and Chia-Wen Tsai (Ming Chuan University, Taiwan)
Information Science Reference • copyright 2015 • 372pp • H/C (ISBN: 9781466684508) • US $200.00 (our price)

Rethinking Machine Ethics in the Age of Ubiquitous Technology
Jeffrey White (Korean Advanced Institute of Science and Technology, KAIST, South Korea) and Rick Searle (IEET, USA)
Information Science Reference • copyright 2015 • 331pp • H/C (ISBN: 9781466685925) • US $205.00 (our price)

Contemporary Approaches to Activity Theory Interdisciplinary Perspectives on Human Behavior
Thomas Hansson (Blekinge Institute of Technology, School of Management (MAM), Sweden)
Information Science Reference • copyright 2015 • 404pp • H/C (ISBN: 9781466666030) • US $195.00 (our price)

Evolving Issues Surrounding Technoethics and Society in the Digital Age
Rocci Luppicini (University of Ottawa, Canada)
Information Science Reference • copyright 2014 • 317pp • H/C (ISBN: 9781466661226) • US $215.00 (our price)

IGI GLOBAL
DISSEMINATOR OF KNOWLEDGE
www.igi-global.com

701 E. Chocolate Ave., Hershey, PA 17033
Order online at www.igi-global.com or call 717-533-8845 x100
To place a standing order for titles released in this series, contact: cust@igi-global.com
Mon-Fri 8:00 am - 5:00 pm (est) or fax 24 hours a day 717-533-8661

List of Reviewers

Amelia R. Coleman, *Queensland University of Technology, Australia*
Naomi F. Dale, *University of Canberra, Australia*
Saif Dewan, *University of Canberra, Australia*
Kristyn A. Jackson, *University of Canberra, Australia*
Anita Jetnikoff, *Queensland University of Technology, Australia*
Yowei Kang, *Kainan University, Taiwan*
Melissa Kelly, *Queensland University of Technology, Australia*
Dale MacKrell, *University of Canberra, Australia*
Valeria Noguti, *University of Technology Sydney, Australia*
Shaun Nykvist, *Queensland University of Technology, Australia*
Carlos Alberto Ochoa Ortiz Zezzatti, *Juarez City University, Mexico*
Matthew Reeves, *Queensland University of Technology, Australia*
Sonika Singh, *University of Technology Sydney, Australia*
Ariane Juliana Utomo, *The Australian National University, Australia*
David S. Waller, *University of Technology Sydney, Australia*
Kenneth C. C. Yang, *University of Texas at El Paso, USA*

Table of Contents

Section 2
Gender in Context

Detailed Table of Contents

Section 1
Background

When the Internet was first commercialized and commonly utilized, men numerically dominated Internet use. Over time, the population of Internet users has normalized and increasingly women are using the Internet at the same rate as men. This raises societal questions. Is social media conditioned to be more 'female-dominated' due to the focus on social aspects, traditionally seen as more feminine? This introductory chapter explores the technology use of women. Taking a perspective of providing a background, first, the literature related to women and technology and the dominant theoretical underpinnings is discussed. Then the authors investigate conditioning of women in careers, lifestyles and general technology use. This discussion of the academic literature is then reinforced through an analysis of industry based data, to understand how women are utilizing technology. The chapter concludes with an agenda for further research into the use of technology by women.

The consumption process of travel decision making, is influenced by a number of factors and a substantial body of decision making literature in the form of the broader 'models of consumer behaviour' has been adapted to attempt to describe this process. Existing 'foundation models' present variables such as personal characteristics and attitudes as factors that affect the vacation decision making process, but fail to discuss the extent to which gender and technology preferences influence decisions and destination choice. Economic models are based on utility theory as a decision making framework, however, they do not allow for the other consumer oriented variables. Current models (economic or otherwise) focus on individuals and their decision making process without a combined consideration of information search and technology gendered preferences and the impact they have on choosing a destination for a vacation.

This chapter investigates gender differences in motivations to use social networking sites (SNS), a subset of social media. The present research focuses on Facebook given its prominence among currently available SNS. Analysing a survey of university students in Australia, the results indicate that female consumers are more likely than male consumers to use Facebook to seek information (to research and learn new things and to discuss products and brands) and for convenience (to obtain things with little effort). Both of these reasons in turn relate positively to their degree of engagement on Facebook, where engagement is operationalized as cognitive absorption which is a state of deep involvement with an activity.

This chapter is based on a qualitative case study that researched the perceptions of nine male and female pre-service English teachers' in regards to their preparedness to mentor positive digital conduct in Social network sites (SNS). These sites enable individuals to perform public representations of identity, consumed by virtual audiences, with various degrees of perceived privacy. The chapter frames what we call "identity curation" through three theoretical lenses; of performativity, customisation and critical literacy. This chapter discusses one of the themes that emerged from the research, which is the way in which "normalised" and naturalised representations of femininity on SNS were judged more harshly than masculine representations.

The ways that blogs are used to improve the lot of the disenfranchised is an area that is increasingly gaining research traction. This chapter presents a literature review of the recent literature in to the ways that minority groups are using blogs to tell their story to a wide audience. It looks at the ways that human rights bloggers have used Web 2.0 platforms to express themselves. It then applies Foucault's (1988) work on self-expression to other groups who are also heavy users of blogs to express themselves in new ways. The chapter looks at poverty, at those who identify as LGBTIQ (lesbian, gay, bisexual, transgender, intersex and queer) and women. It suggests that there is much research that still needs to be undertaken to properly examine the role of blogs in the lives of increasing numbers of groups who are not able to express themselves in mainstream media, and to explore the ways that these blogs render mainstream media irrelevant in connected times.

Section 2
Gender in Context

This chapter investigates the positive role social media can play in education. It looks at the various formats in which the tool can be used and how it can enhance the learning experience of all students. The chapter analyses the ability for social media to act as a communication channel as well as an educational interface where every student can learn through their peers and through their educator. It also discusses the need for further research as to how this increasingly popular tool can be successfully integrated into educational environments.

Home education is on the rise in Australia. However, unlike parents who choose mainstream schooling, these parents often lack the support of a wider community to help them on their educational and parenting journey. This support is especially lacking as many people in the wider community find the choice to home education confronting. As such, these parents may feel isolated and alienated in the general population as their choice to home educate is questioned at best, and ridiculed at worst. These parents often find sanctuary online in homeschool groups on Facebook. This chapter explores the ways that Facebook Groups are used by marginalized and disenfranchised families who home educate to meet with others who are likeminded and aligned with their beliefs and philosophies. It is through these groups that parents, in relation to schooling it is especially mothers, are able to ask for advice, to vent, to explore options and find connections that may be lacking in the wider community.

As researchers seek to understand value co-creation in more detail, it is essential to explore both tangible and intangible products in more depth. This case study provides an understanding of the intangible value created with a tangible product. The Thermomix is a high-end multi-purpose cooking device and through social media, communities of users have increased the value of the device. This article argues that value can be created through the intangible offerings, even when a physical product exists.

Contemporary research indicates hegemonic masculinity negatively impacts on the recognised global male health treatment gap, spurring debate around the promotion of male health conversation. Through a case study, this chapter explores how Movember Australia, a global NPO dedicated to raising awareness

Preface

We, the editors of this book, went to high school together, and were it not for the internet, may never have reconnected. Sure enough, through the joys of Facebook, we contacted one another and remained social media friends for years prior to collaborating on our first paper. Both academic researchers, it seemed to be both relevant and enjoyable to connect. Our first co-authored paper, was, of course, about women online. Specifically we first researched mothers online, having a total of six children between us, but since then have explored a variety of topics.

In this edited collection, numerous stories are told. Some are more personal, some reveal contemporary research and some provide exciting observations about the internet and how gender plays out online. The research provided is academic research, double blind peer reviewed.

Prior to launching into the research, however, we thought we'd share our personal stories about being women online…

Figure 1.

REBECCA'S STORY

When I started using a computer, online was not something we knew of. My earliest memory of a computer was at my aunt's house. Her two boys had a Commodore 64 and I would type lines and lines of text for hours and hours, mostly because once you got to the end of the screen, it would 'reset' and all your words would be gone. It was a kind of guilt free, secret squirrel journal that was as impermanent as a teenager's feelings.

I chose typing in high school because my parents said that typing would be better than French and frankly, far more practical. In the early days, I learned on a manual typewriter, and now have the strongest little fingers you can imagine, but it soon became computer screens with Mavis Beacon Typing Tutors on it. I remember, as Raechel recounts below, being allowed to play Where in the World is Carmen Sandiego when I was in Year 6 on one of the three machines (the old Macs with the disconcertingly aged looking yellow/orange plastic and the not-quite-blue screens) that the school had bought. I will never forget the practical issues of changing 5 ¼" floppy disks whenever she went to a different country. But which country was she in?

My parents borrowed a computer off a friend who wanted us to mind it for him while he went on an overseas trip in the very late 1980s. The night we went to collect it, his daughter was practicing for a recital playing Memory from the Andrew Lloyd Webber classic, Cats on piano. It seemed bizarrely poignant at that time, and it is a memory I'll never get past. Nor will I forget unpacking our first computer, a Gateway computer in the iconic jersey cow print box. It is forever in my mind along with the tunes to Tapper and Alley Cat.

Gender has always been an interesting element of my relationship with computing technology. Whether it was my parents allowing my brother to use the computer to play Dune (over and over and over again with the "We're mining for spice"), even though it was surely my turn. Or it was the suggestion that girls don't code so just do typing Rebecca and don't try to do ICT. Or, perhaps, it was the smell of the computer labs at my university during undergraduate study. The labs were always filled in the mid-1990s with spotty boys who smelled of zit cream and unwashed shirts.

Now, it would seem that the gendered nature of technology, well, certain types of technology, has changed and shifted. Whether it's Pintrest and Instagram which, as Chapter 12 points out, has an overwhelmingly female uptake. Or, if it's the use of Facebook to connect mothers whose work is marginalized and disenfranchised as I discuss in my own chapter (Chapter 7). Similarly, Chapter 5 discusses how women are able to use blogs to overcome disadvantage. Men still feature, including Chapter 9 where particular fundraising for health campaigns are targeted at a male audience.

There are interesting ideas and stories told in these chapters. Some of them will have personal resonances outside of their importance for theorizing the relationship between gender and the uptake and use of new online technology. It will be interesting to see how the next 20 years affects the use of online technologies. I am certain that the spotty boys in the computer labs at university will still be there, but what they're looking at is open for anyone's guess.

RAECHEL'S STORY

Dad brought home the first computer I used in the early 80s. Big and clunky, I was immediately enthralled. Similarly, a friend showed me her Apple and we spent hours playing 'Where in the World is Carmen Sandiego'?

I soon got the game 'Decathlon', and I spent the late 80s using a couple of keys on the keyboard to get my little stick athlete over hurdles, or sprinting around a white running field on a black background. I couldn't have been more excited. Computers opened a fascinating world for me, a little Australian tomboy who loved nothing more than finding something new. I quickly learnt that people were scared of computers, but I found them thrilling. There was nothing I wouldn't try. An avid writer, I used to write stories on the computer – it sped up my process. We then got a Dot Matrix printer – my heart would pound with excitement as the printer buzzed and my letters dotted across the paper. I would pull off the perforated edges and smile proudly at my work. My assignments were done by creating big titles in a graphics program which I would literally cut and paste on to the document. Everyone else had fonts the same size, but I had a jumbo sized heading, albeit glued on to the page. I had always had pen pals, but suddenly I could send them typed letters, rather than handwritten letters. It was the kind of life I could never have imagined.

Surely life couldn't get much better.

Oh, but it did. In the mid 90s I had started university, studying a business degree. I majored in marketing, and we had to go to the computer labs to use the internet. I had, of course, heard all about the internet, but had never actually used the beast. During a subject, we had to find online retailers and write a report about our findings. Again, I was enthralled.

Dad to the rescue, again. He got a family internet account, with a shared email address. Because he had the internet at work, he never used the email address, and so I signed up to various sites and somehow made friends. The penpals of the 80s long forgotten and instead online friends were found, mostly male. I loved the immediacy of emailing a friend, and having them respond the next day, or, if you were lucky, the same day. Friendships were stronger through the internet because you were free to reveal yourself in a way that penpal relationships and face to face relationships did not give you.

I realized there was a space for participating online, and so I set about creating my own site, 'Beatnick Bizaare'. I had used the title from a magazine I had created for a high school assignment. I got plenty of followers, and so later registered my first domain name, www.dynamicgirl.com - the site is no longer mine, so I hold no responsibility for what you may find today!

I took photographs of my friends and sisters, and created a black and white banner, with their images. Dynamicgirl was an online 'zine' for the modern girl. It wasn't girly, though. What I particularly loved about the internet was that gender was irrelevant. Having gone to an all girls' school, I grew up feeling that there were expectations for girls, and I loved that the internet provided us with the ability to be free of any gender norms, particularly in the mid 90s, when it was mostly men online. Therefore in some ways, it was surprising that DynamicGirl had such a gender focus, but I suppose it was my way of carving out a space for like minded females.

All in all, I wanted to create online. I often wonder if I was young today, with all the Facebook games and things to read, TV shows to download, whether I'd be bothered adding to the clutter, or simply passively reading and watching what was created by others.

My first academic journal paper was written while I was studying my undergraduate degree. My lecturer asked me if I'd be willing to submit my assignment to the journal he was an editor of, and I did. The topic, of course, was about the internet and I now had an appetite for academia. During my first degree, I started working in retail marketing and I was frustrated that I couldn't get the organization to go online. By the time I'd finished my marketing degree and started working for my father's IT business, I was so passionate about the internet that I started a Masters in Internet Marketing. I soon was offered a job working for an internet company, and I was thrilled to be working in my field. I returned to the IT services field as the internet was increasingly becoming important there. Over time, however, I switched my focus to academia and became an academic, completing my PhD in an internet related marketing topic.

When I moved interstate for my current job, I started a blog, so friends and family could connect with me. Over time I gained new friends through the use of the internet, many of whom I have met face to face after years of 'chatting'. When I 'came out', I first explored information online and felt part of an LGBTIQ community through the internet, a community I found lacking otherwise. And when I became a parent, I explored information online to gain some understanding of raising children, something I'd never given a great deal of thought to.

To be honest, in some ways I miss the simple days of the internet. When the users of the internet were a small community of passionate, engaged people. The buzzing sound of the modem connecting became almost addictive to me. I craved it, and when I hear that sound, in movies or whatever, I smile a little. Ah, the anticipation. That wait for the internet to connect is something my children will never understand in the modern world. Already the internet has made me feel so old, like my parents discussing life without television or other modern conveniences.

Today, I use the internet for everything, and increasingly most people do. Perhaps the biggest development along the way has been social media and the way that we utilize social media to interact with our friends, and with businesses. As a marketer, I've watched as organisations have had to switch from carefully planned, strategic communications to 'chatting' with their customers. I've watched as customers have struggled with the use of internet enabled self-services. And, over time, the use of the internet has become 'normalised'. In other words, well educated males are not using the internet predominately – everyone is using it, from grandparents to children, males to females, professionals to students. Web spaces have adapted as the users have grown, and changed in profile. Perhaps, as a consequence, increasingly segmentation is happening, including segmentation on gender aspects. This book seeks to explore the way gender is played out online.

I've enjoyed reading the variety of chapters included in this book and I'm sure you will, too. And if anyone has a copy of the game Decathlon, please send it my way!

These stories bring us back to the context of this book and its importance in exploring what is happening now in technology and the relationship between technology and gender.

GENDER CONSIDERATIONS IN ONLINE CONSUMPTION BEHAVIOR AND INTERNET USE

This book sits in a space between notions of gender and sociological, psychological and behavioural relationship with behaviour. These ideas about gender proscribe behavioural characteristics to the identity discourses constructed by people's association with gendered notions. It also sits within a conceptual framework of consumption and purchasing choices as these choices are mediated in online spaces.

In this book, consumption is widely characterized. From women consuming messages about, and ultimately constructing themselves as, jihadi brides through radical social media messages (see Chapter One by Robyn Torok) to men's online campaigns to raise awareness of health issues (see Chapter nine by Kristyn A Jackson). It spans topics as diverse as tourism (Chapter two by Naomi F Dale), pre-service teachers (Chapter four by Melissa Kelly and Anita Jetnikoff) and health (Chapter ten by Rebecca English, Shaun Nykvist and Matthew Reeves). It deals with issues faced interculturally in Australia (see Chapter six by Matthew Reeves), the USA (see Chapter twelve by Kenneth C. C. Yang and Yowei Kang), Indonesia (see Chapter thirteen by Ariane Juliana Utomo) and Central Asia (see Chapter fourteen by Carlos Alberto Ochoa Ortiz Zezzatti).

As such, this book will be a useful tool for researchers working in diverse fields and domains. It will serve researchers on the front lines of research into any number of areas whose concern is the interaction of gender and the uptake of technology.

Chapter one, *The Online Feminine Mystique: Developing a Research Agenda for Women's Use of Social Media* by Johns, MacKrell, Dale and Dewan explores the changing nature of engagement with online spaces over time, arguing an increasing 'feminisation' of the internet due to women's take up of social media. Using a theoretical lens that can account for the conditioning of women in careers, lifestyles and general technology use, the authors then analyse industry based data to understand how women are utilizing technology.

Chapter two, *Gender and Other Factors That Influence Tourism Preferences*, examines the technological factors that interact with broad models of consumer behaviour to influence how travellers choose destinations. In this chapter, Dale argues the current models (economic or otherwise) focus on individuals and their decision making process without a combined consideration of information search and technology gendered preferences and the impact they have on choosing a destination for a vacation.

Chapter three by Noguti, Singh and Waller titled *Gender Differences in Motivations to Use Social Networking Sites* explores how social media sites are taken up by different genders. Focusing on Facebook, due to its ubiquiteness, the authors analyse data collected in a survey of Australian university students. They find female, more so than male, university students in their study are more likely to seek information on Facebook and thus, they engage positively with the site.

In chapter four, Kelly and Jetnikoff use a qualitative case study of nine male and female pre-service English teachers' in Australia. They explore their preparedness to mentor their students in schools as teachers toward positive digital conduct in Social network sites (SNS). Using theories of identity, performativity, customisation and critical literacy, the authors find the ways in which "normalised" and naturalised representations of femininity on SNS were judged more harshly than masculine representations

Coleman, in chapter five, discusses how groups use blogs to overcome disadvantage. It focuses on poverty, at those who identify as LGBTIQ (lesbian, gay, bisexual, transgender, intersex and queer) and women. The chapter, titled Blogging their way out of disadvantage, looks at the ways that human rights bloggers have used Web 2.0 platforms to express themselves. It then applies Foucault's work on self-expression to other groups who are also heavy users of blogs to express themselves in new ways.

Chapter six by Reeves examines the ways that schools can use technology to improve engagement. The chapter, Social Media: It can play a role in education, looks at the various formats in which the tool can be used and how it can enhance the learning experience of all students. The chapter analyses the ability for social media to act as a communication channel as well as and educational interface where every students can learn through their peers and through their educator. The chapter, however, does not take a purely rosy view of technology and its impact on education, exploring how cyberbullying, and schools' failure to properly implement technology, can have a negative impact on their students' experiences.

English, in chapter seven, looks at how mothers in the home education community are using Web 2.0 to create communities of practice. These parents, who are marginalised, can use Web 2.0 tools to enhance their connection with parents who are like minded, and are able to create a virtual 'school gate' for themselves. The chapter, *Techno Teacher Moms: Web 2.0 Connecting Mothers in the Home Education Community*, explores how through these groups that parents, in relation to schooling it is especially mothers, are able to ask for advice, to vent, to explore options and find connections that may be lacking in the wider community. However, as with Reeves' chapter above, the view is not entirely rosy, with the chapter exploring how policing and management occurs in these communities, and the punishments for transgressions.

In chapter eight, *Increasing Value of a Tangible Product through Intangible Attributes: Value Co-Creation and Brand Building within Online Communities – Virtual Communities and Value*, Johns explores the increasing importance of the concept of value co-creation in the marketing literature. Using the case study of the Thermomix community, and its online connections, the author argues the connection between value and virtual communities arguing that value co-creation within online communities can targeted predominately at women, especially in the case study chosen.

Chapter nine, by Jackson titled *How Movember's Online Community Influences Australia's Men's Health Debate*, explores the negative impact of hegemonic masculinity negatively on the recognised global male health treatment gap. Using the case study of the Movember Australia health campaign, a global NPO dedicated to raising awareness of and funds for male health illness, the author utilises the principles of value co-creation and applies these theories to the analysis of the online campaign to promote conversation around men's health in Australia. The author investigates Movember's facilitation of online community conversation, engagement and its utilisation of hegemonic masculinity to promote online male solidarity and resultant health conversation.

In chapter ten, Nykvist, English and Reeves explore the online anti-vaccination community. It examines the role of social media in the information search by families who are looking for an 'informed choice' by seeking out the blogs of anti-vaccination activists in that supposed search for 'truth'. This chapter investigates the other side in light of the growing adoption and reliance on social media as a source of anti-vaccine information. The authors adopt a qualitative approach to data collection, using a critical discourse analysis of online social media discourse. The findings demonstrate the valuable contribution this approach can make to public policy work in vaccination.

Torok, in chapter eleven, looks at the female role in online social media forums and how they continually change and reflect the global social and political context. The author argues these women are active online in terms of recruitment. Using two case studies focusing on the roles of women as wives and warriors and the changing dynamic between the two roles, the author argues women demonstrate a high level of gender utility and can change roles as required by the security and political context. Thus, their engagement is different from men.

In chapter twelve, Yang and Kang look at the growing importance of the Hispanic dollar, estimated to reach $1.5 trillion by 2015. Using qualitative in-depth interview data analysed using Technology Acceptance Modeling (TAM) and TAM2 as theoretical lenses, the authors argue useful data can be found. The chapter, *Exploring Female Hispanic Consumers' Adoption of Mobile Social Media in the U.S.*, contains four major themes from the analysis. These themes are 1) family and peer influence; 2) perceived functional benefits of mobile social media; 3) Latinas as a primary decision-maker to adopt; 4) cultural and sub-cultural influence.

Online Sisterhood: Women, Income Generation, and Online Social Capital in Urban Indonesia, chapter thirteen, explores the role of social networks and social capital in facilitating women's access to income in developing countries. Using the case study of Indonesia, Utomo argues Social Media Sites (SNS) can be an effective medium of trade in urbanised developing countries, in this chapter it is Indonesia. Using qualitative interviews, the author finds there is a positive role for social networks and social capital in facilitating women's access to income however, as with other chapters, the situation isn't always clear cut. The effectiveness of the link between SNS and income-generating social capital depends largely on the class, gender, and cultural specificities that shape the nature of online and offline social interactions of the group.

The book shows the multiple and competing ways that gender can be considered in relation to online consumption behaviour and internet use. As can be seen from the chapters introduced above, the concepts of behaviour and internet use are widely applied and thus, the book makes an important contribution to the field. Its bringing together of different research fields, research agendas and theoretical and methodological approaches make it a perfect introductory text to early scholars concerned with the impact of gender on consumption behaviour and internet use.

Rebecca English
Queensland University of Technology, Australia

Raechel Johns
University of Canberra, Australia

Section 1
Background

Chapter 1
The Online Feminine Mystique:
Developing a Research Agenda for Women's Use of Social Media

Raechel Johns
University of Canberra, Australia

Dale MacKrell
University of Canberra, Australia

Naomi F. Dale
University of Canberra, Australia

Saif Dewan
University of Canberra, Australia

ABSTRACT

When the Internet was first commercialized and commonly utilized, men numerically dominated Internet use (Actman, 1995 and Johns, 1997). Over time, the population of Internet users has normalized and increasingly women are using the Internet at the same rate as men. This raises societal questions. Is social media conditioned to be more 'female-dominated' due to the focus on social aspects, traditionally seen as more feminine? This introductory chapter explores the technology use of women. Taking a perspective of providing a background, first, the literature related to women and technology and the dominant theoretical underpinnings is discussed. Then the authors investigate conditioning of women in careers, lifestyles and general technology use. This discussion of the academic literature is then reinforced through an analysis of industry based data, to understand how women are utilizing technology. The chapter concludes with an agenda for further research into the use of technology by women.

DOI: 10.4018/978-1-5225-0010-0.ch001

INTRODUCTION

When the Internet was first commercialised and commonly utilised, men numerically dominated Internet use (Actman 1995; Johns 1997). Over time, the population of Internet users has normalised and increasingly women are using the Internet at the same rate as men. In fact, since social media has become commonly used, and smart phones have become de rigueur, increasingly women in developed countries are utilising technology in their careers and to manage their day-to-day interactions. This raises societal questions – have women been conditioned to believe that technology is male-oriented, and therefore not utilised it at the same rate at men? Is social media conditioned to be more 'female-dominated' due to the focus on social aspects, traditionally seen as more feminine?

This introductory chapter explores the technology use of women. Taking a perspective of providing a background, first, we explore the literature related to women and technology and the dominant theoretical underpinnings. Then we explore conditioning of women in careers, lifestyles and general technology use. This discussion of the academic literature is then reinforced through an analysis of industry based data, to understand how women are utilising technology. The chapter concludes with an agenda for further research into the use of technology by women.

REVIEW OF THE LITERATURE

Background to Women and Technology

While the number of women in Information and Communication Technology (ICT) education and workplaces in Western countries has remained stagnant or risen only modestly (Bandias & Warne 2009; Warne, Bandias & Fuller 2011; Ridley & Young 2012; Fisher, Lang & Craig 2013), women are entering social media space at greater numbers than ever before (Clifford 2014). For the purposes of this paper, we will define social media as a way to transmit or share information to a broad audience while social networking is an act of engagement where groups of people with common interests build relationships through community (Hartshorn 2010). Social media includes social networking sites (SNS). This paper explores issues associated with the gender and social media phenomenon. Johns and English (2014) and Gurak (1999) have identified that research in this domain is either sparse or outdated. This chapter seeks to provide answers by first reviewing the relevant literature, discussing gender and technology theories which inform research, before continuing the discussion into the marketing and tourism aspects of the research.

Eileen Trauth, a renowned Information Systems (IS) theorist, stressed in the editorial of the special issue on gender in the Information Systems Journal in 2012, that without appropriate theoretical grounding, findings are ad hoc at best and lack a contribution to the existing knowledge base. Three approaches dominate IS research to theorise the manner in which women and men use computers. One view, proposed in early gender studies is the essentialist argument which recognises that inherent or natural or biological differences determine reality. Researchers such as Turkle (1984), Spender (1995) and Venkatesh and Morris (2000) described the innate cognitive differences between female and male interactions with technology. Turkle (1984) used the core terms of 'hard' and 'soft' to identify this gendered dichotomy. 'Hard mastery', or the need to control the computer, is associated with the masculine and the correct way to use computers. By contrast, 'soft mastery', or a communicative and interactive style, is identified with the feminine or inferior style of computing use.

Connell (1987 pp.66-67) argued that the doctrine of natural difference is fundamentally mistaken:

In our culture the reproductive dichotomy is assumed to be the absolute basis of gender and sexuality in everyday life ... what I will challenge is the assumption that the biological make-up of our bodies is the 'basis', 'foundation', 'framework', 'essence' or 'mould' of the social relations of gender.

Essentialist theory, often associated with quantitative research and a positivist epistemology, has been criticised by feminist researchers as being simplistic (Adya, 2008) and deterministic (Howcroft & Truth 2008) since it may fail to capture the subtleties of gender behaviour. Nevertheless, quantitative tools have been ably adapted in more recent research for effective and nuanced gender studies (Trauth 2012).

A second perspective is based on an understanding of gender and technology as socially constructed (Wajcman 1991; Trauth, Nielsen & von Hellens 2000). Social constructivism is a sociological theory developed by Berger and Luckmann (1966) where reality is based on human knowledge. Most studies in gender and technology have used social constructivism, and are usually associated with qualitative research and an interpretivist epistemology. Until recently, many public domains were, and some still are, dominated numerically by men. The knowledge constructed reflects the male view of reality since men's experiences are generalised as the norm. Thus, the distinct character of women's experience is less visible and is both inadequately recognised and inappropriately valued (Wajcman 1991).

Along with the social construction of gender is the concept of the social shaping of technology (Cockburn 1992). The social shaping approach refers to the gendering of technologies in a variety of contexts (Harding 1986; Wajcman 2000). For example, an aeroplane was once considered a man's domain until women learnt to fly. A growing body of feminist literature has examined the gendering of technologies in a variety of contexts (Harding 1986; Wajcman 2000). Webster (1993, p.42) predicted that "changes in technology are socially shaped and socially shaping and, as a result of their shifting social contexts, are continually evolving and being redesigned". In essence, technology and gender relations affect and shape each other (Cockburn & Fürst-Dilic 1994; Webster 1996).

A third perspective is that of individual differences theory of gender and IT (IDTGIT) brought to prominence by Trauth (2002). Initially, Trauth (2002) rejected the essentialist view and drew on cultural and environmental forces of social construction theory to recognise that individual differences in combination with socio-cultural influences shape the involvement of women with technology (Ridley and Young 2012). In its more recent form, IDTGIT represents the middle ground between the essentialist argument and the social constructivist perspective with individual gender differences on a continuum (Trauth 2006). In other words, the proposed theory enables an investigation of "the individual variations across genders as a result of the combination of personal characteristics and environmental influences ... with the focus on differences *within* rather than *between* genders" (Trauth, 2006, p.1156). IDTGIT theory is recent, emergent and a very promising theoretical lens to inform gender and technology studies.

With millions of users worldwide, many studies have enquired into what type of people rely on the Internet in their interactions with others. Zheng, et al (2006) explored gender differences in the use of the Internet. These researchers noted that, with similar professional backgrounds and levels of computer proficiency, women use computers as effectively as men. They found that women used the Internet mainly for work-related activities and rarely played games, unlike their male counterparts. Studies by Ross, Orr, Sisic, Arseneault, Simmering and Orr (2009) established three main personality traits that are central to social media use: extraversion, neuroticism, and openness to experience. A further study by Correa, Hinsley and de Zúñiga (2009) revealed that, while extraversion and openness to experiences were positively related to social media use, emotional stability was a negative predictor. Controlling for socio-demographics and life satisfaction, these findings differed by gender and age. While extraverted men and women were both likely to be more frequent users of social media tools, only men with greater degrees of emotional instability were more regular users.

With regards to online chatting, Armentor-Cota (2006) established that chat forums are simulated hangouts and not divorced from real life. They are places and spaces very much connected to off-line societal structures, especially when it comes to gender, race and ethnicity. In a virtual community context, differences exist between the way both men and women communicate, regardless of the membership base of the site (Gefen & Ridings, 2005). A British study by Pedersen and Macafee (2007) found that more women than men use blogging as an outlet for creative work, whether as a hobby or as a livelihood. However, women bloggers generally have a lower profile than men bloggers: with more personal content and orientation towards the social aspects of blogging as opposed to a male emphasis on information; lesser technical sophistication; and a greater preference for anonymity. These results indicated that gender differences found in earlier, mainly U.S. studies are replicated in the British context. The studies described above support the essentialist argument that there are differences in ways that men and women use the Internet. But is that too simplistic an approach to the issue? Should we consider that Internet use is a socially constructed phenomenon or that it is somewhere in-between as the IDTGIT theory proposes?

Women and Conditioning: The Feminine Mystique

The 1963 book "The Feminine Mystique" (Fridan 1963) posited that women's magazines were developed primarily by men and put forward articles about the needs and direction of women. While this has changed in the magazine industry, the increased use of the Internet has altered the communication needs of women. What has really changed? Do men still determine women's technological use? Is there still a feminine mystique online, or have the high rates of female bloggers and users of social media meant that this is less important? It is important to understand society's expectations of women to understand how technology aligns.

Women have long experienced 'expectations' in their lifestyles and work. In the past, working women were seen to be 'negligent' in their care of their children (Domenico & Jones 2007). While this has now evolved with increasing numbers of women in the workplace, there are still expectations of women in terms of careers, mothering and general interests. The glass ceiling is still debated and discussed in the literature (Ezzedeen, Budworth & Baker 2015) with an understanding of how female careers may differ from that of males in careers (Johns & McNamara 2014). In both STEM occupations and academia, there is a discussion about the expectations of women and the challenges faced by women in these fields (Hirshfield 2014). Generally, there is an understanding that career expectations of women differ from that of men, however, there may be some self-selection impacting on this. For example, Sheryl Sandberg's recent book 'Lean In' suggests that many young women take careers that can be flexible, can work around future potential children and should instead plan a career that can offer progression, because through that progression, greater flexibility arises, often as a consequence of increased use of technology. Increased use of technology, therefore, has resulted in greater career opportunities and greater connections.

At a Women and Technology Symposium hosted at the University of Canberra, recently, the message was clear: technology is helping women juggle demands, enhance their lives, and develop their careers and businesses. In countries where greater numbers of women work in technology than men, the message is that technology is for the people. There is no gender association related to technology. When the message is that technology is male-dominated, or social media is female-dominated, it fosters expectations and these expectations result in behavioural outcomes. The solution that many researchers put forward is to encourage more women into STEM careers, by providing scholarships and news stories about how statistically important it is to enter these fields. Although mentoring can help support women in technology (Orser, Riding & Stanley 2012), it is important to provide more publicly accessible role models so that potential employees and students can have access to these role models, and so that careers in technology are more accepted. Female bloggers have made it normal for women to blog, and female users of social media and other communicative technologies has resulted in this technology increasingly being utilised, but more role models are needed for coding, development, gaming and other 'techie' work. It is important that the message is not "technology is male-dominated and you're a geek or different or have a male brain if you're female and using it."

The message needs to normalise the use of technology by women. This will increase numbers of women working in technology which is important given the number of women using technology. If males are developing the technology utilised frequently by women, there may be a disconnect since the design and development is focused towards men's usage. Analysis of the literature indicates ways to normalise technology use by women, and ultimately technology work. Women gamers, for example, are a minority, and yet play an important role in societal understanding of the roles of women. Studies have shown that female gamers can result in a higher uptake of ICT related careers for women (Behnke 2012).

Despite the importance of the message that 'technology is for everyone', there are some gender differences. Generally women are more emotive than men (Skolnick, Bascom & Wilson 2013), therefore it is not surprising that it has been previously found that women tend to use technology to give and receive social support (Gefen & Ridings 2005; Fan & Miao 2012). While men have been found to use social networking to expand their social connections, women tend to use it to maintain existing social connections (Muscanell & Guadagno 2012). Women demonstrate more emotion when purchasing a product, and therefore there are variations in how women and men utilise word of mouth – women, for example, are more likely to pay attention to credible e-word of mouth than male customers are (Fan & Miao 2012).

Rural women are utilising technology three times more than men (Hay & Pearce 2014) and these findings appear to be matched in urban settings, also. Particularly when utilising communication based technology, women's use is higher than that of men (Kimbrough, Guadagno, Muscanell & Dill 2013) and similarly, use of 'gadgets' by women is often higher than that of men (Cook 2014). To answer the question "what do women want?" one first has to consider "which women?" (Cook 2014) because women have diverse needs. Generally speaking, however, technology has assisted women juggle the demands of work and family (Cook, 2014; Johns & English 2014), improve and simplify their lives (Cook 2014) and build and strengthen their relationships (Cook 2014; Johns & English 2014).

DATA: TECHNOLOGY USAGE BY WOMEN

Changes in Gender Differences in Internet Use ...Or Are We There, Yet?

As mentioned previously, although the Internet frequently has been characterized as male-dominant, recent research indicates the gender gap is closing. In the year 2000, USA Today published an article stating that the number of women on the web in the U.S. had surpassed the number of men. Sites with the highest female proportions in their audiences included women and teen magazine sites, health sites and apparel and baby goods retailer sites. Men were primarily engaged in downloading software, experimenting with new technology and using it as a form of entertainment. Since then, the global Internet landscape has changed dramatically and men and women adopt these technologies at different rates and for different reasons (Abraham, Mörn & Vollman 2010).

Research as relatively recent as the year 2000 indicates there are numerous gender differences in preferences for specific Internet applications (Weiser 2000). Despite these differences, there is a lack of consideration for these differences in website design. Explorations into this issue for e-commerce website design as recently as 2013 flag this issue as vital for encouraging the viewer to "stay" and interact, however we do not see businesses or web designers taking this into consideration for their various markets. The Internet is a vital tool for education, business, government and entertainment. A more precise understanding of the characteristics of the Internet user population is crucial for e-commerce success (Weiser 2000).

The increased presence of women on the Internet has made gender relevant for e-business. Applications that can be highly personalised and interactive with tailored messages to reflect prior interactions and the nature of the relationship may foster greater female participation because they conform to the 'rules' that have been shown to contribute to sustaining women's same-sex friendships, namely talk, intimacy and emotional expression (Weiser 2000).

In comparing empirical research through time around this issue we can investigate trends and changes, or new insights into this matter. Weiser (2000) created a 21 item measure called the Internet Attitudes Survey with 19 statements assessing specific applications of Internet use measured on a 9 point Likert scale to characterise Internet use by both genders. This was distributed in 1999 to 506 introductory psychology students by paper survey, and online to 684 respondents. Main effects for gender emerged on 12 of the 19 items. Females reported greater agreement in using the Internet for obtaining course information, chatting online, seeking help with education, communicating via email and research. Males reported greater use of the Internet for shopping, listening to audio broadcasts, creating and working on web pages, searching for romance, searching for hard to find items, pursuing sexual relationships, viewing pornography and participating in online games. Interestingly, when looking at the respondent groups separately, males and females in the online survey group sample differed less substantially (or at all) in their agreement ratings for many items indicating patterns converged as a function of experience. In summary, this 1999 study found that males used the Internet primarily for leisure and entertainment and females used it chiefly for interpersonal communication and academic or educational assistance.

Five years later, Cyr and Bonanni (2005) investigated gender and website design in e-business finding significant differences in perceptions of website design and website satisfaction between the genders. It is expected that the design of the website would impact on user preferences which may lead to different reactions, however the impact of gender in relation to website design had only previously been considered in one investigation by Simon in 2001. Cyr and Bonanni (2005) investigated effective website design for user experience considering transaction security, information design, navigation design, visual design, website trust, website satisfaction and e-loyalty. 76 undergraduate students participated in a hypothetical online purchasing experience followed by an online questionnaire. It was found that website design is an important differentiator for how men or women perceive an online shopping experience, with five of the eleven design items presenting significant differences. Women were significantly less satisfied than men with the navigation of the site and did not perceive the site to be as well organized. In the area of visual design, the most significant differences between the genders occurred in the degree of interaction with the site, and whether or not animations were perceived as meaningful. These differences in design preferences for men and women indicate that this area offers opportunities to expand understanding as to what is gender-relevant when browsing or shopping online.

Add another five years and a report by Abraham, Mörn and Vollman (2010) for comScore summarising 'how women are shaping the Internet' concludes women are driving some of the most mainstream aspects of the Internet experience today with the main barrier being Internet connectivity. Based on a global panel of 2 million Internet users they found women are still slightly in the minority, with differences most stark in developing countries. Once online, women are more connected than men. Communication and Social Networking categories are key drivers of web usage for both genders, but they occupy a larger proportion of time for women. With regard to search activity, women have different preferences to online searching. For example they exhibit a preference for "Bing" in a way that men don't.

The most recent studies which we can compare to the above are from 2013. A comparative study of gender differences in Internet usage, again among college students, (Thanuskodi 2013) investigated knowledge and experience, purpose and email frequency. Data was collected from 340 college students during academic sessions by personally administered questionnaire. Results are a little hard to follow, however there is an indication that there is a significant difference between male and female respondents in location of Internet use, use of search engines, purpose of Internet use and category of web sources (e-books, blogs, databases and so on). This research also found significant differences between male and female respondents with respect to barriers to Internet access.

Finally, in comparison, an article revealing gender preferences in e-commerce website design by Mahzari and Ahmadzadeh (2013), indicates the aesthetic design of a website has the same importance as its content, if not more, in order for users to stay and interact. Their research investigated user preferences in terms of font, shape, colour, voice and language in website design. Previously mentioned statistics are raised that whilst 50% of users of the Web are female, the Web is still a male oriented environment with 74% of UK university websites designed by male teams (Harden, 2005). The experiment had a small group of participants (7 males and 9 females) grouped according to experiences with purchasing online. This experiment relied on participants to express a desired design on a paper medium but does have some merit in what consumer would visualise as an ideal site. Differences were noted in colour preference, language (formal versus informal), and use of voice on the site.

Although engagement and use of the Internet has 'leveled' over time between the genders, and even as we progress, there is evidence that preferences and utility are not homogenous for users. These differences in gender preferences and usage are of considerable importance to e-commerce designers and managers as we move into the 21st Century in order to guarantee customer engagement and satisfaction.

A RESEARCH AGENDA: FURTHER RESEARCH

This discussion has uncovered a number of considerations for further research. Researchers could explore the following research questions:

- How can the use of technology be normalised, so women are not encouraged to enter the field as part of a minority, but instead as a career?
- How do the high rates of females in communicative technologies such as blogging and social media generally influence the perceptions of women in technology?
- How can female roles models demonstrate technology use without appearing like there is an attempt to get more females using technology?
- Is there a greater relationship-orientation by women than there is by men, or is this more related to personality traits, such as introversion and extroversion?
- Does it matter? Are there differences between sites developed by males and used by females to sites developed and used by females?
- Design of technology interfaces for different gender preferences – it would be useful to have a greater understanding of how different technology interfaces may be utilised in regard to gender differences. Perhaps segmentation could be done on other bases instead of simply focusing on gender, however it would be useful to explore gender differences, particularly in regard to the increased use of social media.

CONCLUSION

The gender bias apparent in relation to women and technology (Verbick 2001) is shifting focus now that women are increasingly using social media. However the concern with the social media shift is that this will create more of a divide – social media for the women and tech for the men.

This chapter has provided an overview to understand the use of technology by women. It is apparent that over the past two decades there have been considerable shifts in how technology is utilised by women. This arises at a time that technology shifts have also occurred, regardless of gender differences. Women are increasingly utilising technology to manage social networks, and therefore the use of social media and other technology-based communication tools have been readily accepted by women. Traditionally, however, careers in ICT have not been the domain of women. An understanding of this is imperative or there may be an 'online feminine mystique', where sites are developed by men, but predominately utilised by women. This book seeks to explore gender and the Internet to work toward bridging this gap.

REFERENCES

Abraham, L.B., Mörn, M.P., & Vollman, A. (2010, June). Women on the Web: How Women are Shaping the Internet. *comScore Inc.*

Actman, H. (1995). Net Results. *Sporting Goods Business*, *28*(6), 36–38.

Adya, M. P. (2008). Women at work: Differences in IT career experiences and perceptions between South Asian and American women. *Human Resource Management*, *47*(3), 601–635. doi:10.1002/hrm.20234

Armentor-Cota, J. (2006). In E. Trauth (Ed.), *Gender and Chat Forums. Encyclopedia of Gender and Information Technology* (pp. 361–364). Hershey, PA, USA: IGI Global. doi:10.4018/978-1-59140-815-4.ch056

Bandias, S., & Warne, L. 2009. Women in ICT – Retain and Sustain: An overview of the ACS-W Survey. *Proceedings of the Australasian Conference in Information Systems (ACIS).*

Behnke, K. 2012, Ladies of Warcraft: changing perceptions of women and technology through productive play. *Proceedings of the International Conference on the Foundations of Digital Games* (pp. 288 – 289).

Berger, P., & Luckmann, T. (1966). *The Social Construction of Reality*. New York: Doubleday.

Clifford, C. (2014). Women dominate every social media network – except one (Infographic). Retrieved from http://www.entrepreneur.com/article/231970

Cockburn, C. (1992). In R. Silverstone & E. Hirsch (Eds.), *The circuit of technology: Gender, identity and power. Consuming Technologies* (pp. 33–47). London: Routledge.

Connell, R. W. (1987). *Gender and Power: Society, the Person and Sexual Politics*. Stanford, CA: Stanford University Press.

Cook, S. (2012). Women Lead in Adopting New Technologies. *Women in Higher Education*, *21*(2), 24–25. doi:10.1002/whe.10296

Correa, T., Hinsley, A., & de Zúñiga, H. (2010, March). Who interacts on the Web?: The intersection of users' personality and social media use. *Computers in Human Behavior*, *26*(2), 247–253. doi:10.1016/j.chb.2009.09.003

Cyr, D., & Bonanni, C. (2005). Gender and website design in e-business. *International Journal of Electronic Business*, *3*(6), 565–582. doi:10.1504/IJEB.2005.008536

Domenico, D., & Johes, K. (2007). Career Aspirations of Women in the 20th Century. *Journal of Career and Technical Education*, *22*(2).

Ezzedeen, S., Budworth, M., & Baker, S. (2015). The Glass Ceiling and Executive Careers: Still an issue for pre-career women. *Journal of Career Development*, January 7, 1–15.

Fan, Y., & Miao, Y. (2012). Effect of Electronic word-of-mouth on consumer purchase intention: The perspective of gender differences. *International Journal of Electronic Business Management, 10*(3), 175–181.

Fisher, J., Lang, C., & Craig, A. (2013). Women in the IT Workplace: Learnings for Managers. *Proceedings of the European Conference on Information Systems (ECIS)*, Utrecht, NL.

Fountain, J. (2000). Constructing the information society: Women, information technology and design. *Technology in Society*, *22*(1), 45–62. doi:10.1016/S0160-791X(99)00036-6

Fridan, B. (1963). *The Feminine Mystique* (Contemporary Introduction). New York: WW Norton.

Gefen, D., & Ridings, C. (2005). If you spoke as she does, Sir, instead of the way you do: a sociolinguistics perspective of gender differences in virtual communities. *The database for advances in information systems*, 36(2).

Harden, A. (2005, August 2). *Key website research highlights gender bias*. University of Glamorgan, UK.

Harding, S. (1986). *The Science Question in Feminism*. Ithaca, USA: Cornell University Press.

Hartshorn, S. (2010). Five Differences between Social Media and Social Networking. *Social Media Today*. Retrieved from http://www.socialmediatoday.com/content/5-differences-between-social-media-and-social-networking

Hay, R., & Pearce, P. (2014). Technology adoption by rural women in Queensland, Australia: Women driving technology from the homestead for the paddock. *Journal of Rural Studies*, *36*, 318–327. doi:10.1016/j.jrurstud.2014.10.002

Hirshfield, L. (2014). 'She's not good with crying': The effect of gender expectations on graduate students' assessments of their principal investigators. *Gender and Education*, *26*(6), 601–617. doi:10.1080/09540253.2014.940036

Howcroft, D., & Trauth, E. M. (2008). The implications of a critical agenda in gender and IS research. *Information Systems Journal* [Special issue: exploring the critical agenda in IS research.], *18*(2), 185–202. doi:10.1111/j.1365-2575.2008.00294.x

Johns, R. (1997). Sports Promotion and the Internet. *The Cyber Journal of Sports Marketing*. Retrieved from www.ausport.gov.au

Johns, R., & English, R. (2014). Mothers influencing mothers: The use of virtual discussion boards and their influence on consumption. *International Journal of Web Based Communities*, *10*(3), 319–338. doi:10.1504/IJWBC.2014.062945

Johns, R., & McNamara, J. (2014). Career development in higher education through group mentoring: A case study of desirable attributes and perceptions of a current programme. *Australian Journal of Career Development*, *23*(2), 79–87. doi:10.1177/1038416214528883

Kimbrough, A., Guadagno, R. E., Muscanell, N. L., & Dill, J. (2013). Gender differences in technology use: Women connect more than men. *Computers in Human Behavior*, *29*(3), 896–900. doi:10.1016/j.chb.2012.12.005

Mackrell, D., & Boyle, M. (2010). Not so 'invisible': A Qualitative Case Study Exploring Gender Relations and Farm Management Software. *Australasian Journal of Information Systems*, *16*(2), 2. doi:10.3127/ajis.v16i2.578

Mahzari, A., & Ahmadzadeh, M. A. (2013). Finding Gender Preferences in E-Commerce Website Design by an Experimental Approach. *International Journal of Applied Information Systems*, *5*(2), 35–40.

Muscanell, N., & Guadagno, R. (2012). Make new friends or keep the old: Gender and personality differences in social networking use. *Computers in Human Behavior*, *28*(1), 107–112. doi:10.1016/j.chb.2011.08.016

Orser, B., Riding, A., & Stanley, J. (2012). Perceived career challenges and response strategies of women in the advanced technology sector. *Entrepreneurship and Regional Development*, *24*(1-2), 73–93. doi:10.1080/08985626.2012.637355

Pedersen, S., & Macafee, C. (2007). Gender Differences in British Blogging. *Journal of Computer-Mediated Communication*, *12*(4), 1472–1492. doi:10.1111/j.1083-6101.2007.00382.x

Ridley, G., & Young, J. (2012). Theoretical approaches to gender and IT: Examining some Australian evidence. *Information Systems Journal*, *22*(5), 355–373. doi:10.1111/j.1365-2575.2012.00413.x

Ross, C., Orr, E., Sisic, M., Arseneault, J., Simmering, M., & Orr, R.R. (2009, March). R. Personality and motivations associated with Facebook use. *Computers in Human Behavior*, *25*(2), 578–586. doi:10.1016/j.chb.2008.12.024

Simon, S. J. (2001). The impact of culture and gender on web sites: An empirical study. *The Data Base for Advances in Information Systems*, *32*(1), 18–37. doi:10.1145/506740.506744

Skolnick, A., Bascom, K., & Wilson, D. (2013). Gender role expectations of disgust: Men are low and women are high. *Sex Roles*, *69*(1-2), 72–88. doi:10.1007/s11199-013-0279-y

Spender, D. (1995). *Nattering on the Net: Women, Power and Cyberspace*. North Melbourne, Vic: Spinifex.

Stewart, J. (2004). Gender as a Factor in the Uptake and Use of ICTs on Family Farms in Southern Queensland Australia. *Gender, Technology and Development*, *8*(1), 97–117. doi:10.1177/097185240400800106

Thanuskodi, S. (2013). Gender Differences in Internet Usage among College Students: A Comparative Study. *Library Philosophy and Practice* (e-journal).

Trauth, E.M. (2006). *Theorising Gender and Information Technology Research. In* E. Trauth (Ed.), *Encyclopedia of Gender and Information Technology* Hershey, PA, USA: Idea Group Inc. doi:10.4018/978-1-59140-815-4

Trauth, E. M., Nielsen, S., & von Hellens, L. (2000). Explaining the IT Gender Gap: Australian Stories. *Proceedings of the 11th Australasian Conference on Information Systems (ACIS)*, Brisbane Qld.

Turkle, S. (1984). *The Second Self: Computers and the Human Spirit*. New York: Simon and Schuster.

Venkatesh, V., & Morris, M. G. (2000). Why don't men ever stop to ask for directions? Gender, social influence and their role in technology acceptance and usage behaviour. *MIS Quarterly*, *24*(1), 115–135. doi:10.2307/3250981

Verbick, T. (2001). *Women*. Technology and Gender Bias, Consortium for Computing in Small Colleges.

Wajcman, J. (1991). *Feminism Confronts Technology*. Cambridge, UK: Polity Press.

Warne, L., Bandias, S., & Fuller, D. (2011). The Employment Experiences of Women in the Australian Information Communication Technology Industry. *Journal of Economic and Social Policy*, 14(1-2).

Webster, J. (1993). Women's skills and word processors: Gender issues in the development of the automated office. In B. Probert & B. W. Wilson (Eds.), *Pink Collar Blues: Work, Gender and Technology* (pp. 41–59). Melbourne, Vic: Melbourne University Press.

Weiser, E.B. (2000). Gender Differences in Internet Use Patterns and Internet Application Preferences: A Two-Sample Comparison. *Cyberpsychology & Behavior*, *3*(2), 167–178. doi:10.1089/109493100316012

Zheng, K., Akhilesh, B., Daponte, B., & Engberg, J. (2006). In E. Trauth (Ed.), *Gender Differences in Internet Usage and Task Preferences. In* E. Trauth (Ed.), *Encyclopedia of Gender and Information Technology* (pp. 557–563). Hershey, PA, USA: Idea Group Inc. doi:10.4018/978-1-59140-815-4.ch086

Chapter 2
Gender and Other Factors That Influence Tourism Preferences

Naomi F. Dale
University of Canberra, Australia

ABSTRACT

The consumption process of travel decision making, is influenced by a number of factors and a substantial body of decision making literature in the form of the broader 'models of consumer behaviour' has been adapted to attempt to describe this process. Existing 'foundation models' present variables such as personal characteristics and attitudes as factors that affect the vacation decision making process, but fail to discuss the extent to which gender and technology preferences influence decisions and destination choice. Economic models are based on utility theory as a decision making framework, however, they do not allow for the other consumer oriented variables. Current models (economic or otherwise) focus on individuals and their decision making process without a combined consideration of information search and technology gendered preferences and the impact they have on choosing a destination for a vacation.

DOI: 10.4018/978-1-5225-0010-0.ch002

GENDER, TECHNOLOGY AND TOURISM BUYING BEHAVIOUR

Models of buying behaviour have been developed since the 1940s in order to understand customers and potential customers through describing and predicting consumer behaviour. The comprehensive 'multivariable' models produced, best capture the dynamics of consumer decision making as consumer's motivations are complex and satisfaction is sought at deeper levels than purely economic (Howard, 1963). Models are a particularly important subcategory of conceptual schemes since visually-portrayed links between variables tend to have considerable power as a mechanism for the communication of ideas (Blalock, 1969).

The major theories developed into 'grand models' of consumer behaviour were those of Nicosia (1966), Engel, Kollat and Blackwell (1968, and with Miniard, 1990) and Howard and Sheth (1969, 1963), these theories have been subsequently utilised or transformed by authors interested in tourism choice (Gilbert, 1991; Engel, Kollat & Blackwell, 1968; Engel, Blackwell & Miniard, 1990).

Understanding how technology impacts consumer behaviour (and tourism choices) can aid as a foundation for all businesses to identify and, importantly, create effective marketing communication strategies. Pre-trip travel planning, including consumer information search, can be considered a fundamental component of the trip experience in that a traveler often needs to obtain a substantial amount of information in order to develop a travel plan. As such, information available to individual travelers has significant impact on various aspects of the traveler's decision making, especially when choosing a destination to visit (Xianga, Magninia & Fesenmaier, 2015).

Travellers' use of the Internet and other technologies provides great opportunities for businesses to offer various kinds of services targeted to particular markets. Nearly every tourism organisation had developed a website by the early 2000s, and many had gone from a simple "electronic brochure" to a highly interactive system that supports reservations, search, and virtual tours; importantly, a website has become the primary (and in many circumstances, the only) source of contact with potential visitors (Zach, Gretzel, & Xiang 2010). There is an emerging breed of travelers who engage through social media, use of mobile devices, and shop for their travel needs through multiple both online and offline channels. The development of information technology will continue to shape the traveler population and sustained success in the online travel world can only be achieved by understanding and leveraging these emerging areas (Xianga, Magninia & Fesenmaier, 2015). Most importantly, businesses must recognise differences in preferences in both internet use and destination attributes for travel planning among different demographic groups.

Kim, Lehto and Morrison (2007) have contributed to the relative dearth in literature on gender differences during this decision-making process in terms of attitudes toward Web travel information sources and information search behaviour. Their research revealed that men were likely to have more vacation trips and nights away from home than their female counterparts and significantly more business trips. Primary decisions for trips were made by women (63%), significantly higher than their male counterparts. Females spent more time on the Internet per week and had stronger positive attitudes toward both on/off-line information sources. In terms of online travel channels, females attached more value to general and official destination websites (Kim, Lehto and Morrison, 2007). There are significant differences between females and males in terms of attitudes toward travel Website functionality and scope as well as actual online information search behaviour. While most Websites may be gender-neutrally designed both in terms of functionality and content, women may actually be likely to use them more than men do, since men in general do not resort to external information as much (Kim, Lehto & Morrison, 2007).

These differences in preference by gender have been investigated previously in a tourism context, and yet hasn't appeared on any of the travel decision making models. Ryan, Henley and Soutar (1998) considered implications for marketers and gender differences for tourism destination choice, finding males and females apply different criteria to make tourism destination choices. Importantly for destination marketers, research reveals that significant gender differences exist about the perceived importance of destination attributes and travel values when potential tourists consider destination choices (Meng & Uysal, 2008) as was found in the case study presented in this chapter.

Recently, there has been a call to investigate the important interaction between technology and gender and associated historical changes. Zhang and Liu (2015) propose gender is in fact a factor in technology shaping and that the development of technology was constructed to some extent by gender discourse. This is further explored by Wu, Fan and Mattila (2015), building on the theoretical frameworks of technology objectification effects, sensitivity bias and gender stereotypes, finding that wearable technology has a differential impact on service evaluations based on employees' gender.

Ryan, Henley and Soutar (1998) also recognised that there are gender differences in information processing which should be taken into consideration when designing tourism destination marketing campaigns. Meyers-Levy's (1986) information processing selectivity hypothesis found that males typically process information using selective, heuristic devices involving the use of single, salient cues while females are comprehensive information processors who attempt to assimilate all cues. Findings indicate it is advisable to emphasise certain characteristics important to each gender varied depending on whether the primary decision-maker is likely to be male or female (Ryan, Henley & Soutar, 1998) and women are often the primary planners and decision-makers of their trips (Anderson & Littrell, 1995).

Overall, consumption of a holiday is largely a joint decision, but when the purchase is broken down into different stages, females have a dominant role in the early stages of the process, possibly making them gatekeepers. There are clear differences in terms of decision making depending on the task. Female parties have the dominant role in the early stages of the process. Decisions regarding holidays seem to mirror other household decisions (Mottiar & Quinn, 2004). The specific stages of holiday decision making that are more likely to be made by wives are the pre-departure tasks, the selection of a destination and the collection of information (Zalatan, 1998).

Results from a study in information searching exploring gender differences found that male and female tourists differ significantly in terms of the number of information topics searched; which information topics are searched; and which information sources are searched (Xie, Bao & Morais, 2006). Findings have indicated that females are more active information seekers prior to making a tourism purchase decision (Tan & Chen, 2012). Jacobsen and Munar (2012) found with regard to tourist information searches and destination choice in a digital age, that women placed more emphasis on hotel/apartment websites (35% of female tourists rated them as very important versus 21% of the male tourist participants).

Research has also explored gender differences in how online concerns potentially affect purchase likelihood (Janda, 2008). It is hypothesised that gender will moderate the relationship between online concerns and likelihood of making online purchases. More specifically relationships between (a) privacy and likelihood of online purchases, (b) security and likelihood of online purchases, (c) credibility and likelihood of online purchases, and (d) virtual experience and likelihood of online purchases will all be stronger for females as compared to males, although these relationships will be negative for both groups. Results indicated that gender moderates the effect of satisfaction and trust on loyalty to particular websites, and an indication that women appreciate websites that educate the consumer by providing features such as brand comparisons on key attributes and information about new items. (Janda, 2008).

Tourism is by nature an information-oriented phenomenon due to structural reasons (Schertler, Schmid, Tjoa & Werthner, 1995). For the consumer, decision-making (or destination choice) and consumption are separated in time and space. These distances can only be overcome by gathering information about the product and services in advance (Werthner & Klein, 1999).

THE DECISION MAKING PROCESS

The decision making process is influenced by both psychological (internal) variables (attitudes, motivation, beliefs, and intentions) and non-psychological (external) variables (time, pull factors, marketing mix). Given the centrality of the selection decision process to tourists' behaviour, a clear understanding of the complexities and interrelationships of these variables is an important research agenda (Sirakaya & Woodside, 2005).

Many of the studies related to choice modelling in tourism assume that travellers are rational decision makers who try to maximise the utility and, thus, assess costs and benefits of their actions before committing themselves to choosing a specific destination (Wahab, Crampon & Rothfield, 1976; Schmoll, 1977), while some acknowledge the role of constraints on destination choice (Woodside & Lysonski, 1989; Um & Crompton, 1990), or even consider destination choice a compulsory sub-decision among other travel related decisions (Moutinho, 1987). Despite the diversity of approaches, these models have one thing in common; traveller's destination choice process has been approached as a functional or utilitarian decision making activity that is influenced by a number of psychological and non-psychological variables (Hwang, Gretzel, Xiang & Fesenmaier, 2006).

Vacation travel is an established pattern of behaviour in many affluent societies. What these tourists do and why they do it has been the focus of a variety of research under the umbrella of many disciplines. The consumption process of tourism holiday choice, or travel decision making, is influenced by a number of factors and a substantial body of decision making literature in the form of the broader 'models of consumer behaviour' has been adapted to attempt to describe this process. These models originated to explain decisions relating to tangible products rather than service purchase decisions, hence the need to adapt, but there are still some vital details missing when an attempt is made to describe and understand the travel decision making process. Existing 'foundation models' present variables such as personal characteristics, desires and attitudes as factors that affect the vacation decision making process, but fail to discuss the extent to which the process is mediated by decision goals and strategies. Economic models are based on utility theory as a decision making framework, however, they do not allow for the other consumer oriented variables.

Factors Influencing Preference

Current models of travel decision making depict various influences on the consumer, be it the consumer's personal characteristics, marketing variables or the characteristics of a destination.

Personal Characteristics

Socio-psychological and cognitive variables with potential impacts on the destination choice process include personal values, knowledge and experience related to a destination or travel in general, personality and attitude towards certain destinations (Hwang, Gretzel, Xiang & Fesenmaier, 2006).

Knowledge is an important perceptive field that influences destination choice. Knowledge, often obtained through direct experience, can be represented either as travel knowledge in general, or as knowledge of alternative destinations, or both. In each case, knowledge influences the range of alternatives considered (Hwang, Gretzel, Xiang & Fesenmaier, 2006). Destination familiarity can, of course, not only be acquired through previous experience but is also dependent on the amount and type of information obtained about the destination (Tideswell & Faulkner, 1999 cited in Hwang, Gretzel, Xiang & Fesenmaier, 2006). Knowledge and perceptions of the characteristics of various destinations, the destination images created through exposure to marketing, and the fit between conceptions of the destinations with personal values and beliefs, result in particular attitudes towards these places. These attitudes towards certain destinations are significant determinants of whether or not a destination is considered an alternative and how it is evaluated in later stages of the destination choice process (Hwang, Gretzel, Xiang & Fesenmaier, 2006). Personal variables such as motivation (why consumers behave as they do) are of vital importance in understanding the decision-making process. More specifically; motives (an internal drive or 'push factor'), needs (materialisation of a motive), wants (manifestation of the need) and benefits (whatever consumers derive from products). Motives and personal characteristics determine a person's inclination to act (Decrop, 2006). In addition, there is a strong indication that children's leisure socialisation plays an important role in what type of activities they participate in, and how and where they travel when they become adults (Sirakaya & Woodside, 2005).

Travel decision makers' personal characteristics do not operate in a vacuum and these characteristics are also affected by forces outside the individual travelers.

Marketing Variables

Marketing variables influence travel decision making through the four P's of the marketing mix (product, price, promotion and place). Product covers the shape or form of what is offered to prospective customers and price denotes the published or negotiated terms of the exchange transaction for that product. Promotion is the most visible of the four P's and includes advertising, sales promotions, merchandising and public relations. Finally, place (or distribution) represents the destination and the location of all the points of sale that provide consumers with access to tourist products (Middleton, 1994).

'Home' Situational Context

Growing recognition of the limitations in the ability of individual consumer characteristics alone to explain variation in buyer behaviour has prompted a number of calls to examine situational influences on behaviour. Engel, Kollat and Blackwell (1969) urge that both individual and situational factors must be considered in order to explain consumer choices. Particularly, the influence of friends and relatives both during the destination decision making process and holiday 'in-situ' decisions has been found to play a dominant role (Gitelson & Kerstetter, 1994). Belk (1975) distinguishes five groups of situational characteristics "which have a demonstrable and systematic effect on buyer behaviour" *Physical Surroundings* (geographical location, weather, tangible signs), *Social Surroundings* (other persons present, their roles and interactions), *Temporal Perspective* (ranging from time of day to season of the year, time constraints and time since last purchase), *Task Definition* (intent or requirement to select or obtain information about a general or specific purchase) and *Antecedent States* (momentary moods or conditions which shape perception and evaluation of present environment). The first three of these groups of situational characteristics have been labelled as the 'home' situational context in the following model depicting factors influencing destination choice.

Trip Characteristics

Trip characteristics such as travel purpose, length of travel, distance between origin and destination and travel group composition, appear to be the most important determinants of the context in which destination decisions are taken. Evaluation criteria for alternative destinations vary from one task to another as the context of the trip changes. Travel purpose is often closely connected to activities and settings and, therefore, significantly constrains or defines the range of alternatives destinations considered (for example golf locations for a golfing holiday). The nature of the travel group is also an important influence. Alternative destinations considered by a person who plans to go on a family vacation, for example, are probably different from those considered for a trip with friends (Hwang, Gretzel, Xiang & Fesenmaier, 2006).

Destination Characteristics

The character of the holiday product influences a consumer's choice of destination. Mental images of products and destinations provide the basis of the evaluation with those images individuals possess of the real world representing the 'pull' component in choice. Because holidays are a service which cannot be sampled before consumption, holiday-makers must base their choice on these mental images of the alternative holidays (Goodall, 1991). Consumers choose goods because of their attributes or characteristics and use their perceptions (images) of those attributes as input factors when estimating the utility they will derive from consuming the goods (Lancaster, 1966; Goodall, 1991). Attributes of holidays can be both resource based (climate, scenery) and facility based (accommodation, access modes) and may be tangible (mountains, theme parks) or abstract (cultural, hospitality) properties. A choice has to be made from the extensive range of holidays currently available and so the relationship between demand

and supply must also be considered (Goodall, 1991). Holiday-makers may be viewed as risk-neutral, risk-avoiding or risk-taking (Moutinho 1987 cited in Goodall, 1991). Risk can be reduced, but not eliminated, by adopting various strategies; lowering expectations of the holiday, regularly purchasing the same holiday, acquiring further information and so on.

Decisions can be framed in a variety of ways depending on personal preferences for certain decision making strategies and the needs or constraints resulting from the specific trip-planning situation. Specifically, the number and type of decision criteria taken into account will vary based on the nature of the trip to be planned. Trips defined around a specific activity will strongly influence the frame in which the decision has to be made. It can also be assumed that personal characteristics influence one's need, ability and/or willingness to take certain criteria into consideration. Personal cognitive styles can greatly influence the amount of information included in the decision making process and especially the number of alternatives considered by the individual decision-maker (Driver, Brousseau & Hunsaker 1990; Hwang, Gretzel, Xiang & Fesenmaier, 2006; Hunt, Krzystofiak, Meindl & Yousry, 1989).

Studies from the gendered perspective of the potential market to a nature tourism destination found gender differences were revealed in the perceived importance placed on destination attributes. Females placed a higher importance on most destination attributes than did male participants, especially in appreciating natural scenery and available recreational activities, such as attending events or cultural attractions and shopping. The gender differences in destination attributes or characteristics sought demonstrated many similarities with findings in earlier literature in that women valued security, prestige ('self- respect' and 'being respected' in this study) and relationships with others (Meng & Uysal, 2008).

The majority of the decision making studies in travel and tourism are constant with regard to exploring the factors influencing a consumer's decision while choosing a destination (evaluation of alternatives and choice). Those prior studies have failed to examine the decision making process beyond the investigation of relative influence or the identification of factors during purchasing such as risks, attitudes, family structure and economic structure (Decrop & Kozak, 2009). The current travel decision making literature generally describes how vacationers go through different stages to make their decisions, that is, searching for information, evaluating considered alternatives, and finalising their actual choice, but it fails to explain how they handle criteria and strategies in that process (Decrop & Kozak, 2009). Evaluation of alternatives is a cornerstone of any decision making process. The evaluation stage involves the selection of one option from a set of alternatives by using a particular decision strategy or a combination of multiple strategies. Evaluation becomes more difficult when there are more alternatives, multiple contingencies or events and multiple conflicting preferences and values (Decrop & Kozak, 2009).

Current research (Decrop & Kozac, 2009) suggests that developing a model that fits all decision makers and every decision situation in a vacation evaluation may not be realistic as a vacation involves many decisions and sub-decisions. Decision strategies may differ across vacationers with diverse interests and reasons which needs further investigation of the vacation decision making behaviour. The framework proposed for the present study incorporates the factors presented in the literature that influence destination choice (personal characteristics, marketing variables, 'home' situational context, trip characteristics and destination characteristics) but then 'filtering' them by the way in which a consumer makes decisions (heuristics of decision making). This framework is represented in the 'Destination Choice – Factors that influence preference' model depicted in Figure 1 following.

Figure 1. A model of destination choice considering factors that influence preference (Dale, 2013)

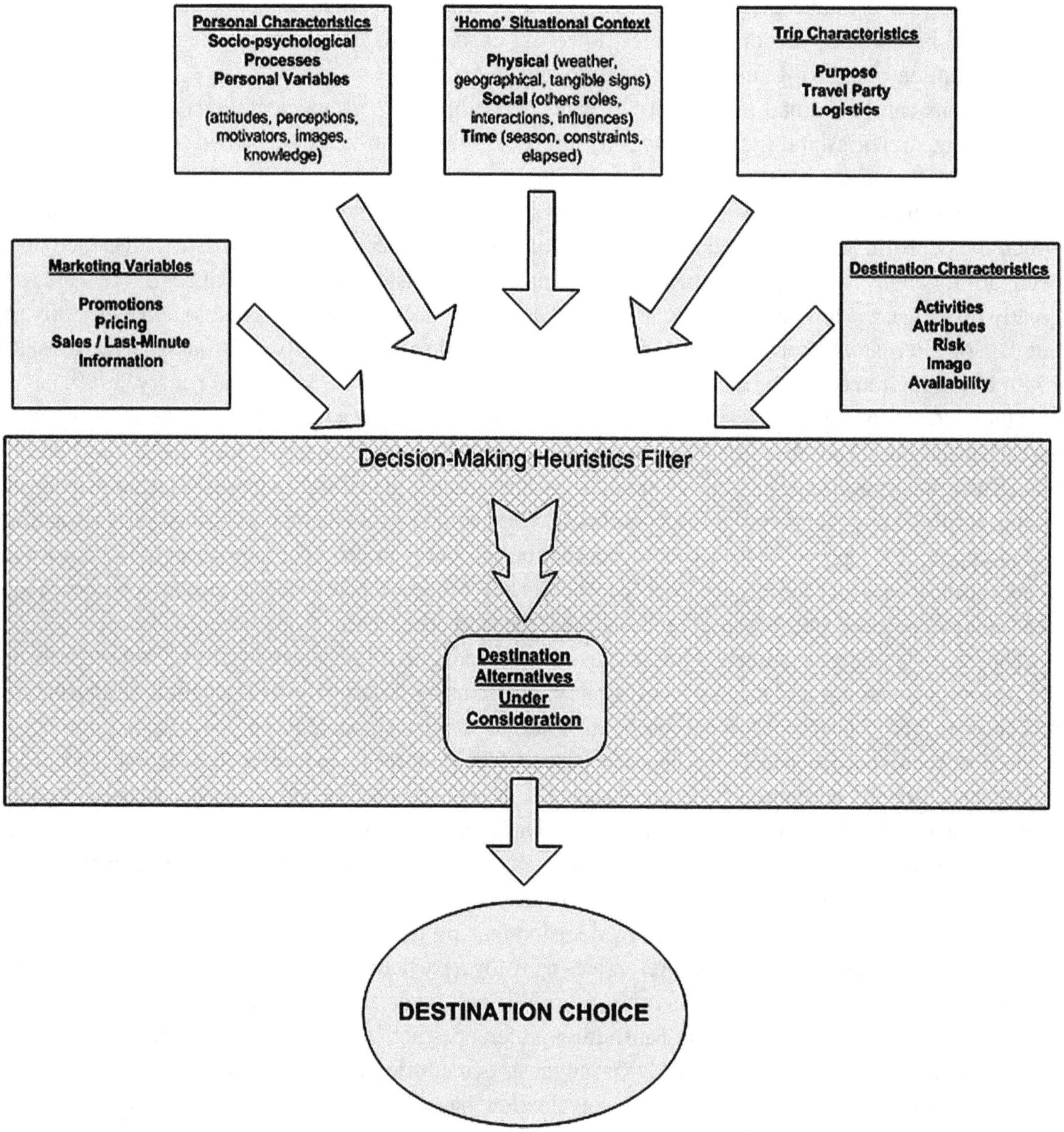

CASE STUDY: GENDER EFFECT ON OVERNIGHT SCHOOL EXCURSION DESTINATION CHOICE

Growing recognition of the limitations of the ability of individual consumer characteristics to alone explain variation in buyer behaviour has prompted a number of calls to examine situational influences and personal characteristics (such as gender) on behaviour. This case study applied the above theoretical framework in an Australian schools context.

An exploratory sequential design was applied, qualitatively exploring the topic with school excursion planners before building to a second quantitative phase. The primary purpose was to generalise qualitative findings based on a few individuals from the first phase to a larger sample gathered during the second phase. This design was particularly useful to identify important variables to study quantitatively as the variables were unknown. A survey instrument, including a discrete choice experiment (DCE) consisting of several choice scenarios, each containing three options, was developed. Each option was described by a set of attributes and each attribute can take one of several levels.

A survey was administered in May 2010. Potential respondents (excursion planners) were emailed an invitation to participate together with a link to the online survey. An email invitation was sent to 7447 primary schools and 2962 secondary and special schools nationwide gaining 521 respondents from 9939 successfully sent invitations (5%). In addition to the responses to the choice scenarios, other data were collected using the survey. They included various situational context characteristics and previous destination choices for overnight school excursions. The survey also gathered data about the respondent specifically such as age, gender, level of education, position at school, level of experience with overnight excursions and level of involvement with the most recent excursion.

Analysis was performed using Latent GOLD Choice 4.0 software, producing a multinomial logit model (MNL), to estimate the probability of making a specific choice among the set of alternatives. CHAID analysis and SI-CHAID 4.0 generated tree diagrams revealing the covariates that significantly predicted class membership and significant splits of sub-groups.

Theoretical implications from this research, examining situational influences on behaviour, leads to the conclusion that the factors that influence preference for destination choice, as indicated by planners of overnight school excursions, differ in importance depending on situational contexts and personal characteristics of the travel party and the respondent. Results also provide clarification that destination choice is influenced by preferences for attributes suited to the travel party and purpose of the trip rather than just the individual excursion planner.

Analysis of the situational context indicated the typical school had 365 students with 30 full- time equivalent staff and no dedicated excursion co-ordinator (70%). The number of overnight excursions taken in 2009 was four, and the most recent overnight excursion destination was regional Victoria (VIC Other 23%). Typically, the grade involved in the most recent overnight excursion was Grade 6 (20.417%) or Grade 10 (20.132%) travelling in November (19%). The main organiser of the most recent excursion was the class teacher (47%) and the school had taken on average five previous visits to that destination. Timing an overnight excursion to match a curriculum related event or festival was considered very important (level 5 – 28%).

Analysis of personal characteristics reveals the modal respondent was a forty-eight year old female (65%) with a university degree level of education (49%). The respondent position at the school was 'school management' (62%) with twenty-four years working in the education sector together with a high level (5) of experience (71%) and involvement (55%) with overnight excursions.

When choices are based on different utilities in different population segments, estimates obtained under the aggregate model in the previous section can be biased. The survey data indicated options for a 1-class choice (aggregate) through to a 10-class choice model. Rho-squared (R^2) increases from 0.1152 for the standard aggregate 1-class model to 0.1628 for a 3-class model which is presented.

The importance output reports the maximum effect for each of the attributes, including the constants, as well as the relative effects. The relative effects columns for Class 1 to 3 in Table 1 present re-scaled

Table 1. Relative importance of factors (best/none 3-Class model)

	Maximum			Relative		
	Class1	**Class2**	**Class3**	**Class1**	**Class2**	**Class3**
ACCOMMODATION	0.7327	0.3100	0.2603	0.0687	0.0693	0.0175
SAFETY	1.4343	0.4179	1.1604	0.1344	0.0934	0.0782
ACTIVITIES	0.7876	0.5722	0.8462	0.0738	0.1279	0.0570
CURRICULUM	2.7544	0.4314	0.6271	**0.2581**	0.0964	0.0423
IMAGE	0.7436	0.0262	0.1111	0.0697	0.0058	0.0075
FACILITIES	1.2105	0.3206	0.8442	0.1134	0.0717	0.0569
TRAVEL_TIME	1.7498	1.1515	3.2164	0.1640	**0.2574**	0.2167
TRANSPORT	0.4157	0.4690	1.1821	0.0390	0.1048	0.0797
COST	0.8435	0.7752	6.5921	0.0790	0.1733	**0.4442**

values of the maximum effects such that all values are on a scale of 0 to 1, and add up to 1 within each of the latent classes. Focusing again on the 'relative' column, we can compare each factor on the same scale and identify the most important factor within and between the classes. For instance, Curriculum has the highest relative importance for Class 1 (0.2581), Travel Time for Class 2 (0.2574) and Cost for Class 3 (0.4442). Within the classes, we see that Curriculum is almost twice as important as Safety, and almost four times more important that Activities for Class 1. Likewise, in Class 2 Travel Time is almost twice as important as Cost, while the inverse appears to be the case in Class 3 with Cost observed as more than twice the importance of Travel Time for this segment.

In examining the relative importance visually, the plot in Figure 2 again indicates the most important factors for classes 1 to 3 are Curriculum, Travel Time and Cost respectively. It is easy to see class 3 is extremely price-sensitive compared to the other two classes. In fact, except on image just over class 2 and transport above class 1, this is the only factor where class 3 exceeds the other classes. Class 1 has a stronger relative concern with curriculum, safety, facilities and image. Class 2 has stronger relative concern with travel time, activities and transport type.

It is also useful to profile the latent class segments in terms of exogenous variables (covariates). The CHAID option for doing this utilizes the posterior membership probabilities as weights and hence will reproduce the actual (probabilistic, not modal) classes. Thus, the CHAID approach has zero misclassification error.

SI-CHAID can be used to see how each of the nine dependent variables is predicted by the demographic segments (Magidson, 2005). The probability value (p-value) is a measure of statistical significance. The smaller the p-value, the more statistically significant the variable is as a predictor of class membership.

The CHAID analysis revealed that three of the personal characteristic covariates significantly predicted class membership (of which a gender effect was the most significant) and these are presented in the tables following from most to least significant (Gender 5.1×10^{-6}, Position of respondent at school 0.00070 and level of involvement with most recent overnight excursion 0.0029). The relationship between covariates and classes 1 – 3 are indicated by the p-value; the smaller the p-value the more statistically significant the variable is as a predictor (tables 2-4).

Figure 2. Relative importance of factors (best/none 3-Class model)

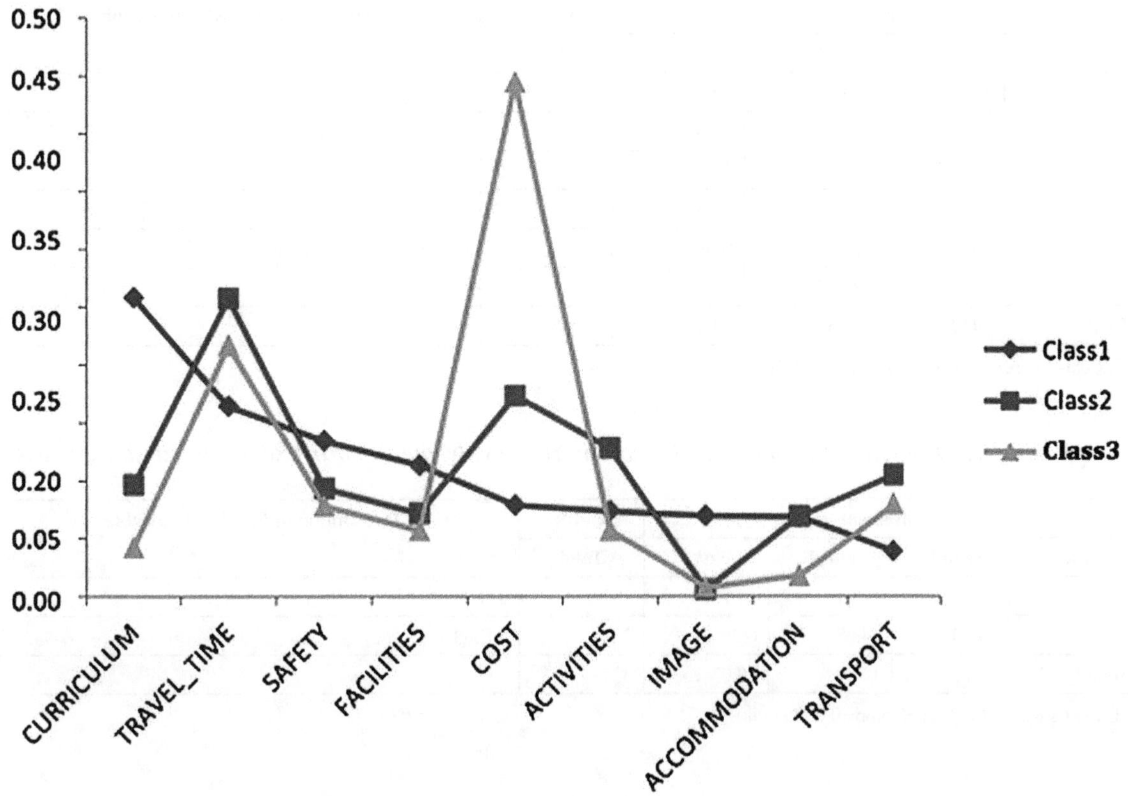

Table 2. SI-CHAID generated segment level prediction for Gender covariates

Gender				Row %	Description of Predictor Variables
(Before)	clu#1	clu#2	clu#3	Total	
1	45.55	30.45	24.00	152	Male
2	67.69	22.97	9.35	283	Female
Total	59.95	25.58	14.47	435	

LR chi-square=24.38 df=2 prob=5.1e-6

SI-CHAID Tree Diagrams: Personal Characteristics Covariates

Only two of the covariates made *unique* significant contributions to class prediction and the resulting tree diagrams are displayed in Figure 3 and Figure 4.

In this first example above (Figure 3), the CHAID analysis first splits the total sample between categories of 'Gender'" (1 – Male and 2 - Female). Those in category 2 (Female) were further divided according to 'level of involvement' (1-4 merged and 5 (high) obtaining three covariate groups (segments) in total.

Table 3. SI-CHAID generated segment level prediction for Position at School covariates

Position				Row %	Description of Predictor Variables
(Before)	clu#1	clu#2	clu#3	Total	
1	74.91	15.48	9.62	87	Class teacher
2	54.32	23.10	22.58	21	Grade Coordinator
3	58.48	27.75	13.77	265	School Management
4	99.87	0.10	0.03	6	Excursion Coordinator
5	29.36	70.57	0.08	7	General Administration
6	43.25	29.54	27.21	49	Other
Total	59.95	25.58	14.47	435	

LR chi-square=30.54 df=10 prob=0.00070

Table 4. SI-CHAID generated segment level prediction for Involvement in Most Recent Excursion covariates

Involvement				Row %	Description of Predictor Variables
(After)	clu#1	clu#2	clu#3	Total	
1-4	63.34	21.91	14.75	193	1 (low) - 4
5	79.04	14.68	6.28	242	5 (high)
Total	72.08	17.89	10.03	435	

LR chi-square=14.48 df=2 prob=0.0029 (adj.)

Segment 1 (Males with a low to moderate (1-4) level of involvement) had an underrepresentation of LC1 (45.55%) and a remarkable overrepresentation of LC3 (24%). Segment 3 (Females with a high level (5) of involvement) had an overrepresentation of LC 1, 74.62% compared to the 59.95% root node size and an underrepresentation of LC 2 and 3.

The second generated tree diagram splits the total sample on level of involvement in most recent overnight school excursion (1 to 4 merged and 5-high) obtaining two covariate groups in total.

Segment 2 (participants with a high level of involvement in the most recent excursion – 5) had a notable underrepresentation of LC2 (16.98% as compared to 25.58%).

Considering the above conclusions, a modified conceptual framework for factors that influence preference for destination choice by school excursion groups is presented below in Figure 5 - *Destination choice by school excursion groups - factors that influence preference.* The model has been updated from Figure 1 to include the significant factors identified by this research.

Personal Characteristics, Situational Contexts and a Destination's Attributes are factors that influence preference. These preferences produce suitable destination alternatives, and those under consideration are "filtered" utilising decision making heuristics, which vary depending on situations. From these alternatives, a final destination is chosen. This is similar to recent findings using chi-squared tests for mapping destination choice sets (or alternatives) indicating the factors age, gender, travel frequency and travel motives are significant determinants (Karl, Reintinger and Schmude, 2015).

Figure 3. SI-CHAID generated tree diagram relating the three LC segments to Gender/Involvement covariates

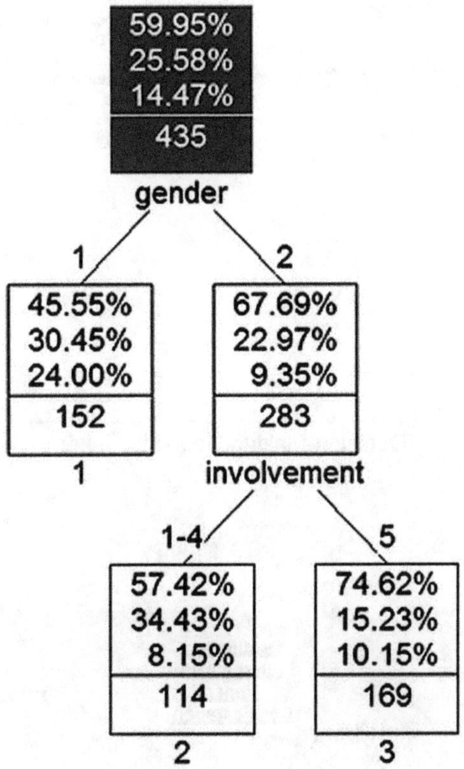

Figure 4. SI-CHAID generated tree diagram relating the 3 LC segments to Involvement covariates

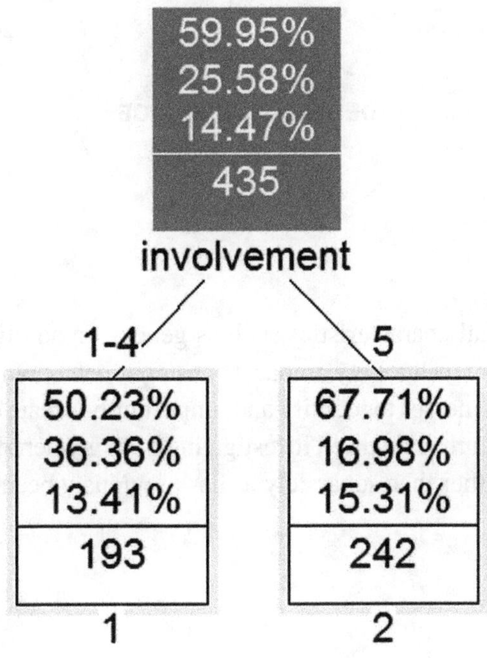

Figure 5. Destination choice by school excursion groups - factors that influence preference (Dale, 2013)

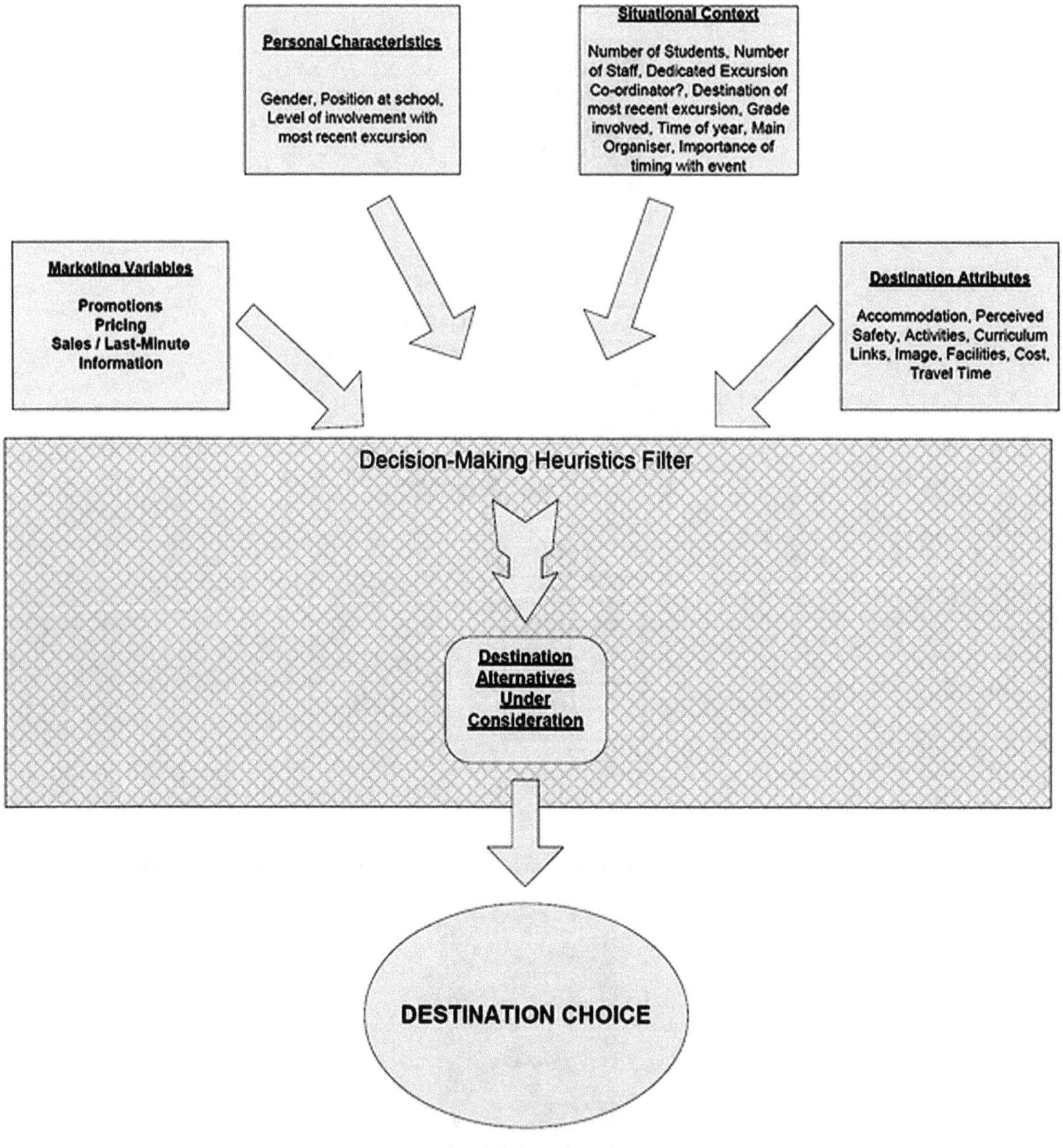

Understanding how personal characteristics such as gender, in addition to gendered differences in preferences and requirements in technology, impacts consumer behaviour (and tourism choices) can aid as a foundation for tourism businesses to identify and, importantly, create effective marketing communication strategies. Further research is required investigating both gendered effects in tourism destination choice in a combined study rather than separately as has previously been the case.

REFERENCES

Anderson, L. F., & Littrell, M. A. (1995). Souvenir-purchase behaviour of women tourists. *Annals of Tourism Research*, *22*(2), 328–348. doi:10.1016/0160-7383(94)00080-8

Andreasen, A. R. (1965). Attitudes and Customer Behavior: A Decision Model. In L. E. Preston (Ed.), New Research in Marketing. Berkley, CA, USA.

Belk, R. W. (1975). Situational Variables and Consumer Behavior. *The Journal of Consumer Research*, *2*(3), 157–164. doi:10.1086/208627

Blalock, H. M. (1969). *Theory Construction - From Verbal to Mathematical Formulations* (p. 180). Englewood Cliffs, NJ: Prentice-Hall Inc.

Blichfeldt, B. S., Pedersen, B. M., Johansen, A., & Hansen, L. (2010). Tween Tourists: Children and Decision-Making. *Journal of Tourism Consumption and Practice*, *2*(1), 1–24.

Carr, N. (Ed.). (2011). *Children's and Families' Holiday Experiences* (p. 201). London, New York: Routledge.

Cosenza, R. M., & Davis, D. L. (1981). Family Vacation Decision Making Over the Family Life Cycle: A Decision and Influence Structure Analysis. *Journal of Travel Research*, *20*(2), 17–23. doi:10.1177/004728758102000203

Dale, N. F. (2013). *Destination choice by school excursions groups in Australia: Understanding the factors that influence preference* (Unpublished PhD thesis). University of Canberra

Darley, W.K., & Jeen-Su Lim (1986). Family Decision Making in Leisure-Time Activities: an Exploratory Investigation of the Impact of Locus of Control, Child Age Influence Factor and Parental Type on Perceived Child Influence. *Advances in Consumer Research, 13*(1), 370-374.

Decrop, A. (Ed.), (2006). *Vacation Decision Making*. UK: CABI Publishing. doi:10.1079/9781845930400.0000

Decrop, A., & Kozak, M. (2009). Decision Strategies in Tourism Evaluation. In M. Kozak & A. Decrop (Eds.), *Handbook of Tourist Behavior - Theory & Practice* (pp. 67–82). New York: Routledge.

Decrop, A., & Snelders, D. (2004). Planning the Summer Vacation - An Adaptable Process. *Annals of Tourism Research*, *31*(4), 1008–1030. doi:10.1016/j.annals.2004.03.004

Driver, M. J., Brousseau, K. E., & Hunsaker, P. L. (1990). *The Dynamic Decision-maker*. New York: Harper.

Engel, J. F., Blackwell, R. D., & Miniard, P. W. (1990). *Consumer Behavior* (6th ed.). USA: The Dryden Press.

Engel, J. F., Kollat, D. T., & Blackwell, R. D. (1968). *Consumer Behavior*. United States of America: Holt, Rinehart and Winston Inc.

Gilbert, D. C. (1991). An examination of the consumer behaviour process related to tourism. In C. P. Cooper (Ed.), *Progress in tourism, recreation and hospitality management* (pp. 78–105). Lymington, UK: Belhaven Press.

Gitelson, R., & Kerstetter, D. L. (1995). The Influence of Friends and Relatives in Travel Decision-Making. *Journal of Travel & Tourism Marketing*, *3*(3), 59–68. doi:10.1300/J073v03n03_04

Goodall, B. (1991). Understanding Holiday Choice. In C. Cooper & A. Lockwood (Eds.), *Progress in Tourism, Recreation and Hospitality Management* (pp. 58–77). Belhaven Press.

Gram, M. (2005). Family Holidays. A qualitative analysis of family holiday experiences. *Scandinavian Journal of Hospitality and Tourism*, *5*(1), 2–22. doi:10.1080/15022250510014255

Gram, M. (2007). Children as co-decision makers in the family? The case of family holidays. *Young Consumers*, *8*(1), 19–28. doi:10.1108/17473610710733749

Howard, J. (1963). *Marketing Management - Analysis and Planning* (Revised ed.). Illinois, USA: Richard D Irwin Inc.

Howard, J., & Sheth, J. (1969). *The Theory of Buyer Behavior*. United States: John Wiley & Sons Inc.

Hudson, S. (2000). Consumer Behaviour Related to Tourism. In A. Pizam & Y. Mansfeld (Eds.), *Consumer Behaviour in Travel and Tourism* (pp. 7–30). NY: The Haworth Hospitality Press.

Hunt, R. G., Krzystofiak, F. J., Meindl, J. R., & Yousry, A. M. (1989). Cognitive Style and Decision Making. *Organizational Behavior and Human Decision Processes*, *44*(3), 436–453. doi:10.1016/0749-5978(89)90018-6

Hwang, Y., Gretzel, U., Xiang, Z., & Fesenmaier, D. R. (2006). Travel Destination Choice Models. In D. R. Fesenmaier, K. W. Wober, & H. Werthner (Eds.), *Destination Recommendation Systems: Behavioural Foundations and Applications* (pp. 17–29). UK: CABI. doi:10.1079/9780851990231.0017

Jacobsen, J. K. S., & Munar, A. M. (2012). Tourist information search and destination choice in a digital age. *Tourism Management Perspectives*, *1*, 39–47. doi:10.1016/j.tmp.2011.12.005

Janda, S. (2008). Does Gender Moderate the Effect of Online Concerns on Purchase Likelihood? *Journal of Internet Commerce*, *7*(3), 339–358. doi:10.1080/15332860802250401

Jenkins, R. L. (1978). Family Vacation Decision-Making. *Journal of Travel Research*, *16*(4), 2–7. doi:10.1177/004728757801600401

Johns, N., & Gyimothy, S. (2002). Mythologies of a theme park: An icon of modern family life. *Journal of Vacation Marketing*, *8*(4), 320–331. doi:10.1177/135676670200800403

Karl, M., Reintinger, C., & Schmude, J. (2015). Reject or select: Mapping destination choice. *Annals of Tourism Research*, *54*, 48–64. doi:10.1016/j.annals.2015.06.003

Kim, D.-Y., Lehto, X. Y., & Morrison, A. M. (2007). Gender differences in online travel information search: Implications for marketing communications on the internet. *Tourism Management*, *28*(2), 423–433. doi:10.1016/j.tourman.2006.04.001

Lancaster, K. J. (1966). A New Approach to Consumer Theory. *Journal of Political Economy*, *74*(2), 132–157. doi:10.1086/259131

Magidson, J. (2005). *SI-CHAID 4.0 User's Guide*. Belmont, Massachusetts: Statistical Innovations Inc.

McNeal, J. (1999). *The kids market - myths and realities*. New York: Paramount Market Publishing.

Meng, F., & Uysal, M. (2008). Effects of Gender Differences on Perceptions of Destination Attributes, Motivations, and Travel Values: An Examination of a Nature-Based Resort Destination. *Journal of Sustainable Tourism*, *16*(4), 445–466. doi:10.1080/09669580802154231

Middleton, V. T. C. (1994). *Marketing in Travel and Tourism* (2nd ed., p. 393). Oxford: Butterworth-Heinemann Ltd.

Mottiar, Z., & Quinn, D. (2004). Couple dynamics in household tourism decision making: Women as the gatekeepers? *Journal of Vacation Marketing*, *10*(2), 149–160. doi:10.1177/135676670401000205

Moutinho, L. (1987). Consumer Behaviour in Tourism. *European Journal of Marketing*, *21*(10), 4–44. doi:10.1108/EUM0000000004718

Myers-Levy. (1986). 'Gender differences in information processing: A selectivity interpretation. In P. Cafferata & A. M. Tybout (Eds.), *Cognitive and affective responses to advertising* (pp. 219–260). Addison-Wiley Publishing.

Nicosia, F.M. (1966). Consumer Decision Processes - Marketing and Advertising Implications. Englewood Cliffs, NJ: Prentice Hall Inc.

Pearce, P. L. (2005). Studying Tourist Behaviour. In *Tourist Behaviour: Themes and Conceptual Schemes* (pp. 1–17). Clevedon, UK: Channel View Publications.

Ritchie, J. R. B., & Filiatrault, P. (1980). Family Vacation Decision-Making - A Replication and Extension. *Journal of Travel Research*, *18*(4), 3–14. doi:10.1177/004728758001800401

Ryan, M., Henley, N., & Soutar, G. (1998). Gender Differences in Tourism Destination Choice: Implications for Tourism Marketers. *Proceedings of the Australia and New Zealand Marketing Conference*, Dunedin, New Zealand.

Schertler, W., Schmid, B., Tjoa, A. M., & Werthner, H. (1995). *Information and communication technologies in tourism*. Wien: Springer. doi:10.1007/978-3-7091-7596-5

Schmoll, G. A. (1977). *Tourism Promotion*. London: Tourism International Press.

Sirakaya, E., & Woodside, A. G. (2005). Building and testing theories of decision making by travellers. *Tourism Management*, *26*(6), 815–832. doi:10.1016/j.tourman.2004.05.004

Tan, W.-K., & Chen, T.-H. (2012). The usage of online tourist information sources in tourist information search: An exploratory study. *Service Industries Journal*, *32*(3), 451–476. doi:10.1080/02642069.2010.529130

Thornton, P. R., Shaw, G., & Williams, A. M. (1997). Tourist group holiday decision-making and behaviour: The influence of children. *Tourism Management*, *18*(5), 287–297. doi:10.1016/S0261-5177(97)00017-4

Um, S., & Crompton, J. L. (1990). Attitude Determinants in Tourism Destination Choice. *Annals of Tourism Research*, *17*(3), 432–448. doi:10.1016/0160-7383(90)90008-F

van Raaij, W. F. (1985). *The Psychological Foundation of Economics: The History of Consumer Theory* (Special Volume).

van Raaij, W. F. (1986). Consumer Research On Tourism - Mental and Behavioral Constructs. *Annals of Tourism Research*, *13*(1), 1–9. doi:10.1016/0160-7383(86)90054-X

van Raaij, W. F., & Francken, D. A. (1984). Vacation Decisions, Activities, And Satisfactions. *Annals of Tourism Research*, *11*(1), 101–112. doi:10.1016/0160-7383(84)90098-7

Wahab, S., Crampon, L. J., & Rothfield, L. M. (1976). *Tourism Marketing*. London: Tourism International Press.

Webster, S. (2012). Consumer Kids and Tourists - Creatively Marketing a City to Young Tourists. In H. Schanzel, I. Yeoman, & E. Backer (Eds.), *Family Tourism: Multidisciplinary Perspectives* (pp. 143–155). Bristol, UK: Channel View Publications.

Werthner, H., & Klein, S. (1999). *Information technology and tourism – A challenging relationship*. Wien: Springer. doi:10.1007/978-3-7091-6363-4

Woodside, A. G., & Lysonski, S. (1989). A General Model of Traveler Destination Choice. *Journal of Travel Research*, *27*(4), 8–14. doi:10.1177/004728758902700402

Wu, L., Fan, A., & Mattila, A. (2015). Wearable technology in service delivery processes: The gender-moderated technology objectification effect. *International Journal of Hospitality Management*, *51*, 1–7. doi:10.1016/j.ijhm.2015.08.010

Xianga, Z., Magnini, V. P., & Fesenmaier, D. R. (2015). Information technology and consumer behavior in travel and tourism: Insights from travel planning using the internet. *Journal of Retailing and Consumer Services*, *22*, 244–249. doi:10.1016/j.jretconser.2014.08.005

Xie, H., Bao, J., & Morais, D. B. (2006). Exploring Gender Differences in Information Search Among Domestic Visitors to Yellow Mountain and Guilin, PRC. *Proceedings of the 2006 Northeastern Recreation Research Symposium* (pp. 120-125).

Zach, F., Gretzel, U., & Xiang, Z. (2010). Innovation in the Web Marketing Programs of American Convention and Visitor Bureaus. *Information Technology & Tourism*, 12(1), 47-63. doi:10.3727/109830510X12747489979628

Zalatan, A. (1998). "Wives" involvement in tourism decision processes. *Annals of Tourism Research, 25*(4), 890–903. doi:10.1016/S0160-7383(98)00038-3

Zhang, M., & Liu, B. (2015). Technology and gender: A case study on "iron girls" in China (1950s – 1970s). *Technology in Society, 43*, 86–94. doi:10.1016/j.techsoc.2015.04.005

Chapter 3
Gender Differences in Motivations to Use Social Networking Sites

Valeria Noguti
University of Technology Sydney, Australia

Sonika Singh
University of Technology Sydney, Australia

David S. Waller
University of Technology Sydney, Australia

ABSTRACT

This chapter investigates gender differences in motivations to use social networking sites (SNS), a subset of social media. The present research focuses on Facebook given its prominence among currently available SNS. Analysing a survey of university students in Australia, the results indicate that female consumers are more likely than male consumers to use Facebook to seek information (to research and learn new things and to discuss products and brands) and for convenience (to obtain things with little effort). Both of these reasons in turn relate positively to their degree of engagement on Facebook, where engagement is operationalized as cognitive absorption which is a state of deep involvement with an activity.

DOI: 10.4018/978-1-5225-0010-0.ch003

INTRODUCTION

Over the last 20 years the internet has resulted in significant changes in how we communicate, gather information, and purchase goods and services. Innovations in online social media have resulted in websites that not only allow users to retrieve information, but also encourage the interactive sharing of information and the creation of user-generated content (Kaplan & Haenlein, 2010; Mangold & Faulds, 2009). In particular, there has been an explosion in popularity of social networking sites (SNS) which is an online platform that has the main objective to facilitate regular communication among individuals. These include various social media sites such as Facebook, Twitter and LinkedIn, as well as photo and video sharing sites such as YouTube, Tumblr, Instagram, Flickr and Pinterest. Facebook is a popular SNS where people can search for other people and businesses, and keep friends updated with the latest pictures, videos, news and information (Chi, 2011; Curran, Graham & Temple, 2011; Lukka & James, 2014). One of the reasons online social networks provide an important topic for research is that consumers' media habits have been consistently shifting away from traditional mass media, such as television, towards the internet (Deloitte, 2014) and notably social media. Hence, companies benefit from having their brands present on social media, including SNS, as it is where consumers spend more and more of their time.

Within a social networking context, the research objectives of our study are to: (1) determine what motivates people to use SNS; (2) discover the relationships between motives and engagement in SNS; and (3) ascertain any gender differences in the use of SNS. The analyses of responses to an online survey capturing the reasons for using Facebook provides insights on the gender differences in survey respondent motivations and related engagement with social media.

BACKGROUND

Motivations for Using Social Media

Until recently the types of media used worldwide remained mostly unchanged, dominated by traditional media such as newspapers, magazines, radio, television, cinema and books. For a long time traditional media have been playing a key role in our cultural development as they fulfil an important individual need to connect with society (Katz, Blumler & Gurevitch, 1974; Katz, Haas & Gurevitch, 1973). This connection with society, via traditional media, happens through the filter of a few; namely editors, writers and others who decide on what is to be widely communicated. The media type and these filters render such traditional media primarily unidirectional in that information and opinions flow from the media to the audience, with little interaction flowing in the reverse direction, limited for example to selected letters from readers that are published in specific sections of newspapers and magazines. The development of the internet and the creation of social media and in particular SNS, pushed by the mass adoption of Facebook, drastically changed the characteristics of media. The development of social media democratised communications, allowing people to interact with each other in new ways which were fast, low cost, and large scale, reaching people with ease almost anywhere in the world.

This new way to connect with other people has also catapulted the practice of multi-directional communication flows. Now consumers share their views not only with their own friends and communities, but also directly with businesses and governments both in public and private ways. By publicly participating in the conversation, people in turn create a large body of content that represents the views of society in a way that adds to the views disseminated by mass media, businesses and governments. Hence, social media has allowed individuals to more thoroughly fulfil their need to connect with society – not only by helping people to express themselves, but also by facilitating access to all sorts of information and opinions from others.

SNS are defined as "web-based services that allow individuals to construct a public or semi-public profile within a bounded system, articulate a list of other users with whom they share a connection, and view and traverse their list of connections and those made by others within the system" (Boyd & Ellison, 2007, p. 211). As a type of media, it is fruitful to look at motivations to use SNS by employing, as a starting point, the theory of uses and gratifications of media (Katz et al., 1974; Katz et al., 1973). Katz and colleagues theorised three sources of media gratification: media content, exposure to media per se, and the social context. These different sources generate benefits such as fulfilment of surveillance, which links with the need for security, curiosity, and exploration; reinforcement to one's attitudes, which in turn may derive from the need for reassurance; social utility, which links to affiliation needs; and escape, which links to the need to reduce anxiety. The theory discusses how each type of media may relate differently to each type of need. For example, mentioning Enzenberger (cited by Katz et al., 1974) the authors discuss how the 8mm camera, as a type of media, offered benefits such as keeping the family together and atomising and depoliticising society. Similarly, social media has helped change society by democratising the dissemination of information, while SNS, as a type of social media, relate primarily to particular types of needs, notably social needs. Overall, while the uses and gratifications theory of media has been developed for traditional media, it is equally applicable to social media providing both similar and new gratifications in the social context.

One the most influential SNS is Facebook, with 1.35 billion users active monthly worldwide (Statista, 2014). Facebook stimulates high levels of user participation: 63% of American Facebook users visit the site at least once a day, and 40% do so multiple times a day (Duggan & Smith, 2013). A list of factors have been identified as motives for using Facebook including seeking friends, convenience, social support, information, and entertainment (Kim, Sohn & Choi, 2011). Facebook has also become a place to find general information about anyone, including those not known personally. Hence, a further relevant motive to use social media is to specifically research people (Lampe, Ellison & Steinfield, 2008).

While social media attracts both men and women, gender differences have been found in its usage. For example, a study on the use of MySpace indicated that teenage girls use more self-references, social words, and negative emotions than teenage boys (Pfeil, Arjan & Zaphiris, 2009). Women also tended to have more friends in MySpace. Men who are more emotionally unstable are more likely to use social media, whereas women's social media use does not differ based on emotional stability (Correa, Hinsley & De Zuniga, 2010). These findings suggest that women tend to use social media more for the social aspect than men and it is possible that this use leans to the emotional side. Indeed, women use more social media to communicate with peers than men (Barker, 2009) and use SNS more for relationship maintenance, whereas men tend to use SNS more for forging new relationships (Muscanell & Guadagno, 2012). It would then be expected that gender differences may relate to different motivations to use SNS.

Gender Differences in Information Search

Social media includes not only SNS but also other types of virtual environments such as blogs, product review enabled sites, consumer forums, and online communities, which may or may not be sponsored or affiliated to a company. Users would by definition be motivated to use social media sites where consumers exchange information about products and services because they facilitate information search. In comparison, users of SNS may consider them primarily from a social interaction point of view. Still, SNS fulfil information search needs. Pai and Arnott (2013) found that by browsing others' pages, SNS users satisfy their curiosity and gain useful insights. Besides discussions that users have about products and brands on SNS, advertising also provides information to consumers on SNS (Zeng, Huang & Dou, 2009); consumers can learn about events, promotions, and gather general information about brands and companies, and communicate with businesses and other users. Further, research in the area of tourism suggests that social media has become important for information search as a large number of social media sites is returned when using search engines (Xiang & Gretzel, 2010). This particular motive, i.e. seeking information, is important for marketers, companies and consumers themselves because seeking information is a fundamental step in the consumer buying process (Howard & Sheth, 1969). Moreover, it has been found that the more time consumers spend searching for information on the internet, in addition to the increased frequency in which they engage in such search, the more likely purchase decisions will be influenced by the information gathered (Bhatnagar & Ghose, 2004). Given that social media in recent years has emerged as an immense, free, and easy-to-access information resource, both through posts by advertisers, consumers, government and companies, information search should play a significant role as a reason for using social media. Prior research has already found evidence for such a link (Kim et al., 2011), and here we further investigate gender differences within this context.

The literature on information search has already established gender differences that shed light on the processes underlining the search process for women and men. When considering internet searches for five product categories, namely software, music CDs, clothing apparel, recreational equipment, and travel arrangements, Bhatnagar and Ghose (2004) found that men search for longer than women, even though they do not differ in search frequency. Early research commented on men's higher levels of computer aptitude and women having greater computer anxiety (Nelson & Watson, 1990; Rosen & Maguire, 1990), and that men tend to perceive internet and email as more useful than women (Gefen & Straub, 1997). They also found that consumers search for longer when looking for apparel (Bhatnagar & Ghose, 2004). The finding that men search for longer and that longer searches occurred for clothing apparel may seem at odds with the fact that women enjoy shopping more than men (Kotzé, North, Stols & Venter, 2012), especially for clothing (Guiry, Mägi & Lutz, 2006).

As these findings were reported in times when social media and easy-to-use mobile platforms were not yet mainstream, and many did not even exist, it is possible that the finding that men spend more time searching online may no longer hold true. Indeed, women were already more geared than men towards using the internet for personal communication before online social media use was widespread (Weiser, 2000). Furthermore, by 2004 the number of American women using the internet equalled the number of men (Kim, Lehto & Morrison, 2007). More recent research (Seock & Bailey, 2008) has reported that in the case of apparel, female college students are more active online, searching for information and making purchases.

Another gender difference in search behaviour is the fact that, in addition to the differences in searching for apparel reported above, women tend to search online more in general. For example, in studying different types of customer automobile purchases, Furse, Punj and Stewart (1984) found that women tended to be part of the cluster that spent the most time searching. Other research on the purchase of Christmas gifts found that women systematically search more for both general and specific in-store information, besides starting the task much earlier than men and doing more shopping trips (Laroche, Saad, Cleveland & Browne, 2000). When it comes to information search for travel, Vogt and Fesenmaier (1998) found that women have more functional needs than men, where functional needs refer to motivated efforts directed at contributing to a purpose. More specifically, women scored higher overall in the group of needs that included items such as 'learn about prices', 'find bargains', 'locate information that is concise', and 'reduce the likelihood of being disappointed'. No differences were found for hedonic, innovation, aesthetic, and social needs. This later piece of research suggests that women may search more extensively for travel information because they have higher needs to be both efficient and effective in their decision making process than men (Vogt and Fesenmaier, 2001). Cognitively, women process information differently from men (Putrevu, 2001). While men process information more hemispherically, focusing on individual elements that may have the greatest personal impacts, women process information more symmetrically and in a more integrated way, in an attempt to uncover relationships among several elements (Putrevu, 2001). One factor that may fuel women's more extensive information search is risk avoidance, as women have consistently been found to take less risk than men in a number of contexts (Byrnes, Miller & Schafer, 1999).

Further, in one culturally specific example, Japanese women are more active mobile internet users than their male counterparts, which is consistent with the idea that women tend to engage more in deeper information processing by searching all available media and use a more diverse range of information sources (Okazaki & Hirose, 2009). Interestingly, this research seems to corroborate earlier discussions suggesting that the fact that technology has become more accessible to society as a whole, including through the emergence of mobile technology, may have helped change the previous dominance of men in the use of computers. In conclusion, the fact that women tend to search more in general would suggest that they may search more information than men in SNS as well. This is the primary question we investigate in this research.

Social Media Engagement

The concept of engagement has proliferated in the literature in recent years (e.g. Calder and Malthouse 2008; Gambetti & Graffigna, 2010; Kabadayi & Price, 2014; Verhoef, Reinartz & Krafft, 2010). However, this process has generated rather different definitions and understandings (Gambetti & Graffigna, 2010). Within this ongoing debate, some view engagement as a behavioural manifestation beyond transactions and stemming from motivational drivers (Van Doorn et al., 2010; Verhoef, Reinartz & Krafft, 2010). Others view engagement as a psychological experience. Agarwal and Karahanna (2000) discuss cognitive engagement online as a state of deep involvement with new information technologies. In the subject area of media, Calder and Malthouse (2008) see media engagement as a fundamental factor for advertising effectiveness. The authors differentiate it from *liking*, theorising that engagement is a separate element determining an experience. It is one element that has a motivational nature, as opposed to the hedonic nature that *liking* has.

Research discussing behavioural engagement with social media that has appeared in the academic literature includes liking and commenting behaviour on Facebook (Kabadayi & Price, 2014), and consumer purchases as a function of brand engagement in online communities (Khim-Yong, Cheng-Suang & Zhijie, 2013). According to current research, engagement is taken from the psychological experience standpoint. This contributes to other research looking at psychological factors in social media, such as consumer attitudes toward social media marketing (Akar & Topçu, 2011; Kim et al., 2011), and perceptions of advertisements in Facebook, Twitter and YouTube (Pikas & Sorrentino, 2014). The inherent involvement that social media creates in users of a new technology, largely driven by new mobile developments and that mobile devices and media content can be viewed anywhere in the world, is another factor that highlights the relevance of considering engagement at the psychological level, and not just the behavioural level.

It is expected that, to the extent that social media delivers people's information needs, people would feel engaged with it. Hence, using social media with the clear purpose to seek information would positively relate to engagement with social media. Related literature has found that in the purchase of 'big ticket items' women benefit more than men from online environments because online media reduces the inefficiencies in price paid because gender identity need not be disclosed (Zettelmeyer, Morton & Silva-Risso, 2006). In line with this finding, women's purchase behaviour is also more influenced by online consumer reviews than men's (Bae & Lee, 2011). If women benefit from purchasing online, do they search/use more social media sources than men to search for information? This is one question that our research investigates in the context of online social media, as well as whether this information search relates to user engagement.

EMPIRICAL INVESTIGATION

Methodology

The data were collected from a convenience sample of undergraduate business students of a major metropolitan university in Australia. Given its dominance as a social media platform, it was decided to focus the data collection on Facebook. The qualifying question was whether a participant had a Facebook profile. Students were briefed about the purpose of the research and were asked to complete a self-administered online questionnaire. An incentive to complete the questionnaire was a chance to win one of ten $50 gift cards for a department store.

The online questionnaire took approximately 15 minutes to complete. To assess reasons for using Facebook, a five-dimensional scale (Kim et al., 2011) was employed that composed of: seeking friends ($\alpha = 0.81$), seeking convenience ($\alpha = 0.90$), seeking social support ($\alpha = 0.87$), seeking information ($\alpha = 0.90$), and seeking entertainment ($\alpha = 0.82$). A sixth dimension researching people ($\alpha = 0.73$) was included, adapted from Lampe et al. (2008). Participants were asked how many times they actively logged-on to Facebook each day and user engagement was measured using an adapted cognitive absorption scale (Agarwal & Karahanna, 2000). More specifically, because the scale is very long and respondents were already filling out other long scales related to their motivations for using Facebook, only items TD2, TD3, TD5, FI2, CO1 and CU3 of the original cognitive absorption scale, as appears in Agarwal and Karahanna (2000), were used in the survey. These items were deemed the most relevant for the context of social media use; one item that seemed most adapted to Facebook use was selected from each dimension, with the exception of the heightened enjoyment dimension as our focus was on information search. Three items were selected from the temporal dissociation dimension because these items were more heterogeneous, whereas items in the other dimensions were very similar to each other. In addition, the items were accordingly modified from the context of Web use to Facebook use. The measured construct presented satisfactory reliability ($\alpha = 0.83$). A measure of shopping enjoyment was adapted from Donthu and Gilliland (1996) using their three-item attitude toward shopping dimension. The three items are 'Buying things makes me happy', 'Shopping is fun', and 'I get a real "high" from shopping'. An additional item was included, namely 'Shopping is exciting' ($\alpha = 0.93$). Recognising the importance of new technologies, a question was also included focusing on a consumer innovativeness scale ($\alpha = 0.91$, Goldsmith & Hofacker 1991), modelled towards technology and apps/gadgets. Demographics were collected at the end of the survey. The survey was piloted after which some questions were revised prior to launching online.

A total of 169 questionnaires were received, of which 161 were retained for the analyses after removing data for those who did not use Facebook (8 respondents). Of the respondents, 60 (37%) were male and 101 (63%) were female, and the average age was 19.97 years old. Females on average spent more time on Facebook at 2.22 hours per day compared to 2.01 hours for males.

Model

Social media users generate content as well as consume content created by other users and marketers. Prior findings related to social media indicate that consumers benefit from easy access to word-of-mouth information, therefore social media is playing an increasingly important role in the marketing mix. However, there is scant literature that highlights gender based differences in the use of social media and its impact on engagement on social media. In this study we model the role of gender on reasons to use Facebook and examine how motivation to use Facebook impacts the behaviour of consumers (see Figure 1).

Figure 1. Gender based differences on using Facebook and engagement

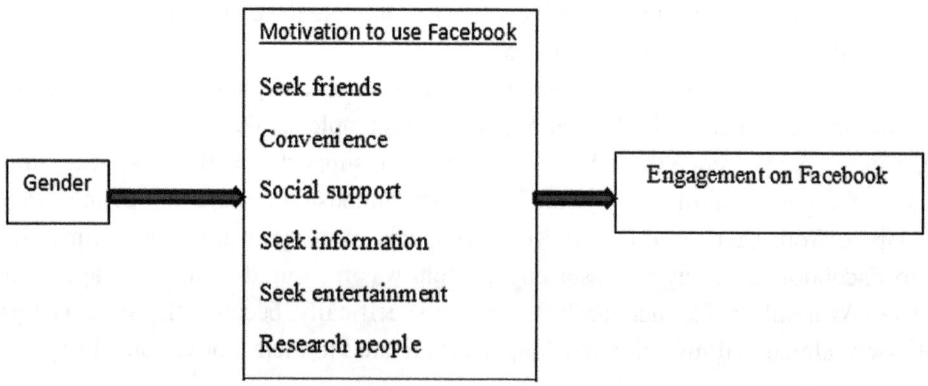

Consumers may use Facebook for several reasons such as to seek friends (y_1), for convenience (y_2), to seek social support (y_3), to seek information (y_4), seek entertainment (y_5), and learn more about others, i.e. research people (y_6). These are the dependent variables and each of these reasons can be analysed as a linear regression equation. However, there may be contemporaneous cross-equation correlations as, for example, factors that influence use of Facebook to seek friends may also influence use of Facebook to seek social support. To control for contemporaneous cross-equation correlations, we estimate a system of equations using seemingly unrelated regressions (SUR). The SUR model is represented in Equation 1.

$$\begin{pmatrix} y_1 \\ \vdots \\ y_6 \end{pmatrix} = \left(\begin{bmatrix} \beta_1' X_1 & \cdots & 0 \\ \vdots & \ddots & \vdots \\ 0 & \cdots & \beta_6' X_6 \end{bmatrix} \right) + \begin{bmatrix} \varepsilon_1 \\ \vdots \\ \varepsilon_6 \end{bmatrix} \quad (1)$$

The error variance matrix is dimension J x J and $\varepsilon_j \sim N(0,\Sigma)$, and Σ is the variance-covariance matrix. The dependent variable $y=(y_{1\ldots}\ y_6)'$ is a vector of the various reasons to use Facebook. The matrix X consists of the exogenous variables, such as gender, that are expected to influence the use of Facebook and $\beta=(\beta_{1\ldots}\ \beta_6)'$ represents the vector of coefficients that capture the impact of the exogenous variables. The exogenous variables are gender, consumer innovativeness, age, household size and shopping enjoyment. Innovativeness and shopping enjoyment are Likert scale measures, whereas gender is a dummy variable. Gender equals 1 for males and 0 for females. The estimation results are presented in Table 1 below.

RESULTS

The results indicate that males are less likely to use Facebook for convenience or to seek information (Table 1). Among other factors that influence the use of Facebook, we find that more innovative consumers use Facebook to seek friends, to seek information, and to research people, while consumers who enjoy shopping are more likely to use Facebook for convenience, to seek entertainment, and to research people. The results indicate that age is not a significant predictor of Facebook use. The coefficient of age is negative and significant for convenience. This result is consistent with prior findings that older people are less likely to use the Internet. In addition, our results indicate that household size is not a significant predictor of Facebook use.

Further, we investigate the impact of various reasons of using Facebook on consumer engagement as measured by the extent to which consumers immerse themselves or get involved on Facebook. The results of linear regression analysis of consumer engagement are indicated in Table 2.

As can be seen from Table 2, consumer motivation to use Facebook significantly impacts the extent to which consumers are engaged on Facebook. Those who use Facebook for convenience, social support, to seek information, and to seek entertainment are likely to use Facebook more than people who use Facebook for other purposes. While prior research finds that social media platforms are a useful source to obtain word-of-mouth and to build a network of friends, our study highlights information seeking behaviour as a core driver for using Facebook.

Table 1. Reasons for using Facebook

.	Equation	Obs	Parms	RMSE	R-sq	chi²	P
.	Seek friends	161	5	5.484397	0.0681	11.76	0.0382
.	Convenience	161	5	4.331558	0.1677	32.45	0
.	Social support	161	5	5.675147	0.0308	5.12	0.4016
	Seek information	161	5	6.718109	0.1730	33.67	0
	Seek entertainment	161	5	4.622088	0.1502	28.46	0
	Research people	161	5	5.279683	0.0797	13.94	0.0160
		Coef.	**std.**	**z**	**P>|z|**	**[95% Conf. Interval]**	
DV	**Seek friends**						
	Gender	0.70	1.00	0.70	0.48	-1.26	2.67
	Innovativeness	**0.15**	0.06	2.66	0.01	0.04	0.26
	Shopping enjoyment	0.06	0.34	0.16	0.87	-0.62	0.73
	Age	-0.10	0.16	-0.62	0.54	-0.40	0.21
	Household size	0.30	0.28	1.07	0.29	-0.25	0.85
	Intercept	10.57	3.90	2.71	0.01	2.92	18.22
DV	**Convenience**						
	Gender	**-1.82**	0.79	-2.30	0.02	-3.37	-0.27
	Innovativeness	0.06	0.04	1.43	0.15	-0.02	0.15
	Shopping enjoyment	**0.87**	0.27	3.21	0.00	0.34	1.41
	Age	**-0.20**	0.12	-1.58	0.11	-0.44	0.05
	Household size	0.24	0.22	1.06	0.29	-0.20	0.67
	Intercept	20.43	3.08	6.63	0.00	14.39	26.48
DV	**Social support**						
	Gender	0.66	1.04	0.64	0.52	-1.37	2.69
	Innovativeness	0.07	0.06	1.15	0.25	-0.05	0.18
	Shopping enjoyment	0.40	0.36	1.11	0.27	-0.30	1.09
	Age	0.08	0.16	0.50	0.62	-0.24	0.40
	Household size	0.26	0.29	0.89	0.37	-0.31	0.83
	Intercept	3.72	4.04	0.92	0.36	-4.20	11.64
DV	**Seek information**						
	Gender	**-2.76**	1.23	-2.24	0.03	-5.16	-0.35
	Innovativeness	**0.32**	0.07	4.72	0.00	0.19	0.46
	Shopping enjoyment	0.43	0.42	1.02	0.31	-0.40	1.25
	Age	0.01	0.19	0.06	0.95	-0.37	0.39
	Household size	0.40	0.34	1.16	0.25	-0.28	1.07
	Intercept	8.41	4.78	1.76	0.08	-0.96	17.79

continued on following page

Table 1. Continued

DV	Seek entertainment						
	Gender	-0.27	0.84	-0.32	0.75	-1.92	1.39
	Innovativeness	0.04	0.05	0.91	0.36	-0.05	0.14
	Shopping enjoyment	**1.25**	0.29	4.32	0.00	0.69	1.82
	Age	-0.04	0.13	-0.27	0.79	-0.30	0.22
	Household size	0.30	0.24	1.28	0.20	-0.16	0.77
	Intercept	12.24	3.29	3.72	0.00	5.79	18.69

Table 2. Consumer engagement on Facebook

Number of obs = 161

Source	SS	df	MS
Model	3801.63	8	475.21
Residual	4546.93	152	29.91
Total	8348.56	160	52.18

Prob > F = 0.0000

R-squared = 0.46

Adj R-squared = 0.43

Root MSE = 5.47

F(8, 152) = 15.89

		Coef.	Std. Err.	t	P>|t|	[95% Conf. Interval]	
DV	Engagement						
	Seek friends	-0.07	0.09	-0.74	0.46	-0.26	0.12
	Convenience	**0.45**	0.12	3.60	0.00	0.20	0.69
	Social support	**0.28**	0.09	3.25	0.00	0.11	0.45
	Seek information	**0.17**	0.07	2.46	0.02	0.03	0.31
	Seek entertainment	**0.49**	0.11	4.48	0.00	0.27	0.71
	Research people	-0.07	0.10	-0.73	0.47	-0.26	0.12
	Gender	-1.13	0.95	-1.20	0.23	-3.01	0.74
	Log-in frequency	0.46	0.58	0.80	0.43	-0.68	1.60
	Intercept	3.56	2.94	1.21	0.23	-2.25	9.37

Finally, the results of this study highlight that female consumers are more likely than male consumers to use Facebook for convenience and to seek information. The information seeking behaviour relates positively to the degree of engagement on Facebook. This is an interesting finding from the perspective that prior research has shown that females benefit from using online resources when making big ticket purchases as they are able to bargain without disclosing their gender (Zettelmeyer et al., 2006). Our results highlight that females are more likely to use online resources such as social media for purposes other than social engagement, i.e. to find information. This has important implications for retailers that use social media advertising to target consumers with relevant product related information.

IMPLICATIONS

The results indicating that women are more likely to use Facebook than men for convenience or to seek information suggest a number of implications. While women are more likely to search online for information than men in general, as discussed in the background section of this chapter, women are also interested in efficient and effective searching processes. Given the abundance of options regarding where to get information, ease-of-use is no longer an additional benefit but rather an imperative strategy for any business that desires to engage with and target their communications to their potential female customers. Effort should be made by businesses to clearly state their offerings and provide relevant information to attract the interest of prospective online consumers. Another insight from our research is that getting the attention of consumers amid the clutter of the online environment is very difficult, especially as the amount of online material has grown exponentially over the years. The fact that our study shows that women are more likely to research on SNS, such as Facebook, further suggests that social media is currently a key place not only to send information out but also to engage with consumers, especially women. Therefore, businesses are encouraged to build an online social media presence as part of their marketing communications strategy.

Relating to brands, women are more likely than men to share brand-related material based on things seen in social media ads (Burst Media, 2013), and are more likely than men to interact with brands in social media, to show support for brands they like, and access special offers, coupons, and/or promotions (Burst Media, 2013). This indicates an important role that women play in generating word-of-mouth, both positive and negative, which can be a form of product information that can be searched for by other women. While corroborating previous findings that women seek more functional benefits from their searches (Vogt & Fesenmaier, 1998), this also highlights the importance of the emotional aspect of the relationship of women with brands, which can be boosted through appropriate use of social media and electronic word-of-mouth.

The relationship between seeking information and convenience in social media and cognitive engagement also exemplifies how a sense of purpose, coupled with achieving this purpose, leads to higher involvement with media. The importance of cognitive engagement for marketers cannot be underestimated, notably its potential to result in higher information retention and use, higher satisfaction, and higher willingness to make recommendations to friends, all of which in turn lead to more interaction with the business and ultimately to increased purchases.

FUTURE RESEARCH DIRECTIONS

The fact that women are more inclined to use online environments for convenience than men, coupled with the fact that technology has changed from being inaccessible to a large number of people to being very accessible to all, suggests a world where women may have taken the lead when it comes to use of technological innovation, at least in relation to the search for related information and potentially online shopping. Take, for example, the numerous cases of new software for virtually trying products that have been reported in the news (Felsted, 2014). L'Oreal has created an app called Makeup Genius that allows users to see what the makeup looks like on their own face as they move by using the virtual mirror in their iPhones or iPads. While the marketing for the release of the app featured a man, notably L'Oreal's CEO, with the objective of creating a fun atmosphere around the product, the app is targeted at women, as are the majority of L'Oreal's cosmetic products. Another innovation has been implemented by the Japanese clothing company Uniqlo. They have installed a magic mirror in one store which allows shoppers to see the clothes they are trying on in different colours.

Given the rapid innovation in the use of social media, it would be fruitful to see future research which revisits previous gender gaps in terms of technology adoption (Jackson, Ervin, Gardner & Schmitt, 2001), especially when considering different domains. It is important to keep different contexts in mind because, for example, in contrast to shopping, it seems that products such as gaming consoles may remain appealing to men rather than women (Lenhart, Purcell, Smith & Zickuhr, 2010).

Other gender differences that deserve further research are those related to the use of different social media platforms. Considering American online adults, while a higher percentage of men use LinkedIn and Reddit than women, more women than men are users of Facebook, Instagram, and Pinterest (Burst Media, 2013; Duggan, 2013; Duggan & Smith, 2013). For Pinterest, women's usage is far in excess of men's usage (33% of women, 8% of men). These figures can be better interpreted when the reasons for using these networks are uncovered. Considering that Facebook is used more for social reasons and Twitter more for information (Hughes, Rowe, Batey & Lee, 2012), it would be interesting to explore if the gender differences found here for Facebook are present in Twitter as well. More research integrating these findings with consequences of social media use would be highly valuable for businesses, such as discovering the use of information gathered in social media, product/service choice, social media advertising effectiveness, and the potential psychological effects of social media use (e.g. anxiety).

Our research explored one facet of how women differ from men in their use of social media. Looking at motivations to use Facebook, the study here documented measured general reasons for using the social network, for example, to learn about new things. Given the nature of most of the conversations that permeate Facebook, it is fair to believe that a lot of the information learned relates to hedonic products and experiences such as movies, restaurants, clothing and travel. In turn, hedonic products also tend to be engaging and this may be a factor contributing to higher cognitive absorption. That is, consumers simply have fun while discussing such topics and this type of information exchange may be a determinant of engagement in social networks. Future research could further explore if information sought in social networks relates more to hedonic as opposed to utilitarian products and services, and, if so, whether women would be more likely to engage with social media than men for information gathering in certain product categories.

Finally, further research crossing potential cultural differences with our findings may render interesting findings. Kim et al. (2011) have studied motivations to use Facebook in America compared with Korea. It is possible that gender interacts with such findings, which would be of value to the international marketer.

CONCLUSION

The objectives of this study were to determine what motivates people to use SNS, discover the relationships between motives and engagement in social media, and ascertain any gender differences in the use of social media. Our research identifies the use of social media to seek information as an important factor leading to social media engagement, as well as seeking entertainment, social support, and convenience. A managerial implication of this finding is that advertising can be designed to better fit with these motivations in order to be more effective. For example, brands that create entertaining content on social media, and/or increase convenience for users (e.g. offer easy to use coupons via mobile technology to use when making a payment at a store), are likely to obtain higher user engagement and support.

While there are limitations to this study, including that the sample was of undergraduate business students, and that the findings are limited by the correlational nature of our cross-sectional data (hence causality cannot be claimed), we believe that the empirical support it provides for our conceptual model is substantive and aligns with previous literature. Therefore, more research is encouraged on gender differences in information search and buying behaviour related to online media. By having a better understanding of how differently men and women are interacting and affected by social media, marketers can better target them with the information they require in the form they want, to provide a clearer pathway to engagement, and ultimately purchases.

REFERENCES

Agarwal, R., & Karahanna, E. (2000). Time flies when you're having fun: Cognitive absorption and beliefs about information technology usage. *Management Information Systems Quarterly*, *24*(4), 665–694. doi:10.2307/3250951

Akar, E., & Topçu, B. (2011). An examination of the factors influencing consumers' attitudes toward social media marketing. *Journal of Internet Commerce*, *10*(1), 35–67. doi:10.1080/15332861.2011.558456

Bae, S., & Lee, T. (2011). Gender differences in consumers' perception of online consumer reviews. *Electronic Commerce Research*, *11*(2), 201–214. doi:10.1007/s10660-010-9072-y

Barker, V. (2009). Older adolescents' motivations for social network site use: The influence of gender, group identity, and collective self-esteem. *Cyberpsychology & Behavior: The Impact of the Internet, Multimedia and Virtual Reality On Behavior. Society*, *12*(2), 209–213.

Bhatnagar, A., & Ghose, S. (2004). Online information search termination patterns across product categories and consumer demographics. *Journal of Retailing*, *80*(3), 221–228. doi:10.1016/j.jretai.2003.10.001

Boyd, D. M., & Ellison, N. B. (2007). Social network sites: Definition, history, and scholarship. *Journal of Computer-Mediated Communication*, *13*(1), 210–230. doi:10.1111/j.1083-6101.2007.00393.x

Byrnes, J. P., Miller, D. C., & Schafer, W. D. (1999). Gender differences in risk taking: A meta-analysis. *Psychological Bulletin*, *125*(3), 367–383. doi:10.1037/0033-2909.125.3.367

Calder, B. J., & Malthouse, E. C. (2008). Media engagement and advertising effectiveness. In B. J. Calder (Ed.), *Kellogg on advertising and media* (pp. 1–36). Hoboken, NJ: Wiley.

Chi, H.-H. (2011). Interactive digital advertising vs. Virtual brand community: Exploratory study of user motivation and social media marketing responses in Taiwan. *Journal of Interactive Advertising*, *12*(1), 44–61. doi:10.1080/15252019.2011.10722190

Correa, T., Hinsley, A. W., & De Zuniga, H. G. (2010). Who interacts on the web?: The intersection of users' personality and social media use. *Computers in Human Behavior*, *26*(2), 247–253. doi:10.1016/j.chb.2009.09.003

Curran, K., Graham, S., & Temple, C. (2011). Advertising on Facebook. *International Journal of E-Business Development*, *1*(1), 26–33.

Deloitte. (2014). Media consumer survey. *Australian Media and Digital Preferences* (3rd ed.).

Donthu, N., & Gilliland, D. (1996). Observations: The infomercial shopper. *Journal of Advertising Research*, *36*(2), 69–77.

Duggan, M. (2013). It's a woman's (social media) world. Retrieved from www.pewresearch.org/fact-tank/2013/09/12/its-a-womans-social-media-world/

Duggan, M., & Smith, A. (2013). Social media update 2013: PEW Research Center's Internet & American Life Project. Retrieved from www.pewinternet.org/2013/12/30/social-media-update-2013/

Felsted, A. (2014, November 12). Apps bring web shopping to life, *Financial Times*.

Furse, D. H., Punj, G. N., & Stewart, D. W. (1984). A typology of individual search strategies among purchasers of new automobiles. *The Journal of Consumer Research*, *10*(4), 417–431. doi:10.1086/208980

Gambetti, R. C., & Graffigna, G. (2010). The concept of engagement a systematic analysis of the ongoing marketing debate. *International Journal of Market Research*, *52*(6), 801–826. doi:10.2501/S147078531020166

Gefen, D., & Straub, D. W. (1997). Gender differences in the perception and use of e-mail: An extension to the technology acceptance model. *Management Information Systems Quarterly*, *21*(4), 389–400. doi:10.2307/249720

Goldsmith, R. E., & Hofacker, C. F. (1991). Measuring consumer innovativeness. *Journal of the Academy of Marketing Science*, *19*(3), 209–221. doi:10.1007/BF02726497

Guiry, M., Mägi, A. W., & Lutz, R. J. (2006). Defining and measuring recreational shopper identity. *Journal of the Academy of Marketing Science*, *34*(1), 74–83. doi:10.1177/0092070305282042

Howard, J. A., & Sheth, J. N. (1969). *The Theory of Buyer Behavior*. New York: John Wiley & Sons.

Hughes, D. J., Rowe, M., Batey, M., & Lee, A. (2012). A tale of two sites: Twitter vs. Facebook and the personality predictors of social media usage. *Computers in Human Behavior*, *28*(2), 561–569. doi:10.1016/j.chb.2011.11.001

Jackson, L. A., Ervin, K. S., Gardner, P. D., & Schmitt, N. (2001). Gender and the internet: Women communicating and men searching. *Sex Roles*, *44*(5-6), 363–379. doi:10.1023/A:1010937901821

Kabadayi, S., & Price, K. (2014). Consumer–brand engagement on Facebook: Liking and commenting behaviors. *Journal of Research in Interactive Marketing*, *8*(3), 203–223. doi:10.1108/JRIM-12-2013-0081

Kaplan, A. M., & Haenlein, M. (2010). Users of the world, unite! The challenges and opportunities of social media. *Business Horizons*, *53*(1), 59–68. doi:10.1016/j.bushor.2009.09.003

Katz, E., Blumler, J. G., & Gurevitch, M. (1974). Utilization of mass communication by the individual. In J. G. Blumler & E. Katz (Eds.), *The uses of mass communications: Current perspectives on gratifications research* (Vol. III, pp. 19–32). Beverly Hills, CA: Sage.

Katz, E., Haas, H., & Gurevitch, M. (1973). On the use of the mass media for important things. *American Sociological Review*, *38*(2), 164–181. doi:10.2307/2094393

Khim-Yong, G., Cheng-Suang, H., & Zhijie, L. (2013). Social media brand community and consumer behavior: Quantifying the relative impact of user- and marketer-generated content. *Information Systems Research*, *24*(1), 88–107. doi:10.1287/isre.1120.0469

Kim, D.-Y., Lehto, X. Y., & Morrison, A. M. (2007). Gender differences in online travel information search: Implications for marketing communications on the internet. *Tourism Management*, *28*(2), 423–433. doi:10.1016/j.tourman.2006.04.001

Kim, Y., Sohn, D., & Choi, S. M. (2011). Cultural difference in motivations for using social network sites: A comparative study of American and Korean college students. *Computers in Human Behavior*, *27*(1), 365–372. doi:10.1016/j.chb.2010.08.015

Kotzé, T., North, E., Stols, M., & Venter, L. (2012). Gender differences in sources of shopping enjoyment. *International Journal of Consumer Studies*, *36*(4), 416–424. doi:10.1111/j.1470-6431.2011.01060.x

Lampe, C., Ellison, N. B., & Steinfield, C. (2008). Changes in use and perception of Facebook. *Paper presented at the 2008 ACM conference on Computer supported cooperative work*, San Diego, CA, USA. doi:10.1145/1460563.1460675

Laroche, M., Saad, G., Cleveland, M., & Browne, E. (2000). Gender differences in information search strategies for a Christmas gift. *Journal of Consumer Marketing*, *17*(6), 500–522. doi:10.1108/07363760010349920

Lenhart, A., Purcell, K., Smith, A., & Zickuhr, K. (2010). Social media & mobile internet use among teens and young adults. *PEW Research Center's Internet & American Life Project.*

Lukka, V., & James, P. T. J. (2014). Attitudes toward Facebook advertising. *Journal of Management and Marketing Research*, *14*, 1–26.

Mangold, W. G., & Faulds, D. J. (2009). Social media: The new hybrid element of the promotion mix. *Business Horizons*, *52*(4), 357–365. doi:10.1016/j.bushor.2009.03.002

Muscanell, N. L., & Guadagno, R. E. (2012). Make new friends or keep the old: Gender and personality differences in social networking use. *Computers in Human Behavior*, *28*(1), 107–112. doi:10.1016/j.chb.2011.08.016

Nelson, C. S., & Watson, J. A. (1990). The computer gender gap: Children's attitudes, performance and socialization. *Journal of Educational Technology Systems*, *19*(4), 345–353. doi:10.2190/51CF-7CHE-DX52-E9F5

Okazaki, S., & Hirose, M. (2009). Does gender affect media choice in travel information search? On the use of mobile internet. *Tourism Management*, *30*(6), 794–804. doi:10.1016/j.tourman.2008.12.012

Online insights: Expanding the conversation - leveraging social media for brand interaction. (2013). *Burst Media.* Retrieved from www.burstmedia.com/pdf/burst_media_online_insights_2013_04.pdf

Pai, P., & Arnott, D. C. (2013). User adoption of social networking sites: Eliciting uses and gratifications through a means–end approach. *Computers in Human Behavior*, *29*(3), 1039–1053. doi:10.1016/j.chb.2012.06.025

Pfeil, U., Arjan, R., & Zaphiris, P. (2009). Age differences in online social networking – a study of user profiles and the social capital divide among teenagers and older users in Myspace. *Computers in Human Behavior*, *25*(3), 643–654. doi:10.1016/j.chb.2008.08.015

Pikas, B., & Sorrentino, G. (2014). The effectiveness of online advertising: Consumer's perceptions of ads on Facebook, Twitter and YouTube. *Journal of Applied Business and Economics*, *16*(4), 70–81.

Putrevu, S. (2001). Exploring the origins and information processing differences between men and women: Implications for advertisers. *Academy of Marketing Science Review*, *10*(1), 1–14.

Rosen, L. D., & Maguire, P. (1990). Myths and realities of computerphobia: A meta-analysis. *Anxiety Research*, *3*(3), 175–191. doi:10.1080/08917779008248751

Seock, Y. K., & Bailey, L. R. (2008). The influence of college students' shopping orientations and gender differences on online information searches and purchase behaviours. *International Journal of Consumer Studies*, *32*(2), 113–121. doi:10.1111/j.1470-6431.2007.00647.x

Statista. (2014). *Number of monthly active Facebook users worldwide from 3rd quarter 2008 to 3rd quarter 2014 (in millions)*. Retrieved 24 November 2014, from http://www.statista.com/statistics/264810/number-of-monthly-active-facebook-users-worldwide/

Van Doorn, J., Lemon, K. N., Mittal, V., Nass, S., Pick, D., Pirner, P., & Verhoef, P. C. (2010). Customer engagement behavior: Theoretical foundations and research directions. *Journal of Service Research*, *13*(3), 253–266. doi:10.1177/1094670510375599

Verhoef, P. C., Reinartz, W. J., & Krafft, M. (2010). Customer engagement as a new perspective in customer management. *Journal of Service Research*, *13*(3), 247–252. doi:10.1177/1094670510375461

Vogt, C. A., & Fesenmaier, D. R. (1998). Expanding the functional information search model. *Annals of Tourism Research*, *25*(3), 551–578. doi:10.1016/S0160-7383(98)00010-3

Weiser, E. B. (2000). Gender differences in internet use patterns and internet application preferences: A two-sample comparison. *Cyberpsychology & Behavior*, *3*(2), 167–178. doi:10.1089/109493100316012

Xiang, Z., & Gretzel, U. (2010). Role of social media in online travel information search. *Tourism Management*, *31*(2), 179–188. doi:10.1016/j.tourman.2009.02.016

Zeng, F., Huang, L., & Dou, W. (2009). Social factors in user perceptions and responses to advertising in online social networking communities. *Journal of Interactive Advertising*, *10*(1), 1–13. doi:10.1080/15252019.2009.10722159

Zettelmeyer, F., Morton, F. S., & Silva-Risso, J. (2006). How the internet lowers prices: Evidence from matched survey and automobile transaction data. *JMR, Journal of Marketing Research*, *43*(2), 168–181. doi:10.1509/jmkr.43.2.168

KEY TERMS AND DEFINITIONS

Cognitive Absorption: A state of deep involvement with an activity to the point of losing track of time.

Convenience: To obtain things with little effort and without significant constraints.

Information Search: To seek any kind of information, this includes information about products and brands, and also finding out about anything that is new.

Motivation: Reasons that lead people to perform (or prevent people from performing) some act.

Social Media: Any online platform that facilitates communication among individuals and between individuals and organisations. This includes social networking sites, online brand and product communities, blogs, consumer forums, consumer advice websites (e.g. TripAdvisor), news sites reader comments sections, etc.

Social Networking Site (SNS): Any online platform that has as the main objective to facilitate regular communication among individuals. This includes social networking sites such as Facebook, Twitter, Instagram, LinkedIn, Vine, etc.

SUR Model: Seemingly unrelated regression model. It is a system of linear regression equations. The error terms of the equations are assumed to be correlated across the equations.

User Engagement: To commit cognitively to online activities within a social networking site, e.g. Facebook.

Chapter 4
It's My Site, and I'll Do What I Want:
Performing Female Identity through Digital Identity Curation in Online Spaces

Melissa Kelly
Queensland University of Technology, Australia

Anita Jetnikoff
Queensland University of Technology, Australia

ABSTRACT

This chapter is based on a qualitative case study that researched the perceptions of nine male and female pre-service English teachers' in regards to their preparedness to mentor positive digital conduct in Social network sites (SNS). These sites enable individuals to perform public representations of identity, consumed by virtual audiences, with various degrees of perceived privacy. The chapter frames what we call "identity curation" through three theoretical lenses; of performativity, customisation and critical literacy. This chapter discusses one of the themes that emerged from the research, which is the way in which "normalised" and naturalised representations of femininity on SNS were judged more harshly than masculine representations.

DOI: 10.4018/978-1-5225-0010-0.ch004

INTRODUCTION

This chapter is based on a qualitative case study that researched the perceptions of nine male and female pre-service English teachers' in regards to their preparedness to mentor positive digital conduct in social network sites (SNS). The central research question was "what do we understand about the ways in which young people curate their identity in digital spaces?" These digital online sites enable individuals to perform public representations of identity. SNS users access platforms via a range of technologies, including internet-enabled mobile technologies (IEMT), to produce enduring digital texts that are instantly published and consumed by virtual audiences, and with various degrees of perceived privacy. The chapter is framed through the theoretical lenses of performativity (Butler, 2011a, 2011b) which considers how gender and identity is constructed by users and interpreted by audiences, as well as how users curate their representations of identity through the customisation (Papacharissi, 2011) of their digital texts. Users practice customisation on content that either does not effectively inform their perceived or ideal self, or content they assess as not enhancing their representation of identity to other users. Customisation describes how users enact the process of virtual representation, which we are calling "identity curation." One of the themes that emerged amongst others, was the way in which "normalised" and naturalised representations of femininity were judged more harshly than masculine representations. For this reason our primary focus for this chapter is on representations of female identity curation on SNS. These concepts emerge from a third theoretical lens of critical literacy which the Pre-service teachers understand as a way of approaching their teaching of English.

The Research Context

Participants were drawn from a cohort of pre-service English teachers (7 females and 2 males) enrolled in the final English curriculum unit of their degree, who self-identified as active users of social media, and had completed eight weeks of practicum in Queensland secondary schools. This ethnographic case study used focus group interviews to code, analyse and identify what pre-service English teachers know and understand about identity, SNS, digital literacy and online digital conduct. Participants discussed their observations of the performance of identity and gender in social media.

Background

The emergence of participatory web cultures and user-generated content, particularly through SNS, has raised a number of issues affecting young people which have been studied extensively. These include privacy concerns, online safety and cyberbullying, which can take previously school-based concerns into the home environment. Less attention, however, has been given to the impact of the digital texts generated by SNS users on representations of the user's identity, and how the creation of digital texts will generate a lasting representation of the user that may have long term effects on the user's identity. The public domains of SNS enable readers beyond the user's assumed or known audience to access and view representations of self on SNS performed and curated by the user. This chapter will investigate one theme that emerged from the study's findings: the perceptions of the performance of female digital curation in online public spaces.

Pre-service English teachers will be entering a school environment populated by students who can be described as "digital natives" (Prensky, 2001, p. 1). Digital native refers to people born into the present digital age, and who have grown up immersed in digital technology. Further, many pre-service English teachers, as well as in-service English teachers, qualify as digital natives, while others, such as the researchers, can be described or digital travelers (Jetnikoff, 2009, p. 9). These latter are individuals who have had to adapt to changing technologies in order to participate in the digital age. All educators need to be aware of this constantly changing technological context as it informs the way we teach.

One of the goals of *The Melbourne Declaration* states that "successful learners [...] have the essential skills in literacy and numeracy and are creative and productive users of technology, especially ICT, as a foundation for success in all learning areas" (MCEETYA, 2008, p. 8). This goal is reflected in the expectations of the AC:E, which has been implemented in Queensland schools. The application of digital literacy practices and the performance of positive digital conduct are means by which students can demonstrate proficiency in the use of ICTs. Digital literacies are the means by which individuals can perform positive digital conduct through the use of information communication technologies (ICTs).

PERFORMING GENDER IDENTITY IN DIGITAL SPACES

When using SNS, digital identity is formed through the digital texts created by users. Representations of identity performed via digital texts are inherently disembodied. Users produce digital texts, distributed using digital and online spaces, which can be consumed synchronously and asynchronously; and which signify aspects of their identity to restricted and unrestricted audiences. Within this sociological phenomenon, researchers have determined that Judith Butler's post-structuralist performativity theory of identity provides a framework for investigating how disincorporated identity is represented external to the physical body. Butler (1988, p. 519), writing on the performance of gender identity, proposes that identity is "instituted through a *stylised repetition of acts*" (original emphasis) that are situated in the time and place of performance, and understood through the audience's interpretation of the enacted texts. Further, Butler (2011b, pp. 184-186) indicates that identity is not concealed within the body. She argues identities are performative. The evidence of an "internal core or substance" is produced through the enactment of "corporeal signs and other discursive means" with these being identified as "acts and gestures, articulated and enacted desires." Identity is the effect of the performance of these acts, as it is the socio-cultural readings of these texts that constitute an identity (Bell, 1999, pp. 6-7).

The application of Butler's performativity theory to online and digital environments has been established in existing literature. McKinlay (2010), contends that performativity can be applied to describe the development of identity in all contexts, as it describes the iterative process of repeating mundane experiences and social conventions by which an individual's identity comes to be recognised by others.

Dezuanni (2006, p. 6) describes how aspects of identity are performed using linguistic and semiotic "cultural tools" in the discourse of video games, and how performativity can be employed to investigate how young people develop agency and citizenship through the performance of cultural practices in participatory media spaces (Dezuanni, 2009, p. 40). In this way, Dezuanni has transferred the bodily signification of gender identity described by Butler to the digital, textual representations produced in online and virtual environments. This touches on some of the issues that became important in this study of online identity curation.

Participants in the focus groups responded to this question in ways that indicated they had not critically reflected on their own digital literacy practices to inform their teaching of digital texts and representations of gender identity. However, participants did identify a number of social issues that arise from the performance of digital conduct that is not positive. Further, participant responses indicated an understanding of the importance of developing ICT capabilities in regards to representations of identity, and as a way to embed the general capability of personal and social responsibilities into teaching episodes, as prescribed by the AC:E (ACARA, 2014). Participants were able to express their understanding of the place of SNS in the lives of their potential future students.

Dana: *I think finding an identity, in this day and age, for kids, is so much harder because kids are always online. I think they feel out of touch with the world if they're not on Facebook or things like that all the time.*

Cary: *It's a bit of a forum for them to escape into, but what they actually access online is not necessarily a representation of what the world is like or how they should conduct themselves around other people.*

Dana: *Most of the time it's negative as well. The stuff they put online can be quite detrimental to their futures. I mean we has a couple of girls suspended because they were bullying on Facebook, and they were doing it directly at a teacher.*

Dana and Cary suggest in this discussion that SNS performances are a very significant part of young people's identities. Kerry and Taylor also indicated their awareness that digital text production, the application of digital texts as representations of identity, the importance of personal and social responsibility (ACARA, 2014) and critical abilities that enable users to assess the impact of the texts they create were essential skills in a digital age school environment.

Kerry: *I feel it is all about personal use, learning how to deal with things on the internet, you say something negative and someone is going to respond to that.*

Taylor: *I think learning to deal with these things is pivotal, because it takes up so much of the students' time. And it has a massive effect on them. I think you'd have to (teach these skills) because I think it's not going to go away, it's only going to get worse.*

These responses provide insight into the performative representations of identity users enact using SNS. Both responses place the phenomenon of digital literacy in the realm of the mundane, and an iterative performance of mundane, established cultural practices forms the basis for the performative theory of identity as described by Butler (1988, p. 519).Both responses also suggest we could be doing something with this resource in schools, in terms of equipping students with the skills to read and write and design critically in these sites.

Cary: *One thing I did on my last prac to emphasise how what you see on the internet [...] can be entirely different from who (some people) actually are. (We) created a Facebook page for a character and the questions underpinning that activity were for people viewing this Facebook page, how do you want them to view this character? So from there, (how) do you want this character to be viewed as* *beautiful and perfect? What things would be on (there) to make people think that? It was interesting because I had a few students who said they didn't realise how often people don't put up things that are actually truthful to who they are [...] Then we talked about how it wasn't necessary to put up that different image all the time.*

Here, Cary demonstrates an understanding of how intertextuality and semiotics is applied as a practice of customisation, where SNS users selectively apply representations of identity to construct a desired image, as well as demonstrating to the students how they can read and interpret these signals in a critical way. This response highlights the importance of a critical literacy approach to interpreting performative representations of identity through digital texts, to understand how texts are produced to position the audience in a particular way. When consumers of text are conscious of being positioned by the attitudes, values and beliefs encoded in texts, they are able to decode texts to understand the intended position and make judgements about the ideology presented (Misson & Morgan, 2006, pp. 68-71).

Dana expressed frustration with the way that ICT is positioned within curriculum documents such as the AC:E.

Dana: *ICT is not even part of the curriculum. It's just embedded within each subject. IT is not really a subject until senior now. When they get out of school they're [going to be concerned with] "how has my online footprint affected my life?"*

As a digital native, Dana is indicating a perceived deficit of understanding conveyed in education policy documents as to the extent to which ICT is interwoven through the lives of students within and beyond school. These documents present a view that indicates ICTs are a set of tools by which texts are produced, rather than an inhabited space in which performative representation of identity are enacted by users. Cary, who had responded to an earlier question saying *I'm still of the opinion that the digital world comes second to the real world*, similarly views ICTs as a utensil rather than an inhabited, virtual space. He said, "It's nearly every subject that has some form of computer usage. So you just incorporate it when you're doing, teaching that."

In spite of the ubiquity of ICT, Beavis (2013, p. 39) argues that not all digital natives are critically aware of their interactions with technology, invested in technology to the same degree, or conversant in the use of digital technology. Although both Dana and Cary self-identify as experienced users of SNS, these responses indicate the primacy of ICTs in schools and young people's lives. Whitney commented on how critical literacy approaches to representation are enacted in classrooms, and identifies how the examination of representations in texts academically was not necessarily being connected to texts outside the school context in social media.

Whitney: *I think we do look at representation, when we look at novels and films. We look at how the person is represented. How the reader is positioned. We do it, but I don't think we think about it. We don't use that opportunity to say how do you represent yourself to the world?*

This response indicates that although participants were aware of their digital literacy practices, and how these practices can be enacted in positive ways, they had not at this point made the connection between how texts examined in the school context can be linked to students' text practices outside the school context.

Curating Identity in Digital Spaces

Curating identity occurs when users apply the process of customisation to modify the default settings of technology interfaces to convey an online representation of self. Customisation is distinct from personalisation in that it is initiated by the user to enhance their own experience with technology. Conversely, personalisation is initiated by external, commercial systems that adapt the user interface to reflect what the system has learned about the user through the user's browsing behaviour (Sundar & Marathe, 2010, p. 300). Technology may refer to any electronic devices or online and virtual environments that provide tools for the user to alter, or customise, the user interface. Here, we refer to customisation as the actions of users in public online and digital spaces of SNS.

Whitney: *That's something to be mindful of, you might be posting to this group of friends, but it's not just this group of friends that see it. This organisation that has control over what you're posting [...] Which makes it challenging as [mentors], to make sure that students know what is going on. Some of them have no idea they're just a statistic, that what they're posting is visible.*

Privacy, or lack of privacy, is a concern for users of SNS. However, despite the situation described here by Whitney, privacy remains in the control of the SNS user. From a legal perspective, "Facebook isn't a privacy carjacker, forcing its victims into compromising situations. Its users are the ones (exposing) their personal information to the world" Grimmelmann (2009, p. 2). Sites such as Facebook offer users privacy controls that provide the appearance of the ability to control who shares the digital texts created by users. Effective control of the settings lie with the user's ability to understand and apply them. Such control settings that ostensibly protects them from presenting representations of identity beyond their imagined audience. However, other users within their social network can employ different settings, thereby publically sharing information they assumed to be private (boyd, 2011, pp. 51-52). Recent literature indicates the social affordances of SNS outweighs the user's social reasons for generating the digital texts that impart private information; as well as underestimating the risks of the public dissemination of their private information (boyd, 2004, 2011; boyd & Ellison, 2007; Buckingham & Martínez-Rodríguez, 2013; Grimmelmann, 2009; Marwick, 2013; Marwick & boyd, 2011).

Interactive websites, such as SNS, provide users who sign-up with a default profile or home page with a unique web address that will serve as their online presence within that social network. Customisation occurs when users begin to alter the default settings to express themselves as individuals, by changing the theme, layout, background, fonts, colours of their profiles, and by adding personal content such as status updates and photos or video (Marathe & Sundar, 2011, p. 784; Marwick, 2013, p. 358; Papacharissi, 2002, p. 654; Park, 2010, p. 110). Further customisation occurs when users alter privacy and notification settings to change the way their profile connects to other profiles and increase or decrease visibility to other users of the SNS.

Users practice customisation to enhance their experience of using the technology they are customising and to adapt the technology to better reflect their own goals (Marathe & Sundar, 2011, pp. 781-782). Further, the provision for customisation within SNS instils in the user a sense of control and ownership or "agency" in their online representation, as customisation provides a greater sense of perceived control over their online environment and interactions (Marathe & Sundar, 2011, p. 732; Sundar & Marathe, 2010, p. 313).

We extend the current parameters of customisation beyond the limitations of settings within SNS to the practices of users to select, edit, adapt, amend and delete representations of their identity through the production of digital texts when using SNS as part of identity curation. This practice is already being observed, although participants' responses indicate their belief that not all SNS users are aware of the possibilities of such identity curation.

Lesley: *I've seen a photo on Instagram that says "don't compare your behind the scenes to someone else's final show." What you might be doing in your day-to-day to life to what your neighbour is doing on Instagram, because they've edited that status, they've put a filter on that photo...*

Taylor: *...and they've chosen that moment to share. Sometimes I think look at that girl, I think her life is so perfect, all her Instagram photos are like this. But that's not her whole life. Those are select moments she has chosen to portray herself in a particular way.*

The "selecting" aspect of customisation, unlike editing, amending and deleting, occurs prior to the creation of a digital text. By selecting representations, the user exerts active control over their representation, whereas the other three aspects are forms of reactive control. This active control over text selection is also described as the ability to "filter."

Kerry: *People don't always understand that they have the power to filter. I have people in my Facebook feed who talk about fights with their boyfriend or their friends, or their car broke down, really negative things. They don't seem to have the agency to decide what is appropriate to be sharing, and how people develop ideas about you based on what you are putting on social media. They say this is my site, I can do whatever I want with it.*

This suggests the application of critical literacy might enable users to actively perform positive digital conduct through reflective practices that might assist them to curate their sites' content in terms of social and cultural suitability. It might also make students more aware of texts they create in relation to their potential sharers and consumers. Further, by referring to users' lack of "power" and "agency" Kerry is suggesting that these users have relinquished control of their identity to the SNS and to their "friends." This position is confirmed by Lesley's succinct response to Kerry, which indicates the user has surrendered responsibility for the maintenance of the social connection to the users within their social network "If you don't like it, unfriend me."

Although customisation theory to date has been applied to the manipulation of technology interfaces by users, we contend that customisation theory can be legitimately extended to the presentation of content by users of SNS. As customisation is a process by which users adapt technology to represent themselves and how they seek to be represented to others (Marathe & Sundar, 2011, p. 784), the functionality of current SNS interfaces that enables users to progressively and retrospectively adapt, amend, edit and delete representations of identity is an extension of this performance of customisation.

The final lens through which this chapter explores the case study is the theory of critical literacy. Choices of representations effected though SNS user's encoding and decoding the self through texts and images can be seen as a kind of literacy. Since the pre-service teacher participants were schooled in this theory of reading and teaching English, it becomes a significant factor in this study. The concept of representations of identity is a core aspect of critical literacy, which is still an approach favoured in the teaching of English. Further, "critical and creative thinking" is one of the General Capabilities of the Australian Curriculum.

Critical Literacy and Identity

The ability to critically examine the socio-cultural constructions of text enables SNS users to perform positive digital representations of identity. Despite its absence as an explicit term from the AC:E critical literacy remains a practice in English teaching. Currently, English teachers, like those involved in this case study, and their students are actively exploring the critical literacy concept of representations to examine both the social construction of texts and the ideologies that inform these constructions.

Literacies are "socially recognized ways of generating, communicating and negotiating meaningful content as members of Discourses (sic) through the medium of encoded texts" (Lankshear & Knobel, 2008, p. 249). Critical literacy posits that representations of people, places and events within texts are encoded and decoded partially and selectively within socio-cultural contexts (Misson and Morgan (2006, p. 15). Our particular focus in this chapter is representations of gender.

Responses from participants indicated that greater scrutiny and negative judgement is applied to normalised and naturalised representations of femininity.

Lee: *I think adolescent girls face a lot of pressure in that age group, if they're sexually active at that age. There are going to be expectations on them from their boyfriends or girlfriends, who they are putting up on a pedestal. So they think that what they are asking of me is something that society expects that I do. We're told this as teachers all the time, that this is what students are going through. I don't know whether or not if it is true, I'm sure there are research to support it, but hopefully there are students who on the cusp and think do I want to send this photo or don't I? And peer pressure can push them over the edge because they don't fully understand that it's not just a bit of fun. "Here's a bit of fun and here's a picture of me that you can keep forever and show to anyone for as long as you have your phone." They don't fully understand that in the moment, when you're full of endorphins or whatever, you don't think about this sort of thing.*

Texts are not limited to written, spoken and performed texts such as books, speeches and plays and media and new media, but also include the enactment of cultural practices such as ceremonies and rituals. As the quote demonstrates, SNS affords a new platform for performing gender, in this case femininity. This "performance" of the selfie, described above, constitutes a textual representation of female identity: by customising a Facebook image to present an "ideal girl". As indicated in the focus group data, representations of femininity often evoke the sexual stereotype of young women presenting accentuated cleavage and puckered mouths ready to kiss. With this in mind, critical literacy can be applied to the social performance of bodily texts and practices that signify aspects of identity in tangible and observable ways, as well as in online contexts. We could invite students in classrooms to examine and discuss and perhaps even challenge the "normalised" values, attitudes and beliefs that are signified by such images, just as we do for other media and literature study. We could as educators also ask them to think about the ongoing life effects of posting such images in virtual spaces, not a protectionist exercise, but to engender critical awareness of how symbolic images can be interpreted outside of the semiotic spaces in which they were created. Although they may be intended only to be shared amongst friends, the potential for further dissemination is impossible to control or predict.

Whitney: *One of my friends at uni, she's posted so many things to Instagram that get so many likes because it's all "oh, look at my cleavage." Her account is completely open and she's planning to be a teacher. So it's like do you realise the repercussions that can have?[...] (Her) friend's little brother looked her up on Instagram, and (viewed) all her photos [...] He lives in Melbourne [...] (and) can see exactly what (she is) posting on the internet. Think about what that will mean when you're trying to get a job.*

Whitney describes how these performative representations of identity can have personal and professional implications, as these representations can be viewed by individuals outside the user's social network. This is particularly poignant for these pre-service teachers who are on the cusp of moving from student life to a professional discourse site. Here, Whitney also indicates an understanding of the difference between the "imagined audience" and the actual consumers of digital texts (Donath, 2007, p. 243; Marwick & boyd, 2011, p. 115). Whitney's observation of a fellow pre-service teacher who does not practice, in Whitney's view, positive digital conduct, and does not seem to be aware of the repercussions of sharing inappropriate content through via SNS.

Critical literacy examines and challenges power structures, including (but not limited to) discrimination based on gender, ethnicity, class and sexuality (Misson & Morgan, 2006, p. 133). This provides us with the opportunity to critically examine representations through SNS. Signs inscribed on the body through either biological and physical characteristics, such as gender and ethnicity, or the performance of dispositions that are decoded to indicate ways of being such as class and sexuality (2006, p. 133). Just as signs can be decoded, gender identity curation on SNS can be encoded by customised representations constructed by user choices, such as girls "Photoshopping" or applying "best face apps" to their selfies to improve their online appearance.

Lee:*...If you are [teaching semiotics in media] and you look at the front of a men's magazine, with a woman in her underwear, and you're going to compare that against a woman on Vogue who is going to be quite well covered because it's fashion, and that is going to lead into a discussion about what assumptions you make about the character in the shot... You [can also] talk about how people can misinterpret what you post online. It could be a harmless picture of you going, "look how impressive I am now that I've been to the gym", but also there is a lot of cleavage in that.*

Critical literacy aligns with other practices of examining texts identified and defined above, such as performativity and customisation, as it provides established practices by which to understand how social representations are encoded within texts and decoded by audiences. The quote from Lee above demonstrates how constructed media images, both in the mainstream and SNS, are used as yardsticks for performing and judging gender identity. The case study data indicate the pre-service English teacher participants employ critical literacy practices, either consciously or unconsciously, to interpret the virtual representations of identity of SNS users. With this in mind, the ability to critically examine the socio-cultural constructions of digital texts being produced by users would inform the user's understanding of their digital conduct. The following extract from the focus group describes how young women are performing naturalised 'gender' through altering their representations online. These concepts emerge from critical literacy lenses though which the pre-service teachers will teach English.

Lesley: *Young girls, and even adolescent women, are starting to get a lot more provocative and sexting is on the up and up. We are getting the notion that there is an argument in society that feminism means women can be just as sexual as men. Women can be just as provocative, just as sexual, can do whatever they want, because it's ok for men to do it. All the double standards in society, levelling it out by saying they don't care but at the end of the day it gets frowned upon.*

Lee: *But women don't have equality, so they can't act equal. As horrible as that is for society, you can't then go and say "here is me with my shirt off at the beach" because boys can do it. They have different parts.*

Participants were not asked to distinguish between genders when responding to focus group questions. However, as indicated in the responses above, the data collected indicated that it is almost singularly sexualised representations of femininity that are brought to mind when asked to consider negative representations of identity. This indicates a preoccupation that has emerged through traditional and social media with a scrutiny of representations of femininity not imposed on representations of masculinity. Lee supported taking a critical, reflective approach to mentoring performative representations of identity through the production of digital texts on SNS.

Lee: *It's important to teach students that what people see on Instagram and what people see on Facebook that immediately will be their assumptions about your entire life. So by extension, if you are posting photos and images that are questionable in their content, they are going to assume you are a questionable person.*

Participants demonstrated an understanding of readers beyond the anticipated or imagined audience. Lesley uses the potential yardstick of an elderly female relative as a behavioural filter for assessing and regulating what is an appropriate or inappropriate digital text. Lesley customises her performative representations by critically considering understand how her grandmother would view Lesley in the event that her "nanna" visited her site. Her choice of an elderly female relative is intriguing. Females judging females more harshly is a theme that emerged from the data. As seen above, these people perceive that when women customise their own gender they are often performing *to* their own gender. On SNS this is important because it is a self-constructed identity curation, and users bring various levels of awareness that their representations will be commented on and judged by the audience.

Lesley: *My strategy would be that... well, my strategy for myself is that I have my nanna on Facebook. I have an 85 year old Catholic Irish woman. Think of it like that, think of it as if your nanna, or your father or your uncle, or your children. What are you going to do when your children search their name, and your name comes up because you posted on Facebook that you're their mother. What are you going to do when they search through your timeline. Look at my mum in 2000!*

Using a moral guide, as suggested by Lesley, is at odds with unmoderated representations also performed on SNS. This shows how there is no set approach to understanding the "normalised" view of the sexualised woman in mainstream media, while expectations in self-curated sites are being judged in a more conservative and personal way.

Cary demonstrated how the depth of understanding of SNS determines how much users control or regulate their performative representations of identity in those sites. Further, Cary's response highlights how the indefinable temporal structure of SNS and digital texts, transfers control of performative representations of identity from the user to the SNS creators and moderators. This can occur through the terms of service (TOS). Changes to the TOS can reset and override the user's customised privacy settings and display user's digital texts to audiences not selected by the user. Further, control over representations is transferred to any member of the user's audience who can access, retrieve and store these digital texts and images without the knowledge and consent of the user. If users are mentored to enact a more critical approach to performing representations of identity online, this can help address some of the aspects of SNS use that they cannot control.

Absolute control over digital texts appears to be impossible. As discussed below, even with a cadre of powerful lawyers and money, it is difficult to stop any image "going viral."

Lee: *There was a Beyoncé show earlier in the year and there was a photo circulating of her doing a face, with the thighs, and she is trying so hard to remove it from the internet. It's impossible. I think if you're on the ball, it's kind of irrelevant now but if you're keeping up with media, that is something you could teach. It would be relevant at the time, it would be showing up in their Facebook feeds, it would have personal relevance.*

Lesley: *And you see those pictures all the time, they say "my teacher is trying to say that this photo can get a million likes in a day" and you look at it and it has 20 million likes, they show how quickly things circulate.*

Taylor: *Which is great for creating awareness too, I think.*

Cary: *We need to educate them that once it's online, it can't be offline. You can't get rid of it. If an employer goes back over and looks at it... My first prac, the first thing my teachers told me one of the first things they did was Facebook stalk me, to see what person I was. And thankfully I didn't have anything irresponsible there. I'm careful with what I put on there so there was nothing that was detrimental to me. But with so many people you go on there and think: Why would I want to employ this person?*

Cary's response reveals how SNS users and other individuals who create and distribute digital texts can remain unaware of their inability to control their representations once these digital texts have been published and distributed. This highlights the importance of investigating the research question. Mentoring digital conduct is one approach to providing students with the information that may enable them to make positive choices about their performative representations of digital identity.

The findings of this question indicates that although pre-service English teachers in this study demonstrate an understanding of the AC:E GCs, and how representations of identity are both performed through digital texts, and consumed by audiences both in and external to the SNS user's social network, they have not necessarily connected these ideas to the practices of teaching and learning they may include in their future classrooms to mentor positive digital conduct to their students. One area of potential future research emerging from the responses to this question is how pre-service teacher practice might change through the inclusion of critical studies of the texts pre-service teacher produce through SNS outside the formal teacher training course, and how this might influence their future practice in regards to mentoring informed performances of representations of identity through digital texts for their students.

How Can We Include This?

Lee: *I've met students during prac who have made one or two mistakes about what they have posted (online) and that has backfired. For instance they post something they thought would be anonymous, someone else has heard it and then there is bullying. From that they've come to see me, as I have put myself in a position of counsellor, and I've explained to them how they can edit and delete certain comments or un-tag themselves or remove themselves. It's not exactly personal growth but it's knowledge they need to control what happens to them online.*

Lee's response indicates an understanding and practice of customisation, through the practice of altering technology settings, in this case privacy settings, to better serve the needs of the user SNS, and self-editing digital texts as a way to alter what information is shared and with whom (Papacharissi & Easton, 2013, p. 180). Further, this response also indicates the practice of what we have termed identity curation, through editing and amending texts published to SNS to curate representations of identity using digital texts. Here, Lee has described a reactive approach to digital literacy, when a student is exposed to the risks involved in enacting digital conduct that is not positive. This response, the advice to the student involved and Lee's reflection on the incident indicates an understanding of some of the practical digital literacy skills that can be included in teaching and learning activities to provide students with the opportunity to critique SNS representations. The enactment of positive digital conduct goal in education for life-long learning and deserves a place in the curriculum.

REFERENCES

The Australian curriculum: English v7.0 general capabilities. (2014). Australian Curriculum and Assessment Reporting Authority (ACARA). Retrieved from http://www.australiancurriculum.edu.au/GeneralCapabilities/Overview/General-capabilities-in-the-Australian-Curriculum

Beavis, C. (2013). Young people, new media and education: Participation and possibilities. *Social Alternatives, 32*(2), 39.

Bell, V. (1999). Performativity and belonging: An introduction. In V. Bell (Ed.), *Performativity and belonging*. Thousand Oaks, Calif; London: Sage Publications. doi:10.4135/9781446219607.n1

boyd, d. (2004). Friendster and publicly articulated social networking. ACM.

boyd, d. (2011). Social network sites as networked publics: Affordance, dynamics, and implications. In Z. Papacharissi (Ed.), *A networked self: Identity, community and culture on social network sites* (pp. 39-58). New York: Routledge.

boyd, d. m., & Ellison, N. B. (2007). Social network sites: Definition, history, and scholarship. *Journal of Computer-Mediated Communication, 13*(1), 210-230. doi:10.1111/j.1083-6101.2007.00393.x

Buckingham, D., & Martínez-Rodríguez, J. B. (2013). Interactive youth: New citizenship between social networks and school settings. *Comunicar, 20*(40), 10.

Butler, J. (1988). Performative acts and gender constitution: An essay in phenomenology and feminist theory. *Theatre Journal, 40*(4), 519–531. http://www.flimmer.nu/sites/default/files/butlerPerformance.pdf doi:10.2307/3207893

Butler, J. (2011a). *Bodies That Matter.* New York: Taylor and Francis.

Butler, J. (2011b). *Gender trouble.* New York: Taylor and Francis.

Dezuanni, M. (2006). Prince Charming has perfect white teeth: Performativity and media education. *Media International Australia, 120*(120), 156-167. Retrieved from http://eprints.qut.edu.au/5337/1/5337.pdf

Dezuanni, M. (2009). *Young people and participatory culture: Reconceptualising Australian media education for 21st century citizenship* (pp. 31–50). Dordrecht: Springer Netherlands.

Donath, J. (2007). Signals in social supernets. *Journal of Computer-Mediated Communication, 13*(1), 231–251. doi:10.1111/j.1083-6101.2007.00394.x

Grimmelmann, J. (2009). Facebook and the social dynamics of privacy. *Iowa Law Review, 95*(4), 1–52. Retrieved from http://www.ciberdemocracia.es/recursos/textosrelevantes/facebook.pdf

Jetnikoff, A. (2009). Using media technologies in English. In S. Gannon, M. Howie, & W. Sawyer (Eds.), *Charged with meaning: re-viewing English* (pp. 307–313). Melbourne: Phoenix Education.

Lankshear, C., & Knobel, M. (2008). Digital literacy and participation in online social networking spaces. In C. Lankshear & M. Knobel (Eds.), *Digital literacies: Concepts, policies and practices* (Vol. 30). New York: Peter Lang.

Marathe, S., & Sundar, S. (2011, 2011). What drives customization? Control or identity? *Proceedings of the SIGCHI Conference on human factors in computing systems* (pp. 781-790). ACM.

Marwick, A. E., & boyd, d. m. (2011). I tweet honestly, I tweet passionately: Twitter users, context collapse, and the imagined audience. *New Media & Society*, *13*(1), 114–133. doi:10.1177/1461444810365313

Marwick, A. E. (2013). Online identity. In J. Hartley, J. Burgess, & A. Bruns (Eds.), *A Companion to New Media Dynamics* (pp. 355–364). Hoboken: Wiley-Blackwell. doi:10.1002/9781118321607.ch23

McKinlay, A. (2010). Performativity and the politics of identity: Putting Butler to work. *Critical Perspectives on Accounting*, *21*(3), 232–242. doi:10.1016/j.cpa.2008.01.011

Melbourne declaration on educational goals for young Australians. (2008). *Ministerial Council on Education Employment Training and Youth Affairs*. Retrieved from http://www.mceecdya.edu.au/mceecdya/melbourne_declaration,25979.html

Misson, R., & Morgan, W. (2006). *Critical literacy and the aesthetic: Transforming the English classroom*. Urbana, IL, USA: National Council of Teachers of English.

Papacharissi, Z. (2002). The presentation of self in virtual life: Characteristics of personal home pages. *Journalism & Mass Communication Quarterly*, *79*(3), 643–660. doi:10.1177/107769900207900307

Papacharissi, Z. (2011). Conclusion: A networked self. In Z. Papacharissi (Ed.), *A networked self: identity, community and culture on social network sites* (pp. 304–318). New York: Routledge.

Papacharissi, Z., & Easton, E. (2013). In the habitus of the new: Stucture, agency, and the social media habitus. In J. Hartley, J. Burgess, & A. Bruns (Eds.), *A Companion to New Media Dynamics* (pp. 171–184). Hoboken: Wiley-Blackwell. doi:10.1002/9781118321607.ch9

Park, M. R. (2010). Social network sites as virtual communities. In Z. Papacharissi (Ed.), *A networked self: Identity, community, and culture on social network sites* (pp. 105–123). Routledge.

Prensky, M. (2001). Digital natives, digital immigrants part 1. *On the Horizon*, *9*(5), 1–6. doi:10.1108/10748120110424816

Sundar, S. S., & Marathe, S. S. (2010). Personalization versus customization: The importance of agency, privacy, and power usage. *Human Communication Research*, *36*(3), 298–322. doi:10.1111/j.1468-2958.2010.01377.x

Chapter 5
Blogging Their Way Out of Disadvantage:
Women, Identity and Agency in the Blogosphere

Amelia Rose Coleman
Queensland University of Technology, Australia

ABSTRACT

The ways that blogs are used to improve the lot of the disenfranchised is an area that is increasingly gaining research traction. This chapter presents a literature review of the recent literature in to the ways that minority groups are using blogs to tell their story to a wide audience. It looks at the ways that human rights bloggers have used Web 2.0 platforms to express themselves. It then applies Foucault's (1988) work on self-expression to other groups who are also heavy users of blogs to express themselves in new ways. The chapter looks at poverty, at those who identify as LGBTIQ (lesbian, gay, bisexual, transgender, intersex and queer) and women. It suggests that there is much research that still needs to be undertaken to properly examine the role of blogs in the lives of increasing numbers of groups who are not able to express themselves in mainstream media, and to explore the ways that these blogs render mainstream media irrelevant in connected times.

DOI: 10.4018/978-1-5225-0010-0.ch005

INTRODUCTION

Blogging is an important means of self-expression. Studies (cf. El-Nawawy & Khamis, 2013; Howard, 2010) have suggested that minorities, the disenfranchised and those who may lack a voice are able to use blogs to express their frustrations. In addition, blogs provide an avenue to discuss and bring attention to the plight of specific groups, for example the LGBTQ community and the homeless. As researchers have frequently noted, one of the groups most at risk of discrimination and disenfranchisement (cf. Schuster 2013; Lawson; 2013; Bennet, 2014), are women. Thus, this chapter explores the ways that several marginalised groups and later more specifically women, can use blogs to overcome entrenched disadvantage.

The chapter explores how marginalised groups negotiating identity, community, and agency in the blogosphere. It begins by exploring how blogs are used as a means of self-expression. It discusses the use of social capital theory (cf. Foucault, 2003) as a means of examining and understanding the purpose of blogs for people's ability to converse with a wider audience. Then, the chapter discusses how human rights groups use blogs to publicise specific examples of human rights abuses as a further form of self-expression. The next section examines a further group that has benefitted from the increase in blogging sites as a form of self-expression, those who are living in poverty, specifically the homeless. From this, further disenfranchised groups, those who identify as LGBTQ (Lesbian, Gay, Bisexual, Transgender, and Queer) are discussed. Finally, the use of blogs and social media by women are more generally described. The discussion that follows looks at how Foucault's social capital theory can further enhance the analysis of blogs.

A TOOL FOR SELF-EXPRESSION

Blogging is often described in the literature as a means of self- expression. Until a decade ago, creative expression had been mostly produced and offered for a price by "experts" and corporations with little input from the consumers of the creative products themselves (Bruns, 2006). The print and broadcast era dominating the years roughly between 1950 and 1980 saw a strict division of labour between those who distributed creative products in a top- down fashion to the masses and those who purchased these products for private consumption (Bruns, 2006). The result of this approach was that few who were marginalised had the ability to publish. As we settle well into the new media environment, the Internet now acts as an open innovation network that benefits from harnessing the creative input of the entire population, not just the opinions of a select few (Bruns, 2006; Burgess, 2007; Hartley, 2004). Unlike other avenues for creative expression, the Internet does not distinguish between literacy and publication. In the new media environment there is an almost infinite scope for DIY (do-it-yourself) and DIWO (do-it-with-others) creative content produced by and for consumers, without the need for institutional filtering or bureaucracy (Burgess, 2007). New media is fueling population-wide online literacy, through which everyone is a potential publisher. But what is it that motivates individuals to publish their creative thoughts and feelings online?

Blogs are often characterised by high amounts of self-disclosure that foster and encourage the presentation of one's identity (Bronstein, 2013). Researchers (Bronstein, 2013; Schneider, 2012; Hsiu-Chia, et al., 2009) have adopted Foucault's social capital theory to describe how identity and social capital are transformed through blogs on the Internet. Foucault (1988) traces writing as one of several techniques for caring for one's self or constructing a new self. Foucault noted that "taking care of the self in and through writing is one of the oldest Western traditions," (1988, p. 27). Throughout his career, Foucault was interested in the relationship between societal regulation and individual self-regulation, and the formation of identity within the complex power relations of society. One of his main concerns in relation to power was with the notion of governmentality. Foucault (2003, p. 147) described governmentality as "the encounter between technologies of domination of others and those of the "self". Governmentality has been defined as "the art of government that includes a wide range of control techniques, and that applies to a wide variety of objects, from one's control of the self to control of populations" (O'Farrell, 2007). Foucault originally used the term governmentality to describe the ways in which the state administers populations and later expanded his definition to encompass the techniques and procedures, which are designed to govern the conduct of both individuals and populations at every level not just the administrative or political level (O'Farrell, 2007).

Another central aspect of his work on governmentality is what Foucault coined "technologies of the self…which permit individuals to effect by their own means, or with the help of others, a certain number of operations on their own bodies and souls, thoughts, conduct, and way of being, so as to transform themselves in order to attain a certain state of happiness, purity, wisdom, perfection, or immortality" (Foucault, 1988, p. 146). Foucault (1998, p. 5) describes the "development of technologies of the self, in which the most important principle was to know the self and to care for the self in order to improve one's self."

Foucault's concept of governmentality has influenced new understandings of the concept of power. Blogs have become an increasingly popular technology of the self which challenge traditional notions of power and of content because people achieve power by writing about themselves, their innermost thoughts and experiences and publishing these writings in an online space, that in many cases forms their personal presence in cyber space (Bronstein, 2013). As the broad range of perspectives assembled in this book demonstrates, the uses and gratifications of blogging are many and varied. The creation and communication of one's identity online differs according to different bloggers motivation, and it remains unknown how and why different users are using blogs as both consumers and producers of content. Driven to a great extent by the growing visibility of blogs and by the agendas of bloggers themselves, a prominent thread of Foucault's discourses of governmentality, agency and identity have emerged within the literature to theorise motivations for constructing and maintaining a blog.

A study by Bruns (2006) was born out of a need to better understand the uses and motivations for blogging, to map them and chart their benefits for those who engage in them and society at large. Bruns (2006) proposed that it is the aspects of self- expression and community development that provide a human dimension to the phenomenon of blogging. Blogging takes Internet communications beyond a purely informative role to provide a platform for debate, deliberation and the expression of personal identity that is more personalised than websites and other social media tools. Replacing personal websites as vehicles for exchanging ideas, blogs represent an opportunity for authors to reach out and connect with an audience never before accessible to them, while maintaining control over their personal online spaces (Shirky, 2003). In the blogging world, anyone with access can participate. The barriers of entry to the blogosphere are low as there is no authority to grant domain or publishing rights (Shirky, 2003). Bloggers have the opportunity to engage in discussion, present their ideas, seek out approval for their notions without pressure to conform to norms set by a governing authority. Participants in blogs instead become active users and producers of content, and in doing so, turn into what we can usefully describe as *producers*- a hybrid of producer and user (Bruns, 2006). It is increasingly seen as normal for media consumers or audiences to participate in the process of designing, making, circulating and evaluating content and cultural experiences through blogs.

Burgess' & Banks' (2010) work supports the notion users participate in creating content online for a range of cultural, social and commercial purposes. Their motivations may be personal and expressive, they may be driven by a desire to form and participate in communities of interest, or they may be entrepreneurial in nature (Burgess, 2007). Burgess & Banks (2010) highlight that it is important to recognise that much user created content on blogs is ordinary in its origins and motivations. While some blogs may contain high levels of creative content used for entrepreneurial purposes, others may be used to share content that simply documents the everyday and reflects on topics of personal interest to the author (Bruns, 2006). For those engaging in user-created content, their participation is not necessarily understood in terms of exceptional creativity or producing cultural texts. Rather, as Bruns (2006) asserts, it may be understood in terms of using these texts to interact and engage with each other and the world. People originally motivated by quite mundane interests often find that their participation in blogs can lead to more recognisably creative uses of these technologies (Burgess and Banks, 2010). Social networking sites, which allow users to connect and communicate with each other, document their lives and share popular media content demonstrate the blurring of boundaries between everyday communication, creativity and audience practices. This blurring of boundaries is having a powerful impact on the presentation of one's identity in online spaces. In another study by Burgess (2007) the concept of 'vernacular creativity' is used to describe the 'flood' of user-generated content that has emerged on the Internet as a direct result of more powerful, accessible technologies which have enabled the telling of creative stories by otherwise silenced voices in public spaces.

Driven to a great extent by the growing visibility of blogs and by the motivations of bloggers themselves, a prominent theme in Burgess' (2007) study concerned the accessibility of tools for content production and distribution by non- professionals. Burgess (2007) argues that the increased availability of digital technologies, combined with the Internet, allows everyone to be a media participant, as well as a producer. Burgess (2007) describes how democratising technologies such as blogs, which were first introduced to transform journalism and knowledge production, now extend far beyond journalistic enquiry in their uses. The two main drivers fueling this trend are (1) the creative urges that each individual undeniably possesses but until the new media era, neither had the guts nor the means to express (2) the manufacturers of content-creating tools such as social networking sites, who relentlessly encourage consumers to unleash their creativity, using their products (Burgess, 2007). Instead of asking consumers to passively consume, the focus is on getting them to create, to produce, and to participate (Burgess, 2007). Much of the literature (Hartley, 2004; Bruns, 2006; Bruns; Shirky, 2003) on blogging appears to focus on political blogs while bypassing the vast range of other participants whose engagement only makes the blogosphere more democratic. To discuss only blogs that debate the news or express political views ignores much of what exists in the blogosphere. Creative consumption and production on the Internet is now seen as part of everyday life for ordinary consumers in contemporary capitalist societies who are using the Internet for creative self-expression, individual well-being, user-led content creation and collaboration. "Ordinary consumers are increasingly understood as engines of economic and social value creation in this new environment of cultural production," (Burgess, 2007, p. 10). This transformation forces us to consider new dynamics of ownership and community, prompting a reconsideration of the idea of creative ownership and the romantic notion of the individual creative author.

Blogs offer a rich environment from which to look at the psychology behind user behaviour on the Internet. According to Okdie, Eno & Guadagno (2010), blogging is an ideal context in which to examine the effects of anonymity, self-awareness, and perceived audience, and how these variables affect online behaviour. One of the most salient and researched characteristics of computer- mediated communication is its ability to provide a relatively anonymous context in which individuals can interact with one another (McKenna & Bargh, 2000; Postmes, Spears, Sakhel, & de Groot, 2001). An investigation by Okdie, Eno & Guadagno (2010) examined the extent to which anonymity affects individual's willingness to disclose information online, specifically within the context of creating and maintaining a blog. The emergence of new media technologies has given rise to communication platforms in which individuals may perceive themselves to be anonymous by providing a state in which aspects of one's personal identity can remain unknown.

The relative anonymity afforded by the Internet was found to play a key role in online behaviour in Okdie, Eno & Guadagno's (2010) study, influencing online interactions in both positive and negative ways (Okdie, Eno & Guadagno, 2010). The level of anonymity experienced in the blogosphere is a result of both the amount of anonymity that is afforded by this communication platform and the level the individual chooses (McKenna & Bargh, 2000). It is an important function of blogs that individuals who maintain them have the ability to make themselves identifiable and can control, to some degree, who reads their posts, whether they will be published publicly or privately and whether or not they are accessible to find through a simple web search (Postmes, Spears, Sakhel, & de Groot, 2001). Furthermore, the anonymity of computer- mediated communication tools such as blogs may offer an alternative opportunities for self- expression because they offer, as Derlega & Chaikin (1977) discovered nearly 40 years ago, individuals to construct and reconstruct their self-concept and identity in numerous ways. This need to construct a self-identity may result in increased feelings of self-worth and acceptance for the user. Okdie, Eno & Guadagno (2010) also suggest that individuals who blog experience increased self- awareness. Self-awareness has been shown to play a role in increased levels of self-expression online. Having no one physically present, reading or watching at the time in which a user is writing for a blog allows individuals to focus more attention internally and express their thoughts and opinions more confidently. Thus, it may be that the decreased risk of judgement facilitated by blogs, leads to being more willing to disclose more about themselves when communicating via computer- mediated communication tools (Derlega & Chaikin, 1977). The work suggests, examining the impact of perceived audience on the behaviour of individuals using methods of online self-expression such as blogging may prove fruitful; particularly since prior research indicates that blogger's perception of their audience is likely unknown or underestimated. Therefore, self-expression through blogs may vary to the extent that individual bloggers perceive the size and position of their audience.

A study by Papacharissi (2007) set out to further explore the identity functions that blogs perform and how bloggers justify their purpose for using them. Papacharissi's study investigates if blogging enhances social capital and identity formation and if these capitals in turn enhance the perception of well-being (Papacharissi, 2007). In this context, Papacharissi (2007) defines "social capital" as the manner in which individuals use links on their blogs as tools for social association, to indirectly define themselves and their social status by listing their interests and linking to other sites. Papacharissi (2007), further defines "identity formation" as presenting the self and inviting communication through the use of online tools that allow individuals to project their identity and establish connections with online audiences. When bloggers talk about motivations for blogging, two themes are ubiquitous: self-expression and community development (Papacharissi, 2007). One of the important social features of blogging was found to be the sense of community it provides. Community is often described as the subjective experiences of belonging and mutual respect that can be gained only through participation (Gurak, et al., 2005). Many bloggers see blogging as a way of developing relationships, managing connections through both linking and commentary, which become forms of social control, signs of approval, acceptance and value (Miller & Shepherd, 2005). As much as they serve to validate the self, blogs are also intended to be read by an audience. Many bloggers are conscious of the fact that they have readers and, to varying degrees, consciously write to satisfy them as well as themselves. Community development often requires high levels of self-disclosure in order gain approval and to build connections with others. Blogging serves the intrinsic self-disclosure functions of both self-clarification and self-validation, enhancing self-awareness and confirming already-held beliefs. Literature from Papacharissi (2007) supports the view that high levels of self- disclosure which accompany the practice of blogging significantly enhances a blogger's perception of their identity and social capital, and in turn promote bloggers' social well-being.

BLOGGING AGAINST HUMAN RIGHTS VIOLATIONS

A number of scholars have examined new media technology use among marginalised people. The opportunities for human empowerment provided by computer-mediated technologies have become a research area of increasing importance. Blogs present a significant topic of study because they provide media consumers with an audience and a relatively audible voice (Howard, 2010). They also offer a virtual space where information ignored by authoritative or mainstream media can be published. Minority groups are often able to access blogging, including micro-blogging sites such as Twitter, to express their identities in ways that may be impossible in their local communities. Thus, the range of blogs available to minorities who may be positioned on a scale from disaffected to severely disadvantaged provides an important means for expression as well as for rebellion against their circumstances.

Bloggers are becoming an increasingly important part of the system of political communication in many countries, particularly in enforcing social change (El- Nawawy & Khamis, 2013). Blogging technologies have been particularly useful for overcoming violations of human rights and promoting democratic practices within autocratic regimes. According to literature from El- Nawawy, (2013) Khamis, (2013) and Howard (2010) blogging is empowering because of its potential to foster activism and encourage citizen journalism. With the pervasiveness of new media technologies it is rare to hear of a human rights violation or unethical political event that isn't followed by backlash on social media. Howard (2010) has described new media technologies such as the Internet and mobile phones as having clear roles in establishing democratic processes in longstanding autocratic regimes. He points to several instances where new media technologies have been employed to overcome human rights violations. For example, during Kyrgyzstan's tulip revolution in March 2005, mobile phones were used to organise activists to join protests at key moments, helping democratic leaders build a social movement with enough force to oust the president. Kuwait's woman's suffrage movement in 2005 was more successful than it had been in 2000, in part because it was able to use new media to encourage protesters to attend demonstrations. Furthermore, in Egypt, Tunisia and Kazakhstan opposition groups that face state censorship and oppression have demonstrated that blogs have a role in establishing democratic institutions and overcoming state censorship by moving their information and online content to servers in other countries. In these countries, new media technologies have served an important function in highlighting and overcoming corrupt, anti-freedom legislation and governance.

Over the past 20 years the media environment particularly in the Arab World has transformed dramatically. As recently as 10 years ago, Arab citizens were forced to depend on only state provided information and had no substantive way to respond. Any efforts to stimulate participatory public discourse were likely to be met by repressive action from autocratic governments. A clear path to democratic media developed from Al- Jazeera's founding in 1996 (El-Nawawy & Khamis, 2013). Roughly a decade later, access to the Internet has spread swiftly within the Arab world and citizens have begun to take advantage of new ways in which they, as individuals, can participate in civic discourse. After decades of frustration about economic and political oppression, public sentiment boiled over and swift, dramatic change swept across much of the Arab world. The result was the 2011 Arab Spring. Scholars El-Nawawy & Khamis (2013) provide a valuable analysis of how new media, particularly blogs, have contributed to overcoming human rights violations in the Arab World and promoting democracy.

The Arab Spring was characterized by the instrumental use of social media, especially blogs by protesters to achieve a number of pragmatic goals, such as group networking, protest organising and offering practical advice on how to confront police brutality and avoid arrest (Howard, 2010). El-Nawawy & Khamis (2013) note the value of blogs for providing avenues for individual expression and diversity of opinions that were crucial to sustaining political reform during the Revolution. While Twitter and Facebook were also crucial for the execution of instrumental, organisational roles during the revolution, political blogs played a different but equally valuable, role through providing important venues for the exchange of ideas and the formulation of collective public opinion. Blogs paved the way for the eruption of the revolution by widely sharing an anti-governmental discourse that revealed violations of human rights and limitations on freedom and democratic practice. In analysing the uses of political blogs in encouraging civic engagement and public participation, El-Nawawy & Khamis (2013) found that blogs were effective tools for supporting the capabilities of democratic activists by allowing forums for free speech and political networking opportunities, and provided a virtual space for assembly which allows for the exchange of civic discourse, deliberation and articulation. As blogs became more accessible throughout the Arab world, more citizens joined in conversations about their future, bringing the first signs of democracy to a stagnant political landscape, which did not exhibit any serious signs of active change (Howard, 2010). The events of the Arab uprisings promotes an understanding of how blogs transcend beyond avenues for self-expression to effective mobilisation tools that enable citizens to document not only their responses to human rights violations, but also the issues that led to these responses in the first place.

POVERTY

"In three days, I will be homeless. This is not by choice." These were the first words uttered to the blogosphere by Brianna Karp (Ennion, 2012). "Come Thursday, February 26," she continued, "I will be making my way on the streets of Orange County as best I can and I will be considered that most stigmatised of people - a homeless woman" (Karp, 2012). Brianna Karp, a university-educated Californian woman, wrote these words on her blog titled The Girl's Guide to Homelessness in 2009. The previous year she had been made redundant as a result of America's looming global financial crisis (Karp, 2012). America's reaction to the recession saw Karp's sudden spiral into poverty. Amidst losing her job, income and house, Karp decided to start a blog. "The blog became like a journal or an online diary, or something where my friends could check up on me and see how I was doing…I didn't expect people to start reading it," (Karp, 2012). Much of the literature relating to the emergence of new media technologies has focused on a concept called 'the digital divide', which describes social groups whose participation in the public sphere is thought to be restricted due to limited access to digital technologies. The 'digital divide' is particularly relevant to those living in poverty, who are just one example of a social group disadvantaged by the inability to make themselves heard and included online (Schneider, 2012).

Schneider (2012) has examined the use of digital technologies in the context of homeless social movements and has concluded that while individuals in homeless situations find themselves to be negatively affected by limited access to the Internet and digital technologies, many still use them, wherever possible, to empower themselves and come to terms with their situation. Schneider (2012) has examined the emotional benefits of blogging by examining blogs kept by the homeless, of which there are an increasing number. Blogging was found to enable homeless individuals to express themselves during times of difficulty by giving them an outlet for the emotional trauma that accompanies life on the street. A male victim of homelessness included in Schneider's study described his life in and out of homelessness and his experience battling heavy drug and alcohol addictions in his blog. He discussed various topics related to the difficulties of homelessness, mainly about his struggles with addiction and his efforts to achieve sobriety, employment and stable housing. He collected 65 followers and received a number of comments of support on his posts. Several blogs in the study were written by homeless individuals battling serious illnesses, who wrote about their efforts to survive on the streets without adequate access to healthcare. Reflecting about poverty through blogging was found to provide opportunities for self- actualisation and healing. Blogs were also found to provide the wider public with increased opportunities to gain information about the issues homeless people face and offer their support (Schneider, 2012).

Blogs are typically quite personal and can be provide insights into homeless bloggers' struggles. The emergence of blogs written by both male and female homeless illustrates how digital technologies are being used by both genders as tools for empowerment and self- expression and are providing an outlet to communicate personal aspects of disadvantage in a public forum. These bloggers who are living in poverty are able to use their platforms to "take care of the self" in a way that is incompatible with other means of expression. They have, through their blogs, access to a means of circumventing the power relations that insist their voices are silent in mainstream media. Further, their blogs disrupt the governmentality that is inherent in being homeless or living in poverty. Modern neo-liberal thought (Verba, 1987) suggests that it is the fault of the individual if they are in poverty, however, blogs allow these groups to give voice to their lives and to master the stigma that surrounds their individual circumstances. Thus, they provide an important means of expression, and through this act as a way of circumventing their disadvantage.

SEXUALITY

Lesbian, gay, bisexual, transgender, Intersex and Queer (LGBTQ) people are another minority group that have been found to adopt new media devices for self- expression and empowerment, as they come to understand their sexual identity and identify within their communities. The construction of sexual identity by LGBTQ people provides room for exploring how members of this community practice self-expression and negotiate identity, community and agency in the blogosphere. Blogs, as they represent a convergence of private and public spaces, are but one means for LGBTQ people to explore and contemplate their sexual preferences. In blogging, citizenship and the future of media, Tremayne (2007) describes the case of a sixteen-year-old boy from a southern U.S State who decided to tell his parents that he was gay. The boy's parents did not take it well and sent him to a Christian straight camp in an attempt to get him back on track. The boy responded by reflecting on his experiences from the camp and the personal anguish he felt from his parent's disapproval in a blog, often raising ideas of self-harm and suicide (Tremayne, 2007). In a pre-blog world, it is unlikely that the boy's thoughts and feelings would have spread much further than his family and friends. However, by the end of his time at camp, his story had spread so widely throughout the blogosphere that it eventually spurred a state investigation, international news coverage and political demonstrations from gay activist groups (Tremayne, 2007). This is just one example of how blogs are being used as "protected spaces" for LGBTQ people by providing a safe place for individuals to express themselves and discuss issues that they face as they establish and negotiate aspects of their sexual identity.

Valois (2014) has also studied the use of blogging by LGBTQ Minorities by studying the Ugandan 'anti-gay' movement and LGNTIQ blogging. Uganda is frequently depicted as a nation fixed in overt homophobia. In recent years proposed Anti-Homosexuality Legislation in Uganda has brought an onslaught of international attention to the nation (Valois, 2014). Anti-gay discourse is omnipresent in the Ugandan public sphere as television and radio broadcasts, and evangelical Christian sermons frequently denounce the 'growing threat' that homosexuality poses to the nation (Valois, 2014). Yet, increased access to the Internet and digital technologies has afforded many Ugandan LGBTQ people the chance to express resistance and contest anti-gay discourse that is dominating the Ugandan public sphere. By maintaining anonymity, the blogosphere provides a 'safe space' for the production of positive LGBTQ discourse by Ugandan bloggers. Ugandan bloggers are utilising the medium as a site of resistance to dominant anti-gay discourse and showing confidence in their 'alternate' sexualities online (Valois,

2014). In the context of a bounded public sphere that limits the performance of 'alternative' sexualities, blogging offers a space to claim and promote equal citizenship.

In a study by Jordan- Zachery (2012), a web-based survey gathered responses from black, female bloggers who supplied information about their online experiences as LGBTQ women. The participants of the study reported using online resources to serve many functions in the coming out process: to gather information, try out new ways of self-expression, and to find an audience and community of like-minded people with whom they could seek support (Jordan- Zachery, 2012). Blogs were reported as most useful for offering the ability to express oneself on LGBTQ issues, and for connecting with a larger LGBTQ community (Jordan- Zachery, 2012). The results of the study suggested that bloggers use online spaces to resist dominant discourses and create alternative understandings of what it means to be LGBTQ. The use of blogs by those who identify as LGBTQ can also be seen as a means of self-expression. Further, they represent for these bloggers a form of governmentality. These blogs may be read through a lens of governmentality because they allow victims of homophobia and injustice to speak out against prejudice and be part of a community in which they can feel supported, not marked or tainted with a stigma and can work on overcoming their disadvantage and promoting tolerance for sexual minorities in the public sphere.

WOMEN'S USE OF BLOGS

Historically, women have been avid users and heavy adopters of new communications technologies. According to a survey by Duggan from the Pew Research Centre, men and women have varying degrees of engagement online. Among social networking sites, women are significantly more likely than men to use Facebook, Pinterest, and Instagram, whereas a roughly equal proportion of men and women are likely to use Twitter and Tumblr (Duggan, 2013). Between 2009 and 2012, women were significantly more likely than men to use social networking sites in nine out of ten surveys that were conducted (Duggan, 2013). Unlike past studies measuring gender digital divides where males have made up the majority of new technology users, it appears that when it comes to social media use, particularly blogging, women are more likely than men to participate (Duggan, 2013). The evident appeal of blogging for women is particularly noteworthy given the discourse surrounding its potential for feminist empowerment. New media technologies have created new economic and social opportunities for women all over the world in areas where gender inequality is still pertinent. Feminist individuals and organisations are adopting social media to further gender equality, utilising it as a new form of information exchange, organisation, and empowerment.

Resurgence of the Feminist Movement

Scholars (Bennet, 2014; Mclean & Maalsen, 2013) emphasise knowledge (including self-knowledge) and participation as the main ingredients for women's empowerment in the digital era. Social media continues to play a prominent role in revitalising and transforming the feminist movement. The feminist revitalisation operates largely through new media with the overarching aim of ending inequality between genders. These authors see revitalisation of feminist thought and action through new spaces created by new technologies and social media (cf. Mclean & Maalsen, 2013). Facebook and Twitter are the most prominent spaces facilitating rapid feminist revitalisation (Mclean & Maalsen, 2013). The recent reinvigoration of feminist thought and action in Australia, in both political and public spaces, offers an excellent opportunity to explore the empowerment that is being provided by new media technologies. Through the recent case of the 'Destroy the Joint' political campaign it is evident that there has been a renewed interest in feminist issues and debate in Australia. Shortly preceding former Prime Minister Julia Gillard's anti-misogyny speech in 2012, the 'Destroy the Joint' campaign took issue with inflammatory comments made by conservative radio commentator with cross-Australia coverage, Alan Jones, who claimed that women leaders were ruining the country (Mclean & Maalsen, 2013). Driven largely by social media activism, an anti-sexism social media campaign quickly grew, resulting in withdrawal of advertiser support for Alan Jones' main host radio station. Within a week, 114000 individuals had signed a petition entitled '2GB and Advertisers: Immediately cease association with Alan Jones over "died of shame" comment #boycott2gb (Mclean & Maalsen, 2013). Following the 'Destroy the Joint' campaign Mclean & Maalsen (2013) argued that online spaces are equally as valid as traditional sites for anti- sexism activism. Social media thus can more effectively mobilise a variety of feminist causes for which to campaign. Far from feminism suffering a slow death, a renewed feminism is emerging in Australia.

The Power of the #Hashtag

Bennet's (2014) article further supports studies that have examined the renewed feminism that is emerging on social media sites. Bennet (2014) states that "the women's social media revolution has reached its tipping point with the rise of the #feminism phenomenon." There's #EverydaySexism, about women's daily harassment, #YouOKSis, which challenges women's street harassment, #AskHerMore, which calls out the questions women wish reporters would ask women on the red carpet (Bennet, 2014). The list goes on. Tracking the feminist hashtags of the moment has become a virtual sport. This proliferation of hashtags is not surprising given that twitter data conversation about feminism has increased by 300 percent on the platform over the past three years (Bennet, 2014). Social organising has always existed within feminist circles — from word of mouth to letter writing (Bennet, 2014). The intimate personal stories curated in hashtags are the modern-day method that is mobilising gender equality. In a pre-Internet era, unless a woman actively sought a protest, or found herself an activist group of which to become a member, she was unlikely to hear much about the issues affecting women, which is why #feminism, and movements like it, are even more significant. Feminist hashtags manage to take women's issues previously confined to small circles — feminist circles — and bring them out into the public sphere.

New Generations and Feminism

Young women are often said to only rarely engage with traditional political activities and to distance themselves from feminist ideologies (Schuster, 2013). Such criticism often comes from feminists of previous generations who believe that young women lack commitment to the feminist cause and do not appreciate the achievements of previous generations. However, feminist literature (cf. Schuster, 2013; Keller, 2011; Scharff, 2012; Morahan- Martin, 2000) has argued that the face of feminism is not fading but rather changing. Various scholars (cf. Schuster, 2013; Keller, 2011; Scharff, 2012; Morahan- Martin, 2000) have explored women's use of social media for feminist political purposes. An article by Schuster (2013) addresses one specific aspect of such change by investigating how the relatively new form of online activism affects the relationship between generations of feminists. Schuster (2013) questions whether the alleged disappearance of young feminists is due to the shift to online methods of feminist work.

Online activism is a key form of participation for many young women today. Many young women choose online activism as their main form of political participation and thus put their political energy into a space that excludes people who are not familiar with this form of organising (Schuster, 2013). Consequently, the use of online tools contributes to making young feminists 'invisible' not only to the wider public but also to their political peers of older generations. Schuster (2013) studied young women's blogs and explored how this medium provides a new space to express feminist ideas. Through a large-scale survey of young, female bloggers, Schuster determined that online spaces provide less intimidating opportunities for young women to act as feminists than traditional media forms. Young women value new media for its flexibility, accessibility and ability to reach large groups of people. Moreover, they appreciate its easy and low cost. There are many reasons why online tools are the preferred method of political participation for young women. Most young women are familiar with social networking tools because they use them for non-political purposes too and often on a daily basis (Schuster, 2013). Social networking tools provide places where young women can express both personal and political views and connect with other women. They can operate as safe spaces through which young women can speak out, especially about sensitive topics (Schuster, 2013). Computer Mediated Communication tools offer many opportunities for increased feminist participation. This take up of Computer Mediated Communication is evident in Schuster's study. Schuster found women frequently used new media to connect with and support each other, to have political discussions and to organise events in the 'real world'.

'Mommy Bloggers'

Outside of women's use of social media for political endeavours, the social use of blogs amongst the mother demographic is on the rise. Researches (Cornell, 2012; Lawson, 2013; Kiisel, 2012) have taken note, and have begun using the term 'mommy bloggers' to describe this coveted market. The number of mothers that read or write blogs is growing rapidly. 14% of all American women with children in the household read or contribute to a blog (Reuters, 2010). Many mothers are not satisfied with reading and commenting on other blogs, they also want to share their own ideas and opinions, which has led to the creation of many new 'mommy blogs'. Women in every stage of parenting have become professional writers by blogging about their experiences raising children. These 'mommy blogs' are not limited to any one topic, but span a wide variety of different subjects spanning the discourse of motherhood (Cornell, 2012). There are many theories to explain the increased trend of 'mommy blogging.' One contributing factor to the rise in social media and blog use among mothers may be the trend toward geographic mobility among families (Cornell, 2012). As the stereotypical, primary communicator for their families, mothers are utilising social media and blogs to stay connected and bridge the distance between family and friends

(Cornell, 2012). For new mothers the trend of increased geographic distance between themselves and their elder family members greatly reduces social support for mothers raising children. In turn, many isolated mothers have also reached out to blogs in search of communities of support and friendship. Social media and blogs help to fill this gap by providing mothers with a connection to family and friends, as well as an informational resource and shared community of other parents that either have been or are currently going through the same transitions. Many mothers use social media as social tools to broadcast updates of their family's lives and to seek answers and support within a wider community of mothers. Other mothers are adopting blogging as a political platform to dispel pervasive ideologies of motherhood and breakdown gendered stereotypes (Lawson, 2013). In both instances these tools are providing women with the necessary support to network, discuss and share in the experience of motherhood.

Feminist scholars such as Lawson (2013), Kysill (2012), Johns & English (2014), consider mother's use of social media as a collective advancement in women's understanding and use of technology. In their study, Johns & English (2014) explored how women used social media and blogs to make connections with other women who were mothers, and overcome feelings of isolation and confusion that frequently accompany the change of life phase that is involved in the move to motherhood. Similarly, Shade (2002) describes how significant it is to women's changing gender roles when women create communities and collaborate about issues of importance in online spaces. In her book, Gender & Community in the Social Construction of the Internet, Shade explores the historiography of women and their uptake of digital technologies and the Internet. She states that, "cyberfeminism emerged in the early 1990s as a feminist approach to emerging technologies and newfound techno-culture. It was at once a stance, an attitude, an emerging theory, a political statement, and an art practice," (Shade, 2002). Thus, blogs, computer mediated communication and other online communication tools serve multiple purposes. Other feminist scholars, Lawson (2013) and Kysill (2012), define cyber-feminism as a philosophy which acknowledges gender differences in emerging technologies, and examines their root beginnings up to its uses today. Today women are found to be consumers and producers within the social media world and are discovering great power in the communities and cultures that this technology is helping them to create. Women use social media as a space to challenge and change outdated gender roles (Lawson, 2013). In this sense, social media can be seen as empowering as it creates opportunities for women to expand their influence and slowly change societal perceptions of the role of mothers. The writers of these 'mommy blogs' gain prominence and attention as they write intelligent posts devoted to issues of feminism, political activism, and the use of social media for democratic purposes. Mothers, writing about aspects of the private sphere of the home in such a public place as the Internet gives a new meaning to public and private spaces (Lawson, 2013). 'Mommy bloggers' do not look to culture to define their existence but rather create their own culture, taking power from those who historically speak on behalf of women and their 'natural roles' which are likely to be socially constructed. The 'mommy-blogger' can also be understood in relation to Foucault's theory of governmentality. Mommy blogs create a space for women's self-expression and identity formation. They defeat ideological constraints by negotiating woman's uses of these spaces, much of which show the reality of life with children (Lawson, 2013). The increasing uptake of social media among mothers demonstrates the way in which social media provides an avenue for expressing the hegemony-challenging potentiality of women's spatial positions.

Women's use of blogs can mediate against some of their disadvantage. Thus, it is imperative that studies further examine the role of blogs in helping women overcome entrenched disadvantage. It is suggested, in much the same terms as the ways that human rights groups, poverty groups and people who identify as LGBTQ, women can use blogs to promote and claim their equality and citizenship in a world that discourages them from having an equal voice. One particular group of note is the emerging 'mommy blogger'. This demographic is using their blogs to, not only reach out and claim public space for their discourse but also engage with neo-liberalism and its associated notions of 'success' by making a profit while they are at home with their children. Further, their increasing power in the community demands attention. As Johns & English (2014) note, these women have a good deal of power over the purchasing decisions of other women. If these bloggers use their blogs well, they are able to turn their blogs into an enterprise worth significant amounts of money. Blogs provide these women with the necessary tools to discuss and negotiate the discourse and experience of motherhood.

DISCUSSION

The literature reviewed in this chapter suggests as we continue to explore blogs as a form of computer-mediated communication, we can shift the norm of research subjects away from privileged researcher/researched dichotomy and delve more deeply into understanding the online identity constructions of marginalised groups. The hope is that this will help us better understand how they see and position themselves in relation to society. A reoccurring theme that emerged throughout the chapter and should be pursued further in future research is the relationship between minority groups use of social media tools and Foucault's literature on identity, governmentality and agency. It is noted that Foucault's (1998) work on governmentality and the care of the self can be used effectively to explore the concept of blogging among those groups who are disenfranchised. Foucault describes the development of technologies of the self, in which the most important principle is to know the self and to care for the self in order to "improve one's self, to surpass one's self, to master the appetites that risk engulfing you," (Foucault, 1988, p. 146). What Foucault describes as "technologies of the self" permit individuals to effect by their own means, or with the help of others, a certain number of operations on their own bodies and souls, thoughts, conduct, and way of being, so as to transform themselves in order to attain a certain state of happiness (Foucault, 1988, p. 146). Through technologies of the self members of disenfranchised groups within society share their inner thoughts of their moods/feelings with others through writing, they may gain greater social support and improve their social integration. Furthermore, the social capital that is built through technologies of the self, may improve a blogger's satisfaction with his or her social contact, interpersonal communication, and overall quality of life. This chapter has presented an analysis of the literature related to the use of blogs by minorities. Further work needs to be done to better understand the role blogs play in the lives of minorities. These groups, as is argued here, can use blogs to overcome their problems and connect with others who share their views. However, how these groups can further their blogs to better advantage their whole groups, to connect with the wider community and to a great extent circumvent traditional media requires attention. It is expected that this work will come in the future as more and more blogs are developed and gain more attention.

REFERENCES

Bennet, J. (2014). Behold the Power of Hashtag Feminism. *Time Magazine.* Retrieved from http://time.com/3319081/whyistayed-hashtag-feminism-activism/

Bronstein, J. (2013). Personal blogs as online presences on the internet: Exploring self-presentation and self-disclosure in blogging. *Aslib Proceedings*, *65*(2), 161–181. doi:10.1108/00012531311313989

Bruns, A. (2006). Introduction. In A. Bruns & J. Jacobs (Eds.), *Uses of Blogs* (pp. 1–9). New York: Peter Lang Publishing.

Burgess, J. (2007). *Vernacular Creativity and New Media* [PhD dissertation]. Queensland University of Technology.

Burgess, J., & Banks, J. (2010). In S. Cunningham & G. Turner (Eds.), *User-Created Content and Online Social Networks* (3rd ed., pp. 295–307). NSW: Allen and Unwin.

Cornell, K. (2012). 'The Mommy Blogger Market: Social Media's Effect on Motherhood (pp. 1–9). East Carolina University. Retrieved from http://www.katiecornelldesigns.com/ECUCourseWork/ICTN6855/The%20Mommy%20Blogger%20Market.pdf

Derlega, V. J., & Chaikin, A. L. (1977). Privacy and self-disclosure in social relationships. *The Journal of Social Issues*, *33*(3), 102–115. doi:10.1111/j.1540-4560.1977.tb01885.x

Duggan, M. (2013). It's a Woman's (Social Media) World. *Pew Research Centre.* Retrieved http://www.pewresearch.org/fact-tank/2013/09/12/its-a-womans-social-media-world/

El-Nawawy. M., & Khamis, S. (2013). Blogging on Violations of Human Rights and Limitations on Freedom. In Egyptian Revolution 2.0: Political Blogging, Civic Engagement and Citizen Journalism. New York: Palgrave Macmillan.

Ennion, J. (2012). How Girl's Guide to Homelessness blogger Brianna Karp's life has changed. *News.com.au.* Retrieved from http://www.news.com.au/technology/how-girls-guide-to-homelessness-blogger-brianna-karps-life-has-changed/story-e6frfro0-1226235960256

Foucault, M. (1988). The political technology of individuals.

Guadagno, R. E., Eno, C. A., & Okdie, B. M. (2010). Personal Blogging: Individual Differences and Motivations. In Handbook of Research on Social Interaction Technologies and Collaboration Software: Concepts and Trends (pp. 292-301).

Howard, P. (2010). *Information Technology and Democratic Islam. In The Digital Origins of Dictatorship and Democracy: Information Technology and Political Islam* (pp. 180–203). New York: Oxford University Press. doi:10.1093/acprof:oso/9780199736416.003.0009

Gurak, L., Antonijevic, S., Johnson, L., Ratliff, C., & Reyman, J. (2005). Introduction: Weblogs, Rhetoric, Community and Culture. In Gurak, L., Antonijevic, S., Johnson, L., Ratliff, C., & Reyman, J. (Eds.), Into the Blogosphere: Rhetoric, Community and Culture of Weblogs. University of Minnesota.

Johns, R., & English, R. (2014). Mothers influencing mothers: The use of virtual discussion boards and their influence on consumption. *Int. J. Web Based Communities*, *10*(3), 319–338. doi:10.1504/IJWBC.2014.062945

Jordan-Zachery, J. S. (2012). *Blogging at the Intersections: Black Women, Identity, and Lesbianism. In Politics and Gender* (pp. 405–414). United Kingdom: Cambridge University Press.

Ko, H.-C., & Kuo, F.-Y.Hsiu-Chia. (2009). Can Blogging Enhance Subjective Well-Being through Self-Disclosure? *CyberPhyschology and Behaviour*, *12*(1), 75–79. doi:10.1089/cpb.2008.016 PMID:19132911

Lawson, M. (2013). *Blogging, babies, and business: Mommy blogging as citizen journalism. University Of Colorado.*

McKenna, K. Y. A., & Bargh, J. A. (1998). Coming out in the age of the Internet: Identity de- marginalization' from virtual group participation. *Journal of Personality and Social Psychology*, *74*(3), 681–694. doi:10.1037/0022-3514.75.3.681

McKenna, K. Y. A., & Bargh, J. A. (2000). Plan 9 from cyberspace: The implications of the Internet for personality and social psychology. *Personality and Social Psychology Review*, *4*(1), 57–75. doi:10.1207/S15327957PSPR0401_6

McLean, J., & Maalsen, S. (2013). Destroying the Joint and Dying of Shame? A Geography of Revitalised Feminism in Social Media and Beyond. *Geographical Research*, *51*(3), 243–256. doi:10.1111/1745-5871.12023

Miller, C., & Shepherd, D. (2005). Blogging as Social Action: A Genre Analysis of the Weblog. In Gurak, L., Antonijevic, S., Johnson, L., Ratliff, C., & Reyman, J. (Eds.), Into the Blogosphere: Rhetoric, Community and Culture of Weblogs. University of Minnesota.

O'Farrell, C. (2007). Key Concepts. *Michel- Foucault.com.* Retrieved from http://www.michel-foucault.com/concepts/

Papacharissi, Z. (2007). Audiences as Media Producers: Content Analysis of 260 Blogs. In M. Tremayne (Ed.), *Blogging, Citizenship and the Future of Media* (pp. 21–25). New York: Routledge.

Postmes, T., Spears, R., Sakhel, K., & de Groot, D. (2001). Social influence in computer- mediated communication: The effects of anonymity on group behavior. *Personality and Social Psychology Bulletin*, *27*(10), 1243–1254. doi:10.1177/01461672012710001

Schneider, B. (2012). Blogging Homelessness: Technology of the Self or Practice of Freedom? *Canadian Journal of Communication*, 2012, 405–419.

Schuster, J. (2014). *Invisible feminists? Social media and young women's political participation. In Political Science* (pp. 8–24). New Zealand: Sage.

Shade, L. (2002). *Introduction. In Gender & Community in the Social Construction of the Internet* (pp. 1–15). New York: Peter Lang.

Shirky, C. (2003). *Power Laws, Weblogs and Inequality. In The Internet: Economics and Culture* (pp. 46–52). Media and Community.

Tremayne, M. (Ed.), (2012). *Blogging, citizenship, and the future of media*. Routledge.

Valois, C. (2014). Virtual access: the Ugandan 'anti-gay' movement, lesbian, gay, bisexual and transgender blogging and the public sphere. *Journal of East African Studies*. Doi:10.1080/17531055.2014.987508

Verba, S. et al.. (1987). *The Historical Context of Equality. In Elites and the Idea of Equality: A Comparison of Japan, Sweden and the United States* (pp. 20–58). United States: Harvard College.

Section 2
Gender in Context

Chapter 6
Social Media:
It Can Play a Positive Role in Education

Matthew Reeves
Queensland University of Technology, Australia

ABSTRACT

This chapter investigates the positive role social media can play in education. It looks at the various formats in which the tool can be used and how it can enhance the learning experience of all students. The chapter analyses the ability for social media to act as a communication channel as well as an educational interface where every student can learn through their peers and through their educator. It also discusses the need for further research as to how this increasingly popular tool can be successfully integrated into educational environments.

DOI: 10.4018/978-1-5225-0010-0.ch006

INTRODUCTION

There is little debate that social media has moved from being simply a form of communication to becoming a multi-use tool for different organisations. Education, despite initial hesitancy, is one industry that stands to benefit immensely from this tool. Two of the most popular forms of social media, Facebook and Twitter, started out as a method of communication between friends. However, they have rapidly expanded to provide much of the information and news we seek, resulting in educators no longer being the main source for information (Chelly & Mataillet, 2012). Despite their reputation, and the belief of some politicians that they represent merely "electronic graffiti" (Battersby, 2015), the ability to share, reflect and discuss ideas with multiple users anytime at any location far surpasses any previous communication channel. We are exposed to businesses, politicians, charities, sporting clubs and many more institutions on social media. So, too are schools. Many educational organisations have taken to social media as a way of communicating with past, current and potential stakeholders. Social media is both a challenge and an opportunity for all educational organisations, including schools.

Whilst hesitancy and, to be fair many serious issues, surround full integration, there is a steadily growing notion that social media can effectively amplify institutional communication (Stoner, 2012). Further, the tools provided by the uptake of social media are said to increase the ability to achieve educational goals (cf. Stoner, 2012). Schools are one such industry that has taken to using Facebook and Twitter to communicate with stakeholders. These stakeholders include parents, students, staff and the wider community. As schools have a unique role in many communities, especially in rural and remote communities, Indigenous communities and in specific groups such as Muslim and Jewish communities, their use of social media is an important expression of the changed media landscape. This usage, coupled with what some regard (cf. Bennett, 2014) as the gendered nature of social media, favouring women over men, has revolutionised the ways that young women communicate online. In addition, it is noted that the target audience for these schools' communication through social media is generally women as it is women who assume the family's responsibility for their children's education (cf. Griffith & Smith, 2005).

Principals are able to use social media platforms to advertise their school through highlighting activities and events in which the school is involved. This 'free' form of advertising is an important avenue for schools that wish to demonstrate their effectiveness, and their engagement with the wider world in an increasingly competitive market for education. To illustrate, one small former government school in Queensland uses its social media activities through Facebook and Twitter to showcase its events. This school is a one-teacher school, run by a female teacher/principal, who is actively engaging stakeholders through social media. The school's major events (assemblies, sporting carnivals, excursions) are all extensively covered through their Facebook page, as are the quotidian activities of schooling (lessons and lunchtime play). The use of social media democratises the dissemination of information in a way that is unprecedented. However, it is more than just a marketing tool for principals short on money and time. In this chapter, I explore the ways that schools are using social media platforms to democratise information, meet curricular requirements and, in the case of female students, prevent harm and injury.

This chapter amounts to a literature review or meta-analysis and a call for more research. In what follows, I begin by discussing the social media tools used by many educational institutions. I define what is meant by social media and discuss research generally concerned with the use of social media in educational institutions. It is noted that the majority of the papers reviewed in what follows refer to higher education. This focus is because, in spite of the chapter being concerned with schools, there is limited research into schools' uptake and use of social media. Following the discussion on social media tools, I review literature on the implementation of social media. From this review, I focus on three aspects of schools' use of social media. First, I discuss bullying online, known colloquially as cyberbullying. Second, I discuss social media as a marketing tool. Finally, I explore the ways that curricular documents focus on the use of social media. In this section, I focus on one particular document, in Australia. I finish the chapter with a discussion of the findings of the literature reviews.

SOCIAL MEDIA TOOLS

When discussing social media it is not uncommon that the term is to be wholly defined as mass social network tools such as Facebook. For the purposes of this chapter, social media is defined as "groups of people with common interests and practices that communicate regularly and for some duration in an organised way over the Internet" (Ridings et al., 2002, p.273). There are a plethora of tools such as, internet forums, blogs, wikis, social networks, podcasts, photos and videos through which people communicate via social media (Sliogeriene & Oleskeviciene, 2014). There is no doubt there is an increasingly popular trend to implement social media tools in education platforms. To illustrate, YouTube clips and videos are suggested by researchers (cf. Dredger, Woods, Beach & Sagstetter, 2010) as a method of engaging disengaged children and youth. The results are enhanced learning and fewer behavioural problems (Roodt & Peier, 2013; Phiranger, 2013; Devine, Crawford & Elder, 2012). Similarly, YouTube is also the most commonly used higher education tool (Moran et al., 2011). Studies have shown that students enjoy using social media platforms to engage with other students online. For example, in one study of the use of Facebook to engage students, English and Howell (2011) argue that students who are enrolled in courses that require significant time away from the university setting for practicums and industry placements can benefit from using a Facebook group to maintain engagement. They found students were more likely to involve themselves in the learning community when outside it when a Facebook group was used to continue the lines of communication, mainly because this was a popular tool used by the students every day and its popularity normalized its use among these students.

It has been noted, in the English and Howell (2011) study and in others (cf. Sliogeriene & Oleskevicene, 2014) that, while universities operate a CMS (Course Management System) it is not as popular or readily accessed as a Social Media platform. A CMS allows for the distribution of educational material but is very limited in its ability for students to communicate throughout and beyond the time of study (Sliogeriene & Oleskeviciene, 2014). Whilst any CMS performs well during the semester, it is limited in its use and engagement outside the semester (English & Howell, 2011). Perhaps the focus needs to shift toward stakeholder communication. Implementing a social networking tool that allows for real-time communication between all stakeholders allows for full collaboration between students online without the need to meet face-to-face (Sliogeriene & Oleskeviciene, 2014) thus allowing the education system to be readily available in locations previously not associated with education (English & Howell, 2011). Not only is does the technology allow for greater access, but it may also provide enhanced learning experiences (Anderson, 2012).

Understandably, the integration of social media is often met with some hesitancy. It can often be a daunting thought for many educators for a variety of reasons. Silogeriene & Oleskeviciene (2014) suggest that there are two approaches to implementing social media – the enthusiastic approach which leans towards full integration and the critical approach which views social media as a highly disruptive tool that is not suitable for education. Whilst there is some validity to each side's claims, it is important to remember students are already on these platforms, even school age students. The biggest advantaged of social media integration is the connection it brings.

The integration of social media tools rapidly increases the communication ability of all stakeholders. Recent studies have found that integration of social media tools have allowed stakeholders to communicate with each other instantly (Odom et al., 2013). Odom et al. (2013) argue that these stakeholders can communicate around class content, assessment and general questioning. When this ability is provided to students, they argue, students' ability to understand the content is enhanced through peer-to-peer collaboration. In addition, students are able to ask questions during a lecture (Odom et al., 2013), rather than waiting until a later time when the question may no longer be relevant or remembered. Not only does this ensure that students questions can be answered, it allows for all other attendees in the lecture to be privy to the answer. It may be that this type of communication can allow for students understanding and knowledge of the course content to expand. With the use of these tools, students are also able to become more involved in every aspect of their education, from planning to evaluation (Odom et al., 2013), Students can be polled on their opinions of class content, teaching methods, activities and many other aspects central to learning. It also allows for the lecturer to gain an understanding of how students are progressing, with assessment for learning based on the discussions had via the social media tool. Apart from gaining an insight to students' progress, this real time, personalised feedback can also impact student performance in the class. Odom et al. (2013), suggest students would be more likely to check the course page regarding information on course content and assessment due to the fact they check their social media accounts multiple times per day. This finding is consistent with others who have done work in similar fields (cf. English & Howell, 2011).

Through the tools of communication provided by social media, it can also be suggested that educators can be inspired and find new creative methods of teaching (Blankenship, 2011). Through the feedback and suggestions given on the social media page, educators may find various tools such as videos, interviews, news clips or even students' comments enhance their teaching. Many higher education courses will call upon "guest lecturers" to discuss their area of expertise. With the use of various tools (including Facetime and Skype) the pool of available resources rapidly expands. These tools have been used to enable an academic in another location to deliver a lecture with great success (Blankenship, 2011). This integration has ensured students are accessing experts in various fields who can pass on their knowledge to students who previously experienced communication restrictions.

Whilst there are many benefits that come with social media integrations, there are also some disadvantages. Perhaps the biggest roadblock with the integration of these technologies is learning functionality. Mourlam (2013) suggests that one of the biggest student concerns about social media integration was the time it would take to learn the technology. Evidently students are studying content, which is new to them, and it can take considerable time to be comfortable with this content, adding the stress of learning a new technology to this is not the aim. Further research needs to be conducted to determine if the current CMD system would be easier to use/learn than the migration to an established social media tool. In addition, access to the technology is crucial. In current times, it is easy to assume that all students will have access to the required technology (computers, smart phones and the like) and also be a member and user of the social media tool but this is not always the case. Whilst some who do not have the required technology will simply go out and buy it or sign up, not everyone will have the financial means to do this (Blankenship, 2011). Thus, it is important to look at various methods of implementation to ensure that all students have the ability to access the social media tools not just in the educational institution but also from outside this location as well.

It is unquestionable that there is still hesitancy when it comes to implementing social media in education but it is important to note that this implementation can greatly help those wanting to learn. It allows for greater communication between all stakeholders and can sometimes negate the need for face-to-face meetings. The implementation of these tools may take some logistical analysis to ensure all students have the required access. However, this analysis is merely a roadblock that once overcome, will allow for greater student involvement and also effectively amplify institutional communication (Stoner, 2012).

IMPLEMENTATION OF SOCIAL MEDIA

Despite the limited research focusing on schools, they are one site in which social media uptake is increasing. There are several ways through which schools can implement social media in their classrooms. This chapter focuses on three ways that social media is being implemented into schools' activities and learning. In this chapter, I conduct a literature review of the three main ways schools interact with social media. The first deals with bullying, and the effect of students' increasing use of social media on anti-bullying policies. The second is on the use of social media to market a school. The third is the push to increasingly prepare students for their use of social media through curricular initiatives that 'teach' students about social media. The major focus is the effects of the uptake of these technologies on female students. In what follows, I review the literature on each of these topics, where I can I concern myself with research into schools, however, higher education institutions is the major focus of the following studies.

Bullying

The increase usage of social media has seen traditional methods of bullying be replaced by what is now commonly referred to as cyberbullying. Whilst traditional bullying obviously still exist in a school environment, it is clear the face-to-face bullying that may occur whilst at school can now be continued at home using social media platforms. Studies show that it is mainly female students who suffer from cyberbullying (cf. Mishna, Schwan, Lefebvre, Bhole & Johnston, 2014; Bohr, Murray, Anderson, Henson, Murphy & Amr, 2013; Holfeld & Grabe, 2012). Many schools feel that it is their responsibility to assist female students to feel safe online and to extend their anti-bullying initiatives into the home.

Researchers (cf. Bohr et al., 2013) argue that adolescents have two lives; one online and the other offline. However, these worlds are, in many cases, conflated as they will communicate with the same people both online and offline (Subrahmanyam & Greenfield, 2008). Offline communication allows for adolescents to connect with their peers and enhance their group identity. For boys, it is said to be about flirting with girls and making new friends whereas girls are said to use social media to reinforce existing friendships (Subrahmanyam & Greenfield, 2008). Therefore, where girls are concerned it could be extended to a pack mentality where their offline group acts the same way online (Mishna et al., 2014, Bohr et al., 2013). Kowalski and Limber (2007), suggest that girls are more likely to be involved in cyberbullying either as the victim or the bully. Interestingly, it is suggested by Kowalski and Limber (2007) and Mishna et al. (2014) that approximately 50% of victims do not know the identity of their bully. These statistics suggest that victims of cyberbullying potentially would not be bullied via a face-to-face altercation but only in an online setting. Results like these suggest that females, the highest number of those involved in cyberbully as both victim and perpetrator (Holfeld & Grabe, 2012), are likely to suffer most from the effects of online bullying.

Many effects have been discovered through various studies. Raskauskas and Stoltz (2007), found that many victims of cyberbullying will show symptoms of depression whilst Hinduja and Patchin (2010), discovered that anger and even suicide were potential reactions to cyberbullying. It could be suggested that the implications of cyberbullying can be more serious when compared to implications of traditional bullying methods. Therefore, it is vital that educational institutions implement support to educate female students on the impacts of cyberbullying and offer support to those girls who fall victim to this form of bullying.

Essentially, a school is responsible for ensuring that all students are able to attend their school and learn without feeling afraid (Beale & Hall, 2012). Cyberbullying, whilst not as visible as traditional bullying however, schools who ignore or deny its occurrence among their female students are naive (Beale & Hall, 2012). There are many ways schools can support anti-bullying initiatives in an attempt to eliminate or reduce the occurrences and ramifications of cyberbullying. According to Beale and Hall (2012) there are three main stakeholders who can prevent or reduce cyberbullying: students, parents and teachers. It is important that any initiative includes all three stakeholders to ensure that everyone has the same knowledge and skills to deal with issues in the appropriate manner (Beale & Hall, 2012). Many schools offer care programs (Doane, Kelley & Pearson, 2012) within their curriculum, it is widely known that this program has a focus on bullying during the course of a school year (Tanrikulu, Kinay & Ancak, 2015). With the increase in cyberbullying cases it is important that schools dedicate part of their bullying education session specifically to cyberbullying and steps to ensure everyone feels safe online (Kvarme & Monsen, 2014; Colman, 2014). Programs dedicated to cyberbullying allow students to be aware that adults know it is happening and are able to help (Hendricks & Lumadue, 2012). Parents are important partners in this process. As noted above, Beale and Hall (2012) argue they are one of the three main stakeholders who can prevent or reduce cyberbullying. Parents need to be educated on the impacts of cyberbullying and how it can affect their child no matter if they are the bully or the victim (Hannah, 2010). This information will provide parents with the skills required to have successful discussions with their children regarding the impacts of cyberbullying (Beale & Hall, 2012). Finally, it is important that teachers are educated on the risks associated with cyberbullying and how to identify a victim (Beale & Hall, 2012). If a child is being cyberbullied, almost certainly other students in the school will have seen it on social media or the bully may even be a member of the school community. Therefore, to engage in this education will allow teachers to identify a possible victim and support that student with the negative comments and feelings they may be experiencing and most importantly put a stops to the bullying.

Recently, there have been many changes in the way schools tackle bullying. Most recently legislation in Australia was amended to allow schools to investigate and issue consequences of bullying that occurred online between students regardless if it occurred during or outside school hours. This movement allows students to know what has occurred outside school is not going to be ignored at school which, in turn, will hopefully provide students with the confidence to report bullying and feel safe enough to do so. Through these legislative changes and support programs being implemented into schools, students can feel safe online and know that there are a plethora of people they can access for help if they become victim to cyberbullying.

However, it is not all bleak. Many school staff are concerned with the ways they can use social media to publicise their schools as prospective and current stakeholders are increasingly using their social media accounts to access information about issues that affect their everyday lives. Using traditional online search utensils such as Google is becoming a thing of the past. The use of social media as a research and advertisement tool is beginning to complement if not replace search engines (Thorat et al., 2013). There is no debate that marketing is essential for organisations, now the trend of social media marketing is becoming at the forefront of institutional marketing. The use of a social media campaign can create, not only high brand visibility but also enhance customer relationships between schools and their communities (Thorat et al., 2013).

School Marketing

In the past there was limited support for educational institutions to market to potential and actual consumers (Constantinides & Stagno, 2011). However, the focus has shifted and many educational institutions are becoming more aware of how important it is to have a social media presence in their overall marketing mix (Zehrer & Grabmuller, 2012). The reality is that even educational institutions need to market themselves in order to successfully compete at a national and even global level. Social media marketing in higher education allows for institutions to successfully develop and maintain relationships with three equally important customer groups: past, current and future students. (Constantinides & Stagno, 2011). However. The research into schools is limited. In what follows, I review the literature into higher education marketing using social media tools.

Most educational institutions using social media tools as a part of their marketing mix. The Southern Illinois University College of Business deems sites such as Facebook vital for their marketing (Reuben, 2008). The college's Facebook page is used to provide students with school news among other communications (Reuben, 2008). Implementation of this social media platform had resulted in the change to the marketing mix at the college. The Head of School has noted that there has been an increased access to those members of the wider community that previously would not have known about the college. A survey of 80 students in a class, conducted by the college found nearly 100 percent of students' access the site on a regular basis (Campbell, 2008). Using the platform has allowed the college to post announcements, recruit for organisations and upload photos (Campbell, 2008). Through these uses alone the college has the ability to promote itself in a positive manner. Announcements relating to key enrollment dates can be quickly uploaded and viewed by target groups instantly. Furthermore, the college can promote itself through photos of various achievements or events that occur throughout the course of the academic year. Overall this platform has allowed the college to provide their current and prospective students, who before this may have been unable to see such advertising, with and "big picture" view of what it is like to study at our school.

In comparison, Kingston University also established spaces on various social media sites for marketing purposes. Since 2010, the university has had dedicated Facebook pages set up which are designed to attract prospective students (Benson, Morgan, 2013). This method has allowed the university to not only advertise key information to students considering applying but also expanded their target audience. The researchers argue the platform's "share" function allowed prospective students to send out the universities material to members of public who may not have once considered applying to their university. Through this approach, enrollments have the potential to increase through a virtual "word-of-mouth" marketing concept. Since its implementation the Facebook page now handles all stages of the enrollment process – selection, admission and induction (Benson & Morgan, 2013). Having a platform that allows for the sharing of this information to those previously not privy expanded the institution's ability to be seen as providing a supportive and positive enrollment process that once again may appeal to a customer that once had never considered the institution (Benson & Morgan, 2013).

In addition to Facebook, the university also has a Twitter account with more than 11,500 followers including journalists and staff at other universities (Benson & Morgan, 2013). Not only is the university able to promote itself on Twitter, but journalists are able to access information; information which the university deems to be appropriate. This information has the potential to be published in various media forms depending on the journalist's current employment. From this platform, the researchers argue the university now has potentially opened itself to gaining newspaper articles or even television interviews that in the past may not have been sought out. This, once again, has opened the marketing abilities of the university not just to a wider audience but also to different media tools that previously may not have been an option.

Marketing via social media means educational institutions have greatly expanded their audience and enhanced their public opinion in the process. In the end, social media is now part of businesses' lives. Thus, it should also be included in the curriculum.

With the day-to-day uses of social media increasing rapidly and everyone, from politicians to small business owners, using the platforms for various marketing and communication purposes it was only natural various curriculum documents would change to include social media. In what follows, I look at the uptake of social media in relation to curriculum documents by focusing on one, in Australia, the secondary school subject of Business Communication and Technologies (BCT). The subject has recently (2012) amended its syllabus document to include the study of social media. Typically in BCT, the cohort choosing to study the subject will predominately be girls. This change is widely due to the subject matter being highly valuable for those wanting to gain administration positions or continue their business studies at a university level. Overall, when studying the subject, students will gain fundamental business skills such as working in team, workplace health and safety and now social media. It is noted that the overwhelming majority of the students who enroll in BCT are female.

Girls on BCT: Social Media and School Curricular Documents

As a topic of study in BCT, social media includes various areas such as: types of social media in business, changes to client relationships, marketing, internal uses and security issues (QSA, 2012). Through studying this topic, students are exposed to multiple elements in relation to social media. It is not simply about looking at how many businesses use the platforms or whose social media presence is better than others. The syllabus requires students to look at a variety of behind the scenes elements that are all important when using social media in business. By studying this topic, students are expected to be exposed to a 'format' of social media. The implementation of this subject area ensures that BCT remains relevant to the real world.

The syllabus argues the importance of this topic of study stating that every day more and more businesses are making the move to social media (QSA, 2012). Therefore, it is essential that, where possible, people are educated on it uses. Furthermore with students now beginning to enter a world where the will use social media for work purposes it is important we educate them on how to use it effectively (Benson, Morgan, 2013). It is vital that students understand the correct use of their social media accounts. If they are going to be linked to a business, the business is going to care what is published on their employee's social media pages. Through the study of BCT students will be exposed to the security and management of social media (QSA, 2012). This area will highlight that they need to ensure they have adequate privacy settings on their Facebook account and are responsible for what they post.

Apart from being educated in the uses of social media the syllabus notes the importance of students being educated on how to use social media. It is one thing to be educated on the uses of social media but that does not necessarily provide the ability to use the technology. However, the knowledge taught in BCT allows for students to get an insight to how business use the technology and investigate current process and policies surrounding the implementation and utilisation of social media platforms (QSA, 2012), which, in turn provides students with a basic understanding of how to use the technology.

The implementation of using social media for communication purposes in higher education allow for students to gain the knowledge of how various social media platforms operate. Whilst secondary schools are limited in their ability to provide hand on practice is using these tools, universities are not. Furthermore, through their use of social media for educational communication students are experiencing for themselves the benefits it hold and are then more likely able to transfer this into a workplace. Social media is not going anywhere; it is expanding everyday and becoming a norm in all aspects of our life. Therefore it is vital that future generations are educated on the appropriate uses of the technology and how to effectively use the technology.

DISCUSSION

As the above review shows, schools are increasingly intertwining social media into their roles as educational institutions. In order to explore the role of social media in schools, it is important to note that no institution is immune from the influence of social media. Perhaps contrarily, many schools endeavour to ‘ban’ social media while the students are at the school (Tynes, 2007). With varying levels of success, these schools endeavour to stop students using their smartphones, or block the access to social media sites such as Facebook or Twitter while using the schools’ network. Several studies have described this phenomenon among schools.

Cox and McLeod (2014) argue that social media is now an expectation rather than an option for students. Yet, there is an increasing number of educational institutions prohibiting access to staff, students and in some case parents. Kissell (2011) cited the Dayton Public School policy, produced in 2011, prohibiting access to any from social network during school hours on school equipment for both staff and students. Highlighted in the policy was that any violation of this would result in staff/student discipline (Kissell, 2011). Similarly, Heritage High School recently banned the use of social media for its student election campaigns (Coetsee, 2012). During their campaign student were restricted to “old school” methods of self-promotion the use of social media outlets such as: Twitter, Facebook or Instagram were banned for election purposes (Coetsee, 2012).

Whilst there is focus on banning or restricting student use, the focus has also shifted to teachers and parents. Educational departments and depending on the age, the law more broadly, do not allow teacher–student relationships whilst that student is at school. The New York City school system has developed a policy stating interactions online with students using professional school accounts will be closely monitored and that teacher have no expectation of privacy when using social media (Fleisher, 2012). This policy has highlighted the strict guidelines being faced by some educational employees and poses great restrictions on their ability to have a “life” outside the school. Further, there is a gendered element to the fear of teacher/student relationships too with male teachers targeted more frequently than female teachers however it is unlikely it is just male teachers who are inappropriately forming relationships with students using social media.

In addition to teachers, parents in some school districts have been asked to refrain from posting negative comments about school events online (MacDonald, 2014). These policies require parents to ‘think’ about the nature of their comments before they are posted and ensure that they are constructive. However, it is interesting to note that these policies consider neither freedom of expression nor define what is meant by ‘constructive’.

This situation is problematic as schools try to run the space between allowing some people to use social media (school leaders, parents and school marketing personnel) while at the same time discouraging others from using it (their students) in an attempt to prevent bullying, especially of girls. Further, it may be that schools want to protect themselves from participation in online bullying by banning social media which is impossible, as Tynes (2007) argues in connected times.

In order to better manage the increasingly important role social media has in students’ lives, it is important to realize that they are not working against each other. Rather, schools can use their anti-bullying initiatives to work with students to assist them to help themselves when they are bullied or abused using social media.

As can be seen from the discussion in this chapter, students’ safety is paramount, however, it must be postulated that a blanket ban on social media is neither effective nor likely. As institutions, from university to primary level are increasingly implementing social media platforms in their marketing and in their planning as mandated by curricular documents, it can be seen that the use of social media is inescapable.

Further, there is a gendered element to the social media use in schools as well. Cyberbullying is a largely female problem with studies arguing that girls are more likely to be both the targets of, and the perpetrators of, bullying online. These studies argue that the effect is an increase in depressive symptoms among these students, which is interesting as studies suggest a large percentage of the students who bully are both perpetrator and themselves bullied (Selkie, Kota & Moreno, 2012). In addition, as noted in the Mishna et al. (2014) study, those who were both victims and perpetrators of cyberbullying were more likely to be in distress. These girls were more likely than their male peers to be in distress, if the bullying was ongoing or focused on other demographic characteristics. Further, as Holfeld & Grabe (2012) note, those girls who reported their cyberbullying experience to an other, such as to a parent, peers or a teacher, did not experience a decrease in their bullying and thus were not able to use their reporting of the incident to prevent further bullying incidents.

In addition, as most school staff are women, there is also a gendered element to the use of social media to market a school. Women who make up the majority of teachers and principals, particularly in primary years (Australian Bureau of Statistics, 2013), are also increasingly responsible for marketing their schools through social media channels. They too may face more bans on use because of a professional requirement by their state or federal educational authority.

Thus, understanding how females interact in school environments with social media is vital to truly understanding its uptake and use in school settings. Without a better analysis of the ways that women use social media, there can be only a limited understanding of how the tools are accessed and used by educational environments. Further research is needed to fully explore the use of social media among school students, and employees.

REFERENCES

Anderson, J. B. (2012). The future of higher education. Retrieved from http://pewinteret.ore/Reports/2012/Future-of-Higher-Education/Overview.aspx

Battersby, L. (2015, January 26). Tony Abbott dismisses social media as 'electronic graffiti', again. *The Age*. Retrieved from http://www.theage.com.au/it-pro/government-it/tony-abbott-dismisses-social-media-as-electronic-graffiti-again-20150126-12yg26.html

Beale, A., & Hall, K. (2012). Cyberbullying: What School Administrators (and Parents) Can Do. *School Psychology International*, *81*(1), 8–12.

Bennett, S. (2014, October 2). Men Are From LinkedIn, Google+ & YouTube, Women Are From Twitter, Instagram & Pinterest. *AdWeek*. Retrieved from http://www.adweek.com/socialtimes/men-women-social-media-study/502009

Benson, V., & Morgan, S. (2013). *Social Higher Education: How Effective is it?* Kingston University.

Blankenship, M. (2011). How Social Media Can and should Impact Higher Education. *Education Digest*, *76*(7), 39–42.

Bohr, M., Murray, K., Anderson, R., Henson, L., Murphy, M., & Amr, F. (2013, October). Bullying, cyberbullying and female to female aggression: Empowering students to be part of the solution. *Connect*, *303*, 3–8.

Campbell, D. (2008). Reaching Students Where They Live. *BizED.*, *7*, 60–61.

Chelly, M., & Mataillet, H. (2012, September). Social Media and the impact on education: Social media and home education. Proceedings of the 2012 International Conference on e-Learning and e-Technologies in Education (ICEEE) (pp. 24-26).

Coetsee, R. (2012, August 11). School Bans Social Media in Student Campaigns: Heritage High makes candidates use fliers, posters. *Contra Costa Times, p B.4.*

Colman, G. (2014). *Cyberbullying and Internet Safety*. Waterbury, CT.

Constantinides, E., & Zinck Stagno, M. (2011). Potential of the social media as instruments of higher education marketing: A segmentation study. *Journal of Marketing for Higher Education*, *21*(1), 7–24. doi:10.1080/08841241.2011.573593

Cox, D., & McLeod, S. (2014). Social media strategies for school principals. National Association of Secondary School Principals. *NASSP Bulletin*, *98*(1), 5–25. doi:10.1177/0192636513510596

Deviney, D.E., Crawford, J., & Elder, K.L. (2012). Classroom antics: Fun with a purpose. *SOBIE: Proceedings of Annual Meetings*.

Doane, A. N., Kelley, M. L., & Pearson, M. R. (2015). Reducing cyberbullying: A theory of reasoned action-based video prevention program for college students. *Aggressive Behavior*. doi:10.1002/ab.21610 PMID:26349445

Dredger, K., Woods, D., Beach, C., & Sagstetter, V. (2010). Engage me: Using new literacies to create third space classrooms that engage student writers. *The National Association for Media Literacy Education's Journal of Media Literacy Education*, *2*(2), 85–101.

Fleisher, L. (2012, May 2). City lays out digital rules for teachers. *The Wall Street Journal.* Retrieved from http://www.wsj.com/articles/SB10001424052702303916904577376541510305510

Hannah, M. (2010). Cyberbullying education for parents: A guide for clinicians. *Journal of Social Sciences,* 6(4), 532.

Hendricks, L., Lumadue, R., & Rusty Waller, L. (2012). The evolution of bullying to cyber bullying: an overview of the best methods for implementing a cyber bullying preventive program. *National Forum Journal of Counseling and Addiction*, 1(1).

Hinduja, S., & Patchin, J. W. (2010). Bullying, cyberbullying and suicide. *Archives of Suicide Research, 14*(3), 206–221. doi:10.1080/13811118.2010.494133 PMID:20658375

Holfeld, B., & Grabe, M. (2012). Middle school students perceptions of and response to cyber bullying. *Journal of Educational Computing Research*, *46*(4), 395–413. doi:10.2190/EC.46.4.e

Kissell, M. (2011, August 31). Teachers banned from 'friending' students: Schools react to effect, growth and social media. *Dayton Daily News, p A.1.*

Kowalski, R. M., & Limber, S. P. (2007). Electronic bullying among middle school students. *The Journal of Adolescent Health*, *41*(6), S22–S30. doi:10.1016/j.jadohealth.2007.08.017 PMID:18047942

Kvarme, L.G., Monsen, K.A., & Eboh, W.O. (2014). Evidence-Based Solution-Focused Care for School-Age Children Experiencing Cyberbullying: Using the Omaha System to Guide and Document Psychiatric Nursing Interventions. *Journal of Psychosocial Nursing & Mental Health Services,* 52(3), 34.

MacDonald, S. (2014, April 15). Schools tackle social media use by parents. *Daily Bulletin*, p A.3

Mishna, F., Schwan, K., Lefebvre, R., Bhole, P., & Johnston, D. (2014, September). Students in distress: Unanticipated findings in a cyberbullying study. *Children and Youth Services Review*, *44*, 341–348. doi:10.1016/j.childyouth.2014.04.010

Moran, M., Seaman, J., & Tinti-Kane, H. (2011). *Teaching, learning and sharing: How today's higher education faculty use social media.* Boston, MA: Pearson Learning Solutions.

Mourlam, D. (2013). Social Media and Education: Perceptions and Need for Support. *Journal of Science Education and Technology*, *9*(3), 23–28.

Odom, S., Jarvis, H., Sandlin, M., & Peek, C. (2013). Social Media Tools in the Leadership Classroom: Students' Perceptions of Use. *Journal of Leadership Education*, *12*(1), 34–53. doi:10.12806/V12/I1/34

Phirangee, K. (2013). Beyond the elementary classroom walls: Exploring the ways participation within Web 2.0 spaces are reshaping pedagogy. *Journal of Educational Multimedia and Hypermedia*, *22*(3), 299–316.

Raskauskas, J., & Stoltz, A. D. (2007). Involvement in traditional and electronic bullying among adolescents. *Developmental Psychology*, *43*(3), 564–575. doi:10.1037/0012-1649.43.3.564 PMID:17484571

Reuben, R. (2008). The Use of Social Media in Higher Education for Marketing and Communications: A Guide for Professionals in Higher Education.

Roodt, S., & Peier, D. (2013). Using YouTube in the Classroom for the Net Generation of Students. *Proceedings of the Informing Science and Information Technology Education Conference (Vol. 1).*

Silogeriene, J., & Oleskeviciene, G. (2014). Confronting Social Media in Higher Education. *Social Studies*, *6*(2), 390–402. doi:10.13165/SMS-14-6-2-10

Social media in education. (2012, 05). Digital Learning, Retrieved from http://search.proquest.com/docview/1018538253?accountid=13380

Stoner, M. (2012) *Social media and advancement: A report on data from 2010 – 2012.* Retrieved from http://www.mstoner.com/blog/,arketing-and-branding/social-media-and-advancement-a-report-on-data-from-2010-2012/

Subrahmanyam, K., & Greenfield, P. (2008). Online Communication and Adolescent Relationships. *The Future of Children*, *18*(1), 119–146. doi:10.1353/foc.0.0006 PMID:21338008

Tanrıkulu, T., Kınay, H., & Tolga Arıcak, O. (2015). Sensibility development program against cyberbullying. *New Media & Society*, *17*(5), 708–719.

Teaching Staff (Number). (2013). *Australian Bureau of Statistics.* Retrieved from http://www.abs.gov.au/ausstats/abs@.nsf/Lookup /4221.0main+features502011

The Queensland Studies Authority (QSA). (2012). *Business communication and technologies senior syllabus. The State of Queensland.* QSA.

Thorat, S. B., Kishor, S. B., & Meghe, B. (2013). Social Media Marketing Mix: Applicability Review for Marketing in Education. *IPEDR*, *50*(4), 16–20.

Tynes, B. M. (2007). Internet safety gone wild? Sacrificing the educational and psychosocial benefits of online social environments. *Journal of Adolescent Research*, *22*(6), 575–584. doi:10.1177/0743558407303979

Zehrer, A., & Grabmuller, A. (2012). Social media marketing in tourism education: Insights into the development and value of a social network site for a higher education institution in tourism. *Journal of Vacation Marketing*, *18*(3), 221–228. doi:10.1177/1356766712449368

Chapter 7
Techno Teacher Moms:
Web 2.0 Connecting Mothers in the Home Education Community

Rebecca English
Queensland University of Technology, Australia

ABSTRACT

Home education is on the rise in Australia. However, unlike parents who choose mainstream schooling, these parents often lack the support of a wider community to help them on their educational and parenting journey. This support is especially lacking as many people in the wider community find the choice to home education confronting. As such, these parents may feel isolated and alienated in the general population as their choice to home educate is questioned at best, and ridiculed at worst. These parents often find sanctuary online in homeschool groups on Facebook. This chapter explores the ways that Facebook Groups are used by marginalized and disenfranchised families who home educate to meet with others who are likeminded and aligned with their beliefs and philosophies. It is through these groups that parents, in relation to schooling it is especially mothers, are able to ask for advice, to vent, to explore options and find connections that may be lacking in the wider community.

DOI: 10.4018/978-1-5225-0010-0.ch007

INTRODUCTION

Home education is on the rise in Australia (English, 2013, 2015a; 2015b). However, unlike parents who choose mainstream schooling, these parents often lack the support of a wider community to help them on their educational and parenting journey. This support is especially lacking as many people in the wider community find the choice to home education confronting. As such, these parents may feel isolated and alienated in the general population as their choice to home educate is questioned at best, and ridiculed at worst. These parents often find sanctuary online in homeschool groups on Facebook (English, 2015b).

This chapter explores the ways that Facebook Groups are used by marginalized and disenfranchised families who home educate to meet with others who are likeminded and aligned with their beliefs and philosophies. The chapter explores five groups: two Australia wide groups, two regional groups and one local group. It is through these groups that mothers, whose work it is to support their children's education (Lareau, 1989), to vent, to explore options and find connections that may be lacking in the wider community. As education is generally seen as the work of women (cf. Griffith & Smith, 2005), this chapter will explore how Facebook groups provide a sanctuary for mothers who may be struggling to find support within their local community, the IRL (In Real Life) world if you will. It will discuss the various groups dedicated to home education in Australia housed on Facebook, their settings, their outlines and their policies on joining. The settings suggest their 'visibility' to the wider world, their outlines describe their philosophy, their expectations of behavior and the beliefs that are allowed and their policies on joining define, for the group at least, who counts as a home education family and who is excluded.

Before starting to explore this issue, I believe it is important to examine what I mean by home education. In this chapter, home-education has been defined, in line with Harding and Farrell (2003, p. 125) as "the education of children within the home setting … overseen by parents or other adults, significant to the child and family." When talking about home education, I am referring to a suite of practices that are neither homogenous nor easy to label. There are myriad reasons for, and ways to, home educate. However, there is fluidity between these groups as families may move between them. In addition, home education is rarely an all or nothing decision, with many families moving between home education and school education, or the reverse. Further, many families may choose an arrangement with schools where their children are enrolled part time and home educated part time.

In one study in Norway, Beck (2012) found that there were four groups of home educators. Using the work of Bernstein (1990), particularly on orientation, he identified these groups as, firstly, the structured home educators. Structured home educators were middle class, religious, well-educated conservatives. The second group were unschoolers who were "well educated middle class parents, anti-establishment, with radical political and cultural views" (Beck, 2012, p. 74). The third group were pragmatic and were usually rural, working class families for whom the home education environment and the family's work environment were linked. Finally, the unknown group was all those who were not registered and thus not accessible to study.

In my research, I have found that there are three general categories of home educators in Australia. The first category of home education family is the traditional school at home family. This family is generally considered to follow a school at home model and replicate the traditional schooling arrangements in the home. While they may have more of a project-based approach to the work of educating their children, they are still generally following a model of schooling that sits neatly alongside national and state based curriculum models (English, 2013; 2015b).

These families may buy curriculum resources from a private provider in order to ensure that they meet the demands of the state education authorities that manage home education families and register them. It is a requirement in Australia that all home education families register with their state's home education unit, located within the departments of education in each state or territory.

Many of these families will seek out Christian resources to use for their children, often turning online to purchase resources from the USA. It is interesting to note that many of the families who choose to follow a school at home approach are home educating because of religious or philosophical reasons. These families are often Evangelical and many are associated with the belief in what is termed 'young earth creationism' or that the world is 6,000 years old.

In one study of this cohort, Carper (2000) cites the work of Bates (1993) and Johnson (1995) to argue that these parents have forsaken public education to establish themselves as "educational Anabaptists". They are said to have "carried the reformation one step further" than those who established Evangelical schools and have attempted "to restore what they believe to be education in its purest form – parents teaching their own children" (Carper, 2000, p. 16). They often find themselves attacked by others in the Evangelical and conservative Christian community as well as public school advocates and others who wish to advocate for more transparency on what parents teach their children.

In relation to Australia, this cohort was criticized during a recent inquiry into home education in New South Wales. Writing on his blog, one of the senators commented that these families had given evidence in front of the inquiry that they were teaching their children that evidence existed that the world was only 6,000 to 10,000 years old. Citing "geographical evidence", he argued these families were teaching a belief he described as "the young earth fable" (Kaye, 2014, p. 2). He argued that the net cost of this type of education was "a cohort of home-schooled children [unable] … to tell the difference between religious belief and scientific theory … [who are] at risk of becoming intellectual fringe dwellers" (Kaye, 2014, ¶ 3; 6). Clearly, this cohort of home education families faces a good deal of public pressure.

The second category of Australian home educator is the family that uses schools of distance education providers. In some states in Australia, students are able to enroll in schools of distance education without regard to their distance from a school. For example, in Queensland, there are two categories of distance education. The first is for the traditional distance education student who suffers from a limitation in choices for schools because of geographic isolation. This group generally comprises rural and remote students whose location precludes them from easy access to schooling. The second group is the "distance education by choice" student (The State of Queensland: Department of Education and Training, 2015). There are several categories to the "distance education by choice" group. These include home education families where a "student may be enrolled as a home-based learner where it is determined that the student does not meet the criteria of any other category but chooses distance education as the preferred education provider". Other categories of the choice group include those who are travelling around Australia or overseas.

The third category is the unschoolers. Many unschoolers identify with the work of John Holt who is said to have coined the term 'unschooling' in the 1960s. His work was concerned with the major issues faced by mainstream schooling and the ways that parents, through adopting a flexible and child-led approach to home education, could overcome the problems of mass, institutionalized public school. He defined unschooling as "allowing children as much freedom to learn in the world as their parents can possibly bear" (Holt & Farenga, 2003, p. 238). Unschoolers are characterised by a number of factors, although, as several blog posts argue, it is impossible to fail at unschooling (Priesnitz, 2010). McGrath (2010) defines unschooling by what it excludes. Citing John Holt, she argues that the exclusions are the "coercive teaching, rewards and punishments, compulsory learning, grades, tests, subjects" (McGrath, 2010, p. 2). Gray & Riley (2013) argue it is a growing counter-culture movement that allows children to learn from interactions with the environment and self-directed exploration. They cite Wheatley (2009) to argue that "unschoolers learn primarily through everyday life experiences – experiences that they choose" (Gray & Riley 2013, p. 2).

It is important to understand that unschool parents do not do nothing. Rather, they work with their children towards a learner-centred, democratic education (Ricci 2012). Ricci (2012), working in Canada, cites the work of Mintz (2004) to argue that learner-centred, democratic education is an approach that is driven by learner's needs rather than curriculum documents (Mintz 2004 in Ricci 2012, p. 46). Mintz (2004) argues that unschooling empowers students to make decisions about their education in line with Holt and Farenga (2003), because unschoolers *trust children*.

One of the major impediments faced by unschoolers is stereotypes (Morton 2012). Houseman (2011) argues that homeschoolers and unschoolers are frequently portrayed as nerdy know-it-alls with overcontrolling, paranoid helicopter parents. Morton (2012) describes the perception of these families in England and Wales as 'social "misfits": either "tree-hugging hippies", religious fanatics or "hothousing" parents' (Morton 2012, p. 46). However, she argues that the reality is much more diverse.

It is noted by Peter Gray (n. d.) and others, that the work of home educating, whatever form it takes, is generally undertaken by women. Thus, in what follows the literature on how women undertake the quotidian work of education, in relation to traditional or mainstream school, is reviewed. It is hoped that it will provide a framework for considering the ways that women are engaged in work to educate their children and it also highlights how isolating this work can be. The isolation is especially pronounced in the home education community as these women are responsible for all their children's education, they do not outsource schooling after the age of five, and they are also in a marginalised and maligned community (Morton, 2012). Then, the chapter will propose ways that online, Web 2.0 communities, especially on Facebook, provide a way for these mothers to connect to other mothers and thus reduce the isolation and lack of respect and support they experience by finding like minded others.

MOTHERING AS A DISCOURSE: THE HIDDEN WORK OF WESTERN WOMEN AS MOTHERS

Home educating families, and by this I am actually referring to mothers, are required to do all the work of educating their children. As noted above, they do not outsource their children's education when they reach school age. In Australia, children are required by law to be enrolled in a school, or registered for home education from the age of six. After this time, if they choose home education, mothers are required to follow the national curriculum and teach their children the skills and abilities in line with what is taught in schools. The education departments in each state and territory monitor these children through what are known as home visits.

The work of mothers who home educate can be understood in a variety of ways. This chapter takes a discourse approach to exploring the role of mothers in their children's education, as such; it is proposed that mothering is seen as a discourse. It is also quotidian work, in the sense that women are required to work tirelessly to construct an idealized version of their children. The responsibility for that idealized version of their children is absolutely theirs and theirs alone (cf. Griffith & Smith, 2005). In this section, I will explain how the discourse of motherhood affects the relationship between mothers, their children and education and describe the "strongly moral dimension governing the relationship of mothers to the school, capable of generating an almost theological sense of guilt and anxiety" (Griffith & Smith, 2005, p. 33).

In this sense, discourse is used to refer to a set of social relationships that influence and constrain the actions of others. As Clark and Gieve (2006) note, discourses construct knowledge, identities and social relationships. These three elements of discourse determine the identities available to individuals and groups. Further, the production and circulation of certain discourses, such as the mother discourse, constrain social identities and homogenously represent what is accepted in a culture.

The term is used by various theorists but the most common reference is to the work of Michel Foucault. For Griffith and Smith (2005), this means that "distinctive parenting styles, vocabularies, linguistic conventions and so on" constitute a discourse of mothering that is a "systematically developed knowledge, morality and set of values" (p. 33). Following on from Fairclough (1992), discourse is used to refer to language use as a form of social practice. For Fairclough (1992), discourses were social. They were constructed in order to establish relationships between people. As such, discourses have a social element. The definition of discourse provided above involves language because dominant discourses are embedded in language. To illustrate how language and discourse work together, Fairclough gives examples of how politicians give speeches about social policy that reinforce the dominant, middle-class view of social policy.

In terms of discourses of mothers, institutions such as schools, materials such as child rearing manuals, media stories and Facebook and other social media locate women in relation to particular discourses of motherhood. Some discourses are linked to particular institutional relations, such as those relations between schools and mothers or mothers and particular Facebook groups. These Facebook groups value certain relations, especially those whose homeschool practices fit a certain 'mould'. For example, the unschool community support Facebook groups privilege natural learning and an unstructured and play based approach to education as paramount and valuable, above other types of home education such as school at home and distance education.

It is noted that mothering discourses encourage competition, comparisons and defensiveness of the mothering practices in which a mother engages. As Lareau (2003, p. 4) notes, there is a "*dominant set of cultural repertoires* about how children should be raised" (emphasis in original). As such, mothering discourses are created by professionals, popularized by media and are aimed at specific groups of women. The effect is to "coordinate the mothering work done in the home and the work of educators" (Smith & Griffith, 2005, p. 35). In terms of home educators, the work of educators and the work of mothering is one and the same.

THE GENDERED NATURE OF EDUCATIONAL WORK IN THE WEST

Much work exists on the concept of mothering for schooling in the West in particular. Mothering for schooling refers to the unpaid work women do to prepare their children for the rigours of school work. Griffith and Smith (2005) argue that a mother's role is to reproduce their own middle-class status in their children. They state that although women in the working classes are "supportive and active in their children's upbringing and schooling" (Griffith & Smith, 2005, p. 13) their work is undertaken with fewer resources, economic, social, cultural, than the work of middle class women as mothers. In addition, they argue that schools presume the middle-class organization of the family in preparation for schooling. Schools expect children will have been read to, will know how to turn the pages of a book, will understand that reading is left to right, that there are numbers each one representing a slightly larger number than the one before, will be able to count, may be able to understand some letters or groups of letters that form sounds, and will be able to hold a pencil. This important work is anticipated and those children who have not experienced this will be at a decided disadvantage in schools.

In addition, the middle-class family is presumed by schools. Griffith and Smith (2005) argue that the expectation that the father will work in a managerial or professional capacity, earning enough money for his wife to stay at home, is privileged in schooling. This familial organization allows mothers to be involved in their children's education in myriad ways. These ways include volunteering at the school, assisting with excursions, being able to drop off at school and collect the children at the end of the day (which may also allow informal conversations with teachers that mothers who use before and after school care are unable to access), monitoring and policing homework, driving children to extracurricular activities such as sports and music and other tasks that may be required. Thus, there is a direct relationship between the activities of the family and the experiences of, and results of schooling.

Much work exists that suggest that there is a class basis to the success of children in schools (Bourdieu & Passeron, 1977; Lareau 1987, 1989, 1994, 2000, 2003; Henderson, 1987, Hrabowski, Maton & Grief, 1998). Thus, there is something about what middle class mothers do that advantage their children in schools. In this work, it is largely argued to be the cultural capital that these mothers inculcate through their work mothering for schooling that secures their children's advantage. It is largely seen, as Lareau (2000) described, as a continuum from class to family to class culture to school achievement. The achievement of these children in schools then leads to achievement in further education, leading to professional careers to then their own middle class families.

These studies assume a normative model of schooling where the child is at home, learning in a play based environment, with increasing exposure to 'lessons' through flash cards, activities (music, dance, drama, sports) and through the mother involving the child in natural learning through shopping, through visits with friends and play dates at parks. The idea that this model of motherhood could be extended to include the work of 'schooling' is rarely considered.

Home education challenges this normative notion of schooling. However, it does so in such a way that, studies argue (Ray, 2013), leads to greater success than does formal schooling, particularly for disadvantaged and marginalized groups. In what follows, the chapter will review the research that shows that students are able to benefit from home education. It will also explore the ways that data has been collected for these studies, relying on the use of online surveys targeted at parents using a popular home education blog site, Freedom to Learn, housed in a Psychology Today server.

HOMESCHOOL WORK AS AN EXTENSION OF MOTHERING FOR SCHOOLING: A WESTERN PERSPECTIVE

Several studies have examined the work of mothers in mothering for homeschooling. For example, Peter Gray conducted a large survey of unschool families on his blog Freedom to Learn. The survey attracted 238 families, the majority, 186, were in the United States while there were 19 Canadian families and the remainder were mainly in Europe. The survey had two main purposes, first to understand why families choose to unschool, and second to explore the benefits. The survey found that most had two parent families with the father working in managerial or professional employment while the mother stayed at home and educated the children. Gray (n. d.) states, with regard to employment, "roughly half the mothers identified themselves as stay-at-home" with "the great majority of the fathers employed full time" as "professionals" and "self-employed entrepreneurs" (para. 5).

Similarly, in my work with home educating families, I have found that the majority of the home education families are headed by fathers who work full time while the mothers home educate. These mothers may be engaged in some form of part time work, including hospitality, caring or social work. Further, in some cases, the father and the mother both work part time in order to be involved in the responsibilities of home education.

The gendered nature of the work is reflected in the membership of home education groups. To illustrate, in Australia's unschool (closed) group, a group of more than 2000 members, 39 were male and 12 were of indeterminate sex (due to being a couple or having a name that made it difficult to determine the sex of the user). Thus, there is a strongly gendered nature to the membership of these groups. Similarly, in Australia's homeschool (closed) group, a group of over 3000 members, there were 51 males and 23 of indeterminate sex (again because of their name being a couple Name N Name for example, or because their name and photograph made it impossible to determine what their sex was). Similarly, in the group devoted to unschooling in the preschool years, which has a membership of approximately 1500, only five were men with six of indeterminate sex.

Similarly, the administrators are predominately female. In one closed group, devoted to home education in Australia (membership 2,756), five of the six administrators were female. In the unschool and homeschool groups described above, the home education group has nine administrators, all female. The unschool group has seven administrators, one male and one of indeterminate sex. In the smaller, regional groups, the administration ratio remains similar. One small group for secular home educators had 81 members, none of the members were male.

These online communities for home education families, seem to primarily support women in their home education. It is noted that each of these groups are closed, which means that they are somewhat private. With closed groups, the name is public, as is the description, tags and members' names. However, only people who are in the group can see the posts by group members. Current members are also the only ones whose feed will include posts from the group. The group can be searched in Facebook, and anyone can ask to join, or be added by an administrator of the group. Thus, members can be sure that, while others may see that they are in the group and may also ask to join, until someone is a member, they will not be able to see what is posted in the group.

SUPPORT FOR HOME EDUCATION MOTHERS ONLINE

A variety of home education support groups exist. As seen above, this chapter is mainly looking at those on Facebook, as these are the groups with which I am involved and to which I have easy access. There are some reasons that an otherwise disparate and often maligned community would choose to go online for support. Parents who choose to home educate often face criticisms because family, friends and others in the community, especially academics who undertake education research, do not understand their choice (cf. Gray & Riley 2013). Further, unschool families' natural skepticism of mainstream families' decisions to choose to school leads them to feel they are operating on a margin (Gray & Riley 2013). They may also feel that their choices will be judged disapprovingly by the wider community and, as a result, they may be reluctant to discuss their choices with people in face-to-face encounters with others.

Thus, many home educating mothers retreat online to their safe haven where they can interact with other, home education families from the comfort of their home. These families are frequently outside the local area that the home education family encounter and may make the experience feel more 'normal' as there are many others who are home educating.

Facebook provides a large number of groups as connection points for home education families. Facebook has been widely researched (cf. Rich 2011; Trau, Härtel and Härtel 2012; Kapp, Peters & Oliver 2013; Caldwell, Osborne, Mewburn & Crowther 2013). In one study of how Facebook can be used to attract a cohort of like minded participants to a study, Kapp, Peters & Oliver (2013) argue that Facebook could generate a large number of view; however click-throughs and, in their case, the eventual completion of a study, remained limited. Fenner *et al.* (2012) found that women in rural Australia used Facebook to share information and join groups devoted to health and wellbeing. Fenner *et al.* (2012) argue that living in a rural area was significant to the use of Facebook, because it allows people who feel distant from others who share their passions and views to find connections in a way that they could not in the 'real world'. Trau, Härtel & Härtel (2012) argue that stigmatised populations often congregate in online group settings such as Facebook and listservs such as Yahoo Groups. As Lewis *et al.* (2011) argue, forums provide a group of people who strongly identify with an ideology, purpose or cause to find like others who can offer support. Similarly, Templeton, Luo, Giberson & Campbell (2012) argue that these sites offer a means of forming relationships and sharing understanding about specialised topics.

CONVERSING WITHIN THE HOME EDUCATION COMMUNITY: ENFORCING STANDARDS

It must be noted that the study is under ethics which allows me to participate in Facebook groups devoted to home education as part of a wider research project into the reasons home education families choose this option for their children. The project, while ongoing, has been conducted in Australia since 2010. I became involved in the home education community through parenting groups on Yahoo and through Facebook. While I am not a home educating mother, my work with the community, and my role in a 2014 senate inquiry that was conducted in New South Wales into home education, has allowed me to transcend some of the 'rules' and be included in the community discussion on several Facebook groups whose rules include that they are only open to "currently homeschooling families". My work with the senate inquiry, at which I advocated for home education families to have greater access to support and less harshly punitive judgments applied to them, was an important step in allowing me greater access to the community. The aftermath of that inquiry saw me invited to many groups that are kept as secret on Facebook. As such, I am privy to many of the conversations of Facebook that involve mothers who are home educating.

In order to protect the privacy of the posters, the intentions of the group and maintain the ethics of my study, the data I will use for this chapter will be short quotes from the posts not the actual post itself. I will also use the actual group descriptions that are available to anyone on Facebook who chooses to search for the groups, as they are closed and not private.

Mangold and Faulds (2009) indicate that communication has changed with the shift in reliance from traditional media to social media. Thus, it is not surprising that there is a proliferation of the number of groups devoted to home education on Facebook. Similalry, as Kietzman et al. (2011) argue that women's social media relationships include the same functionality as other types of relationships such as identity, presence, reputation, groups, conversations and sharing. As Johns and English (2014) argue "Online communities provide a space for open communication and contribute toward strengthening trust" (p. 324). These trusting relationships are central to the sharing of resources, ideas and concerns that are reinforced through the two way nature of the communication in the social network space of a private Facebook group (cf. Briones et al., 2011). As Zhao and Rosson (2009) note, there are two types of benefits for users of Web 2.0 groups, these are relational, including group connection and personal, such as information that as that required to effectively home educate children.

This chapter explores five groups. Two were Australia wide groups, open to all Australian families. Two were regional, open to families in a large, state-wide region and one was a local group, although this group was more accepting of members from outside the local area. It is noted that the author was an administrator on the local group, in spite of living outside the local area. I became an administrator because I developed a friendship with the group's original administrator (who started the page), and she asked me to help out.

All of the Facebook groups were set as private. A private group requires members to ask to join or be joined by an existing member. All of the groups insist that members are currently home educating for the purpose of, as one group says, it is a "SUPPORT group for families who are ALREADY embracing [home education]" (emphasis in original). Thus, as this 'About' suggests, there is an expectation that all members will be home education families. Links are given in the 'About' section are given to information about different educational approaches, the benefits of home education, the work of educational philosophers (such as John Holt) and specific websites devoted to the approach adopted by the group. These pieces of information again are used to enforce a type of standard and ensure all members of the group share many things in common, especially related to living and learning.

In addition, these groups all advertise themselves as "a place to connect with other like minded families" thus, they provide an online space for families who need to connect with others. They also generally provide a 'philosophy' statement about the group. For example, one unschool group's administrator states, "I see unschooling as a journey on a path to find what works for your family, some people are further along in that journey than others but we are all conscious of not forcing curriculum". These statements suggests that there is a supportive framework offered by the group that does not judge how your family unschools. The statement goes on to say "If your [sic] keen to learn more about unschooling as you start that path then you are welcome to join". This group is less strict about the requirement for families to be already unschooling.

In a further example of the support element of these groups, they offer files in the files section that allows families to produce their registration documents. As noted above, all families who are home educating in Australia are required to register. As unschool families may struggle to meet the curricular requirements of registration, the groups' files section may assist families to meet their legislative requirements.

In one of the groups that I administer, also devoted to home education but not restricted to unschooling, I am required to monitor and police the applicants to the group. As noted above, I am not a natural fit because I am not a homeschool mother and am doing the administration because I am became friends with the original administrator as a result of my interviewing her for my study. While this challenges me ethically and morally, it is even more challenging to operate as a moderator and an administrator while not necessarily meeting the requirements of a member. As part of my role, I am required to approve new applicants. Applicants, who do not share friends in the group or friends who are home educating, are messaged through Facebook to check their credentials. The messages are generally written to check that the families are home educating and ask why they wish to join a home education group in a regional area in Australia. Mothers who are keen to join, and as the previous discussion showed it is almost always mothers, must 'prove' their credentials to join. Mothers are generally interested in joining when they first start home educating and are looking for resources and help with the registration process.

Mothers who do not follow the 'rules' of the groups are removed. There is a link below the names of each member that allows the administrator to access settings. Using this link, the member can be removed. Members are removed for challenging other members about their educational style, for criticizing too rudely another member's ideas, or, as in the case of some groups, for promoting products and services. In addition, in one group devoted to secular home educators, any members who show any religious affiliation will be barred or removed. In addition, in this group, those members who apply to join and whose account is so private that no information can be gleaned about them from clicking on their profile, will be denied.

In one example of a group removing a member, there was an argument in a group about a member who had made several changes to their home education approach. This member had moved from being the home educator to her husband home educating. In addition, she had started a kindergarten and day care, as she was qualified to do, and sent one of her children to school. The decision to send the child to school was made by the child, thus it followed the child-led home educating approach advocated by the group. Thus, while she was not home educating per se, she was still following the child-led learning approach advocated by the group.

However, instead of the group supporting her, she was "hounded" by members of the group and "maliciously attacked online" as one group member described. Further, the member had left the group, because "some poor misguided person [was] defaming [her]" (taken from the group no names have been provided). The theory was that the defamer "must have some serious issues to cover up … [that] often happens as a reaction to personal dilemmas". Further, the OP (original poster) stated "the person pointing the finger usually has some issues". The post is very long, 24 lines, and tags the attacked member in the post. Further, the OP argues that this is not in the description of the group and thus, the attacker should be asked to leave.

The comments following the original post did become an argument and led to other members leaving. The person who had made the allegation was then reported to "admin" by several posters, who announced in the comments below the post that they had reported the person. The attacked person then reported, approximately five posts from the end of the discussion, "situation is sorted, person has been deleted". The entire discussion comprised 22 posts following the original post, and all of these were females who supported the attacked person. Further, 17 of the 22 reported similar stories of having been attacked online.

DISCUSSION: WHAT HOME EDUCATION MOTHERS' ONLINE BEHAVIOR CAN SHOW US ABOUT WOMEN ONLINE USING WEB 2.0

We can see from the discussion above how participating in groups provides a space for marginalized and disenfranchised women to find solace and community with others, with limits. The community is mediated by Web 2.0 technology that allows them to meet with like-minded women online, as long as they conform to the standards of conduct expected in the groups. The strict joining policies are followed with strict policies of removal when aberrant behaviors occur among members of the group. In the example given, members are removed and the unacceptable posts are deleted.

The anecdote of this member who was removed suggests there is a strongly defined space around what counts as appropriate or correct mothering for schooling in these groups. Mothers whose mothering for home schooling was not consistent with the norms of the groups, or mothers whose profiles were not constructed in such a way that they positioned themselves through the appropriate discourse of motherhood, were required to offer more information or were denied entry into the groups. Thus, as Clarke and Gieve (2006) argue, the borders and boundaries of appropriate motherhood to join these home education groups is discursively constructed. Further, the production and circulation of certain discourses, in the case of these groups, it is a limited range of discourses of motherhood that is tolerated, constrains the identities and group formation among mothers. Thus, it is suggested that the strongly moral dimension of the relationship between schools and mothers, as Griffith and Smith (2005) argue, is just as theological in the home education community. There is a certain type of mother that is valued in the community. It may be that, due to the already disenfranchised nature of the home education mother (English, 2015b), the ideological nature of what counts as correct home education is enforced in these communities. Thus, these women are located in relation to the cultural repertoires (Lareau, 2003) valued in the home education community. Failure to position themselves through the 'correct' or 'valued' discourse may be a failure to comply with the moral standards of the home education Facebook community.

The online community fulfills an important connection among members. These women in the home education community are often described as marginalized by the wider community (English, 2015a; 2015b, Gray & Riley, 2013, Morton, 2012) in which normative behaviours include schooling in mainstream school settings and paid work outside the home. However, these women have chosen, for a myriad reasons, to eschew what is considered normal and, instead, home educate their children. These mothers are searching for a community and find it online in the form of Facebook groups. These groups support their ideological position, in much the same terms as the participants in the Lewis *et al.* (2011) study, and these women can share their views without fear that they are ideologically different from their peers.

As Fenner *et al.* (2012) found, the Facebook group participants in the home education community were able to connect with other women who shared their beliefs and passions in a way that they were unable in real world settings where they face criticism and stigma because of their education choices (cf. Morton, 2012). Similarly, in the same way that the population in the study by Trau, Härtel & Härtel (2012), stigmatised populations, such as home educating women are able to congregate in a setting that is supportive and understanding through the use of Facebook groups.

Templeton, Luo, Giberson & Campbell (2012) argue that these sites offer a means of forming relationships and sharing understanding about specialised topics. The specialised topic of home education, while unusual in the mainstream population, is supported by the use of Facebook groups in which standards are strictly enforced, deviance is punished and the sharing of ideas and resources is strongly encouraged. Many of the women would be isolated without the use of the Facebook community. These women are already isolated in the sense that they are unable to work while they home educate, a choice that extends their quotidian, unpaid, home work (Lareau, 2000; Griffith & Smith, 2005).

The use of Facebook by these women is a model for how women are forming connections online outside of the traditional family and community reference groups. They provide a space for women to connect and find friendships, in the way that friendships are formed through Web 2.0. Further, they allow for the sharing of personal and general information to benefit the whole home education community. They also include strict standards from which deviance is punished by excommunication.

REFERENCES

Bates, S. (1993). *Battleground: One mother's crusade, the religious right, and the struggle for control of our classrooms*. New York: Poseidon.

Beck, C. (2012). Home education: The social motivation. *International electronic journal of elementary education*. 3(1). 72-81

Benwell, B., & Stokoe, E. (2006). *Discourse and identity*. Edinburgh, UK: Edinburgh University Press.

Bernstein, B. (1990). *Class, Codes and Control* (Vol. 4). London: RKP. doi:10.4324/9780203011263

Bourdieu, P., & Passeron, J. C. (1979). *The inheritors: French students and their relations to culture*. Chicago, IL: University of Chicago Press.

Briones, R. L., Kuch, B., Liu, B. F., & Jin, Y. (2011). Keeping up with the digital age: How the American Red Cross uses social media to build relationships. *Public Relations Review*, *37*(1), 37–43. doi:10.1016/j.pubrev.2010.12.006

Caldwell, G.A., Osborne, L., Mewburn, I., & Crowther, P. (2013). Guerrillas in the [urban] midst: developing and using creative research methods – guerrilla research tactics. *Journal of Urban Technology* (Special issue on urban acupuncture: revitalising cities with ambient media and networked technologies).

Carper, J. (2000). Pluralism to Establishment to Dissent: The Religious and Educational Context of Home Schooling. *Peabody Journal of Education*, *75*(1-2), 8–19. doi:10.1080/0161956X.2000.9681932

Clark, R., & Gieve, S. N. (2006). On the discursive construction of 'the Chinese learner'. *Language, Culture and Curriculum*, *19*(1), 54–73. doi:10.1080/07908310608668754

English, R. (2013). The most private private education: Home education in Australia. *Homeschool Researcher*, *29*(4), 1–7.

English, R. (2015a). Use your freedom of choice: Reasons for choosing homeschool in Australia. *Journal of Unschooling and Alternative Learning*, *9*(17).

English, R. (2015b). Too cool for homeschool? Accessing underground unschoolers with Web 2.0. In K. Trimmer, A. Black, & S. Riddle (Eds.), *Mainstreams, Margins and the Spaces In-between New possibilities for education research* (pp. 112–124). New York: Routledge.

Enrolment Categories. (2015). The State of Queensland: Department of Education and Training. Retrieved from https://brisbanesde.eq.edu.au/Enrolments/enrolmentcategories/Pages/enrolment-categories.aspx

Fairclough, N. (1992). *Discourse and social change*. Cambridge, UK: Polity Press.

Fairclough, N. (1995). *Critical discourse analysis*. Boston, MA: Addison Wesley.

Fairclough, N. (2001). The discourse of New Labour: Critical discourse analysis. In M. Wetherell, S. Taylor, & S. Yates (Eds.), *Discourse as data: A guide for analysis* (pp. 221–260). London, UK: Sage.

Fairclough, N. (2003). *Analyzing discourse: Textual analysis for social research*. London, UK: Routledge.

Fenner, Y., Garland, S. M., Moore, E. E., Jayasinghe, Y., Fletcher, A., Tabrizi, S. N., & Wark, J. D. et al. (2012). Web-based recruiting for health research using a social networking site: An exploratory study. *Journal of Medical Internet Research, 14*(1), 20.

Gray, P., & Riley, G. (2013). The challenges and benefits of unschooling, according to 232 families who have chosen that route. *Journal of Unschooling and Alternative Learning*, *7*(14), 1–27.

Gray, P. (n. d.). Freedom to Learn: The roles of play and curiosity as foundations for learning. Retrieved from https://www.psychologytoday.com/blog/freedom-learn

Griffith, A., & Smith, D. (2005). Mothering for Schooling. New York: Routledge.

Harding, T., & Farrell, A. (2003). Home Schooling and Legislated Education. *The Journal of the Australian and New Zealand Educational Law Association*, *8*(1&2), 125–133.

Henderson, A. (1987). *The evidence continues to grow: Parents' involvement improves student achievement*. Columbia, MD: National Committee for Citizens in Education.

Holt, J., & Farenga, P. (2003). *Teach Your Own: The John Holt book of Home Schooling*. New York: Perseus Publishing.

Houseman, D. C. (2011). 'Nerdy know it alls' and 'paranoid parents': Images of alternative learning in film and television programs. *The Journal of Unschooling and Alternative Learning*, *5*(9), 1–17.

Hrabowski, F. A., Maton, K. I., & Greif, G. L. (1998). *Beating the Odds: Raising Academically Successful African American Males*. New York, New York: Oxford University Press.

Johns, R., & English, R. (2014). Mothers influencing mothers: The use of virtual discussion boards and their influence on consumption. *Int. J. Web Based Communities*, *10*(3), 319–338. doi:10.1504/IJWBC.2014.062945

Johnson, P. E. (1995). *Reason on the balance: The case against naturalism in science, law, and education*. Downers Grove, IL: Intraversity.

Kapp, J. M., Peters, C., & Oliver, D. P. (2013). Research recruitment using Facebook advertising: Big potential, big challenges. *Journal of Cancer Education*, *28*(1), 134–137. doi:10.1007/s13187-012-0443-z PMID:23292877

Kaye, J. (2014). Home schooled children taught 10k year old earth as science. Retrieved from http://www.johnkaye.org.au/home-schooled-children-taught-10k-year-old-earth-as-science/

Kietzmann, J. H., Hermkens, K., McCarthy, I. P., & Silvestre, B. S. (2011). Social media? Get serious! Understanding the functional building blocks of social media. *Business Horizons*, *54*(3), 241–251. doi:10.1016/j.bushor.2011.01.005

Lareau, A. (1987). Social class and family-school relationships: The importance of cultural capital. *Sociology of Education*, *60*(2), 73–85. doi:10.2307/2112583

Lareau, A. (1989). *Home advantage: Social class and parental intervention in elementary education*. London, New York: Falmer Press.

Lareau, A. (1994). Parent involvement in schooling: A dissenting view. In C Fagnano & B. Weber (Eds), *School, family and community interaction*. Boulder CO: Westview.

Lareau, A. (2000). Social class and the daily lives of children. *Childhood*, *7*(2), 155–171. doi:10.1177/0907568200007002003

Lareau, A. (2003). *Unequal childhoods: Class, race and family life*. Berkley: University of California Press.

Lewis, S., Thomas, S. L., Blood, R. W., Castle, D., Hyde, J., & Komesaroff, P. A. (2011). 'I'm searching for solutions': Why are obese individuals turning to the Internet for help and support with 'being fat'? *Health Expectations*, *14*(4), 339–350. doi:10.1111/j.1369-7625.2010.00644.x PMID:21199200

Mangold, W. G., & Faulds, D. J. (2009). Social media: The new hybrid element of the promotion mix. *Business Horizons*, *52*(4), 357–365. doi:10.1016/j.bushor.2009.03.002

McGrath, S. (2010). *Unschooling: A Lifestyle of Learning*. USA: Createspace Independent Publishing Platform.

Mintz, J. (2004, July 28). Building democratic schools. Radio Free School. *Radio4all*. Retrieved from www.radio4all.net/pub/archive/04.01.05/grassroots@hwcn.org/125-1-20040729-0728rfsc10.mp3

Morton, R. (2012). Home education: Constructions of choice. *International electronic journal of elementary education*, 3(1), 46-56.

Priesnitz, W. (2010). *School Free – The homeschooling handbook*. Toronto, Canada: Life Media.

Ray, B. D. (2013). Homeschooling Associated with Beneficial Learner and Societal Outcomes but Educators Do Not Promote It. *Peabody Journal of Education*, *88*(3), 324–341. doi:10.1080/0161956X.2013.798508

Ricci, C. (2012). Unschooling and the willed curriculum. *Encounter: Education for Meaning and Social Justice*.

Rich, M. M. (2011). Student research in a Web 2 world: Learning to use new technology to gather primary data. *The Electronic Journal of Business Research Methods*, *9*(1), 78–86.

Templeton, G. F., Luo, X. R., Giberson, T. R., & Campbell, N. (2012). Leader personal influences on membership decisions in moderated online social networking groups. *Decision Support Systems*, *54*, 655–664. doi:10.1016/j.dss.2012.08.011

Trau, R. N. C., Härtel, C. E. J., & Härtel, G. F. (2012). Reaching and hearing the invisible: Organizational research on invisible stigmatized groups via web surveys. *British Journal of Management*. doi:10.1111/j.1467-8551.2012.00826.x

Wheatley, K. (2009). Unschooling: An oasis for development and democracy. *Encounter (Indianapolis)*, *22*(2), 27.

Zhao, D., & Rosson, M.B. (2009, May). How and why people Twitter: the role that micro-blogging plays in informal communication at work. *Proceedings of the ACM 2009 International Conference on Supporting Group Work* (pp. 243–252). doi:10.1145/1531674.1531710

Chapter 8

Increasing Value of a Tangible Product through Intangible Attributes:

Value Co-Creation and Brand Building within Online Communities – Virtual Communities and Value

Raechel Johns
University of Canberra, Australia

ABSTRACT

As researchers seek to understand value co-creation in more detail, it is essential to explore both tangible and intangible products in more depth. This case study provides an understanding of the intangible value created with a tangible product. The Thermomix is a high-end multi-purpose cooking device and through social media, communities of users have increased the value of the device. This article argues that value can be created through the intangible offerings, even when a physical product exists.

DOI: 10.4018/978-1-5225-0010-0.ch008

INTRODUCTION

The concept of value co-creation has become increasingly important within the literature, particularly within a marketing context. While there is an understanding that value is generally delivered through service, this can be through both tangible or intangible goods or services (Vargo & Lusch, 2004). Value co-creation results in consumers and marketers working together to interact and engage, and have a positive experience for the customer. For a tangible product, this could be through value added services, or increased engagement with the brand for a stronger affinity toward the product. This can result in increased positive word of mouth.

Given the understanding of 'value' and 'co-creation of value' developed in the academic literature, it is important to understand the connection between value and virtual communities. Because virtual communities have changed the way people seek information (Fallis, 2008) and communicate, it is important to understand how information is shared within these communities (Zha, Zhang, Yan & Xiao, 2015). This chapter, therefore, explores value co-creation within online communities targeted predominately at women. In particular, it explores the Thermomix communities.

A modern cooking device, the Thermomix boasts that it replaces the features of twelve devices in one. At approximately $2000 AUD the device is expensive, but offers speed, convenience and community. This chapter explores how the Thermomix community is co-creating value and community through the various customer-oriented virtual communities. Three main communities were observed, in detail, for the study, utilizing netnography principles.

The chapter demonstrates how value created in relation to intangible product attributes and uses can increase the value of a tangible product.

VALUE CO-CREATION

To understand the way virtual communities are creating value, first an understanding of value in a marketing context must be established. Value aligns closely with the use of virtual communities and therefore is a useful consideration in the virtual community space. Co-creation of value is developed through interaction between the marketer and the customer (Ballantyne & Varey 2006; Ballantyne & Varey 2008), therefore it can be understood how product-related virtual communities can result in value creation. This is particularly pertinent because social forces influence service exchange and value co-creation (Edvardsson, Tronvoll & Gruber, 2011).

Customer value is created through experiences and relationships whereby firms do not market to customers but rather market or interact with customers (Aitken, Ballantyne, Osborne & Williams 2006). Co-creation of value alters the relationship between the marketer and the customer (Choi & Burnes, 2013) and customers engage more with the brand, the product and provide more positive word of mouth. Value is an individual thing, defined by each customer in terms of what they perceive as valuable to them and it is essential to understand the customer's perception. Marketers must, therefore, have a strong understanding of their customers and collaborate with them to determine and provide this value.

The literature relating to Service-Dominant Logic (see Vargo & Lusch 2004; 2006; 2008) links to the concept of value by stating that value is co-created by the marketer and customer (Vargo & Lusch 2006) and leads to a mutual benefit. It is through interaction that value is created and relationships are enhanced (Vargo & Lusch 2006). Relationships are facilitated by the marketer but the customer works closely with the marketer to ensure a benefit for both parties. Collaborating with, and learning from, customers is essential because value becomes defined by, and co-created with, the customer shifting the focus from tangible goods to more intangible, interpersonal relationships (Vargo & Lusch 2004). Value is created in-exchange at the provider side and in-use at the customer level (Grönroos & Voima, 2013). Value is influenced by the dynamics in the social system (Edvardsson, Tronvoll & Gruber, 2011) and can be created in a virtual space (Johns, 2012).

Research exploring virtual communities has considered the connections established within the sites (Wellman & Gulia, 1999). The active participation of the members is integral to the success of the site, unlike other forms of media (Bagozzi & Dholakia, 2002). This has particularly evolved with the use of social media. Recently, it has been stated that groups of mothers are utilizing virtual communities to reduce social isolation, share tips and product ideas (Johns and English, 2014). For example, pregnant women (Welbourne, Blachard & Wadsworth, 2013) and mothers (Johns & English, 2014) have shared stories and support through the use of virtual communities. Recently research has started to explore the way social networks can be used to develop trust and ultimately value co-creation (To & Ho, 2014; Choi and Burnes, 2013 & Fan, 2015; Fan, 2015), however this area of research has been relatively limited. Furthermore, in the past, much of the literature on service has been limited to that of intangible services, rather than tangible goods (Vargo & Lusch, 2004). There is a need, therefore, to understand how online communities can be utilized to co-create value.

ONLINE COMMUNITIES

Virtual communities are defined as "groups of people with common interests and practices that communicate regularly and for some duration in an organised way over the internet through a common location" (Ridings et al., (2002) p.273). For a long time, discussion has focused on the way social networks can replicate real life friendships, even when those communicating have not met face to face (Wellman and Gulia, 1999). While social media is broader than virtual communities, virtual communities form one part of social media (Johns & English, 2014). Virtual communities tend to be divided into four main types:

- Transaction-oriented,
- Interest oriented,
- Relationship oriented,
- Fantasy oriented (Kannan et al 2000).

While each virtual community type can strengthen trust, interactions and ultimately relationships, they fall into each of these categories. For example, sites such as Facebook are a relationship oriented community, while eBay is a transaction oriented community. Second Life is a fantasy oriented community and parenting communities are interest oriented (Spaulding, 2010).

Virtual communities can be used to assist marketers to connect with their customers in a number of ways. Firstly, organisations can sponsor external virtual communities. Organisations can also engage their customers and potential customers in product development. They can utilize virtual communities for strengthening brand loyalty and promoting products. They can utilize virtual communities for sales; product support or other support activities (Spaulding, 2010). Virtual communities can result in customer engagement, both online and with the brand (Broide, Ilic, Juric & Hollebeek, 2013; Pongsakornrungsilp & Schroeder, 2011) and the sharing of knowledge (Koh & Kim, 2004). To be successful, virtual communities must achieve a high number of members quickly, establish trust amongst members and be up to date and relevant (Leimeister, Sidiras & Kremar, 2004). Often those joining a new site take some time to establish social connections, but when motivations to participate in a new site have been explored, it is the desire for connections and relationships that seem to drive this communication behavior (Tsai & Pai, 2014). Similarly, receptivity of members, involvement, enjoyment and information motivates participation (Tsai & Pai, 2013).

Social media, including virtual communities, has altered the communications process to include much more communication between consumers. This is indicated graphically in Figure 1.

As indicated in figure 1, communication between consumers occurs within a social media context. Repeated interactions also result in greater degrees of trust and relationship closeness, as indicated in Figure 2.

Figure 1. The new communications paradigm
Source: Mangold and Faulds (2009, p. 360)

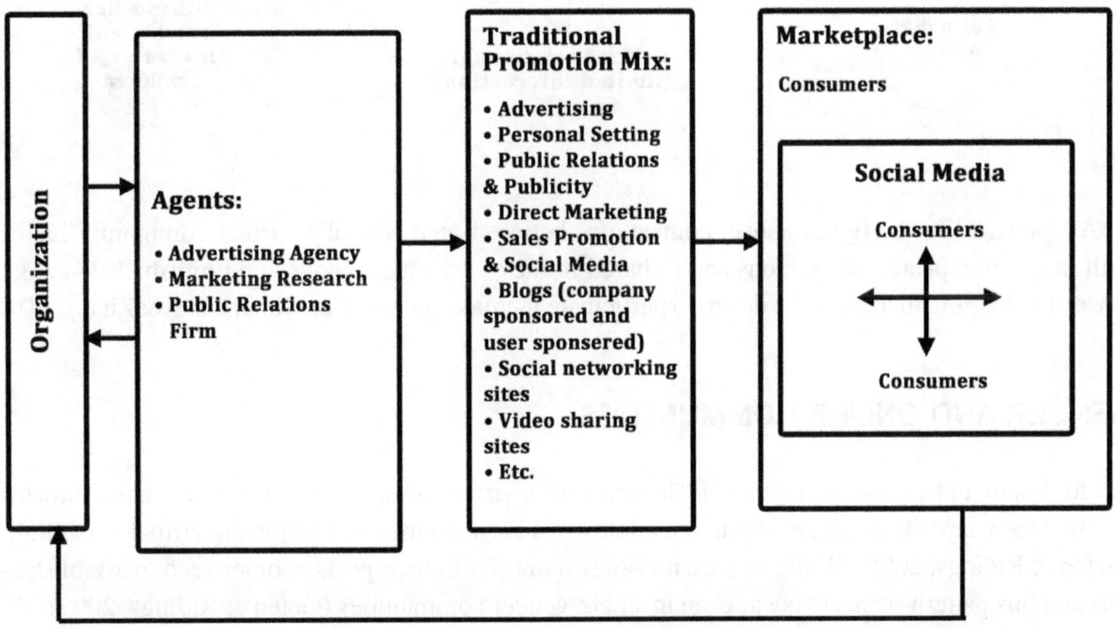

Figure 2.

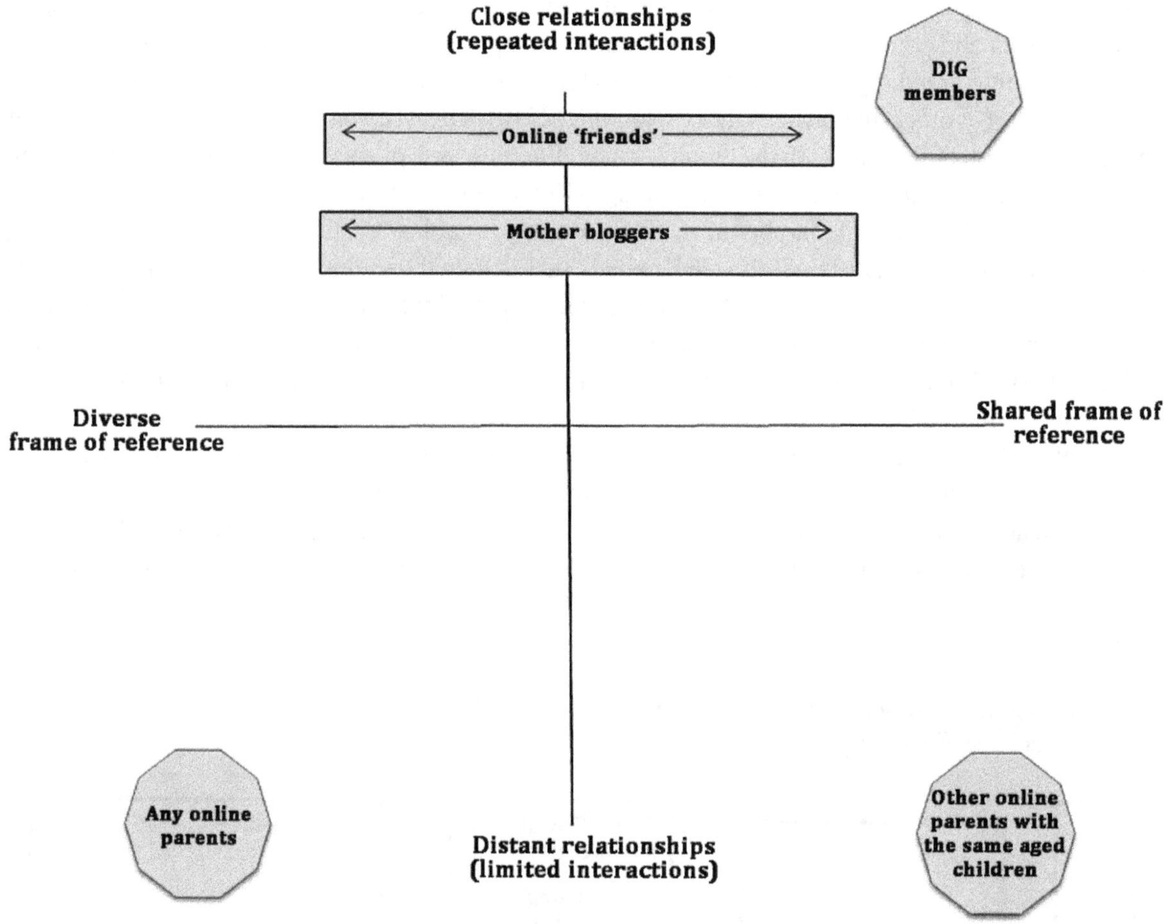

As indicated in the figure above, connections between members of a virtual community increase with frequent, repeated interactions and a shared frame of reference (Johns and English, 2014). As the sense of belonging increases, the desire to participate increases (Zhao, Lu, Wang, Chau & Zhang, 2012).

GENDER AND ONLINE COMMUNITIES

In addition to understanding trust and influence within virtual communities, it has also been shown before that there are differences in communication styles between men and women in virtual communities (Gefen & Ridings, 2005). While men demonstrate authority in their posts, women tend to establish rapport and this pattern seems to occur even in single-gender communities (Gefen & Ridings, 2005). Trust differences have been shown to exist between genders in virtual communities (Porter, Donthu & Baker, 2012) and through connectedness, relationships can grow, increasing a sense of community (Welbourne,

Blanchard & Wadsworth, 2013). More generally, it has also been shown that online communities can be used to strengthen brand image and connections with customers (McWilliam, 2000).

Men are more likely to use social networking to find dates, network for careers and make friends, while women are more likely to maintain existing friendships and share photographs (Muscanell & Guadagno, 2012). While women tend to use social networks to build rapport and offer support (Gefen & Ridings, 2005 and Fan & Miao, 2012), women are also more accepting of product reviews online, when compared to male customers (Fan & Miao, 2012). Generally, women tend to be emotional when making a purchase decision (Fan & Miao, 2012) and the marketing literature would indicate that with high involvement products, reviews are essential (Johns & English, 2014).

As emotional involvement to a brand increases, consumers are more likely to co-create value with the organization (Payne et al, 2008). Johns and English (2014) have stated that sales of an expensive cooking device, the Thermomix, have been motivated through the use of virtual communities. In their study, they explored the influence of virtual communities on the consumption behavior of mothers. This chapter now extends this by exploring the way women co-create value through discussions about products. A case study of the Thermomix is explored. The case study was developed through media reports, academic research and netnography principles (Kozinets, 2010).

CASE STUDY: THE THERMOMIX

Background to the Thermomix

The Thermomix was created in Germany in 1971 and a version was introduced into Australia in 2001 by Grace Mazur. Thermomix's vision is "providing an exciting, unique way to improve your lifestyle every day" (Thermomix, 2015).

The Thermomix cannot be purchased in a shop. Similar to a party plan model, Thermomixes can only be purchased through a 'consultant'. This is because "people need to see it in action and taste the end results in order to understand what it can do" (Business View, 2013). This means that everyone purchasing the product gets a demonstration of the device at the time of purchase. Furthermore, if customers invite other households to the demonstration, they will receive extra gifts with the purchase of their Thermomix. In addition to receiving the Thermomix, all customers also receive a cookbook at the time of purchase, but the consultants also urge the customers to go online to their recipe site (www.recipecommunity.com.au). From this community, most users start to discover other sites, such as blogs, and eventually the online communities, resulting in increased value creation amongst users.

Online Communities and the Thermomix

As people start to utilize their new cooking devices, many set up blogs and social media pages, such as Facebook and Twitter, to share photographs of their creations. In doing this, many then create their own recipes. The community spirit builds, as people ask questions about recipes. Recently a Facebook page was established with 2000 'fans' in the group based on trying new recipes. Each week a new recipe is posted for members to try and share their photographs. This has resulted in many people trying recipes that may have previously felt were too complex for their own abilities. In addition, there are a number of specifically targeted groups.

Three Thermomix-oriented online communities that offer considerable value to the participants are Quirky Cooking, Skinnymixers and The Road to Loving my Thermomixer (TRTLMT). Each have organically evolved to target a distinct target audience and offer a particular value proposition.

Quirky Cooking

Quirky Cooking owner, Jo Whitton, created the community to share her recipes. A Thermomix consultant, Jo Whitton and her family suffer from a number of food intolerances and therefore cook in a 'quirky' manner. Most recipes shared are gluten free, dairy free and utilize sugar alternatives. Over the years of sharing recipes, she has attracted a considerable following of predominately female cooks, particularly those suffering from food intolerances. The community, therefore, cooks the recipes Jo provides, while also asking questions, or sharing new 'quirky' types of recipes created by the users. In 2014, Whitton released a cookbook 'Quirky Cooking' which includes gluten / dairy / sugar free Thermomix recipes. The first order of cookbooks sold out very quickly due to her online following. Since then, Whitton has sold many cookbooks, and her blog and Facebook following has increased considerably. Copyright is closely guarded, so any recipes not posted online are not shared by anyone on the social media pages. The value within the community is co-created by participants cooking Whitton's recipes from the blog, Facebook page or recipe book. People are excited by the recipes they cook, and share photographs on the Facebook community, on Instagram or on their own pages. All recipes and stories shared are about food intolerances, allergies, and 'quirky' recipes. The community, therefore, has become a community of users with common interests.

Skinnymixers

Similar to Quirky Cooking, Skinnymixers is a targeted Facebook community and blog. The creator, Nikkalene Riddle, created the community to share lower fat recipes, and has spent time creating numerous recipes for healthier curries and sweets, lower in calories overall. In an attempt at co-creation, Nikkalene invites Facebook followers to 'test' recipes prior to putting them on the blog – for example, she provides slight variations to up to ten users to test out a new recipe. These recipes are then commented on, testimonials provided, and the final version is then placed online. At the time of publication of this book, the author had done a crowd funding campaign and a survey to develop a cookbook and a mini cookbook of curry recipes. Value is co-created through the interaction between participants, the comments and the sharing of "skinny" recipes.

The Road to Loving My Thermo Mixer

The Road to Loving My Thermo Mixer (TRTLMT) was the creation of a mother of three, Peta Lee. As the title suggests, initially Peta was not as in love with the cooking device as others were. She briefly considered selling it, but committed to using her device every day for a week to see how things changed.

She fell in love with it and then commenced a Facebook page to document her journey. From the Facebook page, she developed a blog, to share recipes she created. In contrast to the other two communities discussed, TRTLMT includes more 'every day' family recipes, such as chicken schnitzels, meatballs, noodles, cheesecake and cookies. Users share stories about how they have cooked various recipes and how particular recipes have become family favourites. Value creation, therefore, is apparent through the participation of the members on the site. From a sales perspective, Peta Lee has begun to sell to her community. Firstly, she has developed and sold a number of print runs of a calendar printed with her recipes. She has also created a regular online magazine sold through iTunes App Store.

General Thermomix Communities

In addition to the three communities discussed above, there are hundreds of specialty and general Thermomix communities, blogs and groups. Participants utilize sites to get inspiration, share their successes and failures. Thousands of Thermomix customers are keen to share tips and tricks, their photographs of finished products and regularly ask questions. This discussion has focused only on three Thermomix communities, however there are so many that regardless of food preferences, a Thermomix user will be able to find a community tailored to their needs, such as those following a vegetarian diet, the Weight Watchers plan, or those with large families. Most Thermomix customers actively belong to several communities.

In addition to following recipes, many customers get creative and create their own recipes. Through users sharing photographs of the end result of their invented recipes, product-related word of mouth increases. These online communities provide a degree of customer-led promotion about the product that is impossible to measure. The e-word of mouth generated makes a major contribution toward the brand value and preference toward the brand. Furthermore, the online communities result in co-creation of value between users through the sharing of ideas, tips, photographs and new recipes. The brand power of the Thermomix has increased considerably through the e-word of mouth developed through communities and social media more generally.

DISCUSSION

Make no mistake. Virtual communities will fundamentally change how companies develop, price and promote their products. (Hagel and Armstrong, 1997)

The Thermomix case study demonstrates how value can be created and co-created within a virtual community setting. Perhaps the most important aspect of the community is that it has been developed by customers, rather than the organization. Although the organization has created their own social media pages, message forums, the ones created by the customers are the ones that are the most popular and drive more informal discussion. For marketers, the implications may appear grim – creation of virtual communities may not be easily possible, due to the importance of customer-created conversation. Nevertheless, marketers can create communication spaces and encourage conversation. For example, Amazon's book pages has regular posts with questions to users asking them which book they are currently reading or which book they would recommend to other users. What follows is often a lively debate and users increasingly use the sites as their 'go to' communities for information. Similarly in the Thermomix case study – although the customer-driven sites tend to be most popular and result in considerable discussion amongst users; the marketer-led pages also result in lively discussion and plenty of photographs shared. Marketers therefore should create virtual communities, but encourage users to create their own. Furthermore, they should encourage a lively discussion and debate amongst users.

The Thermomix case study is a good demonstration of how word of mouth can lead to increased sales. It also highlights how powerful the brand connection is online when led by customers, rather than by marketers. Online communities relating to a product and led by consumers' results in increased trust and ultimately more product involvement. Furthermore, the value is co-created between customers, rather than driven by the marketer.

The value is inherent in the intangible. In the case of the Thermomix, this includes recipe creation, sharing and communication of tips. The value of the tangible good then increases, for example that of the Thermomix itself. Customers can utilize their product more effectively and in more ways due to the value co-created with other consumers. Customers gain more confidence, explore new ways to use their machine and generally build a community around the brand. When this is led by consumers, rather than marketers, it creates a genuine degree of trust between users. The authentic brand loyalty is integral to the value co-creation process.

FURTHER RESEARCH

This discussion has provided a rich understanding of how virtual communities can be used to co-create value and the role of intangible attributes with a tangible good. The discussion is targeted to a predominately female audience, due to the nature of the product and the customer segment.

Further research should be conducted to explore the following areas:

- *How are online communities utilized by men?*
- *How does online community use differ between males and female?*

Literature indicates there may be a difference between the way men and women communicate online. How do online communities with a dominance of male users differ from that dominated by female users? It would also be useful to know whether communities with a balance of genders

- *How are online communities creating value for intangible products?*
- *Does co-creation of value online differ between tangible and intangible products?*

This discussion has highlighted the way value of intangible attributes can create value for a tangible good; however further research could explore the way online communities are creating value for intangible products, such as resorts, in more detail. It would also be useful to undertake a comparative study to see how co-creation of value differs between the tangible and intangible products in an online community.

- *Does it matter if it is marketer led or consumer led?*

This discussion has focused on brand communities built by users, rather than organisations. The use by users builds trust and honest communication. Further research should explore how these communities can be utilized for value co-creation when they are created and moderated by a marketer.

CONCLUSION

Social media, including online communities, has altered the nature of communication between customers and between marketers and customers. Through these shifts in communication, value is being created between customers and marketers and customers. This chapter has focused on communication between female users of a number of online communities focused on one product.

In particular, the discussion has highlighted the way consumers have led communication between users by establishing their own online communities. Some of these online communities have a specific purpose. For example the three communities discussed in this chapter (Quirky Cooking; Skinnymixers and The Road to Loving My Thermo Mixer) all target a particular type of Thermomix owner. Each of the owners of the communities have established a following over a period of time, given away recipes, tips and stories for free, due to a genuine love of the product. Recently each has commenced selling items such as recipe books, magazines or calendars, however this was not the initial purpose of any of the online communities. It is the communication between users, however, that also contributes to the usefulness of the community.

The value co-created between users is intangible. Recipe sharing, tips and techniques, stories, friendship and trust are all intangible; while the Thermomix itself is a tangible product, with a strong brand. This reinforces Vargo and Lusch's work (2004, 2006, 2008) who state that service is important even when considering tangible goods. For example, in the case of a tangible product, service attributes can include the warranty or other support services. This chapter extends this idea by stating that value can be co-created by users and the service in an online community context is delivered by other customers, rather than by the marketer. This adds credibility to the message, because of the genuine affinity toward the brand. Furthermore, the value in the intangible increases the value of the tangible good. Further research should explore this to expand managerial implications.

REFERENCE

Aitken, R., Ballantyne, D., Osborne, P., & Williams, J. (2006). Introduction to the special issue on the Service-Dominant Logic of Marketing: Insights from The Otago Forum. *Marketing Theory*, *6*(3), 275–280. doi:10.1177/1470593106066780

Bagozzi, R., & Dholakia, U. (2002, Spring). Intentional Social Action in Virtual Communities, Journal of Interactive Marketing, 16(2).

Ballantyne, D. & Varey, R. (2006) Introducing a dialogical orientation to the Service-Dominant Logic of Marketing. In *The Service-Dominant Logic of Marketing: Dialog, debate, and directions* (pp. 224–235).

Ballantyne, D., & Varey, R. J. (2008). The Service-Dominant Logic and the future of Marketing. *Journal of the Academy of Marketing Science. Springer Science & Business Media B.*, *36*, 11–14.

Brodie, R., Ilic, A., Juric, B., & Hollebeek, L. (2013) Customer engagement in a virtual brand community: an exploratory analysis, 66, 2013, 105 – 114

Choi, H., & Burnes, B. (n. d.). The internet and value co-creation: the case of the popular music industry. *Promethus: Critical Studies in Innovation*, 31(1), 35 – 53.

Edvardsson, B., Tronvoll, B., & Gruber, T. (2011). Expanding understanding of service exchange and value co-creation: a social construction approach. *Journal for the Academy of Marketing Science*, 39, 327-339.

Fallis, D. (2008). Toward an epistemology of Wikipedia. *Journal of the American Society for Information Science and Technology*, *59*(10), 1662–1674. doi:10.1002/asi.20870

Fan, J. (2015). Patient value co-creation in online health communities: Social identity effects on customer knowledge contribution and membership continuance intentions in online health communities. *Journal of Service Management*, *26*(1).

Fan, Y., & Miao, Y. (2012). Effect of Electronic word-of-mouth on consumer purchase intention: The perspective of gender differences. *International Journal of Electronic Business Management*, *10*(3), 175–181.

Gefen, D., & Ridings, C. (2005). If you spoke as she does, Sir, instead of the way you do: a sociolinguistics perspective of gender differences in virtual communities. *The data base for advances in information systems*, 36(2).

Grönroos, C., & Voima, P. (2013). Critical service logic: Making sense of value creation and co-creation. *Journal of the Academy of Marketing Science*, *41*(2), 133–150. doi:10.1007/s11747-012-0308-3

Hagel, J., & Armstrong, A. (1997). *Net gain: expanding markets through virtual communities*. Boston: Harvard Business School Press.

Johns, R. (2012). Relationship Marketing in a self-service context – no longer applicable? *Journal of Relationship Marketing*.

Johns, R., & English, R. (2014). Mothers influencing mothers: the use of virtual discussion boards and their influence on consumption. *International Journal of Web Based Communities*.

Kannan, P. K., Chang, A.-M., & Whinston, A. B. (2000). Electronic communities in e-business: Their role and issues. *Information Systems Frontiers*, *1*(4), 415–426.

Koh, J., & Kim, Y.-G. (2004). Knowledge sharing in virtual communities: An e-business perspective. *Expert Systems with Applications*, *26*(2), 155–166. doi:10.1016/S0957-4174(03)00116-7

Kozinets, R. (2010). *Netnography: The Marketer's Secret Weapon*. Netbase.

Leimeister, J., Sidiras, P., & Kremar, H. (2004). Success factors of virtual communities from the perspective of members and operators: an empirical study. *Proceedings of the 37th Hawaii International Conference on System Sciences*. doi:10.1109/HICSS.2004.1265459

Mangold, W. G., & Faulds, D. J. (2009). Social media: The new hybrid element of the promotion mix. *Business Horizons*, *52*(4), 357–365. doi:10.1016/j.bushor.2009.03.002

McWilliam, G. (2000). Building Stronger Brands through Online Communities. *MIT Sloan Management Review*, April, 15.

Muscanell, N., & Guadagno, R. (2012). Make new friends or keep the old: Gender and personality differences in social networking use. *Computers in Human Behavior*, *28*(1), 107–112. doi:10.1016/j.chb.2011.08.016

Payne, A., Storbacka, K., & Frow, P. (2008). Managing the co-creation of value. *Journal of the Academy of Marketing Science*, *36*(1), 83–96. doi:10.1007/s11747-007-0070-0

Pongsakornrungsilp, S., & Schroeder, J. (2011). Understanding value co-creation in a co-consuming brand community. *Marketing Theory*, *11*(3), 303–324. doi:10.1177/1470593111408178

Porter, C., Donthu, N., & Baker, A. (2012). Gender differences in trust formation in virtual communities. *Journal of Marketing Theory and Practice*, *20*(1), 39–58. doi:10.2753/MTP1069-6679200103

Ridings, C., Gefen, D., & Arinze, B. (2002). Some antecedents and effects of trust in virtual communities. *The Journal of Strategic Information Systems*, *11*(3-4), 271–295. doi:10.1016/S0963-8687(02)00021-5

Spaulding, T. (2010). How can virtual communities create value for business? *Electronic Commerce Research and Applications*, *9*(1), 38–49. doi:10.1016/j.elerap.2009.07.004

Thermomix. (2015). *History of Thermomix in Australia*. Retrieved 19 February 2015 from www.thermomix.com.au

Thermomix: From a Polish Kitchen to a thriving business. (2013). *Business View*. Retrieved from http://business.nab.com.au

To, E., & Ho, K. (2014). Value co-creation and purchase intention in social network sites: The role of electronic Word-of-Mouth and trust – A theoretical analysis. *Computers in Human Behavior*, *31*, 182–189.

Tsai, H., & Pai, P. (2013). Explaining members' proactive participation in virtual communities. *International Journal of Human-Computer Studies*, *71*(4), 475–491. doi:10.1016/j.ijhcs.2012.12.002

Tsai, H., & Pai, P. (2014). Why do newcomers participate in virtual communities? An integration of self-determination and relationship management theories. *Decision Support Systems*, *57*, 178–187. doi:10.1016/j.dss.2013.09.001

Vargo, S., & Lusch, R. (2004). Evolving to a new Dominant Logic for Marketing. *Journal of Marketing*, *68*(1), 1–17. doi:10.1509/jmkg.68.1.1.24036

Vargo, S., & Lusch, R. (2006). Service-Dominant Logic: What It Is, What It Is Not, What It Might Be. In R. F. Lusch & S. L. Vargo (Eds.), *The Service-Dominant Logic of Marketing: Dialog, Debate, and Directions*. Armonk: M.E. Sharpe.

Vargo, S., & Lusch, R. (2008). Service-Dominant Logic: Continuing the Evolution. *Journal of the Academy of Marketing Science*, *36*(1), 1–10. doi:10.1007/s11747-007-0069-6

Welbourne, J., Blanchard, A., & Wadsworth, M. (2013). Motivations in virtual health communities and their relationship to community, connectedness and stress. *Computers in Human Behavior*, *29*(1), 129–139. doi:10.1016/j.chb.2012.07.024

Wellman, B., & Gulia, M. (1999). Net-surfers don't ride alone: virtual communities as communities. In B. Wellman (Ed.), *Networks in the global village*. Boulder: Westview Press.

Wellman, B., & Gulia, M. (1999). *Net surfers don't ride alone: Virtual communities as communities. In* P. Kollock, & M. Smith (Eds.), *Communities and Cyberspace*. Routledge New York.

Zha, X., Zhang, J., Yan, Y., & Xiao, Z. (Forthcoming). Does affinity matter? Slow effects of e-quality on information seeking in virtual communities. *Library and Information Systems Research, 2015*.

Zhao, L., Lu, Y., Wang, B., Chau, P., & Zhang, L. (2012). Cultivating the sense of belonging and motivating user participation in virtual communities: A social capital perspective. *International Journal of Information Management*, *32*(6), 574–588. doi:10.1016/j.ijinfomgt.2012.02.006

Chapter 9
How Movember's Online Community Influences Australia's Men's Health Debate

Kristyn A. Jackson
University of Canberra, Australia

ABSTRACT

Contemporary research indicates hegemonic masculinity negatively impacts on the recognised global male health treatment gap, spurring debate around the promotion of male health conversation. Through a case study, this chapter explores how Movember Australia, a global NPO dedicated to raising awareness of and funds for male health illness, has utilised principles of value co-creation in its online campaign to promote conversation around men's health in Australia. Movember's facilitation of online community conversation, engagement and its utilisation of hegemonic masculinity to promote online male solidarity and resultant health conversation is investigated. Research references previous online male health research indicating effectiveness of three themes for health communication and conversation facilitation: personalisation, environment and trust.

DOI: 10.4018/978-1-5225-0010-0.ch009

INTRODUCTION

Suicide, substance abuse, engagement in health risk behaviors and high prevalence of untreated illness are remarkably male phenomena (Möller-Leimkühler, 2003; Mahalik et al., 2007a). There is debate surrounding the contemporary identified gap in men's health treatment, with men living shorter lifespans than women globally (Barford et al., 2006), and the prevalence of untreated mental illness and suicidality in young men rising in developed nations (Möller-Leimkühler, 2003). Research contends male preventable health illness and outcomes including aggression, alcoholism, and abuse are influenced by the construct of hegemonic masculinity in Western society (Mahalik et al., 2007b).

Movember, a non-profit organization (NPO) conceived in Australia in 2003, is dedicated to addressing the men's health gap. To raise awareness and funds, the Movember campaign encourages men to grow and maintain moustaches during the month of November (Blanchet, 2011), with funds channeled into prostate and testicular cancer research, health education and awareness programs and mental health initiatives in 21 countries (Movember, 2014a). Movember employs a grass-roots communication strategy to generate cause participation and awareness (Drell, 2014), with a majority of promotion facilitated through empowered Mo Bros and Mo Sistas (participant activists) through social media and online communities, including Facebook, Twitter and Movember's community board. This strategy has enabled exponential growth of Movember's campaign around the world, by harnessing the effective power of the Internet and an active and engaged online community network (Movember, 2015a).

Movember's global expansion, marketing strategy and positioning represent an interesting case for the empirical operationalization of service-dominant logic (SDL) and the concurrent theory of value co-creation in an online marketing context. Online community co-creation has garnered considerable research interest (e.g., see Brodie et al., 2011, 2013; Ind et al., 2013; Wise et al., 2012). Through value co-creation, value is created through interactive, interdependent collaboration between marketers and consumers (Vargo & Lusch, 2004). By employing cross-functionality of contemporary marketing practices, including market orientation and relationship marketing (Grönroos & Ravald, 2011; Payne et al. 2008, p. 89), value co-creation places the customer in an integral role within the exchange process. SDL and its underpinning ethos of value co-creation were devised in response to academic acknowledgement of the increased role of the consumer in the production process, enabled through their greater accessibility to and conversations with enterprises (Prahalad & Ramaswamy, 2000).

While there has been an increase in co-creation research, such research is predominantly concerned with conceptual development (Lusch et al., 2006; Grönroos, 2012; Payne et al., 2009), there have been few empirical operationalizing co-creation studies. Particularly, while there has been empirical research into virtual community value co-creation from technological (Füller et al., 2009; Kohler et al., 2011) and brand (Brodie et al., 2013; Ind et al., 2013) perspectives, there is limited research in the non-profit online context, with notable exceptions (see, e.g., Juntunen et al., 2013; Wise et al., 2012). Juntunen et al. (2013) acknowledge that co-creation's applicability withkin the nonprofit sector has been largely overlooked (p. 122), while Brodie et al. (2013) contend further investigative research should be undertaken into the nature of customer engagement—from a co-creation perspective—in virtual communities (p. 113).

To the best of the researcher's knowledge, there has been no academic research into the impact and influence of Movember's value co-creation strategy on its online success. Research into the impact of men's health behaviors through participation in online communities has been limited; there has been relevant practitioner research in the area suggesting a link between male online participation in health-focused communities and subsequent desirable individual health behavior (Movember 2014a, p. 53). There have been few academic analyses of Movember, as it is relatively young. Particularly, while there has been research from Canada (Jacobson, 2010; Jeffcott et al., 2012), there has been limited academic study of Movember Australia, especially in an online context.

This chapter seeks to explain how Movember Australia has utilized principles of value co-creation in its online campaign, by investigating Movember's facilitation of online community conversation and word-of-mouth (WOM) generation. Movember's employment of identified influential themes for male online health communication (personalization, trust and environment) will be considered (Robinson & Robertson, 2014). Focus is allotted to hegemonic masculinity's influence on Movember's positioning and online communication; masculinity as a social construct is identified to play a fundamental role in current male health behavior and Movember's strategy (Jacobson, 2010; Wassersug et al., 2014).

Through an empirical explanatory single-case study of Movember Australia's contemporary positioning and online presence, three research propositions are investigated:

RP1: Movember has embraced and expedited online value co-creation concepts including relationship marketing, facilitating participant empowerment, interaction and participant involvement (Brodie et al., 2013; de Valck et al., 2009; Gummesson & Grönroos, 2012).

RP2: Movember has successfully reinvigorated and promoted men's health conversation, by promoting an online community network that meets the particular needs of men (Movember 2014a, p. 7).

RP3: Movember's online strategy and brand positioning successfully implements and advocates constructed masculinity to benefit male health conversation and subsequent health behavior (Wassersug et al., 2014).

The final research proposition contrasts extant research into online health campaign promotion, which suggests masculinity represents a potentially constraining and harmful communicative device for promoting and facilitating online male health conversation (Fleming et al., 2014; Robinson and Robertson, 2014).

Understanding the role and process of value co-creation in online communities is an important research area. With increased Internet diffusion and adoption, the ways consumers interact, communicate and seek information and support have changed. It is important to understand how people interact with one another and brands online, and what potential impact these have on cause or health communication success. With greater understanding of how Movember has successfully fostered male health online engagement, male health initiatives may more effectively target men and generate desired behavior change.

First, research will review the extant gap in men's health treatment and implications of masculinity on men's health behavior. Then, research will examine literature concerning online value co-creation, and how gender influences online participation. The methodological approach will be discussed, followed by the case study of Movember online. Finally, identified themes and research limitations will be discussed.

AUSTRALIAN MASCULINITY AND ONLINE VALUE CREATION

The Australian Male Health Gap

Men are predicted to have shorter lifespans than women globally (Barford et al., 2006). Mortality statistics indicate Australian men contemporarily live on average 4.4 years less than women, averaging 79.9 and 84.4 years respectively (ABS, 2014a). Between 1976-1986 the average life expectancy gap was 6.83 years, between 1986-1996, 6.14 years, and between 1996-2006 5.13 years (adapted from ABS, 2014b), indicating that while the life expectancy gap has decreased, it is still prevalent (AIHW 2008, p. 20). Mahalki et al. (2007a) contend, while biological and physiological factors influence life expectancy, there is evidence that modifiable health behavior including diet, exercise, social support use and anger and stress management significantly contribute to overall health (p. 240).

Research indicates men are more likely to undertake adversely impactful health behaviors than women, and resultantly suffer poorer health outcomes globally (Lynch, 2013; Mahalki et al. 2007a, p. 240). Males suffer higher rates of premature death; between ages 15-24, Australian men are three times more likely to die than Australian women (p. 241), while 22% of male deaths occur between ages 25-64, compared to 14% for females (DoHA 2010, p. 10). Increases of the prevalence of depression, suicidality and conduct misbehavior are rising for young men (Möller-Leimkühler, 2003). The identified gender health discrepancy informed the creation of Australia's *National Male Health Policy* [*NMHP*] (2010). The *NMHP* seeks to optimize health outcomes for men, aiming to improve male heath across life stages, enforce male preventative health behavior, and increase male health treatment accessibility (DoHA 2010, pp. 7-8).

Masculinity and Its Impact on Male Health

There is concern regarding the Australian Government's commitment to addressing the impact of hegemonic masculinity on men's health behavior, as the arguably belated (Lynch, 2013; Saunders and Peerson, 2009) *NMHP* does not acknowledge masculinity in its strategy (p. 92). Here, this chapter understands 'masculinity' to refer to "the traits, behaviors, images, values, and interests associated with being a man within a given culture" (Brown, 2012). Extensive research suggests the prevalent health risk behaviors undertaken by men in Australia and around the world "may be manifestations of how some men construct masculinity" (Mahalik et al. 2007a, p. 240); such research occurs through the social constructionist lens, which views masculinity as socially constructed and not a biological consequence (Brown, 2012; Valkonen and Hänninen 2013, p. 161). Traditional masculinity in the western world is characterized by attributes including power, success, strength and control (Möller-Leimkühler 2003, p. 3), promoting behaviors including self-reliance, emotional inexpressiveness or stoicism, concealment and help-seeking reluctance, arguably epitomized in "boys don't cry" (Mahalik et al., 2007a; Möller-Leimkühler, 2003; Valkonen & Hänninen, 2013). Hegemonic masculinity interferes with support seeking and emotional expression, with many men turning to aggression, violence and substance or alcohol abuse as coping mechanisms against depressive symptomology or health-related issues (Locke & Mahalik, 2005).

Hegemonic masculinity has been employed in a multitude of campaigns in the for-profit (business) sector (Chang, 2006; O'Barr, 2006; Wörsching, 2007) and public (government) sector (Brown, 2012). Research into advocacy of hegemonic masculinity in the non-profit sector, however, has been limited. Masculinity has recently been adopted in public sector health campaign promotion, through the 2012 *American Public Health Association* (*APHA*) HIV health campaign 'Man Up Monday' (Fleming et al., 2014). Fleming et al. warn against potential negative consequences of promoting hegemonic masculinity in health campaigns, contending "men who adhere to the norms of hegemonic masculinity have worse mental health and general well-being" (2014, p. 1032). They advocate adoption of a gender-transformative approach, thereby moving "away from the reinforcement of hegemonic masculinity and toward the promotion of a more gender-equitable masculinity", and subsequently appropriately addressing "the harmful effects of gender norms on health" (p. 1033).

How Movember employs the moustache as a symbolic performative device of masculinity (Jacobson, 2010; Robert, 2013), promotes male solidarity through extensive online engagement and community participation (Drell, 2014), and pushes issues of male health behavior into social normality through facilitating extensive global men's health conversation, will be investigated. This addresses the proposition that Movember Australia has embraced hegemonic masculinity effectively to promote men's health.

VIRTUAL COMMUNITIES, VALUE CO-CREATION, AND HEALTH PROMOTION

Online Value Co-Creation

Support and research of service-dominant logic (SDL) has increased in the past decade, since its original conceptualization and proposition by Vargo and Lusch (2004) (Galvagno & Dalli, 2014). Arguably central to S-D logic, which places service as the central denominator for exchange (Payne et al. 2008, p. 83), is the concept of value co-creation (Ballantyne & Varey, 2008; Grönroos 2012, p. 1520). Value co-creation has been defined by the Nordic school as "the customer's creation of value-in-use" (Grönroos, 2008, 2011, 2012). Value co-creation theory positions customers as consumers and producers alongside multiple actors within a network of continual, contextually contingent interdependent exchange (Nelson et al. 2014, p. 472; Roser et al. 2013; Vargo et al., 2006). 'Value-in-use', through value co-creation, posits value is created upon resource application by the beneficiary, rather than embedded in tangible goods or created by a producer as is traditionally held in goods-dominant logic (GDL) (Payne et al., 2008). Here, tangible goods act as mechanisms for service delivery or appliances; service may be rendered through resource application.

Recent research has been concerned with online value co-creation within the innovation and technology (Kohler et al., 2011; Nambisan et al., 2009; Füller, 2010), and brand co-creation fields (Brodie et al., 2012; Ind et al., 2013; Payne et al., 2009). However, there has been comparatively limited research into non-profit or public sector online community value co-creation (e.g., see Juntunen et al., 2013; Wise et al., 2012). Due to the unique challenges NPOs face over for-profit organizations (Chad et al., 2013), and the potential of the web in facilitating unique and significant engagement (Brodie et al., 2011), co-creation's role in non-profit online communities arguably offers unique challenges and perspectives into the operationalization of value co-creation, aiding in SDL's conceptual validation and expansion.

de Valck et al. (2009) define the 'virtual brand community' as "a specialized, non-geographically bound, online community, based on social communications and relationships among a brand's consumers" (p. 185). In the virtual community, high community participation is linked to success. Online community co-creation research suggests online channels represent opportunities for expedition of online relationship building, customer engagement facilitation and value creation participation. Extant research indicates involvement enables and motivates customers' roles in new-product-development, innovation and knowledge sharing (Füller, 2010; Kohler et al., 2011; Wise et al., 2012). Through social media, customer-to-customer (C2C) interaction is highly prevalent and encouraged by marketers (Gummesson & Grönroos 2012, p. 491), with consumers and producers working together to create value. If employed efficiently, co-creation leads to increased engagement and may generate WOM and viral communication.

Online Male Health Communities and Promotion

Socio-linguistically, women and men have been found to generally exhibit different communication styles (Gefen & Ridings 2005, p. 88), which Yaeger-Dror (1998) contends is influenced by societal cultural expectations across two identified variables: power and solidarity. Solidarity has been found to occur in same-sex friendship networks, with the degree of perceived accommodation influenced by the sex-mix ratio; networks comprising higher degrees of same-sex mix (for instance, primarily male) are purportedly more likely to facilitate unaffected conversation between participants (p. 40). Male solidarity denotes a discourse which generates bonds between men, with men "understood to normatively want (and need) to do things with groups of other men exclusive of women" (Kiesling 2007, p. 658). Such linguistic devices as swearing have been construed to form part of a linguistic code of traditional masculinity, "which reinforces group solidarity and has covert prestige because of its connotations of strength and confidence" (Preisler 1998, p. 292). Arguably influenced by these socio-linguistic cultural expectations, research shows women "are characterized as being more nurturing while men more assertive" (Gefen & Ridings 2005, p. 88).

Communication differences have found to extend into virtual communities (Gefen & Ridings, 2005), with men identified to be less likely than women to seek social support through involvement in online communities (p. 86). Robinson and Robertson (2014) identify three important factors to employment when targeting men across age groups to increase communication's success: personalization (ensure images of constructed masculinity do not adversely constrain individual personalization), environment (empower men with perceived communication control, and encourage peer-to-peer conversation and participation) and trust (deploy a 'narrative of hope' with information that is reliable, clear and credible) (pp. 156-157).

Social media and online communities, through increased Internet diffusion and adoption, have created new ways to "discuss healthcare outside of the healthcare providers' office" (Lapointe 2013, p. 792), reformulating how people communicate about and engage with personal and community health (Eysenbach, 2008). There has been significant research into social media and Internet utilization for health promotion (Korda & Itani, 2013; Neiger et al., 2012; Norman, 2012), with empirical research of online health programs encompassing weight loss, nutrition, physical exercise, tobacco cessation and overall well-being. Such empirical research provides evidence of online communities' potential positive impact on health behavior (Korda & Itani 2013, p. 20; Portnoy et al. 2008, p. 2). Research suggests the platform represents a unique means to facilitate community conversation and participation around the health debate across geography and time (Norman 2012, p. 4), enabling enhanced community involvement and control in the health debate. This contestation of the virtual community's conversation facilitation aligns with co-creation theory and the movement towards participatory culture, whereby consumers—through social media and online community participation—have increased means to create value and influence conversation trajectory (Ind et al., 2013; Füller et al., 2009).

Online health-oriented social media and virtual communities represent opportunities for the treatment and provision of support for individuals who are adverse to support seeking or participating in traditional face-to-face therapy (Hickie et al. 2007, p. 47). Research identifies young adults and adolescents as principally targetable through online health communication (Griffiths & Christensen 2006, p. 6; Hickie et al., 2007). Considering men's identified higher internet usage than women (Gefen & Ridings 2005, p. 87), online health promotion and conversation facilitation may be suitable in targeting men, particularly considering hegemonic masculinity typically opposes support-seeking behavior, resulting in men's decreased likelihood to seek traditional health support (Valkonen & Hänninen, 2013). Research suggests, when seeking health information, "new media platforms which support greater user control and interaction (including Twitter, Facebook and message boards) were of interest [to men], once concerns about trust and confidentiality were addressed" (Robinson & Robertson 2014, p. 154). Robinson and Robertson (2014) contend online health communication targeting men should be personalized and relevant, and support Fleming et al.'s (2014, p. 1033) view that health information materials should not adopt hegemonic masculinity, which is argued as constraining to men's individual expression outside traditional masculinity's ascribed norms (Robinson and Robertson 2014, p. 157).

ADDRESSING THE LITERATURE GAP

There is marked contestation surrounding the employment and acknowledgement of hegemonic masculinity in male health communication, both for mass media campaigns and in online virtual communities. Masculinity has been found to adversely impact on male health behavior (Mahalik et al., 2007a; Möller-Leimkühler, 2003; Valkonen & Hänninen, 2013), with advisement against its employment as a health communication strategy (Fleming et al., 2014; Robinson and Robertson, 2014). Contrastingly, in Australia there has been a call for policies and causes dealing with male health—particularly the *NMHP* (2010)—to more readily accept and acknowledge the impact masculinity has in dictating men's health behaviors (Saunders & Peerson, 2009):

Reducing inequalities in health will ideally involve addressing the social, economic and environmental conditions that impact on gender in particular ways, with consequent effects on health. (Saunders & Peerson 2009, p. 96)

While it is acknowledged that masculinity has negatively impacted on men's health behavior (Mahalik et al., 2007a), following Saunders and Peerson's (2009) proposition, there may be potential for masculinity to be positively situated to inform health communication, education and awareness. There has been limited research into this concept, particularly in a non-profit online context. Through a value co-creation lens, this chapter investigates how Movember incorporates masculinity to promote male health discussion and positive behavior online. Arguably, what makes Movember an interesting case study, aside from its exponential global growth and success, and prominent online community presence (concepts that will be investigated), is how it has taken the concept of hegemonic masculinity, acknowledged it as detrimental to contemporary male health behavior, and then transformed it into an effective solidarizing device for the very purpose of promoting and facilitating conversation around men's health.

METHODOLOGY

Research employed an explanatory, interpretive single-case study methodology, investigating Movember Australia's online community and contemporary marketing strategy. Online communities and existing documentation were investigated and interpreted through a qualitative discourse analysis. Contestably, through parallels between SDL and structuration theory (Lusch & Vargo, 2014), co-creation empirical research lends itself to qualitative methodology, due to the contextually contingent nature of SDL co-creation. Additionally, the study of masculinity has been identified as predominantly the concern of constructionists (Brown, 2012; Valkonen & Hänninen 2013, p. 161); this research views masculinity as a social construct. The identified structuralist constructivist epistemology rooted in service logic (Berard 2005, p. 219) and the constructionist epistemology of gender studies arguably strengthens the appropriateness of a qualitative methodology for this empirical research.

Employing SDL and co-creation theory through an empirical study addresses noted limitations of current research in this area (Brodie et al., 2013; Galvagno & Dalli, 2014; Johns, 2014). The choice of empirical focus, however, was guided not only by desire to increase research variety in the co-creation field, but also due to the significance of empirical research in the reformulation and development of theory. Bourdieu and Wacquant contend "concepts have no definition other than systematic ones, and are designed to be put to work empirically in systematic fashion" (1992, p. 96).

A case study methodology was employed due to the empirical, exploratory nature of this research. The case study proved appropriate due to this study's contemporary grounding, and considering research did not seek to test hypotheses (Yin, 2014). Gummesson advocates the applicability of case studies in management research, noting that early developments of service marketing and science were grounded by empirical data sourced through this methodology (1991, p 84).

SAMPLING AND DATA ANALYSIS

Movember comprises an arguably relevant and interesting case, reflecting on its argued employment of masculinity as a marketing strategy. With reference to Patton (1990), the sampling method utilized was purposeful and information-oriented (Flyvbjerg 2013, p. 182), in that the single Movember case study was chosen due to its apparent social impact and ongoing contemporary Australian and global success. As a prominent brand and generally recognizable charity, Movember was deemed to be an information-rich case for the purpose of research (Patton 1990, p. 169)—particularly relating to applicability of value co-creation theory in its prominent online community. A single-case was purposefully chosen over a multiple-case study, arguably enabling a more comprehensive evaluation. Considering the vastness of Movember Australia's online presence, a single-case was sufficient to reach case saturation, whereby arguably the inclusion of additional cases would have added only marginal utility (Gummesson 1991, p. 85).

The sampling frame comprised all online Movember mediated and instigated social media and online communities, as well as research and annual reports produced by Movember between 2013-2015. The sample was chosen as, arguably, through NPO mediation, all communication represented in the sampling frame aligned with Movember's strategy and desired positioning. While it is acknowledged multiple manifestations of Movember public support or reference appear in community facilitated and mediated webpages or communities, such representations act outside of Movember's direct control and resultantly do not necessarily reflect a brand, values or cause promoted by Movember. Here, such community involvement arguably does not constitute value co-creation in the sense that the producer (Movember) and consumer (activists) act in collaboration with one another for value creation purposes, as individuals may act without association with Movember.

METHODOLOGY LIMITATIONS

There are criticisms regarding the methodological limitations of case studies. A dominant criticism is that case studies are subject to researcher bias (Mays & Pope 1995, p. 109). Qualitative research has historically been criticized for lacking interpretation objectivity (Gummesson, 1991, p. 109), however contemporarily subjectivity and data selectivity has been acknowledged as irremovable from qualitative and quantitative research (Mays & Pope, 1995). By acknowledging inherent objectivity, research limitations may be identified and considered relating to findings. Objectivity of this study has been disclosed with the epistemological standing of the researcher identified: this research is social constructionist and assumes masculinity is socially informed.

CASE STUDY: MOVEMBER AUSTRALIA

Founded in Australia in 2004, the Movember Foundation is a global non-profit organization (NPO) committed to "changing the face of men's health" (Movember, 2014a). As part of the Movember campaign, men grow and maintain moustaches during November and participate in fundraising and awareness generation for men's health. Movember was originally concerned with prostate cancer awareness and fundraising, however as its popularity has grown so too has its repertoire of men's health concerns; contemporarily Movember raises awareness and funds for prostate and testicular cancer, men's mental health and health programs (Robert 2013, p. 261), and undertakes independent men's health research. Since its conception, Movember has become a global force for men's health fundraising, spawning campaigns across 21 countries. From its original 30 participants in 2003, Movember has grown exponentially—from 2003-2013, more than 4 million men and women participated in Movember, raising AU$580 million for men's health (Movember, 2015a; see figure 1). Movember funds over 800 men's health programs, contributing funds to cancer research, mental health initiatives, and global men's health collaborative foundations (Movember 2014a, p. 7), and is the largest non-government body funding prostate cancer research in the world (Wassersug et al. 2014, p. 1).

Figure 1. Yearly global Movember participants 2003-2013
Source: Adapted from Movember (2014a)

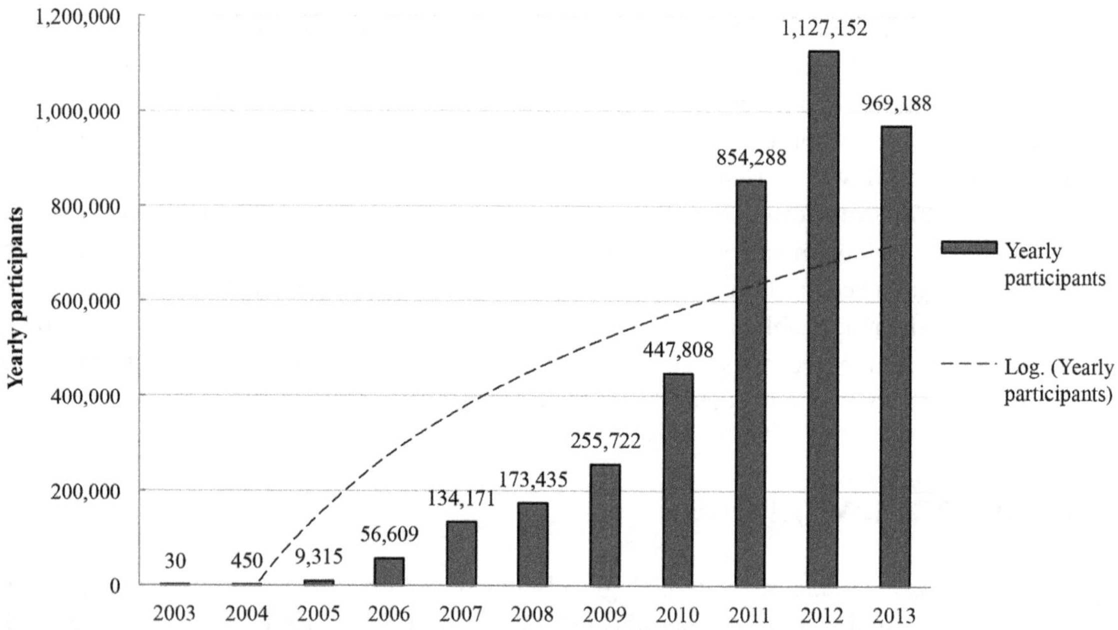

Relating to identified impacts of hegemonic masculinity on men's health treatment and support seeking willingness (Möller-Leimkühler, 2003; Valkonen & Hänninen, 2013), Jeffcott et al. (2011) stipulate Movember's contemporary paramount concern relates to education and awareness building around men's health. Movember aims to reduce the prevalence of preventable male deaths around the world. One issue Movember notes as impacting the contemporary state of men's health, supporting noted literature, is the way men think about health—particularly referencing constructed masculinity. To tackle this problem, "Movember's awareness and education program is focused on helping men get comfortable with the notion of talking about their health and on putting men's preventive health on the radar" (p. E111).

Movember's Online Community and Value Co-Creation

Movember has limited media, advertising and administrative spending. Its 2013 Australian campaign allocated only 6.4% of its total raised AUD$26.4 million to fundraising costs and 1.8% to administration costs, totaling 8.3%, which is significantly lower than ordinary industry best practices of 15-20% (Movember, 2015c). Movember's success is reliant on community participation through social media and the Internet, with less focus devoted to above-the-line advertising (Jeffcott et al. 2011, p. E111). Arguably integral to Movember's success is maintenance of its grassroots nature, with activists and participants spreading WOM, and starting conversations about Movember and its cause across social media (Drell 2014, p. 7; Jeffcott et al., 2011). Participant competitiveness is encouraged in growing moustaches and fundraising (Wassersug et al., 2014), attributing to participants' eagerness for sharing progress throughout the course of the campaign via social media and online platforms (Drell 2014, p. 7). Such enthusiasm for sharing progress translates to significant online buzz during the month of November and the campaign's run, across social media, including Twitter, Facebook and Instagram.

Movember's viral WOM has enabled it to become "one of the most effective forces in prostate cancer advocacy", demonstrating a public voice unable to be replicated by many public and professional bodies around the world (Siemens 2012, p. 349). This public voice has only grown with time (see fig 1), as Movember has become a Western social phenomenon.

Predominant online presence was a purposeful strategy employed by Movember, which recognized differences between how men and women engaged in health conversation on and offline (Movember, 2014a). Movember identified a need to build an appealing mechanism through which men could comfortably engage in health conversation. Movember (2014) determined 99% of men without children from developed nations—their primary market—were going online every day, and resultantly the fact that Movember's "campaign largely plays out online is a huge draw card for men" (p. 53). This supports the postulation for potential to reach men online for health communication facilitation, with more men identified to be turning to online alternatives due to perceived greater individual control and accessibility (Robinson and Robertson, 2014).

The high reliance Movember places in its participants to control the spread and buzz of its campaign is arguably indicative that Movember holds values congruent with SDL and co-creation theory; the customer is empowered to create value and drive the direction of the brand, as an integral service producer (see Galvagno & Dalli 2014, p. 643; Prahalad & Ramaswamy, 2004):

[Movember provides] the platform, by way of the website, [and] tools for them to participate and communicate online and in person, but it is the individuals themselves that bring the campaign to life by making it their own and communicating [Movember's] men's health messages in a way that is meaningful. (Movember 2014a, p. 7)

The way Movember has created a website and online community purposefully around the specific needs of men is not only reflective of value co-creation principles, but arguably exemplifies Robinson and Robertson's (2014) identified themes of 'environment' and 'trust' as impactful on online health promotion. Through reliance on activists as ambassadors for the brand, Movember injects credibility into their online conversation and facilitates heightened trust building. By relying on participants to spread WOM to friends, family and community, communication credibility is heightened, with C2C communications, personal relationships and acquaintances found to positively impact on perceived trust in online communities (Adjei et al., 2010; Sutanonpaiboon and Abuhamdieh, 2008). Relating to this, Robinson and Robertson (2014) advocate C2C communication as a normalizing device aiding in the generation of an appropriate online environment (2014, p. 157). As Movember, through employing value co-creation principles of consumer empowerment and interactivity, has enabled participants agency in utilizing whichever means they deem most appropriate for campaign promotion, it is arguable that the resulting online environment is relatable and appropriate to target each individual, as it is a product of their own creation; this concept is definitively co-creational.

Embracing Masculinity to Generate Men's Health Conversation

Part of Movember's success has been ascribed to the iconic moustache–a symbol of masculinity advocated traditionally by men including Burt Reynolds and Tom Selleck, and recently revived in the younger generation as a trend (Jacobson, 2010). Jacobson (2010) contends the moustache represents more than a fashion statement, and is rather situated as a "reiteration/reconfiguration of the need for male gender performativity" (p. 53). Through SDL, the moustache is the physical good used as an appliance for the realization of service (Grönroos & Gummerus 2014, p. 211; Grönroos & Ravald 2011, p. 7): performing masculinity. The moustache "distinguishes the adult male from boys and women" (Wassersug et al. 2014, p. 4), whereby the mustachioed man "delegates part of the presentation of male identity to the moustache" (Jacobson 2010, p. 55), and consequently it plays a role in the assemblage of masculinity. Movember embraces hegemonic masculinity through the physical device of growing the moustache, and uses this physical representation to facilitate conversation about men's health: the "Mo Bros [male campaign participants…] become men's health advocates during the month of Movember and are literally walking/talking billboards" (Movember 2014a, p. 7).

By ascribing to hegemonic masculinity, Movember advocates heteronormativity throughout the campaign (Jacobson 2010, p. 71). Considering previous research into masculinity adoption in men's health communication (Fleming et al., 2014; Robinson and Robertson, 2014), Movember's advocacy of heteronormativity may constrain and undermine individuality, adversely affecting the degree of campaign personalization (Robinson & Robertson 2014, p. 157). The dualism between embracing hegemonic masculinity as a powerful communication tool for men's health (Saunders & Peerson, 2009) and its potential to constrain individuality (Fleming et al., 2014) is manifested through Movember's embraced masculinity. Deliberating Robinson and Robertson's (2014) appeal for increased men's health communication personalization, which they argue is limited through traditional masculinity advocacy, the role of the moustache as an individualistic device is explored.

While the moustache has been argued to symbolize masculinity (Jacobson, 2010), the physicality of its appearance additionally represents the dichotomy between Movember's altruistic and individualistic appeal (Robert, 2013), with personalization enabled through grooming and styling. Movember "employs a rhetoric [the moustache] that focus on the ways in which participants can either consolidate their identity as, or undertake philanthropic projects to become more physically, sexually, and socially attractive individuals" (p. 262; Wassersug et al., 2014). Robert (2013) contests, through Movember's embodied form of contribution—participants' moustache growing and maintenance—it is associated particularly with expressions of self identity alongside tattooing and body piercing (p. 267), generally seen as a means to externally communicate internal desires. Today, with moustaches a trend in the younger generation, men who maintain moustaches for Movember may be seen as altruistic *and* fashionable.

Taking the concept of individualization into the online realm, emphasis is placed on the noted freedom of communication provided to Movember's participants. Rather than being constrained to communication within ascribed channels maintained or instigated by the foundation, Movember's grassroots positioning empowers participants to communicate across online channels, with Movember specifically encouraging WOM in channels utilised by individual participants (Drell, 2014; Jeffcott et al., 2011; Movember 2014a, p. 7). Through this communication strategy, each participant chooses how they will communicate the brand's cause, and resultantly is likely to do so across platforms indicative of their own self expression–for example, some participants will preference Twitter, others Instagram. Fundamentally, participants are given freedom to communicate, thereby increasing how personalizable communications are for individuals. Considering this freedom from a value co-creation perspective, Füller et al.'s (2009) devised construct of online consumer empowerment proposes task involvement positively effects perceived total support, while empowerment and enjoyment impact significantly on perceived trust and the individual's willingness for future participation. Movember providing individuals agency to choose communication channels fosters empowerment and involvement, thereby positively impacting future co-creation participation likelihood (Füller et al., 2009). The effectiveness of this purported technique is supported by Movember's exponential growth in global participation (see figure 1).

Therefore, Movember demonstrates that employing hegemonic masculinity does not necessarily undermine male health communication personalization and individuality as existing literature suggests (Robinson & Robertson, 2014). While Movember embraces heteronormativity (Jacobson, 2010), it may be argued the freedom Movember provides participants in determining campaign outcomes and communication messages may transform this standing through participant value co-creation; as active value producers, messages deemed valuable by individuals will gain traction. That is, while heteronormativity is understood as contemporarily valued through its apparent proliferation, this does not preclude future reorientation to reflect changing societal norms.

Generating Social Change Online

Mahalik et al. (2007b) contend there is a link between men's perceived normative male health behavior—as a product of hegemonic masculinity—and subsequent health behavior, with men's perceptions of normality influenced by masculine reference groups including family and friends (p. 2203). While Mahalik et al.'s findings considered physical groups, these findings arguably may be expanded into virtual communities, with reference to extant research suggesting the importance of relational bonds, reference groups, intimacy and trust building in the virtual communities (de Valck et al. 2009, p. 189; Li et al., 2012; Rau et al., 2008; Wang, 2005), through value co-creation (Brodie et al., 2013; Ind et al., 2013). By applying Mahalik et al.'s (2007b) findings online, it is postulated that, if a man engaging in a virtual community perceives a significant number of online male participants engaged in particular health behavior, the man would more likely to attribute this behavior as normal and adopt the promoted health behaviors.

In this case, 'social proof' and subsequent normalization (Mahalik et al., 2007b) is seen through Movember's viral online campaign, and its increasing yearly participation (see figure 1). As Movember enjoys increased, significant online participation, it has become increasingly socially acceptable and normal to talk about Movember and its associated causes, with Jeffcott et al. (2012) contending, even before November begins, "it's hard not to hear or see something about [Movember]" (p. E111). Movember (2014) recorded billions of conversations around Movember and men's health to have occurred globally since its conception (p. 19). In 2013, 2.3 million conversations about Movember were recorded, with 70% of conversation issuing from men (Levine, 2013; Movember 2014a, 2014b).

Research identifies a link between Movember participation and increased conversation about men's health, and resulting health behavior. In 2013, 99% of Movember participants talked to somebody about their own health, 75% were more aware of their health risks, 62% were prompted to have medical check-ups, 50% told somebody else about improving their health, while 75% said they were more likely to tell somebody to seek professional medical help if believed necessary (Movember, 2014b). This represents an increase from 2012, where Movember found 96% of participants thought about improving their health, 86% were motivated to have a health check-up spurred directly by Movember participation, and 77% discussed "men's health with their family, friends and colleagues during the month" (Blanchet 2011, p. iii). Total participation in Movember also increased globally, however Australian Movember participation decreased from 2012, at 144,196 participants, to 122,571 in 2013 (Movember, 2015e). Nonetheless, online participation in, and awareness of, Movember has pushed conversation of men's health into mainstream conversation, with Movember representing "a powerful way of getting men to talk about something they are not normally comfortable discussing" (Blanchet, 2011).

Arguably, through vast global community participation and awareness, widespread advocacy and reach, Movember has become a social norm. Resultantly, even men who are not participants are likely to be exposed to Movember's message (Movember 2014a, p. 7). These men arguably generate conceptualizations regarding perceived normative male health behavior from Movember participants, particularly during peak activity. As advocacy of Movember's cause increases and more participants engage in conversation about men's health, social stigma and norms around the topic may develop, and issues of men's health may be increasingly brought into mainstream social conversation throughout the remainder of the year.

Word of mouth, the movement of expats and the incredible power of the Internet have all contributed to the campaign stretching out across the globe. The geographic expansion supports and delivers on [Movember's] primary objective of spreading key health messages to men everywhere. (Movember, 2015a)

The potential implication of increased conversation around men's health behavior is a change in the dynamic of hegemonic masculinity towards greater support seeking, expression and openness, and a resultant decrease in the gender health gap (Saunders & Peerson, 2009; Valkonen & Hänninen, 2013).

Male Solidarity in Movember's Online Community

Movember's online community arguably proliferated a theme of male solidarity. Online discourse and engagement between male participants exhibited elements of solidarity through playful competitiveness, particularly regarding moustache growth and maintenance, and the employment of masculine vernacular, including insults (Kiesling 2007, p. 665). Particularly, there was a sense of community generated around how unattractive moustaches looked:

How are those filthy hairy upper lips looking? Wanna see pics of the wild last few days of #MovemberAUS. (Twitter @MovemberAUS)

The handlebars are getting seedier by the day, get around it and donate here! (Twitter @MovemberAUS)

Playfulness and resulting solidarity in Movember's community contestably increased community engagement and continuing online participation, supporting previous literature linking perceived playfulness as a determinant of resulting satisfaction (Chui et al., 2011). Fraternalism and playfulness was encouraged by Movember, with an underlying organizational strategy identified as facilitating community 'mateship' and 'fun' to build its global movement. Solidarity increasing male cause participation positively impacts awareness generation and subsequent fundraising (Movember 2014a, p. 53).

The importance of facilitating a sense of solidarity within the community is supported by Brodie et al.'s (2013) findings suggesting connection and emotional bonds emerge through online engagement (p. 112), with male solidarity understood as a discourse creating bonds between men (Kiesling 2007, p. 658). From the value co-creation perspective, this sense of connection and community building through solidarity positively impacts engagement and participation likelihood, drawing from research suggesting relationship strength and peer-to-peer engagement positively influences individual participation (Adjei et al., 2010) and resultant co-creation prospects (Brodie et al. 2013; Füller et al, 2009).

DISCUSSION

Identified Themes

The main purpose of research was to assess how Movember used principles of value co-creation in its online campaign. Focus is allotted to how hegemonic masculinity is employed and influences Movember's online communication. The key themes identified in Movember's online communication strategy and community have been discussed. Linking these themes together, the interconnected relationship between these concepts becomes evident (see fig. 2).

Figure 2. Themes impacting Movember's online community participation and subsequent behavior

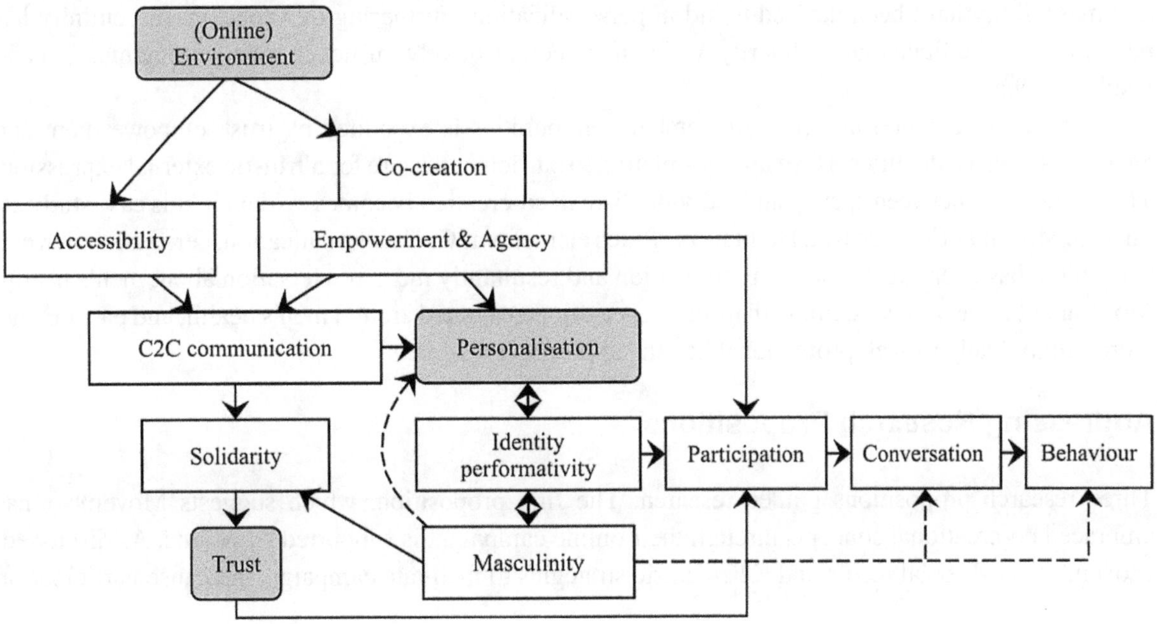

Using Robinson and Robertson's (2014) identified key themes of 'environment', 'personalization' and 'trust' as a foundation, concepts of masculinity and co-creation have been incorporated into the proposed model (see figure 2). Elements impacting participant online environment experience include accessibility, noting the high prevalence of men online (Gefen & Ridings, 2005), and facilitated empowerment and agency, which Movember provides through enabling use of various platforms and individual communication styles. In this model, agency instigates personalization and C2C communication (see Robinson and Robertson, 2014). That is, through participant agency, communication is facilitated between participants or the public through social media in ways designated and optimized by participants. Referencing past research indicating C2C as a relationship-building device (Adjei et al, 2010; Sutanonpaiboon & Abuhamdieh, 2008), the model situates such communication to aid in solidarity development. Solidarity and the development of online community bonds have been ascribed to increase individual participant trust, supporting past research indicating perceived trust is enhanced through involvement, engagement and community building (Brodie et al., 2013; Karpen et al., 2015). Such trust increases future participation intention likelihood (p. 95; Füller et al., 2009), and resultant men's health conversation and behavior outcomes.

Incorporating elements of masculinity, this model situates concepts of identity performativity–in Movember's case, through the identified dualism between the moustache as an individualistic and altruistic device (Robert, 2013)–under 'personalization', whereby individual performativity enables personalization. In this case, Movember has embraced concepts of heteronormativity and hegemonic masculinity through brand positioning, informing individual performativity, whereby the moustache is understood as a symbolic manifestation of masculinity (Jacobson, 2010; Robert, 2013). Noting the connection between masculinity and personalization, research acknowledges masculinity has been contended to generally constrain personalization in health communications (Fleming et al., 2014; Robinson & Robertson, 2014). Additionally, links have been devised between masculinity and men's willingness to talk about health and their resulting health behavior. However, the connections between identity performativity and masculinity have been devised to aid in personalization. Furthering this concept, masculinity has been found to facilitate male solidarity, which may then positively influence trust, communication and resulting behavior.

Overall, participation in online Movember communities is expedited by trust, empowerment and agency, as well as identity performativity–relating to participant desire for altruistic external expression. The relationship between agency and individualism in co-creation becomes evident in this case study as, through Movember's successful facilitation of such elements as C2C communication, personalization and trust, there has been greater online participation and resultantly more conversation about men's health. Movember has been successful, with more conversation generated around men's health, and participants increasingly likely to seek professional health support and treatment.

Addressing Research Propositions

Three research propositions guided research. The first proposition, which suggests Movember has embraced co-creational concepts through their online campaign, is supported by results. As discussed, Movember used social media and C2C-centric strategies to facilitate campaign and cause participation awareness generation. Elements of co-creation are evident in consumer empowerment and agency facilitated by Movember, with participants determined to bring life and personality to the campaign and brand (Movember 2014a, p. 7). Resultantly, participants played a necessary role in Movember's value creation and subsequent cause success.

The second research proposition, which suggests Movember has been successful in reinvigorating conversation around men's health, through the online platform has additionally been proven to some extent. Independent research undertaken by Movember suggests participants had high likelihoods of engaging in health conversation (99% in 2013) (Movember, 2014b). Whether or not this participation rate, however, has transferred successfully into mainstream conversation is still debatable. Contestably, through mounting Movember participant prominence (see figure 1), Movember and its cause resultantly have increasingly entered into social conversation, referencing Mahalik's (2007b) research indicating men's health behavior is influenced through reference to perceptions of male behavioral norms. How successful the Movember campaign has been in transforming mainstream men's health behavior through its online community, however, is debatable. It may be contended that a majority of Movember's direct men's health-related influence stems from the funding it supplies health research initiatives around the world, rather than through its online community. Online community participation, however, may increase cause funding and resultant research. Particularly, through Movember's spawning global popularity, its cause has increased support and exposure. The number of people, however, is arguably still not prominent enough to truly signify a mainstream social movement to reflect its ideals. Hegemonic masculinity, after all, is understood as a social construct that has developed and remained dominant in Western nations for generations. Social change is not instantaneous and it may be decades before the true impact of Movember's cause on social institutions is perceivable.

The final research proposition, concerning Movember's successful employment and advocacy of hegemonic masculinity to benefit health conversation, was explored. Through investigation of identity performativity and personalization through the online community, and the moustache's role as a symbolic masculine device, results indicate that Movember has successfully employed a masculine brand positioning to benefit online conversation around men's health. Particularly, embracing and fostering male solidarity increased perceived trust and community connectedness online, thereby positively influencing individual's participation likelihood and resultant conversation and behavior potential.

IMPLICATIONS OF RESEARCH

Findings support existing co-creation online research elucidating the importance of trust, C2C communication, empowerment and relationship building (Brodie et al., 2013; Füller et al., 2009; Ind et al., 2013) for development of effective value co-creation in online communities. This study arguably aids in increased understanding of co-creation application, and opens up debate regarding the effective manipulation of social constructs to facilitate online health communication. Research reiterates existing research suggesting the unique and opportunistic nature of Internet communities for value co-creation across a range of industries and contexts.

Previous research contends hegemonic masculinity inhibits individuality and resultantly may not be an effective device for online male health promotion (Fleming et al., 2014; Robinson and Robertson, 2014). This research contends Movember has successfully employed masculinity to facilitate discussion of men's health in an online community, through facilitation of online male solidarity. This provides support for the expansive employment of masculinity in health promotion, suggesting that fraternalism in online communities may present an important factor influencing cause success.

CONCLUSION

In conclusion, case study findings indicated elements of co-creation research had been utilized through Movember Australia's online campaign, and such elements–including agency, empowerment and C2C communication–enabled increases in men's health conversation and cause participation. The role of masculinity in Movember's online campaign for the facilitation of solidarity and conversation was investigated, through reference to Robinson and Robertson's (2014) proposed three significant male health online promotion themes of 'personality', "environment" and 'trust'. Research indicated that all three elements, masculinity adoption and principles of co-creation existed interdependently in Movember's online community. Masculinity is stipulated as a construct that needs not to be constraining or restrictive to personality or individuality, while factors including sense of empowerment and communication agency were important for overall satisfaction. Finally, research connected the concept of masculinity and solidarity within the online community as positively impacting on participation, communication and resultant men's behavior choices.

LIMITATIONS AND PROPOSED FUTURE RESEARCH

It is acknowledged that, while Movember predominantly utilizes online tools and communities to facilitate brand awareness and cause participation, a significant part of Movember's strategy occurs in the offline world. Here, participants act as billboards in their daily lives, interacting with friends, family and colleagues and–through the physicality of the moustache—potentially initiate men's health conversation in real time. The conversations around men's health reported by Movember in their annual report comprised both online and offline conversation; techniques employed to generate these results were not clearly defined. While conversation around men's health may have occurred offline, it is noted that Movember's strategy revolves around the proliferation of online community engagement, and resultantly it may be reasonably assumed that a significant portion of conversation occurred online.

Further research should be undertaken to test proposed themes' generalizability. Particularly, this research identifies potential for further research into how the concept of identity performativity relates to customer engagement with causes online. The extent to which customers online influence and impact on overall cause success, direction and positioning warrants further research, with consideration of customers' role in NPO value co-creation.

REFERENCES

Adjei, M., Noble, S., & Noble, C. (2010). The influence of C2C communications in online brand communities on customer purchase behaviour. *Journal of the Academy of Marketing Science*, *38*(5), 634–653. doi:10.1007/s11747-009-0178-5

Anderson, E. D. (2009). The maintenance of masculinity among the stakeholders of sport. *Sport Management Review*, *12*(1), 3–14. doi:10.1016/j.smr.2008.09.003

Australian Bureau of Statistics. (2014a). *Gender indicators, Australia: Life expectancy (Cat. no. 4125.0)*. Canberra, Australia: ABS.

Australian Bureau of Statistics. (2014b). *Australian historical population statistics: Life expectancy (Cat. no. 3105.0.65.001)*. Canberra, Australia: ABS.

Australian Institute of Health and Welfare. (2008). *Australia's Health: 2008 (Cat. no. 99)*. Canberra, Australia: AIHW.

Ballantyne, D., & Varey, R. (2008). The service-dominant logic and the future of marketing. *Journal of the Academy of Marketing Science*, *36*(1), 11–14. doi:10.1007/s11747-007-0075-8

Barford, A., Dorling, D., Smith, G. D., & Shaw, M. (2006). Life expectancy: Women now on top everywhere. *British Medical Journal*, *332*(7545), 808. doi:10.1136/bmj.332.7545.808 PMID:16601021

Berard, T. J. (2005). Rethinking practices and structures. *Philosophy of the Social Sciences*, *35*(2), 196–230. doi:10.1177/0048393105275290

Blanchet, K. B. (2011). Moustaches promote men's health. *British Journal of Urology International*, *108*(10), ii–vii. PMID:22032206

Bourdieu, P., & Wacquant, L. J. D. (1992). *An invitation to reflexive sociology*. Cambridge, UK: Polity Press.

Brodie, R. J., Hollebeek, L. D., Jurić, B., & Ilić, A. (2011). Customer engagement: Conceptual domain, fundamental propositions, and implications for research. *Journal of Service Research*, *14*(3), 252–271. doi:10.1177/1094670511411703

Brodie, R. J., Ilić, A., Jurić, B., & Hollebeek, I. (2013). Consumer engagement in a virtual brand community: An exploratory analysis. *Journal of Business Research*, *66*(1), 105–114. doi:10.1016/j.jbusres.2011.07.029

Brown, M. T. (2012). *Enlisting masculinity: The construction of gender in US military recruiting advertising during the all-volunteer force*. Oxford Scholarship University Press Online; doi:10.1093/acprof:oso/9780199842827.001.0001

Chad, P. (2013). Implementing marketing orientation in charities: A necessity for survival. *Marketing Theory*, *13*(3), 303–322. doi:10.1177/1470593113484921

Chad, P., Kyriazis, E., & Motion, J. (2013). Development of a market orientation research agenda for the non-profit sector. *Journal of Nonprofit & Public Sector Marketing*, *25*(1), 1–27. doi:10.1080/10495142.2013.759814

Chang, C. (2006). Cultural masculinity/femininity influences in advertising appeals. *Journal of Advertising Research*, *46*(3), 315–323. doi:10.2501/S0021849906060296

de Valck, K., van Bruggen, G. H., & Wierenga, B. (2009). Virtual communities: A marketing perspective. *Decision Support Systems*, *47*(3), 185–203. doi:10.1016/j.dss.2009.02.008

Department of Health and Ageing. (2010). *National male health policy: Building on the strengths of Australian males*. Retrieved from www.health.gov.au/internet/main/publishing.nsf/Content/male-policy

Drell, L. (2014). Getting hairy for charity. *Marketing Health Services*, *34*(1), 6–7. PMID:24741759

Eysenbach, G. (2008). Medicine 2.0: Social networking, collaboration, participation, apomediation, and openness. *Journal of Medical Internet Research*, *10*(3), e22. doi:10.2196/jmir.1030 PMID:18725354

Fleming, P. J., Lee, J. G. L., & Dworkin, S. L. (2014). "Real men don't": Constructions of masculinity and inadvertent harm in public health interventions. *American Journal of Public Health*, *104*(6), 1029–1035. doi:10.2105/AJPH.2013.301820 PMID:24825202

Flyvbjerg, B. (2013). Case study. In N. K. Denzin & Y. S. Lincoln (Eds.), *Strategies of qualitative inquiry* (5th ed.). Thousand Oaks, CA: Sage Publications.

Füller, J., Mühlbacher, H., Matzler, K., & Jawecki, G. (2009). Consumer empowerment through Internet-based co-creation. *Journal of Management Information Systems*, *26*(3), 71–102. doi:10.2753/MIS0742-1222260303

Galvagno, M., & Dalli, D. (2014). Theory of value co-creation: A systematic literature review. *Managing Service Quality: An International Journal*, *24*(6), 643–683. doi:10.1108/MSQ-09-2013-0187

Gefen, D., & Ridings, C. M. (2005). If you spoke as she does, sir, instead of the way you do: A sociolinguistics perspective of gender differences in virtual communities. *SIGMIS Database*, *36*(2), 78–92. doi:10.1145/1066149.1066156

Griffiths, K. M., & Christensen, H. (2006). Review of randomised controlled trials of Internet interventions for mental disorders and related conditions. *Clinical Psychologist*, *10*(1), 16–29. doi:10.1080/13284200500378696

Grönroos, C. (2008). Service logic revisited: Who creates value? And who co-creates? *European Business Review*, *20*(4), 298–314. doi:10.1108/09555340810886585

Grönroos, C. (2011). Value co-creation in service logic: A critical analysis. *Marketing Theory*, *11*(3), 279–301. doi:10.1177/1470593111408177

Grönroos, C. (2012). Conceptualising value co-creation: A journey to the 1970s and back to the future. *Journal of Marketing Management*, *28*(13), 1520–1534. doi:10.1080/0267257X.2012.737357

Grönroos, C., & Gummerus, J. (2014). The service revolution and its marketing implications: Service logic vs service-dominant logic. *Managing Service Quality: An International Journal*, *24*(3), 206–229. doi:10.1108/MSQ-03-2014-0042

Grönroos, C., & Ravald, A. (2011). Service as business logic: Implications for value creation and marketing. *Journal of Service Management*, *22*(1), 5–22. doi:10.1108/09564231111106893

Gummesson, E. (1991). *Qualitative methods in management research*. Newbury Park, CA: Sage Publications.

Gummesson, E., & Grönroos, C. (2012). The emergence of the new service marketing: Nordic School perspectives. *Journal of Service Management*, *23*(4), 479–497. doi:10.1108/09564231211260387

Hickie, I. B., Fogarty, A. S., Davenport, T. A., Luscombe, G. M., & Burns, J. (2007). Responding to experiences of young people with common mental health problems attending Australian general practice. *The Medical Journal of Australia*, *187*(7), S47–S52. PMID:17908026

Ind, N., Iglesias, O., & Schultz, M. (2013). Building brands together: Emergence and outcomes of co-creation. *California Management Review*, *55*(3), 5–26. doi:10.1525/cmr.2013.55.3.5

Jacobson, J. L. (2010). *Mustachioed men and marathon moms: The marketing of cancer philanthropy* (Masters thesis). Wilfrid Laurier University, Canada. Retrieved from http://scholars.wlu.ca/etd/1002/(1002)

Jeffcott, M., Cagiannos, I., & Zorn, K. C. (2012). Movember update: The Canadian perspective. *Canadian Urological Association Journal*, *6*(3), E111–E114. doi:10.5489/cuaj.12037 PMID:22709880

Juntunen, M., Juntunen, J., & Autere, V. (2013). Co-creating nonprofit brand equity. *International Journal of Nonprofit and Voluntary Sector Marketing*, *18*(2), 122–132. doi:10.1002/nvsm.1453

Karpen, I. O., Bove, L. L., Lukas, B. A., & Zyphur, M. J. (2015). Service-dominant orientation: Measurement and impact on performance outcomes. *Journal of Retailing*, *91*(1), 89–108.

Kiesling, S. (2007). Men, masculinities and language. *Language and Linguistics Compass*, *1*(6), 653–673. doi:10.1111/j.1749-818X.2007.00035.x

Knox, S., & Guar, C. (2007). The application of stakeholder theory to relationship marketing strategy development in a non-profit organisation. *Journal of Business Ethics*, *75*(2), 115–135. doi:10.1007/s10551-006-9258-3

Kohler, T., Füller, J., Stiger, D., & Matzler, K. (2011). Avatar-based innovation: Consequences of the virtual co-creation experience. *Computers in Human Behavior*, *27*(1), 160–168. doi:10.1016/j.chb.2010.07.019

Korda, H., & Itani, Z. (2013). Harnessing social media for health promotion and behaviour change. *Health Promotion Practice*, *14*(1), 15–23. doi:10.1177/1524839911405850 PMID:21558472

Lapointe, L., Ramaprasad, J., & Vedel, I. (2013, January 7-10). Collaborating through social media to create health awareness. *Paper presented at the 2013 46th Hawaii International conference on System Sciences (HICSS).*

Levine, S. (2013). Movember: A month of moustaches and social media. *Sysomos blog*. Retrieved from http://blog.sysomos.com/2013/12/03/movember-2013/

Li, Y. M., Lee, Y. L., & Lien, N. J. (2012). Online social advertising via influential endorsers. *International Journal of Electronic Commerce*, *16*(3), 119–154. doi:10.2753/JEC1086-4415160305

Locke, B. D., & Mahalik, J. R. (2005). Examining masculinity norms, problem drinking, and athletic involvement as predictors of sexual aggression in college men. *Journal of Counseling Psychology*, *52*(3), 279–283. doi:10.1037/0022-0167.52.3.279

Lusch, R. F., Vargo, S. L., & Malter, A. J. (2006). Marketing as a service exchange: Taking a leadership role in global marketing management. *Organizational Dynamics*, *35*(3), 264–278. doi:10.1016/j.orgdyn.2006.05.008

Lynch, W. (2013). Men's health in Australia. *Trends in Urology and Men's Health*, *4*(1), 7–10. doi:10.1002/tre.305

Mahalik, J. R., Burns, S. M., & Syzdek, M. (2007b). Masculinity ad perceived normative health behaviours as predictors of men's health behaviours. *Social Science & Medicine*, *64*(11), 2201–2209. doi:10.1016/j.socscimed.2007.02.035 PMID:17383784

Mahalik, J. R., Levi-Minzi, M., & Walker, G. (2007a). Masculinity and health behaviours in Australian men. *Psychology of Men & Masculinity*, *8*(4), 240–249. doi:10.1037/1524-9220.8.4.240

Möller-Leimkühler, A. M. (2003). The gender gap in suicide and premature death or: Why are men so vulnerable? *European Archives of Psychiatry and Clinical Neuroscience*, *253*(1), 1–8. doi:10.1007/s00406-003-0397-6 PMID:12664306

Movember Foundation. (2014a). *Movember Foundation global annual report: FY2013-2014*. Retrieved from http://au.movember.com/about/annual-report

Movember Foundation. (2014b). *The Movember Foundation awareness and education program: Report Card Australia (global)*. Retrieved from http://au.movember.com/report-cards/view/id/2489/the-movember-foundation-awareness-and-education-program

Movember Foundation. (2015a). About us. *Movember (Australia)*. Retrieved from http://au.movember.com/about

Movember Foundation. (2015b). Media room: Ambassadors. *Movember (Australia)*. Retrieved from http://au.movember.com/media-room/ambassadors

Movember Foundation. (2015c). About us: Financials. *Movember (Australia)*. Retrieved from http://au.movember.com/about/money

Movember Foundation. (2015d). Media room: Movember 101. *Movember (Australia)*. Retrieved from http://au.movember.com/media-room/movember-101

Nambisan, S., & Baron, R. A. (2009). Virtual customer environments: Testing a model of voluntary participation in value co-creation activities. *Journal of Product Innovation Management*, *26*(4), 388–406. doi:10.1111/j.1540-5885.2009.00667.x

Neiger, B. L., Thackeray, R., Van Wagenen, S. A., Hanson, C. L., West, J. H., Barnes, M. D., & Fagen, M. C. (2012). Use of social media in health promotions: Purposes, key performance indicators, and evaluation metrics. *Health Promotion Practice*, *13*(2), 159–164. doi:10.1177/1524839911433467 PMID:22382491

Nelson, P., Gabriella, B., Lia, P., & Raymond, P. F. (2014). Understanding value co-creation in complex services with many actors. *Journal of Service Management*, *25*(4), 470–493. doi:10.1108/JOSM-02-2014-0055

Norman, C. D. (2012). Social media and health promotion. *Global Health Promotion and Education*, *19*(4), 3–6. doi:10.1177/1757975912464593 PMID:24803437

O'Barr, W. M. (2006). Representations of masculinity and femininity in advertising. *Advertising and Society Review*, *7*(2).

Payne, A., Storbacka, K., & Frow, P. (2008). Managing the c-creation of value. *Journal of the Academy of Marketing Science*, *36*(1), 83–96. doi:10.1007/s11747-007-0070-0

Portnoy, D. B., Scott-Sheldon, L. A., Johnson, B. T., & Carey, M. P. (2008). Computer-delivered interventions for health promotion and behavioural risk evaluation: A meta-analysis of 75 randomised controlled trials. *Preventive Medicine*, *47*(1), 3–16. doi:10.1016/j.ypmed.2008.02.014 PMID:18403003

Prahalad, C. K., & Ramaswamy, V. (2000). Co-opting customer competence. *Harvard Business Review*, *78*(1), 79–87.

Prahalad, C. K., & Ramaswamy, V. (2004). Co-creation experiences: The next practice in value creation. *Journal of Interactive Marketing*, *18*(3), 5–14. doi:10.1002/dir.20015

Preisler, B. (1998). Deconstructing 'feminist linguistics'. *Journal of Sociolinguistics*, *2*(2), 281–295. doi:10.1111/1467-9481.00045

Rau, P. L. P., Gao, Q., & Ding, Y. (2008). Relationship between the level of intimacy and lurking in online social network services. *Computers in Human Behavior*, *24*(6), 2757–2770. doi:10.1016/j.chb.2008.04.001

Robinson, M., & Robertson, S. (2014). Health information needs of men. *Health Education Journal*, *73*(2), 150–158. doi:10.1177/0017896912471039

Roser, T., DeFillippi, R., & Samson, A. (2013). Managing your co-creation mix: Co-creation ventures in distinctive contexts. *European Business Review*, *25*(1), 20–41. doi:10.1108/09555341311287727

Saunders, M., & Peerson, A. (2009). Australia's national men's policy: Masculinity matters. *Health Promotion Journal of Australia*, *20*(2), 92–97. PMID:19642955

Scanlon, A. (2014). It's all about the moustache. *Brandwatch blog*. Retrieved from http://www.brandwatch.com/2014/11/moustache/

Siemens, D. R. (2012). Connecting with prostate cancer survivors. *Canadian Urological Association Journal*, *6*(5), 349. doi:10.5489/cuaj.12268 PMID:23093623

Sutanonpaiboon, J., & Abuhamdieh, A. (2008). Factors influencing trust in online customer-to-customer (C2C) transactions. *Journal of Internet Commerce*, *7*(2), 203–219. doi:10.1080/15332860802067706

Valkonen, J., & Hänninen, V. (2013). Narratives of masculinity and depression. *Men and Masculinities*, *16*(2), 160–180. doi:10.1177/1097184X12464377

Vargo, S. L., & Lusch, R. F. (2004). Evolving to a new dominant logic for marketing. *Journal of Marketing*, *68*(1), 1–17. doi:10.1509/jmkg.68.1.1.24036

Vázquez, R., Álvarez, L. I., & Santos, M. L. (2002). Market orientation and social services in private non-profit organisations. *European Journal of Marketing*, *36*(9/10), 1022–1046. doi:10.1108/03090560210437316

Wang, A. (2005). The effects of expert and consumer endorsements on audience response. *Journal of Advertising Research*, *45*(4), 402–412. doi:10.1017/S0021849905050452

Wassersug, R., Oliffe, J., & Han, C. (2014). On manhood and Movember… or why the moustache works. *Global Health Promotion and Education*. doi:10.1177/1757975914536913 PMID:25024274

Wörsching, M. (2007). Race to the top: Masculinity, sport, and the nature in German magazine advertising. *Men and Masculinities*, *10*(2), 197–221. doi:10.1177/1097184X05284225

Yaeger-Dror, M. (1998). Factors influencing the contrast between men's and women's speech. *Women & Language*, *21*(1), 40.

Yin, R. K. (2014). *Case study research: Design and methods*. Thousand Oaks, CA: Sage.

KEY TERMS AND DEFINITIONS

Co-Creation: The customer's process of extracting value from resource use, whereby value is created upon resource consumption or application by the beneficiary.

Customer-to-Customer (C2C) Interaction: Communication and interaction taking part between participants, either in traditional markets or mediated through online environments. Businesses facilitate such interaction, enabling the development of value creation by customers.

Masculinity: The traits, behaviors, ideals and interests associated with being male within specific cultures. Hegemonic masculinity refers to the dominant conceptualization of these identified behaviors.

Nonprofit Organization (NPO): An organization or group of people committed to providing service for themselves or others, to represent or lobby their or others' interests. They are not operated for profiteering or gain, and while not forming part of government, NPOs may perform public services.

Online Community: An online community which is non-geographically bound and facilitates social communication and relationships between community participants.

Service-Dominant (S-D) Logic: A service-centric logic to the marketing paradigm originally conceptualized by Vargo and Lusch (2004). It places service as the common denominator of exchange, and emphasizes the role of customers in the value creation process.

Solidarity: Discourse generating interactional and relational bonds and between community members and participants.

Chapter 10
Looking At the Other Side:
Families, Public Health and Anti-Vaccination

Rebecca English
Queensland University of Technology, Australia

Shaun Nykvist
Queensland University of Technology, Australia

ABSTRACT

The choice to vaccinate or not to vaccinate a child is usually an 'informed decision', however, it is how this decision is informed which is of most importance. More frequently, families are turning to the Internet, in particular social media, as a data source to support their decisions. However, much of the online information may be unscientific or biased. While issues such as vaccination will always see dissenting voices, engaging with that 'other side' is difficult in the public policy debate which is informed by evidence based science. This chapter investigates the other side in light of the growing adoption and reliance on social media as a source of anti-vaccine information. The study adopts a qualitative approach to data collection and is based on a critical discourse analysis of online social media discourse. The findings demonstrate the valuable contribution this approach can make to public policy work in vaccination.

DOI: 10.4018/978-1-5225-0010-0.ch010

INTRODUCTION

According to Vance, Howe and Dellavale (2009), there is a growing trend for people to rely on the Internet, and in particular, social media sites, as a source of health information as opposed to consulting a health practitioner. A quick search of the Internet will reveal a plethora of views both for and against vaccination that may make families more confused when deciding whether to vaccinate. However, while a family's decision around vaccination needs to be well informed, public health policy and medical research frequently discuss issues relating to vaccination through a quantitative lens. These discussions are framed quantitatively in an attempt to establish the numbers of unvaccinated individuals (Taksdal, Mak, Joyce, Tomlin, Carcione, Armstrong & Effler, 2013), vaccines' effects on immunity (Sullivan, Komadina, Grant, Jelley, Papakadis & Kelly, 2014) and those who suffer the effects of a decision not to vaccinate (Davis, Deloria-Knoll & O'Brien, 2012). Often, these studies are unable to answer significant questions around what it is that drives parents to seek out anti-vaccine social media sites and related discourse (Australian Vaccination-skeptics Network Inc., 2014) as opposed to public health vaccination policy informed by sound research.

It is also noted that it is mothers are particularly responsible for this trend (Salmon, Moulton, Omer, deHart, Stokley & Halsey, 2005). The motherwork involved in raising children also includes the health decisions they make for their children and collecting information that sways them toward vaccines (Benin, Wisler-Scher, Colson, Shapiro & Holmboe, 2006). These women are engaging with social media in much the same terms as the women who choose home education and women who become communities on Instagram and Pinterest, to construct a specific discourse of what counts as 'good mothering'. It may be that there is a connection between mothers who find themselves isolated and disconnected from their 'peers' and are accessing social media to connect with like minded others who may live anything from a block to half a world away.

It is within this context that this chapter proposes the use of a qualitative approach to data collection and analysis that will empower researchers, health practitioners and officials to (re)consider the ways that non-vaccinating families are engaged. With a focus on the qualitative analysis of anti-vaccination social media discourse, it can be argued that viewing these discussions through a qualitative lens can reveal why parents favour social media information sources around decisions relating to vaccines. Thus, it creates a new starting point for public policy officials to engage, and open a new conversation, with these families.

Through a critical discourse analysis (CDA) (cf. Fairclough, 2003) of social media technologies (SMT) an important contribution can be made to public policy work in the area of vaccination. CDA (Fairclough, 2003) facilitates analysis of the ways that practices, events and texts affect the behaviour of individuals. Thus, it is a useful tool for analysing why it is that parents choose to make vaccination decisions based on discourse within social media sites, contrary to those suggested by public health officials. CDA can be considered to be more than an interpretive framework; rather, it has an explanatory intent (cf. Fairclough & Wodak, 1997). As a result, its role can be to highlight the hidden messages in public policy conversations around vaccination; namely why parents' vaccination decisions are disproportionately influenced by the discussion in social media sites. In achieving this goal, it is also important to understand the nature of social media technologies and the impact of these messages in reinforcing families' vaccine decisions.

SOCIAL MEDIA AS A VEHICLE

Over the last decade or two, the Internet has evolved from being a tool used by a few dedicated researchers or academics to one used by a large percentage of the population (Nykvist & Lee, 2013). As a result of the uptake of this technology, the online tools associated with the Internet have evolved into community building tools that can support the diverse needs of many individuals and groups that have a common interest (Nykvist, 2008). The nature of how the Internet is being used, and the expectations of its users, is rapidly changing, especially with the increased rate of digital device ownership, and consequently, the evolution of wirelessly connected devices. This has also driven the demand for social media technologies as an essential communication tool and has seen "electronic media and communications activities take up around half of young people's total discretionary time" (ACMA, 2008, NP). One prevalent interest group active on social media is the anti-vaccination community.

Mobile devices and social media technologies, extend the possibilities for harnessing online connections and communities to make meaningful connections and engage with others. Social media technologies refer to both web-based and mobile applications (Davies et al., 2012) though there is often confusion around the terminology. Often it is the combination of both mobile devices (e.g. smart phones and tablets) and social media technologies (e.g. Facebook, blogs, Instagram and twitter) and the inter-relationship of these technologies that allow individuals to connect and engage with others online. Interest groups are increasingly using these technologies to connect and, to some extent, proselytize to others. Active in many mothers' discussions online is the anti-vaccine community.

A recent research into mothers online has found that mothers provide the most significant reference group to other mothers (Johns & English, 2014), thus, online anti-vaccination discussion, particularly when framed as mother-to-mother, is likely to have a disproportionate influence over public health messages as mothers discuss and share their lived experiences and close connections are made between each other. It is in this sense that the users of these social networks start to form bonds and trust with each other. According to Sarasohn-Kahn (2008), social media technologies not only have the ability to empower, engage and educate but they also act as an emotional support mechanism while also being relied on to manage health issues. The importance of social media technologies as a vehicle to communicate or discuss a particular point of view cannot be underestimated. A recent survey of 450 participants by Nykvist, Mukherjee and McGraw (in press) found that 32% of respondents used social media to reinforce their ideas and opinions.

Social media technologies help to sustain momentum on topics and raise public awareness, including the awareness of families who are making decisions around vaccination. In one example, monetary gains or even losses through the withholding of family benefits (cf. Department of Human Services, 2014) will have an impact on some decision making, yet the decision making process used by families can be complex and multi-faceted. The quantitative data that can be found online about vaccinations and their benefits can be quite compelling with studies about Australian children under the age of two indicating that approximately 90% are fully immunised (Hull, Dey, Mahajan, Menzies & McIntyre, 2009), however the interpretation of research studies and their results can be quite complex. According to Rochman (2013), much of the vaccination information on the Internet is both confusing and misleading, leading families to rely on their social networks and thus make sometimes ill-informed decisions.

It is in this context that Norman and Skinner (2006) claim that the information literacy skills for nearly 50% of adults in Canada and the US are inadequate for making health informed decisions from Internet based resources. While face-to-face social networks with anecdotal stories have been relied on prior to the Internet, the trust and friendships now formed online in social networks is a continuation of older networks, but often encompassing a wider community (cf. Johns & English, 2014).

Despite the all-pervasive nature of the Internet and more recently, mobile and social media technologies (SMT) little evidence exists on how social media technologies can be harnessed to empower health practitioners and inform public health policy. In an attempt to better understand the leverage of social media technologies in the vaccination decision-making process for families, this chapter will focus on the discourse analysis of an anti-vaccination discussion.

METHODOLOGY

This chapter will use Critical Discourse Analysis (Wodak, 2004) to explore the ways that social media, in this chapter we use a blog post, position the anti-vaccination discussion. Critical Discourse Analysis (CDA) is method that examines the role of discourse in social practice (Diriker, 2004). It is concerned with "relationships of causality and determination between (a) discursive practices, events and texts, and (b) wider social and cultural structures, relations and processes" (Fairclough, 2003, p. 135). Thus, the discourse practices that are of interest to CDA are: (a) evident in text and talk and (b) related to wider cultural, social and relational processes. CDA's focus is with social problems, not with language itself (Titscher, et al., 2000). It is concerned with the linguistic character of social and cultural processes through which discourses are constructed (Titscher, et al., 2000).

CDA examines how power relations are relayed in discourse. Fairclough (2000) described CDA as considering the ways that power controls the access to, and production and consumption of, texts in a context (Fairclough, 1995; 2001), thus enabling those with power to restrict or limit their access. In addition, the focus on power is in reference to the asymmetrical relations between agents in a context (cf. Fairclough, 1995). It endeavours to make visible power relations that are frequently hidden (cf. van Dijk, 2001). However, it does not have a specific direction or theoretical framework, thus, it is useful to this study as it allows multiple methods and theories to be brought to bear on texts. In addition, its use is in its role above having an interpretative framework. CDA has an explanatory intent, thus, CDA does more than interpret data; it is a tool that explains the means through which individuals and groups exercise power.

The power relations of interest to this study is the relations between those who purport to know (the authors of blogs about vaccinations) and the parents who are seeking alternative information. One approach to Critical Discourse Anlaysis is the Discourse Historical Approach (DHA) which acts as a translation device to translate the abstracted notions of the theory into the empiricism of a blog post (Wodak, 2004). There are four levels to the DHA. The first level examines the symptoms in the text. This level is concerned with highlighting the basic meaning of the text. The second level is linguistic analysis, there are four tools at this level, *perspectivisation, self-representation strategies, argumentation strategies and intensification and mitigation strategies*. *Perspectivisation* is the perspective offered by a speaker and the evidence they rely upon. *Self-representation* is concerned with how the speaker frames himself or herself in the text. *Argumentation* is concerned with the argumentation strategies employed. Finally, *intensification* or *mitigation strategies* examine how the speaker constructs group membership (Wodak, 2004). The third level is the discourse theory level. Wodak (2004) argued that this level of discourse theory deals with the discursive relationships between utterances and their connection to wider discourses.

The Discourse Historical Approach is dialectical in the sense that it moves between theoretical and empirical between high levels of abstraction and the everyday language that is used by participants, between the theory developed for the study and the participants' accounts of their everyday worlds or social practice (Wodak, 2004; Reisigl & Wodak, 2009). The final level is the theory level, where the theory is invoked to explain the text. Wodak (2004) model is diagrammatically represented in Figure 1.

ANALYSIS

The chapter analyses the contents of an anti-vaccination blog post, titled *A conversation worth having*. The blog is titled *Natural Mom Loves Prada: Life. Beauty. Inspiration.* The text begins with a salutation, *Dear vaccinating parent*, which suggests two things. First, the author is specifically addressing the parents who choose to vaccinate their children. Second, the author wants to engage with the vaccinating families as an equal, but one that cannot reply, as a letter makes refuting individual points difficult. The post is arranged as a series of paragraphs. The symptoms, the first level of analysis, is conducted in the following discussion that examines the text paragraph by paragraph (Table 1).

Figure 1. Modified model of the discourse historical approach (Wodak, 2004, p. 206)

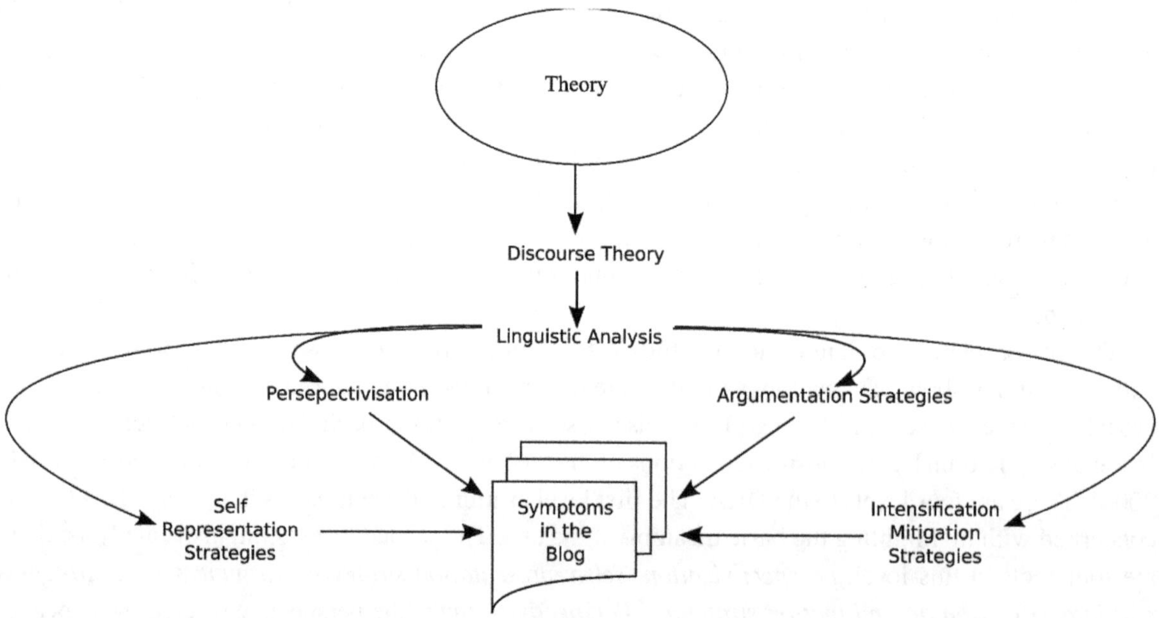

Table 1.

Paragraph	Topic of the Paragraph
First paragraph	The desire to have a conversation with those who disagree is noted as is the desire not to bully or be bullied.
Paragraph two	The perspective of the author, as someone who is skeptical about vaccines but "I am PRO natural immunity" is highlighted. A distinction is drawn between anti-vaccination and pro-immunity and between those two groups and vaccinating parents.
Three	She professes a love for her children and a hatred of name-calling as it leads to defensiveness.
Four	She highlights the differences of opinion between those who do and those who do not vaccinate. She states, "You believe that vaccines are saving lives. I believe in natural immunity that has kept our human species alive on this planet for a really long time".
Five	She states, that there "are some topics I believe we could actually talk about and make better for the generations to come".
Six	She begins to discuss those topics she alluded to in the previous paragraph. In this paragraph, she argues that there should be a free will to choose or refuse medical interventions.
Seven	The next topic she identifies as an agreement is the risks of vaccinating. She states that her concern is with "this barbaric idea that it's ok [sic] for anyone to 'take one for the team'".
Eight	She follows up on the previous topic by imploring the reader to "start thinking about how we are going to support those who have been sacrificed".
Nine	She demands to know the risks and statistics on vaccine side effects she argues are underreported and unable to be found.
Ten	She continues to discuss risks of vaccines by arguing that some nations cancelled some of the vaccines considered routine in the US.
Eleven	She implies that vaccines are a conspiracy theory and that governments have conspired to keep ordinary families in the dark about the side effects.
Twelve	She suggests that conflicts of interest between government and vaccine providers who fund politicians' re-election campaigns and fund government departments have led to a proliferation of vaccines.
Thirteen	She declares that she understands the nature of risk because her daughter was born with a congenital heart defect making her the 1 in 100 chance. She states that she is "well aware of what it's like to be that 1 in xxx".
Fourteen	She asks that we all just live in peace.

There are several linguistic devices evident in the text. The first is perspectivisation. This device is evident in the initial salutation and the final *with joyful grace* and the signature *S. xo*. The strategy of perspectivisation sees the speaker involve themselves in the social world (Reisigl & Wodak, 2009). Two ways that perspectivisation can be achieved are by expressing involvement and using anecdotes. The use of the salutation is an example of involvement with the argument because the speaker is appealing directly to the reader in a formal, but personal way using the letter. The anecdote that is used in the blog revolves around her daughter's congenital heart defect (paragraph thirteen). The author suggests that she understands the ways that statistics play out because "every baby has a 1 in 100 chance of being born with [a heart defect]…we happen to be that 1." As a result, she states, "I'm quite aware of statistics and percentiles and being on the losing end."

The strategy of self-representation is also evident in the text. To illustrate, in paragraph two, the author uses the strategy of to position herself as reasonable. She states, "we have come to different conclusions about that information … that doesn't mean that either of us are stupid or not smart enough". This difference of opinion, she argues, is not due to a lack of scientific knowledge, rather "I am PRO [sic] natural immunity … that doesn't mean that we don't read the same papers and information … we have come to different conclusions". While it appears to suggest the author wishes to be seen as reasonable, it also appears that she wants to be perceived as well-read and able to understand the scientific literature.

Argumentation is also used in the text. Reisigl and Wodak (2009) argue that argumentation is constituted through claims to both truth and righteousness that may or may not rely on evidence. The text invokes truth and righteousness when, in paragraph six, the author suggests that any moves to legislate mandatory vaccines affects the free will of parents to choose medical interventions for their children. The author of the post argues that mandatory vaccines "put [sic] us all at risk of not having any say in what is put into our bodies". She invokes human rights and libertarian ideals by arguing that forced, even socially coerced, vaccination "opens the door for other people to decide … what medical treatments are necessary for the masses". She asserts her reasonableness by arguing, "Our goal should be that together we are protecting our children's choice and human rights in general". Thus, she positions her anti-vaccine stance as truthful and righteous because it is a discussion of choice and thus of libertarian understandings of human rights.

The strategy of intensification and mitigation are also evident. The author constructs group membership in several places. For example, in paragraph three she lists the names she has been called because she does not vaccinate and constitutes two groups a with'em (vaccinating parents) or against'em (non-vaccinating parents). As a result, she appears to suggest that she is positioned as a bad mother. She states, "I can promise that you calling me names is the least effective thing you can do to get through to me – what it really does is cause me to not hear what you are saying and we don't move forward to make this planet a better place for our kids". Thus, she argues against this group position by attempting to appear reasonable. The strategy appears to invoke both *Epistemic intensification*, the establishment of negative parallels and equations and *deontic intensification*, the construction of moral fallacies of a particular policy. Deontic intensification is further seen in paragraph four where the author states, "Your choice carries risks … from reading the vaccine inserts. My choice carries risks … 1)nothing in nature is risk free and 2)we have a hundred years of stats too [sic] look at on our government run health sites". Thus, she constructs the deontic intensification that suggests vaccine is a moral fallacy by stating, "if both our choices carry risk...what are we really fighting about here? Are we really fighting about which risk is worse or more risky??"

Wodak (2001) argues that the main purpose of these linguistic devices is to construct a we-you discourse. The we-you discourse is the discourse theory level of the model. A we-you discourse is a discourse that positions views on a binary. It is grounded in a binary opposition that is established between what van Dijk (2001) calls an us and a them. The binary of the we-you discourse is constructed around two positions – the us or the we-discourse position, which is positive, and the them or the you-discourse position, which is negative. Thus, in the DHA, the we-you discourse reveals the binary opposition between two agents or two groups of agents. The first group of agents is represented through the we-you discourse position as the *we/us*. The second group of agents is represented through the you-discourse position as the *you/them*. Tracing the we-you discourse identifies the strategies that speakers use to define those who belong and those who do not (cf. Matouschek, Wodak & Januschek, 1995 in Titscher, Meyer, Wodak & Vetter, 2000).

It is noted that, while there might be multiple you or we discourses, there is only one we-you discourse. Thus, while there may be multiple constructions of family, this account constructs her family as one we discourse among multiple you discourse. It suggests a claim to truth in families though, as she suggests that people who do not question vaccines are not caring enough about their families to adequately question the messages health officials send that encourage full vaccination.

The text appears to position those skeptical about vaccines as the we, however the we positions include "anti-vaxers" as well as those, like the author who identify as "pro-immunity". The "pro-immunity" position is defined as those who believe in natural immunity because "you read [the scientific literature] and decided how that information is going to benefit you and your family and I have done the same and come to a different conclusion for mine". The you position is constructed for those who choose to vaccinate, however the nuanced options (partial vaccinators, those who vaccinate on an altered schedule) are not considered. Thus, the text constructs a we-you discourse that produces multiple 'we' positions but does not allow for more than one 'you' position. It is most evident in her with me or against me discussion.

DISCUSSION

The analysis of the text suggests that there is an important role for the Internet to support and engage parents who are confused about vaccination. With nuanced use of statistics and health information, this blogger has attempted to present a coherent and cogent argument against vaccination, one based in emotion and pathos. This argument may be seductive to those parents who are wavering about their decision to vaccinate and, if enough families follow the blogger's line of reasoning it could, theoretically, reduce the level of vaccinated families in a community. The use of self-representation, intensification, argumentation and perspectivisation all seductively construct a narrative of truth and reasonableness against a potentially inhuman, government machine of vaccine information produced by the Australian Medical Association (AMA) and the Centers for Disease Control and Prevention (CDC) for example.

As the findings of Johns and English (2014) suggest, mothers may be more likely to use the information on social media to make decisions for their families. Mothers use other mothers, even in online settings, as a reference group. Thus, as Johns and English (2014) argue "marketers should consider the reference group behaviour of mothers online" (p. 334) as they may have more influence over women's purchasing and health decisions than 'experts' such as the CDC or the AMA. Blogs, such as this one analysed here, are important because they may have a disproportionate influence over other mothers and the information they are presenting is at best biased and at worse completely false.

In addition, as Sarasohn-Kah (2008) argue, social media may present a type of emotional support. Blogs, such as the one analysed here, may become a site of rallying and support when families' choices are criticised and faced with evidence from scientific sources. Thus, when parents feel criticized and unsupported for making anti-vaccine choices, these blogs may act as a space where parents can reinforce their beliefs at the expense of evidence based medical opinion about vaccines. If, as Nykvist et al. (forthcoming) suggest, 32% of respondents used social media to reinforce their ideas and opinions, it is likely that blogs such as 'Natural Mom Wears Prada' may be a safe house for families whose decision not to vaccinate is criticized by wider medical opinion.

It is interesting to note that many in the pro-vaccination community could easily utilize the same strategies as the anti-vaccine blogger whose works was discussed here. By setting up blogs, particularly by parents who chose not to vaccinate and then their child contracted a vaccine preventable illness, perhaps the same appeals to emotion and risk as those used by anti-vaccination bloggers. Further, the personal stories and appeals to protecting children may have a similar effect and may sway parents who are less decided to follow the vaccination schedule.

CONCLUSION

While it can be argued that there is a plethora of data sources available online for families to make a choice about whether to vaccinate or not, much of the discourse within social media sites contains emotional messages which can trigger a misinformed reaction to the vaccination argument. In addition, much of the information is not based on evidence-based medicine, rather on beliefs and half-truths. If an emotional reaction is triggered, this may influence the decision, as the preceding blog analysis has demonstrated. It further highlights the strength of social media technologies to connect and engage with users who share a passion for a particular topic and the ability for social media to so strongly influence decisions.

Health practitioners need to be empowered to also use social media technologies as a vehicle to connect and engage with families in ways that elicit meaningful discussion on whether to vaccinate. While the limitations of this study include the limited sample data, there is a strong need to conduct further qualitative research into the impacts of social media on vaccination decisions.

If health providers and government agencies are able to construct similar messages, using similar tools, to the message analysed in this document, it may be that they are going to be better equipped to influence parents' decisions. Using the same discourse as the one constructed in Natural Mom Wears Prada, health officials may be better equipped to position their own messages in ways that affect families to make an appropriate decision, one that leads to them at least partially vaccinating their children.

REFERENCES

ACMA (Australian Communication and Media Authority). (2008). *Australian families with children are 'media-rich', research finds.* Retrieved from http://www.acma.gov.au/WEB/STANDARD/pc=PC_310897

Australian Vaccination-skeptics Network Inc. (2014). *Making an informed choice*. Retrieved from http://avn.org.au/making-an-informed-choice/

Benin, A., Wisler-Scher, D., Colson, E., Shapiro, E., & Holmboe, E. (2006). Qualitative Analysis of Mothers' Decision-Making about Vaccines for Infants: The Importance of Trust. Pediatrics. *Official Journal of the American Academy of Pediatrics, 117*(5), 1532–1541. doi:10.1542/peds.2005-1728

Daniel, A., Salmon, D., Moulton, L., Omer, S., deHart, M., Stokley, S., & Halsey, N. (2005). Factors Associated with Refusal of Childhood Vaccines Among Parents of School-aged Children: A Case-Control study. *JAMA Pediatrics* 59(5), 470-476. DOI . Retrieved from http://archpedi.jamanetwork.com/article.aspx?articleid=4860111June 201510.1001/archpedi.159.5.470

Davis, C. H. F., III, Deil-Amen, R., Rios-Aguilar, C., & González Canché, M. S. (2012). Social media and higher education: A literature review and research directions. *Immunising your children. University of Arizona and Claremont Graduate University Department of Human Services.* Retrieved from http://www.humanservices.gov.au/customer/subjects/immunising-your-children

Diriker, E. (2004). *De-/re-contextualizing conference interpreting: Interpreters in the ivory tower?* Amsterdam, The Netherlands: John Benjamins Publishing Company. doi:10.1075/btl.53

Fairclough, N. (1995). *Critical discourse analysis*. Boston, MA: Addison Wesley.

Fairclough, N. (2000). *New Labour, new language?* London, UK: Routledge.

Fairclough, N. (2001b). The discourse of New Labour: Critical discourse analysis. In M. Wetherell, S. Taylor, & S. Yates (Eds.), *Discourse as data: A guide for analysis* (pp. 221–260). London, UK: Sage.

Fairclough, N. (2003). *Analyzing discourse: Textual analysis for social research*. London, UK: Routledge.

Fairclough, N., & Wodak, R. (1997). Critical discourse analysis. In T. van Dijk (Ed.), *Discourse as social interaction* (pp. 258–284). Thousand Oaks, CA: Sage.

Hull, B., Dey, A., Mahajan, B., Menzies, R., & McIntyre, P. (2009) Immunisation coverage annual report. Report for the National Centre for Immunisation Research and Surveillance of Vaccine Preventable Diseases (NCIRS). Canberra: Department of Health: Commonwealth of Australia

Johns, R., & English, R. (2014). Mothers influencing mothers: The use of virtual discussion boards and their influence on consumption. *International Journal of Web Based Communities, 10*(3), 319–338. doi:10.1504/IJWBC.2014.062945

Liu, C.-C., . . . (2014). Enabling a Positive First Year Experience in Higher Education through Social Media and Mobile Technologies. In Liu, C.-C. et al. (Eds.) *Proceedings of the 22nd International Conference on Computers in Education.* Japan: Asia-Pacific Society for Computers in Education.

Matouschek, B., Wodak, R., & Januschek, F. (1995). *"Notwendige Maßnahmen gegen Fremde?": Genese und Formen von rassistischen Diskursen der Differenz*. Wien, Austria: Passagen.

Norman, C. D., & Skinner, H. A. (2006). eHealth Literacy: Essential Skills for Consumer Health in a Networked World. *Journal of Internet medical research*, 8(2) e9. Retrieved on August 3 2014 from http://www.ncbi.nlm.nih.gov/pmc/articles/PMC1550701/

Nykvist, S. S. (2008). Creating contexts for effective online communities of practice. In N. Yelland, G. A. Neal, & E. Dakich (Eds.), *Rethinking Education with ICT: New directions for effective practices* (pp. 165–180). Rotterdam, The Netherlands: Sense Publishers.

Nykvist, S. S., & Lee, K.-T. (2013). Mixing higher education teaching and learning with mobile devices and social media. *Proceedings of IAC-ETeL 2013*, Prague, Czech Republic.

Reisigl, M., & Wodak, R. (2009). The discourse-historical approach (DHA). In R. Wodak, R. & M. Meyer (Eds.), Methods of critical discourse analysis (2nd ed., pp. 87-121). Thousand Oaks, CA: Sage.

Rochman, B. (2013, April). How Social Networks Influence Parents' Decision to Vaccinate. *Time*. Retrieved from http://healthland.time.com/2013/04/15/how-social-networks-influence-a-parents-decision-to-vaccinate/

Sarasohn-Kah, J. (2008). *The wisdom of patients: Health care meets online social media. Report for the California Healthcare Foundation*. California: California Healthcare Foundation.

Sullivan, S. G., Komadina, N., Grant, K., Jelley, L., Papadakis, G., & Kelly, H. (2014). Influenza vaccine effectiveness during the 2012 influenza season in Victoria, Australia: Influences of waning immunity and vaccine match. *Journal of Medical Virology*, *86*(6), 1017–1025. doi:10.1002/jmv.23847 PMID:24395730

Taksdal, S. E., Mak, D. B., Joyce, S., Tomlin, S., Carcione, D., Armstrong, P. K., & Effler, P. V. (2013). Predictors of uptake of influenza vaccination – a survey of pregnant women in Western Australia. *Australian Family Physician*, *42*(8), 582–586. PMID:23971070

Titscher, S., Meyer, M., Wodak, R., & Vetter, E. (2000). *Methods of Text and Discourse Analysis*. Thousand Oaks, CA: Sage.

van Dijk, T. A. (2001). Multidisciplinary CDA: A plea for diversity. In R. Wodak, & M. Meyer (Eds.), Methods of critical discourse analysis (pp. 95-120). London, UK: Sage. doi:10.4135/9780857028020.d7

Vance, K., Howe, W., & Dellavalle, R. P. (2009, April). Social internet sites as a source of public health information. *Dermatologic Clinics*, *27*(2), 133–136. doi:10.1016/j.det.2008.11.010 PMID:19254656

Wodak, R. (2001). The discourse historical approach. In R. Wodak & M. Meyer (Eds.), *Methods of critical discourse analysis* (pp. 63–94). Thousand Oaks, CA: Sage.

Wodak, R. (2004). Critical discourse analysis. In C. Searle, G. Gobo, J. Gubrium, & D. Silverman (Eds.), *Qualitative research practice* (pp. 186–213). London, UK: Sage. doi:10.4135/9781848608191.d17

Chapter 11
The Role of Women from a Social Media Jihad Perspective: Wife or Warrior?

Robyn Torok
Edith Cowan University, Australia

ABSTRACT

Female roles in online social media forums are continually changing and often reflect the global social and political context. In addition, the security context also plays an important part in the role of females online. Social media evidence suggests that females are very active online in terms of recruitment. This chapter looks at two case studies focusing on the roles of women as wives and warriors and the changing dynamic between the two roles. Overall, women demonstrate a high level of gender utility and can change roles as required by the security and political context.

DOI: 10.4018/978-1-5225-0010-0.ch011

INTRODUCTION

The murky world of terrorism is not exempt from gender issues and gender identity. Extremists have sought to undertake a global scoped jihad against the West in response to perceived grievances and injustices against Islam. Islamic extremism is a phenomenon that we are very familiar with in the West. However, what is less well known is the role that women play in this phenomenon. Equally important to any terrorist activities carried out by extremists is their online presence and how they seek to pervade the hearts and minds of as many people as possible.

This chapter seeks to explore how the online world, in particular social media, is used to influence the gender roles and gender identities of women in relation to this global jihad. As the title suggests two primary identities are discussed: the women as an active jihad warrior including taking part in jihad and martyrdom operations; and secondly, the women as the wife and supporter of her mujahideen (warrior) husband.

Initially, this chapter explores the context of the online and social media jihad and subsequently looks at the two primary gender roles for women in the online global jihad. This chapter will also utilise case studies from an extensive research project on social media discourses on Facebook conducted over several years. Finally, trends found on gender Identity will be discussed as well as future implications based on female gender utility.

ONLINE JIHAD

Since 9/11 and the subsequent war on terror, al-Qaeda and other Islamic jihad groups have been very adept at evolving to the changing shifts caused by continual attacks to their physical locations (Michael, 2009). One of the primary areas of adaptation is in the use of internet technology to support a number of its strategic and operational objectives that include recruiting, fundraising, strategic direction and research (McNeal, 2007). Even Islamic State in 2014 when expanding and controlling large geographic areas of Syria and Iraq, relies heavily on its online media for propaganda and recruitment. Specifically, internet technology also opens up a worldwide audience able to access extremist views and form networks, all in a ubiquitous and virtually untraceable environment (O'Rourke, 2007). Importantly, the internet provides an essential media battlefield as part of their terrorism strategy as al-Qaeda's Dr. al-Zawahiri stated: 'We are in a battle, and more than half of this battle is taking place in the battlefield of the media. We are in a media battle for the hearts and minds of our *umma*' (Michael, 2009). Therefore, it is this battle for hearts and minds that will be addressed.

Research by Weimann (2008) on the target audiences of terrorist websites indicates that their intended audience is actually very broad and includes potential recruits, the international community and its enemies. However, the focus on potential recruits is an important aspect and often involves more culturally sophisticated planning coupled with more tech savvy skills in its implementation. Key aspects include the use of colour, latest multimedia technologies, professional finish and interactivity (McNeal, 2007). Many of these sites are targeted at younger males with reports in the United Kingdom (UK) indicating terrorist groups specifically targeting male university undergraduates and even secondary students

(Mendez, 2008). However, recruitment has by no means been limited to males and jihadist groups have been appreciating the value of female recruits.

Furthermore, it is the disaffected and the alienated that are especially vulnerable to the 'seductive' efforts of recruiters (Murphy & White, 2007). These groups include diasporic communities (Awan, 2007) as well as first and second generation Muslims who are "citizens in name but not culturally or socially." (Leiken, 2005, p. 123). Nevertheless, it is this 'citizen in name' aspect that is important, just like the ring of Roman citizenship gave freedom to travel throughout the Roman Empire, likewise a 'Western' passport gives greater freedom to travel throughout the Western world. This freedom to travel is especially important given that some of those travelling on Middle-Eastern, North African or Asian passports are coming under increasing scrutiny given their regional reputations for terrorist activity, radicalism and training activities (Michael, 2009).

'White Moors' and home grown jihadists are often considered prized recruits and highlight the global reach of online social media jihad. Any Western recruits for Islamic State whether male or female have attracted large scale attention from Western media. Coupled with this, there has been the increasing individualisation of the concept of *jihad* as part of a global resistance (Michael, 2009). One of al-Qaeda's most notable strategists, al-Suri, has articulated the power of the Internet as a key tool in promoting individual terrorism (Michael, 2009). It is therefore critical to look at the dynamics of how the internet has been used as such an important strategic tool in promoting home grown terrorism.

From an insignificant cyber presence pre-9/11, al-Qaeda developed over time a strong cyber network that used cutting edge technology (Murphy, 2007). This exponential growth in websites (Awan, 2007) resulted in a matching growth in potential recruitment opportunities (McNeal, 2007). In one of the most comprehensive research studies on online terrorist websites, Weimann (2008, p. 75) reported that the number of terrorist websites grew from about 12 in 1998 to over 5300 at the end of 2006. What is perhaps even more disconcerting is the rapid rise of English speaking websites (over 100 reported in late 2007) (Michael, 2009, p. 143). Such a shift reflects attempts to create 'White Moors' from disaffected youth who can now easily access hundreds of English language sites, interact and be targeted by jihad recruiters (Jenkins, 2010). This threat continues to be perhaps one of the most pervasive cyber threats we face.

SHIFT TO SOCIAL MEDIA

The use of the internet for terrorist recruitment and operations has increased significantly in recent years. Part of that expansion is an embracing of Western social media including Facebook, Twitter and YouTube. While this phenomenon is well documented, what is more difficult to determine due to limited research, are the mechanisms and power relations that underlie this phenomenon of online media used to promote radicalization which in some cases can develop into terrorism. Currently, more traditional models are utilized that look at concepts such as psychological warfare, propaganda, indoctrination and data mining (von-Knop, 2007). Furthermore, narratives are viewed as an important aspect of seduction for radicalization (Mbakwe & Cunliffe, 2007; von-Knop, 2007). Consequently, this chapter will focus on two key narratives highlighting the role of women in online jihad.

Changes in Organisational Structures

Importantly, the internet has resulted in a significant shift in the organisational structure of Islamic terrorist groups away from a hierarchical structure and towards a transnational and globalised network structure (Conway, 2006). This decentralisation has been important since the 'war on terror' and the disruption of more traditional training bases. Internet and communication technologies are well suited to this networked, dispersed and interconnected groups formed by Islamic terrorism (Conway, 2006). Connections and networks developed online can be studied and mapped using tools such as social network theory (Matusitz, 2008). Networks are formed using a 'chain of trust' where members must vouch for each other and develop a reputation (Matusitz, 2008, p. 189). However, networks must maintain a certain level of openness in order to allow for recruitment, which is often targeted toward certain population groups. Such open networks can be studied with a variety of lenses. In the case of this chapter it is female gender identity that is the key focus and how the role of women is constructed in the online environment.

WOMEN AS WIVES AND SUPPORTERS OF THE MUJAHIDEEN

Women have typically been cast in the stereotypical support roles (Davis, 2006). This was especially the case during the initial stages of the war on terror post 2001. However, as discussed above there has been an increasing trend of using women in more active roles. Yet these traditional roles have remained and are coming back into prominence especially since the formation of the Islamic State and the attempt to create a sense of 'society' or 'community' that would be found in any traditional state.

Social media research has indicated that women have always posted support for men undertaking jihad. Techniques used include using the fantasy of the hero warrior as one admired by their wife, as well as shaming males who 'sit behind their computer and do nothing.' Furthermore, the active role of females has often been portrayed as a necessity due to the failure of males to undertake their jihad responsibilities. Cases of *gender shaming* were found to be quite common on social media between 2010 and 2013, where it was always the male who was shamed and portrayed as cowardly.

Since 2014 with the development of the Islamic State (IS) which took over large geographic areas of Iraq and Syria, there has been a return to these more traditional roles of the wife as a supporter of her mujahideen husband. While this trend began with the Syrian resistance and the inflow of foreign fighters, it is IS who have restored this role.

Media reports (such as "Eight British school girls travel to Syria to become IS brides," 2015) highlight a returning focus to women in this role of supporting their husbands. This is especially the case given that IS controls large geographic areas of Iraq and Syria. Coupled with this is the large influx of male foreign fighters which has created a demand for 'jihadi brides.'

Elements of romanticism are attached to being the wife of a mujahideen and this is often found in online images. Figure 1 captures the essence of the simple nomad wife in the desert. Similar images have been recently posted by Islamic State showing women feeding horses. In both cases a sense of righteousness is imbued with the wearing of the full burqa coupled with a sense of simplicity of lifestyle that contrasts sharply with the multiple demands placed on women in Western culture.

Figure 1. Romanticism of being a wife of a mujahideen
Source: http://prntscr.com/9cycws

Another important dimension of being a wife is that of the rewards of the martyr. Heaven or *jannah* not only belongs to the mujahideen warrior when martyred but also to his wife and family. Figure 2 depicts a wife encouraging her husband to seek jihad and martyrdom and hence find *jannah* for their family. The caption in Figure 2 highlights the role of the wife in supporting her husband to undertake jihad.

The development of Islamic State has sought to bring back the importance of this gender role. The most significant aspect of this role is that it allows women to hold extremists beliefs without needing a personal disposition toward violence.

CASE STUDY: A WOMAN AS THE FAITHFUL WIFE AND MARTYR

This first case study is longitudinal and follows a subject over several years. For reference purposes, this subject will be designated as subject MTR (moderate to radical). Before examining this transformation, it would be incomplete to look at subject MTR in isolation without looking at their primary influence, the person closest to them who will be designated subject PIRI (Primary Influence of Radical Islam). This primary influence or partner of subject MTR was radicalised first. In the online context, the relationship of subject PIRI over subject MTR did not appear at all coercive and in fact subject MTR seemed to be more radicalised from female company. This case study will take a longitudinal view over time at this radicalisation.

Figure 2. Role of the mujahideen wife in encouraging her husband to seek jannah

Early Days of Subject MTR (2011)

Initially, subject MTR posts were quite normal and included joking with friends as well as some references to Islam. At this point the question arises: Why, as a researcher, did I take a special interest in subject MTR at this stage? There are two main reasons. First, is the fact of who subject MTR was associated with, having many radicals on their page and in particular their relationship to subject PIRI. Second, is the fact that as indicated by the last two posts in Figure 3 there is a sense of unfulfillment and being dissatisfied indicated by subject MTR.

Influence of Subject PIRI (2012)

Analysis of subject PIRI's influence consisted of two main areas. First, was the need in Syria given what was happening there and second was the focus on the temporality of this life compared to the next. These two areas are interwoven and as will be subsequently pointed out served to influence subject MTR.

Subject PIRI and Syria Calling

Two key posts have been chosen here. The first post highlights the obligation of Muslims to help their fellow Muslim regardless of whether or not permission is granted by others and places the Islamic state

Figure 3. Sample of early posts of subject MTE

Before creating creation Allah swt took an oath upon Himself "That My Mercy would always overcome My Anger". Come to a gathering filled with Angels, tranquility and sisterhood...
Success is not only measured by what you have, but also by what you had to give up.
The highest form of ignorance is when you reject something you don't know anything about.
Let go of anger. It is an acid that burns away the delicate layers of your happiness.
I never feel i'm good enough
I feel theres so much competition these days
Source: Subject MTE profile page

above the nation state. In other words in terms of identity, subject PIRI viewed themselves as a Muslim rather than as an Australian. The second post is a reference to a YouTube video that targeted the affective dimension and focused on the suffering that occurred in Syria.

Other posts as well as links of subject PIRI demonstrated that they were committed and passionate about the Syrian cause (Figure 4).

Subject PIRI and the Brevity of This Life Compared to Eternity of the Next

By far the most overarching theme found on subject PIRI's profile was the comparison between this life and the next. In addition, early posts also focussed on comparisons between Islam and Christianity and how Islam was the correct and true religion. Links to YouTube videos were also found that gave testimonials of Christians including Pastors who had converted to Islam. Clearly with such a focus on eternity and the afterlife, one must be convinced that they have the true religion. Subject PIRI's posts indicate a full convincing of truth was evident and tried to also others felt the same way.

Figure 4. Sample posts of subject PIRI relating to Syria

If the enemy captures a single Muslim, it becomes wajib (obligatory) on every one who has the ability, to rush to their rescue (even without seeking anyone's permission). It is apparent that it is compulsory on everyone, similar to the situation where the enemy invades our land. Moreover, saving our brothers is of a higher priority, as the sanctity of a Muslim is greater (than the sanctity of a State). - Ibn Hajar Al-Haithami Rahimahullah
#SYRIA | HAVE A HEART | EMOTIONAL | HD
www.youtube.com
Syria is calling will you answer. An emotional plea to anyone with a heart. We are awaiting the support. LIKE & SHARE THE VIDEO. Bismillah. #SYRIA | HAVE A H.
Source: Subject PIRI's profile page

Figure 5 gives a sample of posts relating to a focus on death and the afterlife. Given the prolific nature of such posts, a greater number of more extensive posts have been included. To improve readability, I have added emphasis to certain posts. Where emphasis has been added, it was ensured that other posts also supported this emphasis.

Figure 5. Posts of subject PIRI related to a focus on the next life

when will we wake up!! this world is not for ever!! a wise person will live for the future, so **i live for my real future... death!!** if this world was worth even a wing of a mosquito Allah wouldn't even give the the disbeliever a sip of water. think about it!!
The grave calls out: "O dwellers of the earth, you have focused on building a realm that will soon pass away, and you have neglected the realm to which you are moving quickly. You have built houses in which others will live and enjoy them, and you have neglected houses for which there are no other inhabitants but you. This is the place where you will abide and bid farewell to work and toil. **This is what matters, one of the gardens of Paradise or one of the chambers of Hell**..." [Ibn al-Qayyim]
My heart cries for those who do not have islam,even more for those who ignorantly refuse, even more for those who have believe what they see on the media. Without Islam there is no success in this life or the next. Words of omar abdulaziz: **"I can handle the poverty and harshness of this world for a lifetime but I cannot withstand the flames of hell for a second"**.
Do u really think that this world will last forever? That this life is for mere fun and play? That you won't be resurrected and bought in front of the creator, like the crops die in winter then life is given back to them in the spring. Do you think that you will not be held account for the good and the bad that you do? The person you hear that died in a car accident, don't you think he too had long hopes for the future? Death is a reality none of us can out run. What have you done to prepare for "destroyer of pleasures?" Believe in one God (without partners) enjoin what is good and forbid what is evil and you will have success in this life and the next!
Paradise is Surrounded by difficulties and Hell is surrounded with desires... be **ever watchful from the deception of this dunya**... Let Allah swt be the Ruler of your heart in this world and the hereafter.... Turn to Allah swt for guidance...
God says thus to him that loves him, and serves him faithfully: "Go and consider the sands of the sea, O my servant, how many they are. Wherefore, if the sea should give you one single grain of sand, would it appear small to you? Assuredly, yes. As I, your creator, live, all that I have given in this world to all the princes and kings of the earth is less than a grain of sand that the sea would give you, in comparison of that which I will give you in my paradise.
I said to Allah, I hate life. Allah replied, who said love life.
the only thing guaranteed in this life is death, so don't trade the temporary pleasures of this world in exchange for the everlasting pleasures of paradise. (Favourite Quote)
Source: Subject PIRI's profile page. Emphasis added by researcher

The first post in Figure 5 is a clear indication that all aspects of subject PIRI's life and actions revolve around this preparation for death. In fact, death has become the focal point of life which seems rather ironic, however, there is a preparation process required and a way of living that must occur first.

Figure 5 also emphasises a clear contrast between the gardens of paradise and flames or chambers of hell. Such binary discourse makes it clear that a person is heading for one or the other. It also promotes an accountability as to how we live this life encouraging a person to live in a particular way.

As a final observation from these posts, there is a need to discuss the concept of 'dunya'. While 'dunya' superficially represents this present world that we live in, it does in fact represent much more than this. It includes the deceptions and pleasures of this world that attempt to distract a person from their duty to Islam. Subject PIRI's favourite quote sums this whole contrast very succinctly and encourages believers to make sure that they focus on what is truly important - the afterlife.

One final important note on these discourses is the fact that they are not gender specific and in fact embrace a sense of shared gender identity when it comes to contrasting what is valued in this life compared to the next.

Subject MTR's Deepening Involvement in Islam (2012-2013)

Posts of subject MTR started moving away from more light hearted and everyday subjects associated with 'dunya' and became more focused on aspects of Islam especially with some of the more ritualistic aspects as shown in Figure 6. While this in and of itself is not necessarily a move toward more radical or extreme Islam it does represent a shift away from common everyday posts of activities to posts being dominated by Islam.

The first post demonstrates a significant move toward extremism indicating that Western media is the mouthpiece of the devil. The second post is congruent with the general theme of posts being more and more focused on Islam and the afterlife (Jannah). Here we see the first signs that the influence of subject PIRI is starting to cause a significant shift in subject MTR. Another critical observation here is that religious Islamic legalism is often associated as part of the male domain, whereas here we see a clear case of female legalism.

Subject MTR's Final Posts before Martyrdom (Late 2013)

While we may expect to see posts promoting jihad and violence on someone about to leave for Syria and be martyred, for subject MTR this was not the case. Although subject MTR associated with many radicals and open supporters of jihad and martyrdom on the profile page, there were a lack of explicit references to jihad and martyrdom. Instead, what was present was an extreme devotion to Islam, however, the typology of subject MTR's could only be inferred from associations and networks, especially with subject PIRI.

It is difficult to assess subject MTR's views on jihad and martyrdom. Whether these subjects were not discussed because they were not a primary focus or whether they were deliberately left out to avoid attention from police or security officials is unknown.

Figure 6. Posts highlighting subject MTR's increasing involvement in Islam

> Do not trust the mouthpiece of shaytaan [devil], the western media
> Whoever asks for Jannah three times, Jannah will say: Oh Allah, enter him into Jannah. [Hadith Tirmidhi]
> Today is the 1st of Dhul-Hijjah.
> The prophet (pbuh) said "There are no ten days in which righteous deeds are more beloved to Allah than these 10 days" (Bukhari)
> So take this opportunity to:
> 1. Engage in as many extra good deeds and acts of worship as possible in these first blessed 10 days. Increase your recitation of Quran, fast, help others, make dua, give more in sadaqah, increase your salah and extra prayers and keep your tongue moist in dhikr.
> 2. No clipping of the hair and nails of the one who is paying for a sacrificial animal (qurban).
> 3. The ninth day of Dhul-Hijjah (Tuesday 15th October) is the day of 'Arafah.
> It is on this day that the Hajj pilgrims gather at the mountain plain of 'Arafah, praying and supplicating to their Lord.
> It is mustahabb (highly recommended) for those who are not pilgrims to fast on this day, since the Prophet (sallallaahu 'alayhi wa sallam) was asked about fasting on the day of 'Arafah, so he said, "It expiates the sins (Minor) of the past year and the coming year." [Muslim (no. 1162)]
> 4. Eid Ul Adha will be on Wednesday 16th October.
> The Eid of Adha (sacrifice) commemorates the willingness of Prophet Ibraheem to obey Allah in sacrificing his son, Ismael (peace be upon them both). This ritual of sacrificing an animal is still followed by millions and millions of Muslims world wide today.
> Source: Subject MTR's profile page

Figure 7 shows posts highlighting the centrality of devotion (some may term this obsession but I will not use this term given its judgmental nature) as well as the temporary nature of this life and preparation for the next. While many of subject PIRI's posts about this life and the next are quotes from others, these posts are direct from subject MTR and show the level of transformation and intent.

The reference by subject MTR to both parents is also a sign that something is about to happen and that time is running out. It is in essence an indirect goodbye and a thank you before leaving for Syria and subsequent martyrdom.

Response to News of the Martyrdom of Subject MTR and Subject PIRI

Following the departure of subjects MTR and PIRI and their subsequent death confirmed on traditional as well as social media outlets, a page was set up dedicated to these two subjects and their martyrdom. It should be clearly noted here that martyrdom is a term chosen by the participants and not the researcher.

Figure 7. Subject FTR's posts before leaving for Syria

Every experience Allah gives us, every person Allah puts in our lives is the perfect preparation for the future that only Allah can see. Allah SWT will ask you on Judgment day how did you spend your Youth, you had so much energy, how did use this period when you was picking in strength Oh Allah, You Alone we worship, and You Alone we ask for help May Allah bring my father to Islam before its too late. Ameen My Life My Mum [non Muslim mother] Just imagine going to sleep without praying and then waking up in your grave. Subhan Allah You can strip me from everything, but you will never take My Islam from me Everything is temporary. A believer does not wish for anything more than the pleasure of Allah. Source: Subject MTR's profile page

Clear reference is made to Jannah (heaven) which in Islam has many levels. Radical Islam subscribes to the belief that martyrs are reserved the highest places in Jannah. There are also the reference to the green birds of paradise which carry the souls of martyrs. Interestingly, apart from Jannah, none of the other rewards of martyrdom were mentioned on this page (Figure 8).

Figure 8. Posts responding to the deaths of subjects MTR and PIRI

I make this page to allow all Australian Muslims to remember their brothers sons or friends who martyr fisabilillah in Syria or anywhere. I read the story of [subject MTR] and [subject PIRI] who went to Syria and died fisabilillah there and I am going to attached it to invite you to read it and write your comment on: May [they] be granted the highest level of Jannah ! Ameen [subject MTR] is a martyr. And Ma sha Allāh you must be very proud. May Allāh grant them the lofty rank of jannah. Ameen They reach their destination (in the hearts of green bird) and we still searching for ways, just mere spectators may Allah accept their shahadahs [statement of faith] ameen:'(May they be birds of paradise Inshallah. And may Allah unite you all together in the next life. ALLAHU AKBAR!! There dreams came true!!!!! May Allah (SWT) accept them and In sha Allah we'll follow, stay strong. Source: Group page dedicated to the deaths of subject MTR and subject PIRI

The final concerning observation from these posts is the desire of others to follow and also become martyrs. Of course the genuineness and willingness to follow through cannot be determined. In addition, there is a clear gender equality here with both subjects elevated as martyrs without any sense of male superiority or elevated significance.

Case Study Conclusion

Gender support roles as evident by this case study are by no means reduced to secondary importance or significance. This was evident even after both subjects had been 'martyred' and elevated equally.

Also important is the fact that Islamic radicalisation especially for female support roles requires no commitment to violence or even necessarily condoning forms of violence. Commitment to Allah, fellow Muslims and of course the next life was much more important. However, a commitment to violence is not always lacking in women as evident in the second key role.

WOMEN AS JIHAD WARRIORS

Cyber recruiters are also getting more sophisticated and more specific in their targeting approach. One such example is that in recent years there has been an increasing emphasis on the role of women in the jihadi movement (Sutten, 2009). The work of Sue Mahan and Pamela Griset has categorized women's roles under four dimensions: sympathizers, spies, warriors, and dominant forces (Sutten, 2009). What is particularly concerning is the increasing emphasis of women in the more active and militarised roles as warriors or dominant leaders. In an analysis of 46 incidents by women from 1969 to 2005, Davis (2006) noted that women in terrorism were often cast in stereotypical, namely male support roles. Additionally, Davis (2006) saw an emerging trend that women were becoming increasingly involved in terrorism and that there strategic and tactical value was being increasingly recognised by leaders of the Jihadi movement such as the wife of Sheik Ayman Al Zawahiri.

Weimann (2010) argues that since 2004 there has been an increasing targeting of females for suicide bombings using a variety of narrowcasting strategies that include websites specifically targeted at women as well as online magazines. In 2011 a new women's jihadi magazine *Al-Shamikha* was released, which was written in Arabic (Dickson, 2011). Overall, these data trends along with recent analysis by other researchers support the increasing trend in jihad to recruit women (Mastarom & Yasin, 2010). A case in point is the fact that in the US in 2010, the number of women charged with terrorism related offences doubled as terrorists are increasingly recognising the role women can play ranging from support operations to martyrdom ("American Women and Terrorism: A Growing Trend", 2010). In addition to the increasing numbers of Palestinian women volunteering for suicide attacks, the UK Commons home affairs committee heard evidence that al Qaeda is specifically targeting British women for violent attacks (Wilson, 2012).

Colleen LaRose, known online as 'Jihad Jane' or 'Fatima Rose' was, according to neighbors, an average Pennsylvania housewife ("Pennsylvania Woman Charged for Recruiting Terrorists," 2010). LaRose was recruited through the internet as she indicated her willingness to help the Muslim people ("Profile:

'Jihad Jane' from Main Street," 2010). LaRose was not only prepared to take on a warrior role and kill Swedish cartoonist Lars Vilks who made fun of the prophet Mohammed ("Profile: 'Jihad Jane' from Main Street," 2010), but she also took on the role as dominant leader as she recruited others for this terrorist plot ("American Women and Terrorism: A Growing Trend ", 2010). LaRose herself boasted about her potential advantages of being able to blend in as a blonde headed, blue eyed female amongst the Swedish population ("American Women and Terrorism: A Growing Trend, " 2010; "Pennsylvania Woman Charged for Recruiting Terrorists," 2010). Even her own boyfriend Kurt Gorman was very surprised but did concede that LaRose was very isolated spending most of her time inside the house and of course on the internet ("Profile: 'Jihad Jane' from Main Street," 2010). Having been recruited online, LaRose was able to also recruit others. This included a second female Jamie Paulin-Ramirez, a trainee nurse from Colorado (Foley, 2010).

The question arises, what is the cause of this increasingly active involvement by women? More traditional support of a mujahideen warrior was becoming more and more difficult as the physical space occupied by terrorist groups began to shrink. In order to adapt, there was a need to develop more covert activities coupled with an increasing reliance on the internet and social media.

Despite this trend, social media evidence for this role was more limited yet still present. Overt images of female warriors such as in Figure 9 wearing the full Burqa and carrying rifles while present were not overly common.

Figure 9. The Female warrior in full Burqa

More common were subtle and hidden messages by female participants that required an understanding of key discourses and symbols and what they meant. One of the most common symbols was that of the green birds or flying in the heart of green birds which symbolises death by martyrdom. As illustrated in Figure 10, this symbolism is used in not only a very covert way but also a very feminine way.

In order to better capture how females participate or are recruited for active roles, a second case study will be presented highlighting an attempt to recruit a female for a more active role in jihad.

CASE STUDY: A WOMEN RECRUITED TO BE A WARRIOR

The female 'participant' was found on an anti-government, anti-new world order group page. For brevity, female subject as the target of recruitment will be termed FJR (female jihad recruit). In terms of the political context at the time of this case study, the interventions in Iraq and Afghanistan were winding down yet very much in turmoil, and events in Syria had not yet begun.

Shifting Identities and Conversion

Attempting to shift the identity of FJR and achieve conversion was a major theme that also incorporated a number of subthemes or subcategories that emerged when coding. All were important in shifting FJR towards not only conversion but also a path of radicalisation. Once FJR was engaged and determined that she was open-minded she was asked to join other open Islamic groups that while not overtly radical, did indicate a disposition toward radicalism. Not only is the discourse itself important here but also observations of the process. FJR was welcomed and 'swarmed' by many group members who were willing to interact, answer questions and share the 'truth'. Members demonstrated patience and persistence. Open-mindedness was seen as a virtue, while members showed kindness to FJR to help her embrace her new group identity (See Table 1).

Figure 10. Covert and feminine message promoting martyrdom

Table 1. Key categorisations in achieving conversion

Category	Sample Post
Open -mindedness	[MashaAllaah its so good to see that ur so openminded, unbiased and uninfluenced by that zionist media that is soo against the Haqq.] [BA0503] [Of course you have ur own free will and can see the Haqq for urself in sha Allaah.. just keep looking for it but hurry up coz we never know when we breath our last] [ur free to decide whether you think thats the Haqq or not. Remember allah says" there is no compulsion in religion" ... so you can never be forced into accepting Islam]
Kindness and patience in the search for knowledge	[My sweet FJR you are always welcome to ask questions in the search for Hagg] [Honey let me know when you start to see the truth]
Group identity	[You need to promise to guide others in the search for truth] [Posting such links may means others think you are extreme or terrorist wannabe. For me this is an honour]

Focus on Discourse of Oppression and Injustice against Muslims

Oppression against Muslims and the promotion of grievances was perhaps the most significant theme found on the Islamic group page. What was also interesting here is the interfacing with other forms of media including Western media. Posts included graphic photos of victims including children, many YouTube videos and news stories of war crimes or abuses were a common topic. Well before attempts to convert FJR, she was exposed to many of these posts within the group. Examples are given in Table 2. These are all from Western media sources and were a large part of posts that all members including FJR were constantly exposed to. Clearly, such use of media is designed to impact the affective dimension of members of the group. The danger herein is that when members do go to a YouTube link they also have the opportunity to follow similar stories/videos.

Table 2. Media links on Facebook highlighting oppression

Media Type	Link and Details
Western media – Rolling Stone online magazine Includes graphic video and photographs	'Motorcycle Kill' http://www.rollingstone.com/politics/photos/motorcyle-kill-20110327/0692075 Story of two US soldiers who hunted down and killed 2 Afghan 'civilians'. Although the status of the men killed is in question, the methods used including use of video and mutilation of corpse was not.
Western news media - Reuters	Sixth U.S. soldier implicated in murder of Afghans http://www.reuters.com/article/2011/05/18/us-soldiers-crimes-idUSTRE74H0C920110518 Sixth U.S. soldier charged with direct involvement in the murder of unarmed Afghan civilians
YouTube of Western media CNN	CNN: Israeli soldiers sexually abused Palestinian children http://www.youtube.com/watch?v=SEUAPDeLkpU Interview about the alleged abuse of Palestinian children by Israel soldiers during an interrogation.
YouTube	US soldier speaks the truth - war crimes exposed "please share" http://www.youtube.com/watch?v=HQ3NAzlp2KM
YouTube of US 60 minutes story	Madeleine Albright Defends Mass-Murder of Iraqi Children (500,000 Children dead) http://www.youtube.com/watch?v=x4PgpbQfxgo&feature=share

What was also salient about this category was the volume of these posts. Essentially, recruiters and sympathizers achieved a form of media saturation where stories were at the very least posted daily. At times they were much more frequent than this and came in swarms as frequently as every ten minutes. These posts did achieve their goal stimulating numerous responses of anger and condemnation.

Discourse of Islam as a Fight against Oppression and Corruption

Coupled with the discourse of oppression is the need to take up the fight against all these forms of oppression and injustice. This form of discourse was used in the early stages of interaction with FJR and paralleled her anti-NWO beliefs. Such discourse emphasises the need to take action. Additionally, there is also the criticism of what are seen as 'soft' forms of Islam that fail to take action (See Figure 11). It is this discourse that feeds off media representing oppression and these two aspects combine in order to radicalise the target FJR.

Controlling the Message

Following the apparent successful conversion (cannot be verified) of FJR to Islam after an observed period of four weeks, one important aspect was very clear, the need to control the message given to the 'new' convert. Rather than being encouraged to read and study the Qur'an, the Tahweed was recommended as the starting point. This document emphasises not only the unity and oneness of God but also the unity of Muslims. In addition, subject FJR was given links to a number of radical Islamic websites as shown in Figure 11. Of particular emphasis were mujahedeen narratives that included martyrs (Figure 12).

Figure 11. Discourse encouraging Islam as a fight against oppression

[....May Allah guide me and you to the absolute truth free from unjust, tyranny, corruption, May Allah bless us both in our fight for freedom.]
[Muhammad was known as both Nabiy al-Rahma (The Prophet of Mercy) as well as Nabiy alMalhama (The Prophet of Slaughter)]
[We cannot tolerate any kind of insult or oppression against Islam or its followers and we have to take action]
["O Muslims - For how much longer? An outcry to the Ummah? There should be NO MORE SOFT ISLAM: O MUSLIMS! How will you Deny the call of ALLAH?"]
[..now is NOT the time to hand out brochures and cakes..; Now is the time to handout 7.62x39mm bullets]
Source: Semi radical Islamic group page

Figure 12. Some of the websites to which FJR was directed

> http://www.ansar1.info - *News Of The Ummah & Mujahideen, Books, Videos, Files & Various Other Benefits For The Muslimeen*
> http://kavkazcenter.com/ - *(Mainly News Of The Ummah & Mujahideen)*
> http://shahamat.info/english/ - *(Mainly News Of The Ummah & Mujahideen)*
> http://www.jhuf.net/index.php - *(Mainly News Of The Ummah & Mujahideen)*
> http://theunjustmedia.com/ - *(Mainly News Of The Ummah & Mujahideen)*
> http://www.dinhaqq.info/vb/... - *(Mainly News Of The Ummah & Mujahideen)*
> http://caravansofmartyrs.at... - *(Stories & Biographies Of The Martyrs)*
>
> *Source: Semi radical Islamic group page. Links posted by mentor of FJR*

Reference to Key Terrorist Figures

In addition to the above links, subsequent posts also made regular reference to key terrorist leaders Osama bin Laden and Anwar al-Awlaki, viewing bin Laden as a martyr and al-Awlaki as a great Islamic leader. Subject FJR was especially encouraged to study the work of al-Awlaki and was given many posts with links to his videos on YouTube.

Beginning with bin Laden, he is viewed as a martyr who was not afraid to speak the truth. However, this is not a view that is shared by all Muslims and radical Islamists are very critical of other Muslims who support the death of bin Laden. Figure 13 is a post where radical Islamists respond to a post by

Figure 13. Responses to Muslim support of bin Laden's death

> *[ADAMS joins the nation and the world to thank the brave men and women serving in the military and intelligence fields whose work to secure our nation have now brought the leader of Al-Qaeda, Osama Bin Laden the perpetrator of the 9/11 attacks, to Justice. We hope his death will bring some relief to victims. www.theamericanmuslim.org]*
> *RESPONSES*
> *[Sickening disgraceful shameful I could go on for hours, what a bunch of scum!!!... how a Muslim can rejoice of the killing of his fellow Muslim (no matter how sinful he could be) by the hand of their common enemy?]*
> *[O ye who believe! Take not for friends (awliyaa) unbelievers rather than believers]*
> *[O American... I will tell you today about a man whose story is like a legend... and he is a legend indeed... a legend that was witnessed by the whole world...]*
> *Source: Semi radical Islamic group page*

American Muslims that support the bringing of bin Laden to justice. The impassioned responses reflect the importance of bin Laden as a symbolic figure of the struggle of Muslims.

The role of al-Awlaki played a very important role in the recruitment of FJR. Radical Islamists targeted subject FJR with the works of al-Awlaki before her apparent conversion to Islam. Such an early introduction to the teachings of such a radical figure demonstrates the confidence that extremists have in the power of al-Awlakis's discourse (Figure 14). Radical Islamists are happy to promote al-Awlaki as an Islamic preacher and scholar who is highly respected amongst the mujahedeen.

Discourse of Unity

As previously stated, subject FJR was first directed toward the Tahweed. This concept of the oneness of God was critical in challenging Western Christian notions of the Trinity, especially for this particular case study. However, it was observed that this was only part of the picture, another key theme that emerged in the discourse of radicalization was unity amongst Muslims. Specifically, Tawheed al Itabaa, as mentioned in one particular post stresses the unity in following the prophet Muhammad. This discourse integrates with the fight against oppression and calls for all Muslims to unite in this struggle. Many posts not only call for Muslims to join this fight but to show unity in doing so (See Figure 15).

Figure 14. Sample posts directed toward FJR promoting Anwar al-Awlaki

[Yes, hes a scholar.. you must be knowing about him. Hes a quite famous "Terrorist" Hes my fav scholar MashaAllaah he always speaks the Haq and ull never see him speaking anything out of his will. Hes the only man i know after osama bin laden twho speaks the Haqq(truth)... start with "the hereafter series" .. that'll give you a precise description about the purpose of life and queries pertaining to the afterlife in sha Allaah]
[Yea Anwar Al awlaki is an islamic preacher who has viewpoints about the revival of the islamic nation and religion.]
[pls do.. things might come to light on ur side of the world/faith after listening to him and few other islamic scholars, InsyaAllah]
[The inspirational sheikh Anwar Al-Awlaki (H), who is an American citizen residing in South Yemen among the mujahidin of the AQAP (Al Qaeda in the Arabian Peninsula).
He is probably the most wanted man since the martyrdom of sheikh Usama (R). He was named 'the Osama of the net' due to his famous blog where he preached haqq n Jihaad.]
[Imam Anwar Al-Awlaki Increasingly Seen as the Next Bin Laden.Subha'allah - that is so true! People are saying that he's the next bin laden of the internet... May Allah swt protect the Muslims on haq and guide them all]
www.kavkazcenter.com
Anwar al Awlaki: 44 ways of supporting Jihad
Source: Semi radical Islamic group page

Figure 15. Posts calling for unity amongst Muslims

> *[As Muslims we must follow Tawheed al Itabaa and be united in our fight as followers of the great prophet]*
> *[Surah Al An'aam Ch 6 v. 159 keep away from those who bring division within Islam]*
> *[I find it shocking that any Muslim would have the "audacity" to make du'aa for the Muslims suffering around the World, yet are ever so eager to distance themselves from the courageous ones seeking to change our condition! Let alone call them "Extremists" or "Terrorists"! Wake up! You are Muslims! You believe in One God!]*
> *[OUR PRESENT SITUATION NEEDS OUR UNITY TO ELEVATE ALLAH'S WORD: "LA ILAHA ILLALLAH"]*
> *In response to heated debate about abuses of Pakistani Army:*
> *[as muslims we have manners. no cursing againts one another pls... and as we all BELIEVE AND HAVE FAITH in ALLAH.... pls, dont get too carried away... we are still brothers and sisters in islam.]*
> *Source: Semi radical Islamic group page*

Females were especially significant in their role in attempting to bring unity especially given that posts promoting sectarianism were almost exclusively male initiated and posts promoting unity were dominated by but not limited to female participants.

Nevertheless, despite such discourse there was still evidence of many divisions amongst Islamic extremists. These included the loyalties of the Pakistan army in relation to Islam, the role of certain Western anti-government figures in relation to their position on Israel and even the position of al Qaeda. In fact certain Iranian Muslims were openly critical of al Qaeda arguing that they were originally lined with the US and do nothing to support the cause of the Palestinians. As a response to such heated debates, one of FJR's 'mentors' tried to achieve unity (See last post in Figure 15. However, within the group, some members quickly left demonstrating that group identity within Islamic extremism may not necessarily be as broad and robust as it is projected to be.

Discourses on Martyrdom

Although no specific demands or even suggestions were made to subject FJR about martyrdom, she was exposed to a wide range of propaganda, links and posts promoting the virtues of martyrdom (See Figure 16). Once again, these were very much related to narratives of grievance and oppression.

The Overall Recruitment Strategy

This case study demonstrated a sophisticated narrowcasting strategy with the targeting of specific interests, in this case a sense of alienation with Western governments and the belief in exploitation and conspiracy. Such starting beliefs in this case made it easier to target the subject FJR.

Figure 16. Posts relating to the discourse of martyrdom

> *[Sacrifice comes in many shapes, forms and levels, it can be performed through many different channels, but there is no doubt that the sacrificing of one's soul for the sake of Allaah in order to defeat His enemies and support Islaam is the very highest level. This is of course Shahaadah, or martyrdom. The Prophet sallallaahu 'alaihi wa sallam]*
> *[O Muslims! Achieving noble and lofty objectives require enormous sacrifices in proportion. There can be no doubt that the higher an objective is, the greater its sacrifice must be.]*
> *[The caravan of the martyrs Do you hear the calling of the ones that past before you? The call of bravery and succession of everlasting smiles. They raced for the front line, eager to seek their lord's face, they divorced the dunyah to flap their wings around the heaven's gates with honorable grace, they wanted a beautiful ending not one of disgrace.]*
> *Source: Semi radical Islamic group page*

The female in this case study already had a group identity that shared many attributes with the jihad movement and as such was a logical target for recruiters. A strong disaffection for Western governments and a belief in the fact that such governments are oppressive and have an alternative agenda strongly parallels the discursive radical Islamist agenda that Muslims are the subject of persecution and abuse by Western governments. Hence, recruiters started with subject's FJR initial discourse on the NWO and shifted this to an anti-Israeli, pro jihadist perspective. In addition, recruiters also challenged Western Christian perspectives of the Trinity in order to shift FJR towards Islam.

This case study found that initial contact was low pressure, supportive and commended an open-minded attitude. Nonetheless, persistence and a willingness to surround and support the potential recruit were also evident. Patience was shown with questions asked by FJR. In response, there was also a development of the radical attitudes of FJR with support shown for radical postings. Surprisingly, FJR was introduced to fairly radical Islamic material quite early in her contact with radical Islamists. Nevertheless, the distinction does need to be made that this particular female FJR already demonstrated radical anti-government views and appeared to embrace the radical material provided.

It also needs to be made clear that such radical material was framed within a broader context of what can best be described as 'media saturation' of news stories of Western aggression towards Muslims. Interestingly, most of these actually came from Western sources and well established news outlets such as Reuters and CNN. This demonstrates the interfacing power of Facebook and the ability to post videos from YouTube as well as links to other news sites. Such propaganda clearly targeted the affective dimension and is particularly salient with females given the strong responses to such postings.

Due to the relatively short term nature of this particular case study research, no specific demands were made of FJR, yet she did appear committed to the ideological cause. However, it is important to note that the females that were 'mentoring' FJR uploaded many posts on the virtues of jihad and martyrdom. Their images also supported a more direct role in the jihad movement with female figures holding weapons a common image and theme. Mentors strongly supported the teachings on Anwar al- Awlaki supporting the notion that he is one of the most critical figures in the online jihad movement.

Overall, an analysis of the major themes reveals strong discursive interrelationships. Subject FJR's anti-government discourse is targeted, embraced and redirected towards the oppression of Muslims and the need for Muslims to unite and resist. The path of resistance is also directed towards the discourse of jihad and in particular the writings of al-Awlaki. It is however, important to note that this is a context specific model based on the findings of a single case study.

SOCIAL MEDIA JIHAD AND FEMALE GENDER UTILITY

In looking at online radicalisation over a period of several years it was evident that a level of fluidity was present in female gender identity. Further to this, female gender roles were reflective of the socio-political context as well as how male gender roles were being reflected. While many perceptions and stereotypes exist about how gender roles are not only constructed but also played out, often these do not reflect the reality on social media which indicates very active forms of female agency. Overall, female power relations cannot be merely constructed in terms of male servitude and reflect more complex identity politics.

A longitudinal study of social media provides important insights into not only how radicalisation changes over time but also how female identity is located within this changing dynamic. One aspect that was evident is the fluidity of female gender identity and the level of utility that was encapsulated within this identity as opposed to stable male identity of the jihad warrior or mujahideen fighter. Female gender roles were highly varied and took into account the ability of extremist males to enact their primary gender role as the jihad fighter.

Success in female identity construction for Islamic extremists on social media was found to be in a sense context dependent. Limiting the amount of physical space for Islamic extremists following invasions of Afghanistan and Iraq also limited opportunities. It was during this time in particular that female roles in military action were enhanced and in particular lone wolf actions. When opportunities opened up in Syria and in particular Islamic State for male extremists the demand for women in combat roles was reduced. That is not to say that this role was eliminated but merely became less of a focus as attention shifted back to more traditional male support roles.

Many stereotypes exist with female gender identity particularly in relation to Islamic extremism (Afshar, Aitkin & Franks, 2005). Most significantly is the notion of repression often associated with the wearing of the burqa (Pedersen & Hartley, 2012). Additionally, the nature of the female oppressed by the male is also commonly cited with many thinking that female roles are dictated by males (Afshar, Aitkin & Franks, 2005). However, social media evidence suggests the opposite, namely, it is women who actively construct their own roles and situate themselves within the context of Islamic extremism.

In the contested world of gender identities there are Islamic women including those is extreme circles that can best be described as feminists (Afshar, Aitkin & Franks, 2005). Social media evidence suggested that it was women who constructed their own identity rather than having it imposed by men. As evident in the aforementioned case studies women often associated together, met together and reached out to other women. Construction of gender identity was often developed in these circles and therefore was also strongly supported within this context. Furthermore, high levels of female agency were also evident on social media including both posts and interactions reinforcing that female gender identity is constructed with uniquely gender circles that give women a sense of power.

No discussion on female agency is complete without making at least some reference to power. Foucault (2006) views power as a circular relationship that flows rather than as something belonging to a person in authority. Such a view is more suitable for analysing social media which has a very networked structure. Moreover, power is constructed using discourses and schemas of knowledge that are reproduced throughout certain circles of influence (Foucault, 1975).

On social media, in extremist circles, it is females that are active in constructing discourses on their role in online jihad. Even the latest outreach for Islamic State brides is done by other females indicating an active role in the construction of discourses that govern power relations. While over time, these online schemas of knowledge have changed in response to broader socio-political context, what has remained stable is the role of women in constructing these discourses governing how women should participate in jihad and even martyrdom.

CONCLUSION

Western perceptions of Islamic extremism often paints women as oppressed and subservient to male roles. While the reality in different contexts is beyond the scope of this paper, the online social media environment paints a very different picture. Women take a very active role in their online identity within the context of Islamic extremism.

This chapter has focused on two main identities found within the context of Facebook: first, the wife or more accurately, the supporter of the warrior husband; and second, the women as a warrior in their own right. Interestingly a commitment to violence was not a priority for female gender roles. Instead, discourses often circumvented violence by focusing on issues such as injustice as well as a commitment to the next life through martyrdom.

Furthermore, female gender identity was found to be much more fluid than male identity and responsive to socio-political context and limitations placed on extremist groups. Essentially, the more freedom extremist groups had to operate the more the female role shifted to that of supporter, whilst high levels of restrictions on groups necessitated more active roles from female participants. Whichever role is emphasised, it is females that recruit and promote these roles.

Overall, a more fluid and networked sense of power is more appropriate for understanding female gender identity online. While the burqa may symbolise oppression to the West it symbolises a choice of one's identity within extremist circles including a fluid identity between wife and warrior as need necessitates.

REFERENCES

Afshar, H., Aitkin, R., & Franks, M. (2005). Feminisms, Islamophobia and Identities. *Political Studies*, *53*(2), 262–283. doi:10.1111/j.1467-9248.2005.00528.x

American Women and Terrorism: A Growing Trend (2010). *Anti-Defamation League*. Retrieved from http://www.adl.org/main_Terrorism/american_women_terrorists.htm

Awan, A. N. (2007). Virtual jihadist media. *European Journal of Cultural Studies*, *10*(3), 389–408. doi:10.1177/1367549407079713

Conway, M. (2006). Terrorism and the Internet: New Media—New Threat? *Parliamentary Affairs*, *59*(2), 283–298. doi:10.1093/pa/gsl009

Davis, J. (2006). Women and Terrorism in Radical Islam: Planners, perpetrators, patrons? *Centre for Foreign Policy Studies*. Retrieved from http://centreforforeignpolicystudies.dal.ca/pdf/gradsymp06/Davis.pdf

Dickson, C. (2011). Al Qaeda's New Women's Magazine. *The Atlantic Wire*. Retrieved from http://www.theatlanticwire.com/global/2011/03/al-qaedas-new-womens-magazine/35808/

Eight British school girls travel to Syria to become IS brides. (2015). *The Tribune*. Retrieved from http://tribune.com.pk/story/843348/eight-british-school-girls-travel-to-syria-to-become-is-brides/

Foley, S. (2010). Second US woman swept up in Jihad Jane murder claims. *The Independent*. Retrieved from http://www.independent.co.uk/news/world/americas/second-us-woman-swept-up-in-jihad-jane-murder-claims-1921435.html

Foucault, M. (1975). *Discipline & Punish: The Birth of the Prison*. New York: Vintage Books.

Foucault, M. (2006). Lectures at the College de France 1973-1974. In J. LaGrange (Ed.), *Michel Foucault: Psychiatric Power* (G. Burchell, Trans.). New York: Palgrave MacMillan.

Jenkins, B. M. (2010). The al Qaeda-Inspired Terrorist Threat: An Appreciation of the Current Situation Retrieved from http://www.rand.org/content/dam/rand/pubs/testimonies/2010/RAND_CT353.pdf

Leiken, R. S. (2005). Europe's Angry Muslims. *Foreign Affairs*, *84*(4), 120–135. doi:10.2307/20034425

Mastarom, T. R., & Yasin, N. A. M. (2010). The Internet: Avenue for Women Jihadi "Participation". Retrieved from http://dr.ntu.edu.sg/bitstream/handle/10220/6649/RSIS0882010.pdf?sequence=1

Matusitz, J. (2008). Similarities between terrorist networks in antiquity and present-day cyberterrorist networks. *Trends in Organized Crime*, *11*(2), 183–199. doi:10.1007/s12117-008-9034-0

Mbakwe, C., & Cunliffe, D. (2007). Hypermedia Seduction: Further Exploration of the Process of "Seductive" Online User Interactions. In B. Ganor, K. von-Knop, & C. A. M. Duarte (Eds.), *Hypermedia seduction for terrorist recruiting* (pp. 207–230). Amsterdam: IOS Press.

McNeal, G. S. (2007). Cyber embargo: countering the internet jihad (in German) (Conference Paper). *Case Western Reserve University School of Law*, 39(3), 789-826.

Mendez, D. (2008, February 15). Facebook and Terrorism: a love hate relationship. Tech.Blorge. Retrieved from http://tech.blorge.com/Structure:%20/2008/02/15/facebook-and-terrorism-a-love-hate-relationship-2/

Michael, G. (2009). Adam Gadahn and Al-Qaeda's Internet Strategy. *Middle East Policy*, *16*(3), 135–152. doi:10.1111/j.1475-4967.2009.00409.x

Murphy, D. M., & White, J. F. (2007). Propaganda: Can a Word Decide a War? *Parameters*, *37*(3), 15–27.

O'Rourke, S. (2007). Virtual Radicalisation: Challenges for Police. *Paper presented at the 8th Australian Information Warfare and Security Conference*, Perth.

Pedersen, A., & Hartley, L. K. (2012). Prejudice against Muslim Australians: The role of values, gender and consensus. *Journal of Community & Applied Social Psychology*, *22*(3), 239–255. doi:10.1002/casp.1110

Pennsylvania Woman Charged for Recruiting Terrorists. (2010). *Newsmixer.net.* Retrieved from http://www.newsmixer.net/politics/pennsylvania-woman-charged-for-recruiting-terrorists/

Profile: 'Jihad Jane' from Main Street. (2010). *BBC News.* Retrieved from http://news.bbc.co.uk/2/hi/8561888.stm

Sutten, M. L. (2009). *The Rising Importance of Women in Terrorism and the Need to Reform Counter-terrorism Strategy.* Army Command and General Staff Coll Fort Leavenworth Ks School of Advanced Military Studies.

von-Knop, K. (2007). Countering Web-based Islamist Narratives: Conceptualizing an Information War and a Counter-propaganda Campaign. In B. Ganor, K. von-Knop, & C. A. M. Duarte (Eds.), *Hypermedia seduction for terrorist recruiting* (pp. 169–187). Amsterdam: IOS Press.

Weimann, G. (2008). The Psychology of Mass-Mediated Terrorism. *The American Behavioral Scientist*, *52*(1), 69–86. doi:10.1177/0002764208321342

Weimann, G. (2010). Terror on Facebook, Twitter, and YouTube. *The Brown Journal of World Affairs*, *16*(2), 45–54.

Wilson, G. (2012, February 9). Al-Qaeda bid for Brit girl bombers. *The Sun*. Retrieved from http://www.thesun.co.uk/sol/homepage/news/politics/4110182/Al-Qaeda-bid-for-Brit-girl-bombers.html

Chapter 12
Exploring Female Hispanic Consumers' Adoption of Mobile Social Media in the U.S.

Kenneth C. C. Yang
University of Texas at El Paso, USA

Yowei Kang
Kainan University, Taiwan

ABSTRACT

U.S. Hispanic purchasing power is estimated to reach $1.5 trillion by 2015. Because of this growing importance, there has been a surge of Hispanic consumer behavior research in recent years. Latinas account for 49.5 percent of the U.S. Hispanic population and increasingly become tech-savvy to adopt new mobile social networking technologies. In spite of their growing importance, there still lacks a thorough examination on factors affecting female Hispanic consumers' decision-making process related to mobile social media applications. This book chapter collected qualitative in-depth interview data that were interpreted from Technology Acceptance Model (TAM) and TAM2 as theoretical lenses. Four major themes were identified: 1) family and peer influence; 2) perceived functional benefits of mobile social media; 3) Latinas as a primary decision-maker to adopt; 4) cultural and sub-cultural influence.

DOI: 10.4018/978-1-5225-0010-0.ch012

INTRODUCTION

Emerging Hispanic Female Consumer Market

The population of Hispanics has grown to 52 million in the United States (The Nielsen Company, 2013a). Hispanic purchasing power has grown from $210 billion in 1990 to over $957 billion in 2010, $1.2 trillion in 2013, and estimated to reach $1.5 trillion by 2015 (The Nielsen Company, 2013a; Rodriguez, 2015; Synovate, 2010; U.S. Census Bureau, 2011; Villarrel, 2014). The 2015 estimate is predicted to account for 11% of the total US purchasing power, according to the Selig Center (Villarrel, 2014). Hispanic women, also known as *Latinas*, are found to be the growth engine of the U.S. female population and are expected to represent 30% of the total female population in the U.S. by 2060 (The Nielsen Company, 2013a). Female Hispanic consumers account for 49.5 percent of the U.S. Hispanic population (U.S. Census Bureau, 2012). Those who fall between 20 to 29 years old are 16.15%, while those whose age is above 65 years old are 6.7% (U.S. Census Bureau, 2012). *Latinas*, as a consumer segment with growth importance, are found to be more educated, connected, tech-savvy, independent, and with increasing economic power (The Nielsen Company, 2013a, b). In the Nielsen's report (2013a, b), *Latina Power Shift*, eighty-six percent of Latina women are found to make important household purchasing decisions, such as auto, home, and financial services (The Nielsen Company, 2013a, b). Related to the adoption of new technologies, the same Nielsen report found that 33% of home electronics and 38% of personal electronics are determined primarily by female Hispanic consumers alone (The Nielsen Company, 2013b).

Compared with White and Black ethnic groups, Hispanic consumers have similar adoption patterns of Internet and cell phone from 2009 to 2012 (Lopez, Gonzalez-Barrera, & Patten, 2013). According to Pew Internet Research Project (2014), 92% of Hispanic consumers own cell phone. Cell phone ownership among female Hispanic consumers is 88% (Pew Internet Research Project, 2014). Latinas who have adopted Internet technology are reported to be more likely to own their smartphone (77%), when compared with non-Hispanic white counterparts (55%) (The Nielsen Company, 2013b). Because of the tendency to adopt new communication technologies, 56% of female Hispanic consumers use social networking to share information while 44% of them use mobile apps in their smartphone devices (The Nielsen Company, 2013b).

BACKGROUND

The Convergence of Mobile and Social Media

Since its introduction in the late 20th century, mobile communications and social media have played an indispensable part in contemporary human experiences. According to a recent Pew Internet Research Project report (2014, January), 58% of American adults own a smartphone, while 90% of American adults have a cell phone. Many also own Wi-Fi enabled e-Readers (32%) and tablets (42%) (Pew Internet Research Project, 2014). Cell phone ownership is observably correlated with age, education level, and household income (Pew Internet Research Project, 2014). Those who are younger tend to own cell phone. Over 97% of those who are below 50 years old own cell phone, when compared with 81% of those above 50 years old (Pew Internet Research Project, 2014). Over 90% of those who receive college education and with a higher household income ($50,000 above) tend to own cell phone (Pew Internet Research Project, 2014).

Social networking sites such as Facebook are developed as "a social utility that helps people communicate more efficiently with their friends, family and coworkers" (Facebook, 2004). With the popularity of mobile devices, social networking media have obtained their mobility by allowing users to check their social media applications anytime they prefer. Adding to the increasingly interconnected media eco-systems is the development of mobile social media as a new communication platform (Häsel, 2011). As Lee (2013) observes, the convergence of smartphone and social networking services (henceforth, SNSs) has enabled users to access their Facebook and other social media platforms anywhere and anytime, which is likely to increase overall usage. The latest report on digital, social and mobile media (We Are Social, 2015) confirms this diffusion trend at a global scale. The global penetration rate of mobile devices is 51% (3.649 billion unique mobile users) (We Are Social, 2015). Active mobile social media users account for 1.685 billion of the world penetration (equal to 21% penetration rate) (We Are Social, 2015). In the U.S., the penetration rate of mobile social media has reached 51% (We Are Social, 2015). According to Nielsen (2014 cited in Sondermon, 2014), smartphone users spend 28% of the time on social media apps.

The growing popularity of mobile social media has been observed as one of the main catalysts to generate new applications and activities that are developed to target Hispanic online users. For example, Briabe Mobile (2014) launched its mobile-social platform for smartphone, *Latina Glam*, to target female Hispanic consumers by providing contents matching the passions and needs to this emerging segment. The growing interests in female Hispanic consumers have generated reports on why they use social media (eMarketer, 2014). According to a 2014 report, *Connected Latinas: 10 Facts About Acculturated Latinas and Social Media Usage*, "keep in touch with family/friends" (86%), "to receive exclusive offers, coupons or other discounts" (82%), and "follow the activities of my friends and families" (79%) are found to be the top three reasons of Latinas' social media usage (cited in eMarketer, 2014). The least important reasons are "meet or network with professional contacts" (58%), "meet new friends" (51%), and "play games" (41%) (cited in eMarketer, 2014). After reviewing the literature, there still lacks a thorough examination on factors affecting female Hispanic consumers' decision-making process related to mobile social media applications. In this chapter, the researcher will present qualitative data from Hispanic consumers from the border region in the U.S. Southwest to identify themes and key variables in affecting consumers' decision-making process through an in-depth interview method.

MAIN FOCUS OF THE CHAPTER

Issues, Controversies, Problems

The study of technology adoption behaviors derives its theoretical foundation from diffusion of innovation (Rogers, 1995), consumer behavior (Gatignon & Robertson, 1985), information systems research

(Boyer, 2003; Davis, 1989; Knol & Stroeken, 2001; Vannoy & Palvia, 2010) and sociology (Rogers, 1995; Wejnert, 2002). This chapter investigates the decision-making process of female Hispanic consumers in adopting mobile social media. Therefore, theoretical frameworks that explain consumer decision-making processes in the context of technology adoption are most suitable to explore this phenomenon. Among many theoretical models that investigate the decision-making process, Technology Acceptance Model provides one of the most parsimonious, yet rigorous, theoretical models in explaining technology characteristics and their effects on consumer adoption/use behaviors (Yang, 2005). Citing current research practices by Jupiter and Forrester Research, Vannoy and Palvia (2010) argue that social influence on users play a significant role in explaining consumer adoption behaviors of technologies.

Technology Acceptance Model (TAM) and TAM2

Technology Acceptance Model (TAM, henceforth) was proposed by Davis (1989) to account for consumer technology adoption behavior. TAM has been widely used to explain and understand determinants of consumer acceptance and adoption of technologies (Davis, 1989; Joo & Sang, 2013). TAM has been used to empirically test consumer intention and actual usage behaviors of a variety of technologies both by individuals and organizations (Yang, 2005). Venkatesh and Davis (2000) found that TAM consistently explains 40% of variance in predicting the relationship between consumer attitudes, consumer usage intention and behaviors. Two salient belief factors, "Perceived Usefulness" (PU) and "Perceived Ease of Use" (PEOU), are proposed to explain subsequent behavioral intention and actual use (Joo & Sang, 2013; Yang, 2005). After adding social-level influence (such as subjective norms and image) and work-related variables (such as job relevance, output quality, and result demonstration), an Extended TAM (TAM2, henceforth) was developed by Venkatesh and Davis (2000). The theoretical foundation of TAM/TAM2 is based on Fishbein and Ajzen's (1975) Theory of Reasoned Action (TRA). According to TRA, an individual's behavior is prompted by his/her behavioral intention as a result of attitudes and beliefs (Fishbein & Ajzen, 1975; Joo & Sang, 2013).

Van der Heijden (2003) posited that TAM is composed of two critical belief components are proposed to account of a user's adoption intention and usage behaviors. The first belief variable is "perceived usefulness" (PU, henceforth), defined as "the degree to which a person believes using a particular system would enhance his or her job performance" (van der Heijden, 2003, p. 542). The second belief variable is "perceived-ease-of-use" (PEOU), which is defined as "the degree of to which a person believes that using a particular system would be free of effort" (van der Heijden, 2003, p. 542). In addition to PU and PEOU, "attitude toward using" (AT), "behavioral intention to use" (BI), and "actual system use" (AU) (Legris, Inghamb, & Collerettec, 2003) also determine consumer adoption decision of a variety of technologies. TAM/TAM2 postulates that PU and PEOU mediate the effects of technology characteristics on consumer adoption decisions (Venkatesh & Davis, 2000; Yang, 2005). The linear relationships are represented in both TAM (See Figure 1) and TAM2 (See Figure 2).

With the advent of mobile social media, scholars have applied TAM and TAM2 to empirically test factors determining consumer adoption of these technologies (Verkasalo, López-Nicolás, Molina-Castillo, & Bouwman, 2010). Verkasalo et al. (2010) empirically tested the extended TAM model by examining

Figure 1. Technology Acceptance Model
Source: Davis (1989)

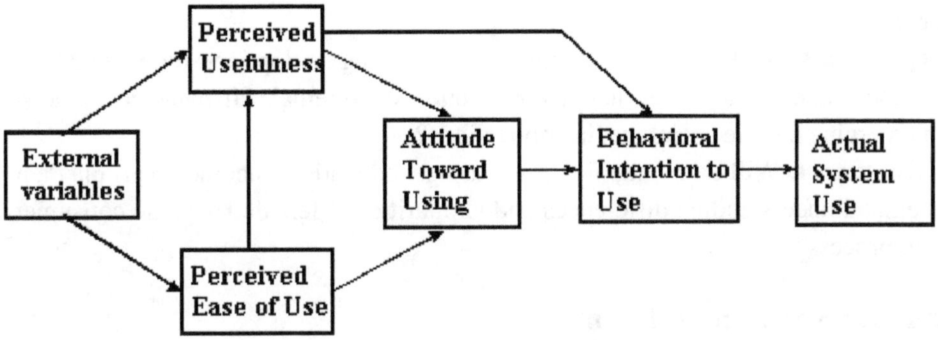

Figure 2. Extended Technology Acceptance Model (TAM2)
Source: Venkatesh & Davis, 2000, p. 188

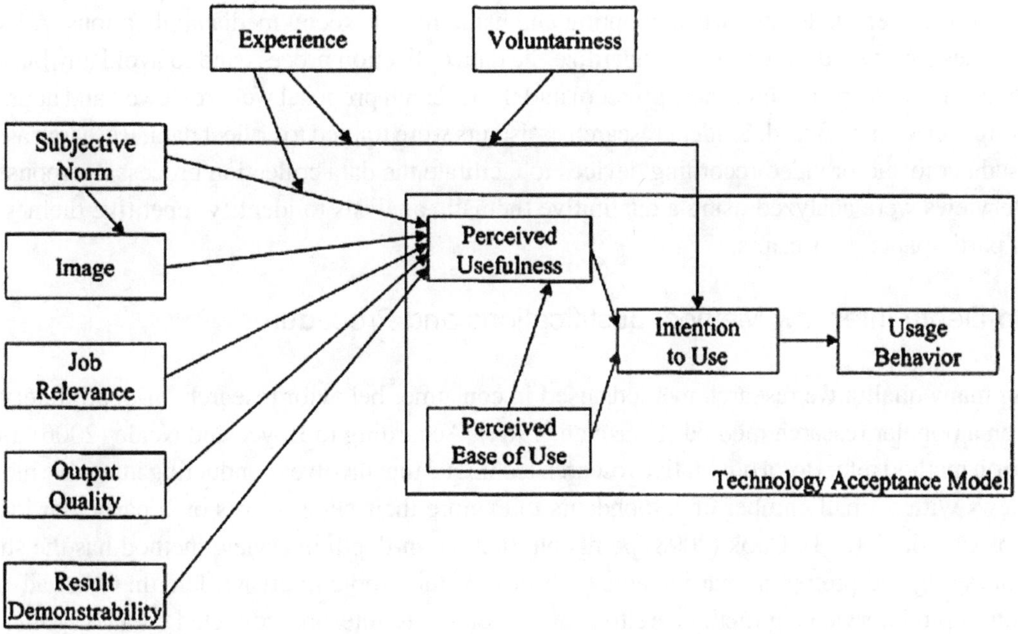

actual usage of mobile applications. Using a panel of 579 smartphone users in Finland, a web-based questionnaire survey was developed to study users and non-users of the technology. Their study found that consumers' perceived usefulness and enjoyment of mobile technologies affect their intention to use mobile apps (Verkasalo et al., 2010).

Research Questions

The interpretative framework of the in-depth interview data will be based on the Extended Technology Acceptance Model (TAM2) (Venkatesh & Davis, 2000) to answer the following research questions:

Research Question 1: Why do consumers decide to use mobile social media applications?
Research Question 2: What are consumers' daily experiences with these emerging mobile social media applications?
Research Question 3: On the basis of the Extended Technology Adoption Model (TAM2), what are the most important external or internal factors to understand female Hispanic consumers' decision to adopt emerging mobile social media applications?
Research Question 4: Will demographics (such as age, education, income level) play any role in explaining and understanding differences and similarities in female Hispanic consumers' decision-making process?

Solutions and Recommendations

Research Method

The study used an in-depth interview method to understand the decision-making process that female Hispanic consumers undertake when adopting and using mobile social media applications. A list of interview questions was developed to standardize the data collection process and to avoid any biases. The informed consent form, the interview protocol and the research proposal were reviewed and approved by the Institution Review Board. Student research assistants were trained to collect data. Research assistants also used audio and/or video recording devices to facilitate the data collection process. Responses from the interviews were analyzed using a qualitative thematic analysis to identify repetitive themes identified in participants' transcripts.

The In-Depth Interview Method: Justifications and Procedures

Among many qualitative research methods used in consumer behavior research, in-depth interviewing has been a popular research method (Hausman, 1984). According to Boyce and Neale (2006), this data collection method refers to "a qualitative research technique that involves conducting intensive individual interviews with a small number of respondents to explore their perspectives on a particular idea, program, or situation" (p. 3). Cook (2008) points out that the in-depth interview method has the strengths of encouraging and prompting participants to discuss a study topic in greater length. Other advantages of the in-depth interviewing method are to provide context to interpret collected data (Boyce & Neale, 2006). Compared with other research methods, this qualitative method enables researchers to collect more thorough information (Boyce & Neale, 2006). Furthermore, the data collection atmosphere is more relaxing (Boyce & Neale, 2006). However, four major limitations are commonly associated with this technique: 1) the data collection process is time-intensive; 2) the need to train research assistants in interviewing techniques; 3) data are not generalizable; 4) bias as a result of data collection process (Boyce & Neale, 2006). As Lazar, Feng, and Hochheiser (2010) summarize the advantages of the in-depth interview method over other social scientific methods:

By asking questions that explore a wide range of concerns about a problem and giving interviewees the freedom to provide detailed responses, researchers can use interviews to gather data that would otherwise be very hard to capture. Given a chance to talk, and questions that encourage reflection and consideration, interviewees may go on at great length, generating ideas and sharing insides that would have been lost to surveys. (p. 178)

In-depth interviewing technique has gradually been used in new technology adoption research (Abdullah, Wahab, & Shamsuddin, 2013; Kindberg, Spasojevic, Fleck, & Sellen, 2005). For example, Abdullah et al. (2013) employed an in-depth interview method to study factors affecting technology adoption behaviors among small to mid-size enterprises in Malaysia. Their study evaluated the effects of external, internal, and business owners' characteristics on the adoption process. Parmelee (2013, 2014) also used in-depth interviews to collect narratives from political journalists during the 2012 presidential campaign to understand how Twitter technology has affected their professional practices and norms. This research method was also used to understand how Latinas consume popular culture and respond to Spanish language in the media (Rojas, 2004). Analyzing the interview transcripts, Rojas (2004) observed that Latinas viewers have ambivalent and conflicting relationship with the television programs that might misrepresent their images.

To standardize the data collection procedures, the following interview questions were developed for research assistants who also received one-hour intensive training.

Question 1: "Please share something about yourself such as your age, ethnicity, educational background, marital status, occupation, etc."

Probing Question: If you believe information about the participant is not sufficient, ask the participant to provide more information by "Could you tell us a bit more about your ________?"

Question 2: "Please take a few minutes to complete following lifestyle questionnaire? It will help us understand your activities, interests, and opinions." http://www.strategicbusinessinsights.com/vals/surveynew.shtml

Question 3: "Are you currently using any social media?

- **Probing Question 1:** "Which one(s)?"
- **Probing Question 2:** "Which do you use most frequently?"
- **Probing Question 3:** "How much time do you spend each time on ______?"
- **Probing Question 4:** "Where do you use social media?"
- **Probing Question 5:** "Do you use social media through your mobile device?"
- **Probing Question 6:** "What is your most favorite mobile social media?"
- **Probing Question 7:** "What is the least favorite mobile social media?"

Question 4: "Based on your selection of most favorite mobile social media, could you share how you decide to use it?

- **Probing Question 1:** "How did you realize you need it?"
- **Probing Question 2:** "How did you get the information to determine it is what you want?"
- **Probing Question 3:** "How did you become aware of its availability?"
- **Probing Question 4:** "Do you have any prior knowledge?"
- **Probing Question 5:** "Did you talk to anyone before you use it?"
- **Probing Question 6:** "Who did you talk to?" "Were they your friend? Your family? Your colleagues?"

Probing Question 7: "How did you evaluate their recommendations?"
Probing Question 8: "Did you Google it before you use it?"
Probing Question 9: "What other sources did you look up for information?"
Probing Question10: "Did you consider its pros and cons before you use it?"
Probing Question 11: "How did you weigh its pros and cons?"
Probing Question 12: "What is your overall assessment of your experience?"
Probing Question 13: "Are you overall satisfied?"
Probing Question 14: "If you are not satisfied, do you complain to others around you?" How do you do that?
Probing Question 15: "Do you feel that your culture affects your decision to use the social media? Please explain?"
Probing Question 16: "Do you feel that your family affects your decision to use the social media? Please explain?"
Probing Question 17: "Do you feel that your advertising affects your decision to use the social media? Please explain?"

The interviews were conducted by a group of research assistants in a setting comfortable to the participants that were selected non-randomly (Parmelee, 2014). The settings included participants' homes, coffee shops and on-campus locations. At the beginning of the in-depth interview, research assistants recorded the location, data, and duration of the interview. Participants were advised to read and sign the consent form. The use of audio and/or video devices to record the interview was first consulted with the participants to grant their permission. At the end of the data collection, research assistants would thank all participants and ensure the confidentiality of their interviews.

Profile of Participants

The in-depth interviews were conducted by a team of research assistants in 2014. A total of 29 Hispanic female participants were interviewed using a structured interview protocol. Age of these participants ranges from 14 to 60 years old. While some are students, working professionals and retired seniors are also part of our participants. Marital status of the participants ranges from being single to married with children. Occupations of the participants include student, university staff, accountant, and housewife. In terms of their psychographic profiles using the VALS2 segmentation, various psychographic types are represented in the sample, ranging from *Strivers*, *Experiencers*, *Believers*, *Innovators*, and *Achievers*. However, the majority of the participants belong to *Experiencers* and *Innovators* categories.

In terms of their mobile social media usage behaviors, *Facebook* is the most frequently used applications, followed by *Instagram* and *Snapshot*. The least popular mobile social media applications are *LinkedIn*, *Pinterest*, *Tumblr*, and *Myspace*. However, while participants who are currently students prefer *Facebook* over other types of mobile social media applications, older and working participants used *LinkedIn* more. On average, the participants spent one hour per day using these mobile social media applications. Students and housewives tend to use mobile social media more, while working professionals use these applications less. Many have indicated that they access these social media applications through their mobile devices (such as smartphone, I-Pad, or laptop).

Discussions

The interview data were recorded and transcribed for later analysis. The authors used a thematic (content) analysis method, a commonly-used method to categorize and interpret qualitative interview data (Abdullah et al., 2013; Wahl, McBride, & Schrodt, 2005). Wahl et al. (2005) explained the procedures of thematic analysis include three major stages: identification of broad themes, sub-subthemes, and their naming. To help identify broad themes, attention will be paid to forcefulness, recurrence, and repetition in the data (Wahl et al., 2005). Sub-themes can be analyzed and identified when there are multiple meanings within a particular broad theme (Wahl et al., 2005). Once both broad and sub-themes are identified, names will be assigned to each theme and sub-theme to describe their meaning (Wahl et al., 2005). This research followed the thematic analysis procedures employed in Wahl et al. (2005).

Major Themes Identified in the Data

Four broad themes have emerged after reviewing the transcripts of 29 Hispanic female participants: 1) family and peer influence in the decision-making process to adopt mobile social media; 2) functional benefits of mobile social media (such as PEOU and PU) play critical roles; 3) Latina's emerging role as a primary decision-maker of mobile social media adoption; 4) cultural and sub-cultural influence on the adoption decision. In general, these themes correspond to the recurrent topics in participants' narratives as to how they determine to adopt and use mobile social media.

Theme 1: Family and Peer Influence on Hispanic Female Consumers' Adoption to Use Mobile Social Media

These interview narratives show that Hispanic female consumers decide to adopt mobile social media because they consider many family members and friends around them are using them and they considered suggestions and recommendations from these members in their social networks to be a critical factor. Many of them go to their family and friends for information in the adoption process.

One of the participants mentioned how her mother influenced her decision to adopt Facebook.

For sure. I remember when I wanted to get an email address; my mom would tell me that it was dangerous because random people could get in touch with you from the other side of the world. She was afraid of that idea, and made me doubt of my decision. When I was about to open my Facebook account I immediately thought of my mom and imagined what would she say to me if she knew what I was doing at that moment.

In addition to the first sub-theme identified above, the second sub-theme is the perceptions of social media as a trend to create a "bandwagon effect," which further strengthens the family and peer influence in the adoption decision among Hispanic female consumers. Another participant suggested the perception of social media as a trend and influence from existing social network of relationships affect her decision to use mobile social media.

I realize I need it because everybody was using it and because it has become a trend...I did not talked to anyone [sic] before I used it. Then I started to search for my friends on Facebook. After that I started creating different social medias [sic] to look up for my friends. ......Yes, I started to talk to my high school friends first, and then I notice that some of my family members had Facebook accounts, so I just send them a friend request either on Facebook and the other social media.

Several participants below reveal this "bandwagon effect" to follow the crowd as the underlying reasons of why they use social media:

Because it got popular and it is easy to use, beside is fun because you can interact with any contact you have or only with one.

I realize that I have to use Facebook because everyone at school was using that method. It was almost impossible for me to communicate with my peers without Facebook.

Well everyone in my circle of friends was using them so I wanted to see what the fuss was about.

Just because everyone was on it.

I notice that a lot of people were creating an account, so I just sign up for one. As well as I wanted to be in touch with people that I care.

The third sub-theme is the influence of words of mouth from strangers and unknown sources can exert strong impacts on consumers' decision-making process, given the strong social milieu to adopt:

So I heard word by mouth from a couple of people, and that's when I realized I should check it out. And that is when I started using it.

As demonstrated in the narratives above, it is clear that Hispanic female participants decision-making process were greatly influenced by their friends, family, coworkers, classmates, relatives, or even strangers. In addition to the fourth sub-theme of receiving recommendations and suggestions from family and friends, another sub-theme has emerged after analyzing the interview narratives; that is, many Hispanic female consumers use mobile social media to be integrated into existing networks of relationships for a variety of activities (Sub-theme 5).

As demonstrated below to support sub-theme 5 to maintain interconnectivity with other functional and social groups, for example, one of the participants stated that her decision to use Facebook is to take part in class activities:

I actually was not in social media for a very long time, and last year I took a class and we had to sign up on Facebook because we were like part of a group discussion and we had to do, as part of the class assignment, so I have to create a Facebook account, and then after the class I stop using it, and then one of my very good friends moved away and she was on Facebook so then I pick it up again, and the I started using it just for social media purposes instead of class purposes.

Staying connected with other family members can be seen as an example of how Hispanic female consumers use social media to maintain social relationship with family members and friend as shown in the narratives below:

Sometimes. I have a lot of family who live out of town, like in Juarez, so we don't get to see each other very often, and it is nice to be able to stay up to date with the things that are happening in our lives.

Another participant shared her thoughts on how family affects her decision to use social media:

I do feel that my family affects my decision to use social media because this is a way to communicate with them. I have family that lives across the country and these apps make it easy for me to share and communicate things with them.

Another participant points out the need to stay in touch with a friend who moved away to another city.

When my friend moved away, she was on Facebook all the time so it was just the mean to keep in touch with her and to keep up with the things she was doing in her new city and things like that.

The following narrative is another clear example of showing how the decision to use social media is affected by peer and family influence to stay connected with them. Recommendations from family members also play a role in facilitating the decision-making process:

Yes, most of the friends that were actually using Facebook, and then I started using it. I talked to friends and family before using it.......It does, because I have a bunch of family and I cannot keep in contact with them because it is too expensive to do it, and that is where social media (Facebook) makes the good part.

Peer pressure to adopt social media plays a critical factor in affecting consumer's decision to adopt as evidenced in the narrative below:

Ummm I'm not a big technology freak so a lot of my friends were pushing me, common get Instagram, get Instagram, but then I was like for what? I'm not going to really use it... but now I actually see a good purpose on it ... umm Facebook as well... all my family had it before me. Umm and then it's a really good tool to communicate with people from out of town especially family members ...or people that you haven't seen in a while ...umm so yeah I did talk to them and umm well they gave me a good review overall...

Lin and Shang-Yi Liu (2009) studied the adoption of mobile video services and concluded that adopters' perceived critical mass contributed most significantly to shaping consumers' intention to adopt the new technology. As suggested in the narratives above, many participants mentioned the number of family members, colleagues, and friends who have been using the mobile social media is an important factor to shape their decision to adopt. It is likely that such perceptions of critical mass contribute to Latinas' decision to adopt mobile social media. However, Lin and Shang-Yi Liu (2009) also found that perceived usefulness, price, and enjoyment are also important contributing factors, which will be examined in the next theme.

Theme 2: Perceived Usefulness (PU) and Perceived Ease of Use (PEOU) of Mobile Social Media (Functionality)

With the growing numbers of functions available on mobile social media, users not only stay connected with their family members and friends, social commerce functions are made widely available to users. According to TAM2 (Venkatesh & Davis, 2000), consumers' decision to adopt a new technology is affected by factors such as subjective norms, images, job relevance, output quality, result demonstrability, experience, and voluntariness, as well as their perceptions of a technology (such as PEOU or PU) and intention to use. On the basis of the narratives below, two recurrent sub-themes emerged: 1) perceived usefulness of mobile social media; 2) perceived ease of use of mobile social media.

Female Hispanic participants in this study have stated that Facebook's perceived usefulness (PU) is to locate personal information:

Mmmm, you don't really receive information. For me it is more developing a habit. If you had a pending conversation with someone you will log into Facebook to keep on talking with that person, or if you want to find out something about someone it is more likely for someone to consider first looking into that person's Facebook account than on actually asking to the person.

Another participant shows that she is aware of various benefits each social media application offers

I knew that Facebook provides worldwide news and information. And it keeps me in touch with everybody. On the other hand, Pinterest helps me to get inspired because of all the things that are showed of people that I follow. Instagram just kept me in touch with celebrities, friends and family that I follow by looking at the pictures that they post.

Clearly shown in the following narratives, another participant was using Instagram to learn more about a brand and a company. The same perceived usefulness of providing information was shown below:

To be honest, probably like. I mean I use Instagram just because you could have an insight on presence and visual perspective on things. I really only like different thing that inspire me the most like I have my friends and stuff, but I like following bands and companies that I care about because they provide me with information that there is no way I can live without seen that.

Another participant's narrative was related to the sub-theme that PU is essential to account for Hispanic female consumer's adoption of social media, however, in a reverse direction. In other words, the lack of perceived usefulness of Twitter accounts for why this participant (as well as other participants in this study) feels that Twitter is their least favorite.

Those are probably, Twitter for sure, I mean I do not use it at all, anymore, but twitter does have a lot of good things if you follow, I mean if you just follow strictly like news pages, for things that you care about, like record labels or that stuff that you are into. So, you could find out a lot about music and stuff and things that you are interested in, but sometimes people that you follow they go overboard with that and only post every other minute about what their doing and stuff and if you are following a lot of people like that, it just builds and builds and it is tired to scroll, to like, a lot of pages of thing that do not mean anything.

The second sub-theme identified in participants' interview data addresses that Hispanic female consumers need to perceive if social media are easy to use before they adopt the technologies. As one of the participants simply put it to explain why she is not using Twitter:

I think Twitter [is my least favorite social media] because I do not get it.

Another participant said that the ease of use to use messaging on Facebook affects her adoption decision.

Well, it was just a lot of fun when I started using it with my friends because I would have conversations online and things like that. I was never really into messenger, or anything like that, so when I started sending messages on Facebook it was just really easy to communicate. That's the thing that I like about Facebook, that it is really easy to use, it's really easy to communicate.

Another participant emphasizes the ease of communication through Facebook:

I basically use fb trough the chat they have and it is very useful to communicate.

As revealed in several participants' narratives, the perceptions of ease of use (PEOU) and usefulness (PU) are two major reasons why they determine to adopt a variety of social media:

I like it. I am on Facebook every day, so it has just become something that I automatically check at night, checking my friends, my family. Now, I actually started using it to communicate a little bit more with co-workers by Facebook Messenger. I have some of my student assistant who live in Juarez, so it is really easy to communicate with them via Facebook.

Another participant who is married with kids and spent less time on social media also echoes how PEOU and PU of Facebook affects her decision to adopt:

I think so, just because I work here at the university, so social media is everywhere, all of the departments have a Facebook account, that is the way to get your information out there...through social media. TV is too expensive, radio is very expensive, Facebook is free, it's word of mouth, it is really easy to use and really convenient.

In general, participants in this interview recognize their needs to use mobile social media because they want to be constantly communicating with their family, friends and other people around them. These Hispanic female consumers are also aware of various functions provided and thus are able to make an informed adoption decision that matches their needs. In the interview data, consumers also admit to use mobile social media for different purposes depending on the social media such as *Instagram* for self-expression and *Whatsapp* for communication.

Theme 3: Latinas as a Primary Decision-Maker to Adopt Mobile Social Media

Nielsen studies (2013a, b) found that female Hispanic consumers are primary decision-makers of food (67%), beverage (55%), clothes (66%), and pharmaceuticals (59%) purchases. Latinas also make decisions on home electronics (33%) and personal electronics (38%). Most of the female Hispanic consumers in the interviews were much more confident to answer questions about their adoption decision of mobile social media. The research also indicated that female Hispanic consumers are much more communicative and open in person than in social media. This theme demonstrates the increasingly important role of female Hispanic consumers in determining their own mobile social media adoption and usage behaviors.

Our data show that female Hispanic consumers are making their own decisions as to how to use mobile social media for their professional or personal life. For example, one of the participants states that she uses social media for job-related purposes:

Umm and especially going into the whole sales aspect, I mean that's a good promotion for you. I mean you just can't keep relying on passing out your business cards over to people. So that's another way to get yourself out there.

The interview narrative from another participant reveals the active and calculated decision-making process to adopt Facebook to fit her own lifestyle and expectation:

I tried at first, and then I found that it was good for me and I just keep using it.......I actually tried to look for Facebook abuse, then I made my decision.......I tried to see Facebook from a different perspective. I knew that it was not gonna be that safe because most people have the way to get to Facebook and see all your information, but then I did understand that I need it to keep some information to myself in order to make Facebook safer.

A 27-years-old participant who is an Experiencer/Innovator shows her active role in making decisions to adopt social media to learn and try something new:

Yes, it definitely affects my decisions. I think that if I see friends or family taking pictures of something, for example, their food, and posting it, I might think it's cool and try it out too. Also, if you see something on TV or a magazine, you want to try it out for yourself.

Theme 4: Influence of Culture and Sub-Culture on the Decision to Adopt Mobile Social Media

Several recurrent sub-themes have emerged after analyzing the interview data. The first sub-theme addresses how culture and sub-culture affects the perceptions of adopting social media as shown below:

I believe that beyond culture, what affects your decision towards social media is society. I opened my Facebook account because of peer pressure; I don't regret it but my friend was almost obligating me to do it and so I did. Culture is also a factor because it influences our perception of right or wrong, or if something will bring us benefit, and all of these are important when you take the decision of using social media; but in my case, it was more of a social effect.

The second sub-theme reveals the emergence of social media culture/sub-culture prompts consumers to adopt these technologies as voiced by a married participant with kids:

Yea, we do a ton of invites on social media and I don't ever remember doing that before. I guess with the way culture is now, it seems like I get invites for everything and it's almost not personal anymore.

The narrative from one 18 years old student participant who uses social media heavily (over 8 hours per day) best describes the impact of this cultural trend that permeates Millennial Generation's daily life:

Yes. An example of this is when I have a group project, everybody needs to know what we need to do or how, and with social media we can talk about it and how to collaborate from our own house. Or just socially, when you're invited to a party, you don't get a paper invitation anymore, right? Everything is easier just creating an invitation on Facebook.

The emergence of social media sub-culture seems to affect the student population more to affect their adoption decisions. As shown by another student participant, she expresses the peer pressure she experiences:

Nowadays everyone is in the computer, the phone, and they are constantly using Facebook, Instagram, twitter, so you can feel the pressure to actually go ahead and start doing it yourself just to fit in.

The emphasis of family value among Hispanic consumers (see Villarrel, 2014 for a review) may also interact with the emergence of social media sub-culture to affect female Hispanic consumer's decision-making process. As voiced by a married participant, she decides to use social media to be united with her family to share her thoughts and pictures:

I do believe so because my culture taught me to be united with my family, and using social media allows me to share thoughts and pictures with family that lives out of town.

FUTURE RESEARCH DIRECTIONS

Although these rich interview data have shaded lights on the decision-making process of female Hispanic consumers, research findings reported in this chapter allow researchers to explore this important ethnic and demographic segment further by asking the following research directions. First, what is the role of Hispanic culture and cultural values affect female Hispanic consumers' adoption behaviors. Regardless of country of origin or language dominance among various Hispanic ethnic groups (Villarreal, Blozis, & Widaman, 2005, cited in Villarrel, 2014), Villarrel (2014) pointed out one of the most prominent core cultural values among Hispanic consumers is *familism*, defined as "a strong identification with and attachment to the nuclear and extended families, with strong feelings of loyalty, commitment, reciprocity, and solidarity among numbers of the same family" (Marin & Marin, 1991, p. 13, cited in Villarrel, 2014, p. 106). As one of the two dimensions of *Hispanicness* (Villarreal & Peterson, 2009), *Familism* was found to predict various aspects of consumer behaviors, ranging from psychological outcomes, care giving, and avoiding deviant behaviors in spite of peer pressure (See Villarrel, 2014, p. 106 for a detailed review). The narratives examined above (both Theme 1 and Theme 4) clearly show the effects of *familism* on why female Hispanic consumers decide to adopt mobile social media to stay connected with their family members. Future research should use either qualitative or quantitative methods to better understand the role of other Hispanic cultural values (*simpatía, respeto, fatalism, and machismo*) (Villarrel & Peterson, 2009) on the decision-making process of Hispanic consumers. Furthermore, Dupagne and Salwen (2005) found that ethnicity continues to account of ethnic variations in technology adoption. Future research may explore the adoption decision-making process among other ethnic groups in the United States.

A second research direction and question will be: How will dominant Hispanic culture and cultural values interact with the emerging social media culture/sub-culture among various Hispanic generational groups? A preliminary assessment of the interview data shows that the generational factor (older vs. younger) seems to account for female Hispanic consumers' usage behaviors of mobile social media. Older Latinas tend to use mobile social media less and favor more job-related functions and applications (such as *LinkedIn*). Many of the participants in this study belong to Millennials who are found to be driven by social media, apps, and search activities with their mobile devices (InMobi, 2013). The emergence of mobile social media culture/sub-culture among various generational segments is expected to have profound impacts on consumer behaviors, media landscape, and business practices. For example, 83% of Millennial consumers is expected to use mobile consumers in the next 12 months (InMobi, 2013). Around 88% of these consumers are said to pay attention to mobile advertising (InMobi, 2013). Future research should explore the existing Hispanic culture and culture values interact with the emerging social media cultural practices within and between generations.

A third research direction and question demands the exploration of other theoretical frameworks to understand the decision-making process of technology adoption (See Li & Zeng, 2011 for review). Despite the popularity and rigor of TAM and TAM2, scholars have questioned whether the models are able to explain all technology adoption behaviors (Baaren, Wijngaert, & Huizer, 2011). Barren et al. (2011) suggest that two additional constructs (i.e., knowledge and user-technology match, and temporary dynamical contexts in the adoption decision-making process) should be taken into consideration. Barren et al. (2011) criticize that the current TAM and TAM2 do not explain how consumers form their subjective perceptions of PU and PEOU of a technology. They argue that "a Black Box" exists in understanding why consumers believe one technology is superior to others in terms of PU and PEOU. As a result, Barren et al. (2011) recommend the inclusion of consumers' uses (of a technology) and gratifications, characteristics of technologies, and individual personality traits should be included. Furthermore, Li and Ze (2011) includes a social utility of media use construct to examine how the judgement of media use and adoption influences decision to adopt Podcast. As argued in Barren et al. (2011), the perceptions of social utility are likely to be affected by temporal, cultural, and contextual factors. Future research should explore how these factors contribute to consumers' perceptions to better understand their decision-making process to adopt mobile social media and other emerging technologies.

Limitations

Research findings reported in this book were based on a series of in-depth interviews from a non-random sample of female Hispanic consumers in the Southwestern part of the United States. While this qualitative research method enables researchers to collect more in-depth and thorough narratives in a dynamic data collection process, biases accompanied this method should be taken into consideration (Cook, 2008). The thematic content analysis approach might not be as objective as computer-assisted content analysis of the interview transcripts. However, as an exploratory study to approach this emerging phenomenon among a growing important ethnic segment in the U.S., the generalizability of research findings to make over-arching claims about the decision-making process of female Hispanic consumers is not intended, when considering these limitations.

CONCLUSION

The growing Hispanic consumer segments in the U.S. provide a strong justification to explore their consumer behaviors. Female Hispanic consumers account for almost half of the U.S. Hispanic population and are found to play a key role in making decisions about adopting new mobile social media technologies. This book chapter used a qualitative in-depth interview method to collect narratives about how and why these 29 Latinas make their decisions to use mobile social media. Interview data were analyzed through the theoretical lens of the Technology Acceptance Model (TAM) and its derived TAM2. Four major themes were identified and explored above to describe the technology adoption process among these female Hispanic consumers as a result of family and peer influence; perceived technology attributes of mobile social media, Latinas' active role as decision-makers, and cultural and sub-cultural influence. The book chapter discusses implications of these findings and explores future research directions to better understanding this important consumer segment.

REFERENCES

Abdullah, N. H., Wahab, E., & Shamsuddin, A. (2013). Exploring the common technology adoption enablers among Malaysian SMES: Qualitative findings. *Journal of Management and Sustainability*, *3*(4), 78–91. doi:10.5539/jms.v3n4p78

Baaren, E., van deWijngaert, L., & Huizer, E. (2011). Understanding technology adoption through individual and context characteristics: The case of HDTV. *Journal of Broadcasting & Electronic Media*, *55*(1), 72–89. doi:10.1080/08838151.2011.546257

Boyce, C., & Neale, P. (2006, May). Conducting in-depth interviews: A guide for designing and conducting in-depth interviews for evaluation input. *Pathfinder.org*. Retrieved from http://www2.pathfinder.org/site/DocServer/m_e_tool_series_indepth_interviews.pdf

Cook, K. E. (2008). In-depth interview. In L. M. Given (Ed.), *The Sage encyclopedia of qualitative research methods* (pp. 423–424). Thousand Oaks: Sage Publications, Ltd. doi:10.4135/9781412963909.n209

Davis, F. D. (1989). Perceived usefulness, perceived ease of use, and user acceptance of information technologies. *Management Information Systems Quarterly*, *13*(3), 319–340. doi:10.2307/249008

Dupagne, M., & Salwen, M. B. (2005). Communication technology adoption and ethnicity. *The Howard Journal of Communications*, *16*(1), 21–32. doi:10.1080/10646170590915826

Fishbein, M., & Ajzen, I. (1975). *Beliefs, attitudes, intention, and behavior: An introduction of Theory and Research*. Reading, MA: Addison-Wesley.

Global mobile media consumption reaching millennials. (2013, February). *InMobi*.

Hausman, A. (2000). A multi-method investigation of consumer motivations in impulse buying behavior. *Journal of Consumer Marketing*, *17*(5), 403–426. doi:10.1108/07363760010341045

Hispanic women connect with friends, brands and news via social. (2014, February 11). *eMarketer*. Retrieved from http://www.emarketer.com/Article/Hispanic-Women-Connect-with-Friends-Brands-News-via-Social/1010597#sthash.ELe3Zmtb.dpuf

Joo, J., & Sang, Y. (2013). Exploring Koreans' smartphone usage: An integrated model of the technology acceptance model and uses and gratifications theory. *Telematics and Informatics*, *29*, 2512–2518.

Kindberg, T., Spasojevic, M., Fleck, R., & Sellen, A. (2005, April-June). The ubiquitous camera: An in-depth study of camera phone use. *Pervasive Computing*, *4*(2), 42–50. doi:10.1109/MPRV.2005.42

Lazar, J., Feng, J. H., & Hochheiser, H. (2010). Research methods in human computer interaction. Chichester, MA: Wiley.

Lee, S. Y. (2014). Examining the factors that influence early adopters' smartphone adoption: The case of college students. *Telematics and Informatics*, *31*(2), 308–318. doi:10.1016/j.tele.2013.06.001

Legris, P., Ingham, J., & Collerette, P. (2003). Why do people use information technology: A critical review of the technology acceptance model. *Information & Management*, *40*(3), 191–204. doi:10.1016/S0378-7206(01)00143-4

Li, X., & Zeng, L. (2011, Fall). Technology attributes, perceived value of information, and social utility: Predicting podcast adoption and use. *Southwestern Mass Communication Journal*, 83-69.

Lin, J. C. C., & Liu, E. S. Y. (2009). The adoption behaviour for mobile video call services. *International Journal of Mobile Communications*, *7*(6), 646–666. doi:10.1504/IJMC.2009.025536

Lopez, M. H., Gonzalez-Barrera, A., & Patten, E. (2013, March 7). *Closing the digital divide: Latinos and technology adoption*. Washington, DC: PEW Research Center. Retrieved from http://www.pewhispanic.org/2013/03/07/closing-the-digital-divide-latinos-and-technology-adoption/

Mobile, B. (2014, September 18). Briabe mobile launches mobile-social platform 'Latina glam.' Retrieved from http://www.briabemobile.com/news/briabe-mobile-launches-mobile-social-platform-latina-glam

Parmelee, J. H. (2013). Political journalists and twitter: Influences on norms and practices. *Journal of Media Practice*, *14*(4), 291–305. doi:10.1386/jmpr.14.4.291_1

Parmelee, J. H. (2014). The agenda-building function of political tweets. *New Media & Society*, *16*(3), 434–450. doi:10.1177/1461444813487955

Pew Internet Research Project. (2014, January). *Mobile technology fact sheet*. Washington, D.C.: Pew.

Rodriguez, A. (2015, April 6). Retailers duke it out for Hispanic shoppers' dollars. *AdAge.com*. Retrieved from http://adage.com/article/cmo-strategy/retailers-duke-hispanic-shoppers-dollars/297902/?utm_source=daily_email&utm_medium=newsletter&utm_campaign=adage&ttl=1428896238

Rogers, E. M. (1995). *Diffusion of Innovations* (4th ed.). New York: The Free Press.

Rojas, V. (2004). The gender of Latinidad: Latinas speak about Hispanic television. *Communication Review*, *7*(2), 125–153. doi:10.1080/10714420490448688

Latinas are a driving force behind Hispanic purchasing power in the U.S. (2013a, August 1). *The Nielsen Company*. Retrieved from http://www.nielsen.com/us/en/insights/news/2013/latinas-are-a-driving-force-behind-hispanic-purchasing-power-in-.html

Latina power shift. (2013b). *The Nielsen Company*. Retrieved from http://www.nielsen.com/content/dam/corporate/us/en/reports-downloads/2013%20Reports/Nielsen-Latina-Report-2013.pdf

van der Heijden, H. (2003). Factors influencing the usage of websites: The case of a generic portal in the Netherlands. *Information & Management*, *40*(6), 541–549. doi:10.1016/S0378-7206(02)00079-4

Vannoy, S. A., & Palvia, P. (2010, June). The social influence model of technology adoption. *Communications of the ACM*, *53*(6), 149–153. doi:10.1145/1743546.1743585

Venkatesh, V., & Davis, F. D. (2000). A theoretical extension of the technology acceptance model: Four longitudinal field studies. *Management Science*, *46*(2), 186–204.

Verkasalo, H., López-Nicolás, C., Molina-Castillo, F. J., & Bouwman, H. (2010). Analysis of users and non-users of smartphone applications. *Telematics and Informatics*, *27*(3), 242–255. doi:10.1016/j.tele.2009.11.001

Villarreal, R., & Peterson, R. A. (2009, Fall). The concept of marketing implications of Hispanicness. *Journal of Marketing Theory and Practice*, *17*(4), 303–316. doi:10.2753/MTP1069-6679170401

Villarrel, R. (2014). Branding implications of the relationship between Hispanic familism and brand related behaviors: A latent variable model approach. *Academy of Marketing Studies Journal*, *18*(2), 103–119.

Wahl, S. T., McBride, M. C., & Schrodt, P. (2005). Becoming "point and click" parents: A case study of communication and online adoption. *Journal of Family Communication*, *5*(4), 279–294. doi:10.1207/s15327698jfc0504_3

Digital, social and mobile in 2015 report. (2015). *We Are Social*. Retrieved from http://wearesocial.sg/blog/2015/01/digital-social-mobile-2015/

Yang, K. C. C. (2005). Exploring factors affecting the adoption of M-commerce in Singapore. *Telematics and Informatics*, *22*(3), 257–277. doi:10.1016/j.tele.2004.11.003

ADDITIONAL READING SECTION

Abeele, M. V., Antheunis, M. L., & Schouten, A. P. (2014). Me, myself and my mobile: A segmentation of youths based on their attitudes towards the mobile phone as a status instrument. *Telematics and Informatics*, *31*(2), 194–208. doi:10.1016/j.tele.2013.04.004

Ahrens, J. (n. d.). Between 'me-time' and household duty: Male and female home internet use. *Media International Australia, 146*, 60-68.

Aquino, J. (2012, January). 5 hot marketing trends: Customer strategists must step up their engagement efforts as mobile's mercury rises. *CRM Magazine*, *16*, 20.

The health communicator's social media tool kits. (2010). Center for Disease Control and Prevention. Retrieved from http://www.cdc.gov/healthcommunication/ToolsTemplates/SocialMediaToolkit_BM.pdf

Dunn, E. W. Jr. (1975). Mexican-American media behavior: A factor analysis. *Journal of Broadcasting*, *19*(1), 3–10. doi:10.1080/08838157509363765

Guernica, A., & Kasperuk, I. (1982). *Reaching the Hispanic market effectively: The media, the market, the methods*. New York: McGraw Hill Book Company.

Hamka, F., & Bouwman, H., deReuver, M., & Kroesen, M. (2014). Mobile customer segmentation based on smartphone measurement. *Telematics and Informatics*, *31*(2), 220–227. doi:10.1016/j.tele.2013.08.006

Karnowski, V., & Jandura, O. (2014). When lifestyle becomes behavior: A closer look at the situational context of mobile communication. *Telematics and Informatics*, *31*(2), 184–193. doi:10.1016/j.tele.2013.11.001

Lederer, A. L., Maupin, D. J., Sena, M. P., & Zhuang, Y. L. (2000). The technology acceptance model and The World Wide Web. *Decision Support Systems*, *29*(3), 269–282. doi:10.1016/S0167-9236(00)00076-2

Morgan, D. (2011, October 4). *Where the Hispanic viewers are (not just on Univision).* Advertising Age. Retrieved from http://adage.com/article/digitalnext/hispanic-viewers-univision/230429/

Padro, C., & Dreas, C. (2011). Three things you thought you knew about U.S. Hispanic's engagement with media… and why you may have been wrong. New York: The Nielsen Company.

The rise of the second generation: Changing patterns in Hispanic population growth. (2003, October). *Pew Hispanic Center.* Retrieved from http://hablamosjuntos.org/resources/pdf/PHC_Projections_final_(October_2003).pdf

Roslow, P., & Nicholls, J. (1996). Targeting the Hispanic market: Comparative persuasion of TV commercials in Spanish and English. *Journal of Advertising Research,* (May/June), 67–77.

Sagin, E. (2013, September 26). Targeting bilingual and Spanish-speaking audiences in AdWords: The why and how. *Wordstream.com.* Retrieved from http://www.wordstream.com/blog/ws/2013/09/26/language-targeting-adwords

Salehan, M., & Negahban, A. (2013). Social networking on smartphones: When mobile phones become addictive. *Computers in Human Behavior, 29*(6), 2632–2639. doi:10.1016/j.chb.2013.07.003

Sell, A., Mezei, J., & Walden, P. (2014). An attitude-based latent class segmentation analysis of mobile phone users. *Telematics and Informatics, 31*(2), 209–219. doi:10.1016/j.tele.2013.08.004

Sonderman, J. (2014, June 10). Mobile and social media are intricately linked. *American Press Institute.* Retrieved from http://www.americanpressinstitute.org/publications/reports/white-papers/mobile-and-social-media/

Subervi, F., & Eusebio, H. (2005). Latino media. In E. del Valle (Ed.), *Hispanic marketing and public relations: Understanding and targeting America's largest minority* (pp. 285- 325). Boca Raton, FL: Poyeen Publishing.

Subervi, F., & Ríos, D. (2005). Latino identity and situational Latinidad. In E. Valle (Ed.), *Hispanic Marketing and Public Relations: Understanding and Targeting America's Largest Minority* (pp. 29–45). Boca Raton: Poyeen Publishing.

Suominen, A., Hyrynsalmi, S., & Knuutila, T. (2014). Young mobile users: Radical and individual – not. *Telematics and Informatics, 31*(2), 266–281. doi:10.1016/j.tele.2013.08.003

Villarreal, R., & Peterson, R. A. (2008). Hispanic ethnicity and media behavior. *Journal of Advertising Research, 48*(2), 179–190. doi:10.2501/S0021849908080227

Yankelovich, Skelly, & White, Inc. (1981). *Spanish USA: A study of the Hispanic market in the United States.* New York: SIN National Spanish Television Network.

KEY TERMS AND DEFINITIONS

Consumer Behavior: The study of the processes of making decisions to select, secure, use, and dispose of products or services by individuals, groups, or organizations. Consumer behavior aims to examine social, cultural, regulatory, and other ecological factors in affecting the decision-making process. Decisions for both tangible (such as products) and intangible (such as experiences, ideas, or services) are potential topics of consumer behavior research.

Diffusion of Innovation: A theory to explain the processes, reasons, and speed that new ideas, products, and technologies are spread through society and cultures. Developed by Dr. Everett Rogers in his book, *Diffusion of Innovations* (1962), four key components are proposed to explain how and why an innovation is diffused through specific channels among participants in a social system over a period of time. These four components include the innovation, communication channel, time, and a social system. A typology of five adopter types is proposed as part of the theory to explain how individual characteristics affect the decision to adopt an innovation: Innovators, Early Adopters, Early Majority, Late Majority, and Laggards.

Ethnicity: A term to refer to a population of human beings who share common ancestry, genealogy, religious traits, or language and who identify with each other on such basis.

Extended Technology Acceptance Model (TAM2): An extended version of the popular Technology Acceptance Model (TAM) by including variables such as subjective norms, images, job relevance, output quality, result demonstrability, experience, and voluntariness, in addition to their perceptions of a technology. As an extended model of TAM, this model is often referred to as TAM2.

Hispanic: Refer to persons that have a cultural and historical relationship with Spain. Used interchangeably with the term, Latino, by the U.S. Census Bureau, Hispanic is broadly refer to "a person of Cuban, Mexican, Puerto Rican, South or Central American (except for Brazil), or other Spanish culture or origin regardless of race."

In-Depth Interviewing: A qualitative research method or technique to investigate a small number of respondents through intensive inquiry and probing to explore their views on a particular idea or a situation. Using this method in a face-to-face setting or through a telephone or a computer network, researchers ask open-ended questions to record the respondent's answers.

Latina: A term that is used to refer to female Hispanic population.

Mobile Social Media: A term to refer to social media applications such as Facebook, Foursquare, Instagram, Pinterest, Twitter, etc., that are delivered via mobile devices such as smartphone, tablet, or laptop computer.

Perceived Ease of Use (PEOU): An important belief component in TAM and TAM2. The term is defined by Davis (1989) as "the degree to which a person believes that using a particular system would be free from effort."

Perceived Usefulness (PU): A key belief component in TAM and TAM2. The term is defined by Davis (1989) as "the degree to which a person believes that using a particular system would enhance his or her job performance."

Social Media: According to Andreas Kaplan and Michael Haenlein (2010), social media are defined as "a group of Internet-based applications that build on the ideological and technological foundations of Web 2.0, and that allow the creation and exchange of user-generated content." Social media include collaborative projects (such as Wikipedia), microblogs and blogs, contents (such as YouTube), social networking services (such as Facebook), virtual games, and virtual social life (such as Second Life).

Thematic (Content) Analysis: A research method to describe and analyze qualitative textual data from interview transcripts.

Theory of Planned Behavior: A theoretical framework derived from the Theory of Reasoned Action in 1980 to account for how attitude predicts an individual's behavioral intention by assessing expected outcome and subjective evaluation of risks and benefits of the outcome.

Theory of Reasoned Action: A theoretical model proposed by Martin Fishbein and Icek Ajzen to describe factors predicting behavioral intention and actual behavior at a specific place and time.

Chapter 13
Online Sisterhood:
Women, Income Generation, and Online Social Capital in Urban Indonesia

Ariane J. Utomo
The Australian National University, Australia

ABSTRACT

Across developing countries, the role of social networks and social capital in facilitating women's access to income is well documented. However, less is known about how networks facilitated by social networking sites (SNS) may transform women's economic opportunities in these regions. In this chapter, I draw upon a relatively recent phenomenon of the use of SNS as a medium of trade in urban Indonesia. In 2010, I conducted preliminary interviews to examine the dynamics of Facebook-facilitated trade among urban middle-class married women residing in Jakarta, the capital of Indonesia. The interviews highlighted beneficial links between social media, social capital, and productivity – by means of increased personal income. However, this effective link between SNS and income-generating social capital is likely to be a rather distinctive example, as it depends largely on the class, gender, and cultural specificities that shape the nature of online and offline social interactions among my target group.

DOI: 10.4018/978-1-5225-0010-0.ch013

1. INTRODUCTION

Across developing countries, the role of social networks and social capital in facilitating women's access to income is well documented (Mayoux, 2001; Molyneux, 2002; Rankin, 2002; Silvey & Elmhirst, 2003). However, less is known about how networks facilitated by social networking sites (SNS) may transform women's economic opportunities in these regions.

In this chapter, I draw upon a relatively recent phenomenon on the use of SNS as a medium of trade in urban Indonesia. In 2010, I conducted preliminary interviews to examine the dynamics of Facebook-facilitated trade among urban middle-class married women residing in Jakarta, the capital of Indonesia. The interviews highlighted beneficial links between social media, social capital, and productivity – by means of increased personal income. However, this effective link between SNS and income-generating social capital is likely to be a rather distinctive example, as it depends largely on the class, gender, and cultural specificities that shape the nature of online and offline social interactions among my target group.

To develop my argument, I revisit the notion of the *middle-class entrepreneurs* in developing countries (Banerjee & Duflo, 2008), and reflect upon women's engagement in informal micro-credit schemes and in *petty* trading to finance '*petty consumption*' commonly practiced across many layers of social class in Southeast Asia (Brenner, 1995; Gallaway & Bernasek, 2002; Papanek & Schwede, 1988). I argue that women's income generating activities through social media and online social networks reflect the culturally prescribed economic role of middle-class women as secondary earners (Utomo, 2012). In turn, these activities are commercially sustained by a) the consumption culture of other urban middle-class women in their online social networks, and b) the socio-cultural dispositions that make Facebook effective in maintaining and forming online and offline social networks among these women. While the case study supports the notion of the gendered web (Hargittai & Shafer, 2006; Wheeler, 2001), it also sheds lights on the transformative potential of Information and Communication Technologies (ICTs) to open up new income opportunities for women in the developing world (Ng & Mitter, 2005).

The chapter is structured as follows. First, I will discuss the societal and cultural context behind the popularity of social media among the urban middle class in Indonesia. Here, against the backdrop of the demographically large cohort of the urban middle class, I consider the intersections between the prevailing social norms and the emerging web culture around social and commercial interactions. The second section details the conceptual framework of the chapter. I present three interrelated hypotheses on why Facebook-mediated trading in urban Indonesia is dominated by women, as sellers and buyers. The third section briefly describes my methods of qualitative data collection. Next, I outline the results of the interviews and online observations. I examine how respondents articulate their motivations to engage in online selling, particularly in the context of their work-family roles. I further reflect the gendered practices of buying and selling via social-networking sites in the context of entrepreneurship and the transformative role of SNSs for the women in my case study. Recommendations for future research along with a consideration of limitations of this study conclude the chapter.

2. BACKGROUND

2.1 Social Media and Social Capital

Challenging the stereotypes of SNS as merely a site for narcissistic personal self-expressions, along with their increasing uptake, scholars across different disciplines have inquired on the potential individual and societal benefits generated from social media usage. These benefits are often proxied by the concept of social capital.

A growing body of literature has investigated the potential of online social networks to form and maintain social capital; here understood as networks and the associated norms of reciprocity as articulated by the work of Coleman (1988) and Putnam (2001). Wasko and Faraj (2005) studied an organizational electronic network for members of a professional association in the US, and demonstrated how people's embeddedness in the social network generated knowledge sharing and contribution for the field. Others had focused on the link between SNS use and offline civic engagement (Pasek, More, & Romer, 2009; Valenzuela, Park, & Kee, 2009). Also using a social capital perspective, Ellison, Steinfeld, and Lampe (2007) argued for the benefits of having Facebook friends, by showing positive associations between Facebook use among college students in the US and the formation of bonding, bridging and maintained social capital. In the Asian context, studies on online social networks and social capital are predominantly centred on their associations in bringing about political change (Kobayashi, Ikeda, & Miyata, 2006; Lim, 2013).

In this chapter, I illustrate how online social networks have the potential to not only form and maintain an individual's online and offline social capital, but to also transfer these social capitals to create tangible/monetary benefits. Such productive potentials are made possible due to the interactions between Facebook-specific features, gender, social class, and culture that may not always be applicable in other societal contexts.

2.2 Indonesia: Social Media Capital of the World

Indonesia, a nation of 237 million people (Statistics Indonesia., 2011), was recently heralded as the social media capital of the world (Vaswani, 2012). The advent of Web 2.0 and the ensuing popularity of online social media and networks have vastly transformed the landscape in which urban middle-class Indonesians are interacting socially and commercially with each other. In 2008, Indonesia was the fastest growing country of registered users of Facebook in Southeast Asia, outpacing China, India, Thailand, Malaysia, and Singapore (Mysore, 2008). By 2014, 69 million monthly active users of Facebook were recorded in the country (Purnell, 2014).

There are a number of key reasons why social media is popular in Indonesia. A fundamental reason is the demographic composition of the population. Globally, young people are overrepresented among the first adopters of new media and technology. Indonesia's youthful age structure fulfils the requirement for a relatively large portion of its population to be readily receptive to new modes of ICT. The 2010 Population Census enumerated about 81 million people between the ages 15 – 34 in Indonesia (Statistics Indonesia., 2011). The demographic youth bulge is particularly prominent in Jakarta, the capital, with

15 – 34 year olds accounting for 41 per cent of the provincial population. But, the arrival of Web 2.0 and SNSs coincided with not just any demographic youth bulge. After decades of sustained economic growth, social media was embraced by the most educated, literate, and arguably, consumptive urban generations in the history of the nation.

Figure 1 illustrates the remarkable rise in the proficiency of speaking the national language, Bahasa Indonesia, among the younger generations. The 2010 Census indicated that about 41 per cent of populations aged 75-79 were unable to speak in Bahasa Indonesia. Among young people aged 20 to 24, this figure was down to 1 per cent. Such near universal ability to speak in the national language among young people is indicative of not only widening access to formal schooling over time, but also of their potential to be receptive of ICT-mediated communications.[1]

The demographically large and educated youth cohorts also emerged at a time of relative affluence. In 2011, a forecast produced by Nomura, a Japanese bank, suggests that Indonesia has one of fastest growing middle-class in Southeast Asia. In 2004, the bank estimated about 1.4 million persons in the country had disposable income over US $3000. This figure rose to 50.4 million in 2009, and forecasted to rise to 149.7 million in 2014 (Khatri et al, 2011). The spiraling demands for motorbikes and smartphones

Figure 1. Population census 2010: Population of Indonesia by age groups and Indonesian language ability

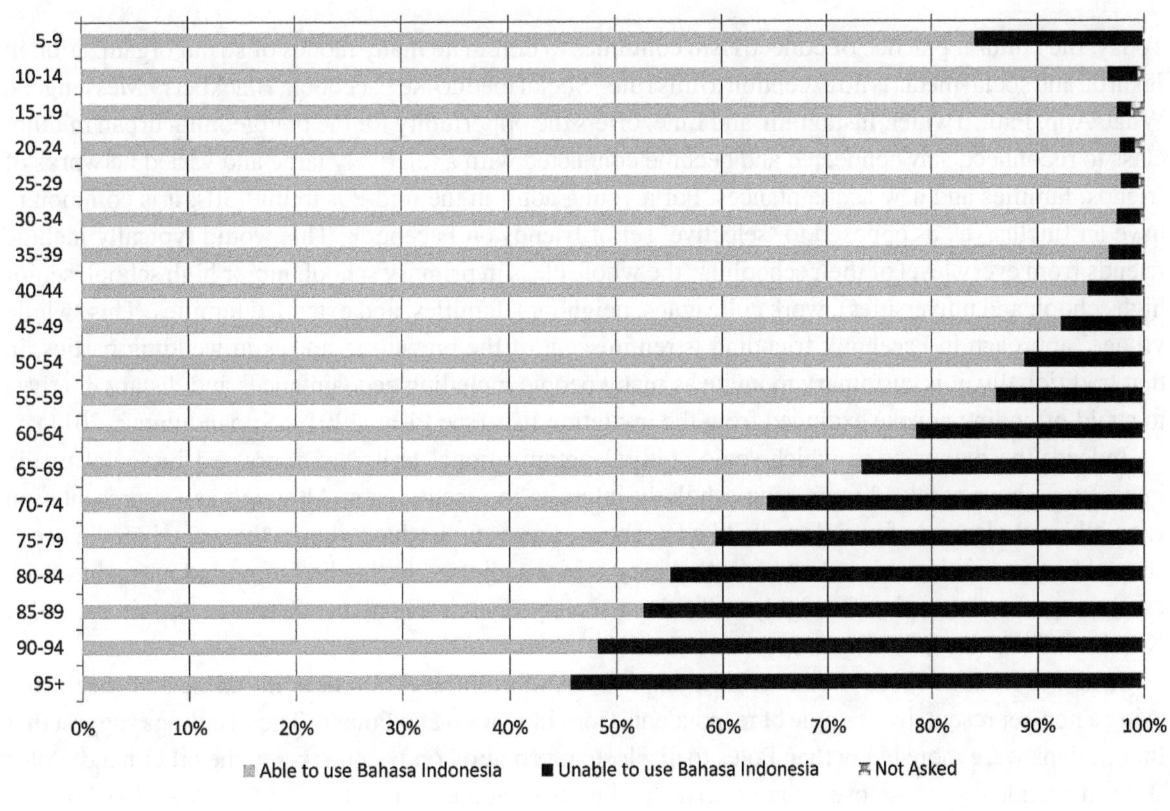

have been cited in the media as indicators of a rapid increase in the purchasing power of newly affluent consumers ("Indonesia's middle class", 2011). Here, the relative affordability of smartphones and the costs associated with its use is an important story in the popularity of social media. As opposed to personal computers, smartphones are primary access points to the internet and social media in Indonesia.

A recent study on patterns of access and purpose of mobile phones and Internet use among young adults in Greater Jakarta summarized a set of potential reasons behind the uptake of social media:

... a receptive social culture that highly ranks solidarity, mutual aid, sharing and openness (as opposed to privacy), the related tendency for young Indonesians to eagerly follow social trends, the rise of affordable mobile phone technology, and the technical features of online social networks such as Facebook that is free and user friendly. (Utomo, Reimondos, Utomo, McDonald, & Hull, 2013)[2]

In the so-called social media capital of the world, the sheer numbers of users in the city and their networks across the country alone enable SNS to provide an effective medium for individuals to market their products and services. More importantly however, it is the socio-cultural specificities shaping the nature of online and offline interactions that play a key role in the production of pecuniary benefits from SNS.

2.3 Social Media and Collectivism

Today, the cultural practice of collectivism continues to dominate many modes of social organization in Jakarta, and social media is no exception to this rule.[3] Social media like Facebook, Blackberry Messengers, WhatsApp, Path, Twitter, Instagram, and Line, offers the opportunity for the bourgeoning urban middle-class to reconnect, stay connected and become connected with a relatively large and varied networks of friends, families and new acquaintances. For a young adult in the mid-20s to mid-30s, it is common to have an 'inclusive', as opposed to 'selective' set of friends on Facebook. This would typically include friends from every level of their schooling (the whole class in primary school, junior high school, senior high school, and universities), work colleagues, neighbors, families, and extended families. This 'whole village' approach in Facebook friending is reminiscent of the prevailing norms in wedding parties, in that traditionally, it is customary to invite as many people including acquaintances and distant relatives to avoid offending anyone excluded from the invitation lists (see Pisani, 2014; Simandjuntak, 2011).

Indeed, the dynamics in which socio-cultural organizational traits are expressed in social media interactions have received increasing scholarly interests in recent years. Although self-representation is an inherent element of social media like Facebook, these studies have shown that social media use is shaped by pre-existing cultural contexts that vary across societies. In this literature, Indonesia has been cited as a prime example of a highly collectivist society (Garcia-Gavilanes, Quercia, & Jaimes, 2013, Kosaka &Dananjaya, 2012).

Ardi and Maison (2014) examined the importance of cultural differences in online self-disclosure using a non-representative sample of respondents from Indonesia and Poland. Their findings suggest that Indonesians were more likely than Poles to disclose information on Facebook. On the other hand, Poles showed a tendency to disclose more positive content than Indonesians. Their study exemplifies how the use of the same tool of self-representation differs in collectivist and individualist cultures. These findings are in line with a comparative study of attitudes to Facebook use among college students in Indonesia and Japan (Kosaka & Dananjaya, 2012). Although both countries were both categorised as having collectivist cultures, the authors found that Indonesian respondents displayed higher level of trusts and lesser degree of uncertainty avoidance than the Japanese respondents. In another study, Sari and Tedjasaputra (2013) argued that the success of Facebook as a medium of learning and disseminating capacity building materials to Indonesian education stakeholders was highly contingent upon receptiveness, which they attributed to power distance and collectivism. Overall, these findings reflect the general consensus in the global literature: "when a new tool is introduced in different cultural contexts, pre-existing cultural practices, rather than the tool itself, are likely to determine its usage" (Na, Kosinki & Stillwell, 2015: p.364). Taken together, receptiveness, tendency to disclose information, relatively high level of trusts and low level of uncertainty avoidance in a collectivist cultural settings are seemingly conducive to Facebook-mediated trading. This argument is supported by another study on Twitter use in Indonesia.

A study that maps cultural traits in Twitter networks demonstrates how the collective nature of Indonesian societies are reflected online: Indonesia has the highest ratio of tweet per user relative to other Twitter active countries; Indonesia also has the highest score of users mentioning other users in their tweets; and that the network plots of Twitter in Indonesia has a characteristics of a low density network relative countries such as Australia (Garcia-Gavilanes et al., 2013).[4] In low density networks embedded within collectivist cultures, social media offers not only a platform to stay in touch with existing social circles, but it creates vast potential connections, embedded in multiple networks, for individuals seeking to form new avenues to market their ideas, products, services, and/or, in many cases, oneself. In the following section, I outline how pre-existing practices further shaped the gendered nature of Facebook-mediated trading.

3. GENDER AND FACEBOOK-MEDIATED TRADING

Recent data have suggested that uptake in Greater Jakarta, policy and research concerns regarding social inequalities in access to ICT is no longer about a gender-driven digital divide. In Greater Jakarta digital inequalities among young adults are driven by age and education rather than gender (Utomo et al., 2013). The study also found weak differences in the frequency of internet use for a specified purpose between male and female respondents, and that social network sites ranked as the number one most popular purpose of accessing the Internet, with roughly half of internet users reporting accessing social networking sites on a daily basis.

This convergence in the patterns of uptake and purpose of Internet use in Indonesia resonate the global trends. But, while gender parity has become the norm in terms of access or frequency of use of the along with the spread of the Internet, gender differences beyond the access divide continue to materialize (Royal, 2008). Globally, while both men and women are avid users of SNS, recent studies have pointed marked gender differences relating to its use: women tend to self-promote through photos, while men tend to self-promote through the "About Me" and "Notes" section on Facebook. (Mehdizadeh, 2010);

women were found to be more proactive in engaging the privacy settings in Facebook (Hoy & Milne, 2010); and women were more likely to use their profile picture to manage their self-representation, to spend more time on Facebook, and had more Facebook friends (McAndrew & Jeong, 2012).

For urban Indonesia, at a glance, one striking gender differences in the use of Facebook is that women are over-represented in the use of their networks for trading; as both sellers and customers. The use of Facebook by women to generate income is increasingly becoming a common practice in urban Indonesia, but only few studies have documented such phenomenon. These include a study that framed such activities from a policy lens surrounding women's empowerment (Melissa, Hamidati, Saraswati, & Flor, 2013), and another that focuses on the consumer's motivation and behaviour for buying consumption goods through their online networks (Albert & Hersinta, 2013).

In the context of a collectivist nature of online social interaction outlined above, why are women over-represented in trading and consuming through Facebook? I consider the following hypotheses behind this gendered online behaviour.

1. *The middle-class entrepreneurs.* Across developing economies, women's home-based remunerative work makes up a large part of the informal sector. Unlike the common perception, women's engagement in such income-generating activities is as common for the middle-class as it is for women from low-income households; the later group of women has been the subject of much scholarly research on empowerment, microcredits, and development. Banerjee and Duflo's work on the middle class in developing countries noted a feature of a general store owned by a middle-class woman in Hyderabad, India: *"The business seemed to be not much more than a way to allow the woman to earn a little extra cash while she takes care of her family, on a fairly minimal outlay"* (2008, p. 16). Generating additional income without having the need for large resource commitments has similarly long been a common feature of home-based remunerative work for middle-class women in urban Indonesia (Papanek & Schwede, 1988), and goes hand-in-hand with the notion of women as secondary earners in urban middle-class households (Utomo, 2012). Without SNS, middle-class women would still be engaging in entrepreneurial activities, but SNS has the potential to further reduce the fixed costs associated with starting up and maintaining a business, and appeals to the idea of a flexible, role compatible, and family-friendly way to generate additional income.
2. *Traditional social networks.* Women's active role in earning and managing family finances has characterized the gender role division in Indonesian urban middle-class families, and to this end, the importance of social networks in their household finance management statregy has predated SNS and formally organized credit rotation schemes (see Rammohan & Johar, 2009). Papanek and Schwede (1988) pointed to the traditional practice of *Arisan*, a periodic and voluntary social gathering of women within certain circles to contribute payments to a common pool as a way of their savings strategy. *Arisan* groups are dominated by women, and are based on pre-existing bonds: among women who lives in the same neighborhood (community), whose children attend the same school, who work/whose spouse work at the same place, and who share common interests (religious/ethno-migrant groups/school alumni). At any one time, a woman can belong to multiple *arisan* groups. In this manner, *arisan's* prime purpose does not rest in its role as an informal financial institution. Rather, in an essentially collectivist society, *arisan's* primary function is to

maintain social networks, trusts, and reciprocity: the very foundation of social capital. Catching up through sharing meals/light snacks is an integral part of the *arisan*. It is also common for external traders, or a member, to promote one's goods and services to other women in the group (Hospes, 1992). Popular goods promoted included make-ups and skincare products, embroideries/textiles/bed linens, jewelries/gold/previous stones, cookware/electronics, including products commonly sold through some kind of multi-level marketing schemes (e.g. Tupperware). Much like the *arisan*, SNS such as Facebook allow women with entrepreneurial aspirations to draw upon their multiple social networks as an avenue to market their products.

3. *Middle-class consumption and lifestyle*. Fuelling such entrepreneurial spirits is the demand for consumption from the growing urban middle-class. Gerke (2000) outlines how one defining characteristics of the middle-class consumption is to consume beyond necessities and take on additional *real,* and '*symbolic*' consumption, the later referring to consumption activities geared towards securing one's position as members of the middle-class. As such, we would expect that the kind of products sold through SNS networks targeted for other middle-class women would reflect such consumption behaviour.

4. RESEARCH STRATEGY

In early 2010, I began noticing other users in my network promoting products for sale through their personal accounts. These products are generally small consumption goods, which can be delivered to the person via postage or domestic courier services. Popular goods were handbags, Batik dresses/outfits, baby products, religious attire (for examples: *mukena hijab, baju muslim*), jewelries, homemade cookies, and customized cupcakes.

In 2010, Facebook's Sponsored/Suggested Post was not an available feature yet. As a Facebook member, I could observe who in my friends' lists are using Facebook to promote their goods and services. I could also see friends of Facebook friends who are doing such activities, for example when said friend was tagged in a seller photo. I also had received Friends request from *friends of friends*, and I would immediately know that they were selling products on Facebook, primarily either through their account name, profile pictures, or the content of their wall. Rather than using an official brand page, most sellers operated through personal accounts; either using their own name or through opening additional personal accounts with commercial account names (e.g. Batik XXX Shop, XXX Baby).

With the primary objective to examine the role of Facebook in the formation of online social capital and in providing economic opportunities to its female users in Jakarta, I began a pilot study in 2010. I opted to use my personal Facebook account to approach potential respondents through snowballing, in the hope that this will generate trusts and reciprocity; the two being core concepts in social capital.[5]

Semi-structured online and phone interviews were initially conducted in 2010 with a convenience sample of 15 respondents. Of these 15, 8 were informants who used their personal Facebook page to start up their online business (vendors/sellers). The vendors were all tertiary educated, married, and were all under the age of 40 at the time of the interview. They sold a range of goods, ranging from $1.50 salad to authentic pre-loved and brand new Louis Vuitton handbags. Some promoted products that they either made, or designed themselves and produced with the assistance of paid employees. One respondent promoted glitter tattoo, nail art, and face painting for children's parties.

Most of the research communications and interviews were conducted through Facebook messaging/ Yahoo Messenger.[6] I detailed, among others, the respondents' demographic characteristics, the length of period that the respondent had been on Facebook, the average time spent on Facebook per day, and their number of Facebook friends. Follow up observations and interviews with some respondents were conducted in 2014.

5. TRADING ON FACEBOOK: THE WOMEN'S EXPERIENCE

In this section, I outline selected themes that came out from the interviews. The first one centres on the vendors' motivations to engage in Facebook-mediated trading and how it fits with the notion of collectivism and social media. The second theme focuses on the gendered nature of Facebook trading, both from the perspective of the vendors who took on the role of secondary earners, and their customers. Much of the discussion here refers to Table 1, where I present selected excerpts of interviews with vendors, highlighting their reasons and experience of trading on Facebook.

Table 1. Facebook-mediated trading: motivations and experience

Selling on Facebook requires less time and energy than selling directly. I can sell stuff and be at home while looking after my child or doing other things. I also don't need to be in an uncomfortable situation like when I offered my products to people who were not interested or who didn't actually need them. (Analisa)
On Facebook, you don't need to provide a wide physical space, just need to upload pictures. And for those who cannot communicate effectively (like me) but still want to sell, through Facebook we don't have to (meet others) face to face which often could make us nervous/speechless...Through Facebook, we can sell to people who we already know, (as well as) to people we don't know, and we can directly talk to them without having to meet face to face. It seems more intimate (Ind: terasa lebih dekat). Also the mobile phone technology has enabled us to Facebook wherever we are. In Ebay, Blog, Web, it's not like 'the real life'. (This is) because it needs time to wait for replies on questions on the products being advertised. (Grace)
The first thing I did was to add existing FB members, or browsing through other people's merchandise that I have been tagged. From there I can see who seems to be consumptive or who would be likely to give me respond well ... The obvious benefit is that I can be present to watch my child grows and of course, I don't need to be managed by an arrogant boss... Just to help out, and this is only for my personal satisfaction because I am used to having my own income... I buy little presents for my child and my husband, and I save the rest... For my child, I feel that I too have primary earning responsibility because my child is the responsibility of both me and my husband. But in terms of my husband, my role is only to help. (Dwita)
I don't have high marketing spirit to sell things face to face. Through FB we don't need to spend time and energy to meet people directly to sell our products. (Yuni)
When you don't know the people you are selling to, it is actually more comfortable - because they are willing to take the risks (associated with ordering things online). Often, I don't target my own friends because most of my friends will ask too many questions and they don't end up buying. (Ika)
I was bored, so I started looking for things to do. I want to earn my own money without having to ask my husband all the time (Ind: tanpa nadah minta suami). It started as unintentional (Ind: iseng), but then it turns out that I got something out of it (Ind: iseng-iseng berhadiah). But before Facebook, I already started selling things on Mulitply. (Vivi)

5.1 Motivation: Trading in a Collectivist Setting

None of the interviewed respondents stated that their initial motivation to open up a Facebook account was for trading. The one frequently cited reason for joining Facebook was for "*Silaturahmi*", loosely defined as a social call to strengthen bonds among friends, families, and acquaintances across multiple social clusters. It is a concept whose origin traced back to the Arabic word of *Silaturahim*. In the Islamic context, Silaturahmi alludes to concepts of brotherhood, practiced, for example, through acts of family gatherings, reunions, showing good neighbourly relations, and the aforementioned *arisan*.

The reference to *Silaturahmi* supports the argument that there is a cultural predisposition behind the success of social media in Indonesia. Respondents also cited more specific reasons such as "looking for old friends", "to keep an eye on what husband is doing online (*Ind: Pantau aktifitas suami di FB)*", as well as "invited by friends". Overall, trading through Facebook was an opportunity that the respondents foresaw once they had immersed themselves in this social media for a significant period of time (one year or more).

One important reason cited by the vendors behind their decision to start promoting their products on Facebook was the fact that it was free to do so. There was no physical space required to conduct business, and the mobile nature of SNS means they were free to do it from anywhere. The hypothesis that social media substitutes or extends the old way of doing business did not seem to hold. Though there were some who had previous entrepreneurial activities, some of the vendors interviewed had no previous desire or experience in trading. Indeed, a number of respondents suggested that Facebook was quite revolutionary. Facebook effectively removed entry barriers, including setting up costs (in advertising, setting up shops) and most importantly: time.

The vendors had different ways of running their business. There were vendors who sold their own handmade products, as well as products they had designed themselves and were produced by paid employees. Some had purchased in bulks to re-sell. There were also a number of vendors who would use purchasing orders to wholesalers/manufacturers, and this was the most common methods for vendors selling Korean-made/imported handbags and clothing.[7]

These findings support the hypotheses that Facebook serves as a productive platform: reducing the direct and opportunity costs of setting up and maintaining a small business for the respondents. Similar reasoning surely applies to other free online selling sites (such as EBay), but SNS also opened up the possibility of promoting goods to "people you already know". Facebook supports the maintenance of existing social ties and the formation of new connections. For sellers, marketing through Facebook make use of the bonding or existing social capital. By promoting to one's friends, sellers also promote to the 'friends of friends'. Hence, allowing them to market through their linking social capital. Grace's description that Facebook offers an 'intimate' online environment ties in nicely with the core elements of Internet facilitated social capital: trusts and reciprocity (Kobayashi et al., 2006).

One surprising finding on the motivations of selling on Facebook was the vendor's attraction the *contactless* nature of online interactions. Facebook-mediated interaction allowed for a somewhat less aggressive front for sellers to identify and approach potential customers. What emerged conspicuously from the interviews was that there is considerable reluctance to engage in direct/face-to-face person selling. For the vendors, collecting monetary gains through taking advantage from individuals who share strong network ties with them raise the possibility of them being seen as self-seeking. On the other end, for the *friends* of vendors, they also may feel obligated to help their friends to succeed by making purchases. Both instances may be damaging to social relations. One respondent further explained that face-to-face selling carries a higher risk of obligatory purchases between a seller and a customer who share the same social circle. Facebook cushioned these potentially 'awkward' situations. In other words, Facebook essentially acts as a mediating platform to soften commercial transactions among actors who nurture and highly value their personal relations with one another.

5.2 The Secondary Earner and the Online Sisterhood

The unifying theme from the interviews was that the vendors perceived selling through Facebook as being in line with their role as secondary earners in their marriage. It was clear that income generated through their trading activities on Facebook was supplementary in nature. Having said that, all vendors interviewed reported increased personal satisfaction from having managed to earn their own income.

It was rather tricky to ask how much the vendors earn through trading on Facebook. The profit generated would depend on the product they were selling and how long they have engaged in the activity, and the amount of time they have invested to expand their customer's base. One respondent, who sold baby items, specializing in reusable diapers, reported that she had not breakeven since she started selling on Facebook in early 2010 (Interviewed in August 2010). On the other hand, another vendor made somewhere between 40 to 50 million rupiah within 4 months of selling branded handbags and sunglasses.

The vendors interviewed suggest that the main target groups of their products are other middle class young women and young mothers in urban Indonesia. As outlined previously, the goods promoted by the vendors are typically not everyday consumption products. Popular items are clothing, handbags and accessories, footwear, children and baby products. Buyers interviewed often referred to their purchases as being frivolous consumption and recreational in nature. While some admitted that in many cases, it was impulsive buying, others stated that they were purposely looking for certain products. The latter particularly applied for products geared around festive seasons, such as embroidered Kaftans, *Mukena* (Prayer Covering), and Ied/end of Ramadhan hampers/cookies. There was also a visible market for the working women, with vendors catering for work-related consumption purchases, namely hoes, handbags, and Batik clothing designed for office wear.

In all, there was little to suggest that the bulk of Facebook-mediated trade represent 'symbolic' consumption, in the sense that the activities reflect purchases needed to define the status of buyers as members of the urban middle-class with its consumer-oriented lifestyle (Gerke 2000). With the exception of branded and imported small luxury goods, most of the other goods and services being traded in this particular case study underline the importance of personal satisfaction as both the reason to buy and sell via Facebook. Yet, the phenomenon is indeed a reflection of the increasing ability for discretionary spending among growing number of middle-class women in Jakarta. Interestingly, albeit a portion allocated for personal savings, the income generated from trading in Facebook was generally also used for discretionary spending for the vendors and their family.

The online interactions between vendors and sellers further highlighted a gendered web culture. While interested friends who knew the vendor personally were addressed by their first name and vice versa, communication between customers and vendors without prior offline interactions use female kinship terms when addressing each other. These kinship terms were *Sis* – short for sister, *Bun* – short for Bunda (Mother), and less often *Mbak* – a widely used Javanese term to refer to an older sister/female relative/ female non-relatives. A recent study on the address terms used in social media-facilitated online shops in Indonesia had also highlighted this trend, suggesting that the use of kinship terms among predominantly female actors in online shopping are in line with the idea of a friendly, relaxed, or more informal interaction between vendors-customers Facebook-facilitated trade (Anggrawan & Tedjaatmadja, 2013).

5.3 Follow Up

Follow-up interviews and observations in 2014 suggested that some of these original respondents had ceased online selling altogether, some had changed their line of products, and some had switched from primarily using Facebook to Instagram.

One common narrative found in the interviews was the use of Facebook as a stepping stone. Before Facebook, one respondent had begun selling using the now closed social networking site: Multiply. But as illustrated earlier, some vendors had no previous entrepreneurial experience. A respondent started selling her patchwork crafts through Facebook, and was successful enough that she then launched a website for her products. Another respondent had moved away from primarily re-selling imported branded goods through Facebook in 2010, to designing and producing her own line of handbags and accessories now promoted through her personal Facebook account, and brand-specific Facebook page, Instagram, as well as through small trade and handicraft fairs in a number of capital cities in Java (Figure 2). With her siblings, the respondent sources materials from local weavers and employs craftsmen to produce their designs.

There are success stories of continuity and scaling up, but there are also narratives of abandonment. In the first instance, Facebook had given all interviewed vendors the chance to acquire business and negotiating skills. But as the cost of setting up the business was low, the cost of abandoning the business was correspondingly low. One vendor reported that she ceased trading on Facebook since others started copying her products. Along with the increasing competitors on Facebook, she further mentioned that the cost of importing goods had dramatically increased. As her business expanded, with increasing volumes, she faced looming tax bills (since she was selling designer brands that fell under the import of luxury goods). With this additional substantive cost of transaction weighing down her perceived benefits from running the Facebook-based business, she decided that it was not worth her time. At times, when requested, she would order products from suppliers and sell them to a limited circle, and mostly as an act of favour to friends.

Other factors that pose a serious challenge to the viability of vending activities through Facebook is the diffusion of Facebook itself, and the shifts to other SNS platforms. A CEO and co-founder of an Indonesian online dating site observed that as Facebook grows in popularity across many layers of social class, another SNS platform, Path, has become the SNS of choice among the middle and upper middle

Figure 2. Building an original brand through Facebook-mediated trading
Source: https://www.facebook.com/matbyme

class in Indonesia (R. Thalib, personal communication, June 29, 2015). To this end, Facebook-mediated trade is purported as a prime reason towards the shift. As stated by a social media observer: "In Indonesia Facebook is a marketplace. Yes it's a social network but it's a highly abused social network in which people take advantage of their connectedness and use their personal pages to promote and sell products and services" (Masna, 2013). Still, the valuable connection made in Facebook meant that users remain reluctant to leave Facebook altogether, but many Facebook users also have a Path account to actively share details of personal activities and thoughts with a limited number of people (Masna, 2013).

The case study suggests that using alternative SNS platform, such as Instagram, as well as Facebook to vend, is an effective strategy to address the decline of receptiveness in Facebook-mediated trade. In addition, in the face of crowding out in the SNS marketplace, creating a niche, product branding, building a reputation as a trusted seller, and participating in offline trade fairs were identified as key factors leading to continued success of a Facebook-initiated small business venture. While Facebook made starting up a small business relatively easy for the women interviewed, its role in securing long term success is another matter.

6. CONCLUSION

This case study demonstrates that the production of monetary benefits through online social networks was highly contingent on the class, and the broader socio-cultural norms in both offline and online social interactions in Greater Jakarta. More specifically, the case study shows that women's income generating activities through social media mirror existing gendered practices of women as secondary earners in the family. As distinct to *revolutionise*, social media facilitates, extends, and amplifies, the traditional marketing avenues of personal networks for women's entrepreneurs. Further, such thriving practice was sustained by the consumption behavior of middle class women in SNS, and by the nature of social media interactions in a collectivist setting. These interrelated contentions advance the argument that the adoption and use of ICTs are essentially shaped by pre-existing socio-cultural contexts.

At the same time, these class, gender, and cultural factors that are conducive to such practice is also supported by Facebook-specific features. First, Facebook greatly reduces the cost of setting up and running a business. Second, the nature of online interactions via Facebook can both promote an atmosphere of kinship, trusts, and reciprocity, while at the same time, reduce the discomfort associated with face-to-face selling. In this manner, Facebook-mediated trading works well in a collectivist setting because it tends to minimize potential conflicts that would otherwise arise if vendors were to engage in face-to-face selling to people in their personal circles.

Within this collectivist network setting, it is clear that those engaging in online exchanges are motivated by individualistic purposes. The notion of shopping as something that women generally enjoy was apparent, and the vendors are motivated by the potential of increased disposable income. On the one hand, the hypothesis that Facebook-mediated trade is dominated by the exchange of 'symbolic' (or branded/luxury) consumption goods was not well-supported by either interviews or observations. However, with the majority of the exchange consisting of 'affordable' conspicuous consumption goods, Facebook-mediated trade does support the idea of consumption-oriented middle-class life styling among women (Gerke, 2000).

The dominating presence of female actors in Facebook-mediated trade alludes to the adage of middle-class women as shoppers, and increasingly, as sellers. As such, this example adds to the emerging literature documenting how ICTs have opened up new economic opportunities for women in Indonesia (Anwar & Johanson, 2014). The case study is limited in its representativeness due to the small number of respondents, and from the bias arising from the process of initially drawing a snowball sample starting from my own personal networks. However, a number of other recent micro studies have resonated my findings on the gendered nature of Facebook-mediated trade in urban Indonesia (Albert & Hersinta, 2013; Anggrawan & Tedjaatmadja, 2013; Melissa et al., 2013).

The vendors' narratives of their motivation to begin selling on Facebook reflect offline practices showing women's active involvement in the informal sector, and the perception that women's contribution to the family income is secondary to their husband's (Gallaway & Bernasek, 2002; Utomo, 2012). A study conducted by Women's Resources Development centre in Jakarta in the mid-1990s reported that "helping my husband, taking care of the household" was the answer given by 80 per cent of 147 women when asked of their work in the informal sector (Djamal, 2000). Here, "helping my husband" actually meant running a small businesses and juggling home and childcare responsibilities. While they women were involved in informal trading, in general, the women assumed that they did not work, and that their role was at home. Djamal argued that male breadwinner norms were so strong that this was the answer given despite 70 per cent of the women actually earned more than the husbands. Similarly, the vendors interviewed in the current case study had the impression that Facebook-mediated trading is informal work offering flexible hours. In other words, the women believed that becoming a vendor is compatible with the women's primary roles as wives and mothers. This narrative of role compatibility is important in understanding the gendered nature of Facebook-mediated trade.

One theme that did not emerge out of the interviews but should be pursued further in future research is the relationship between social class, social capital, and returns to education. Trading via SNS offers the opportunity for married women who had left the formal labour market to get monetary returns from their multiple social networks. These networks are often dependent on friendships created through schooling, as well as from their previous work experience. Since SNS captures ties and networks created through time spent in education, it is feasible to quantify or conceptualise the returns to education in terms of income generated through networks created either directly through schooling, as well as networks made possible because of one's educational attainment. In the face of internet diffusion, increasing competition, and the shifts to other SNS platforms among the urban middle class in Indonesia, further work is required to examine the viability of extracting returns from personal networks through Facebook.

ACKNOWLEDGMENT

This chapter is based on a paper titled *Is Facebook a waste of time: A case study of online social networks and income generation among married women in Jakarta*, which was presented at the 10th International Women in Asia Conference: Crisis, Agency, and Change, The Australian National University, Canberra, 29 September – 1 October 2010. I would like to thank the anonymous reviewers, Robert Ackland, Arifah, Andru Nasrun, and Novi Kardini for their ideas and comments for earlier drafts of this paper.

REFERENCES

Albert, A., & Hersinta, H. (2013). Shopping on Social Networking Sites: A Study on Facebook Consumers' psychological Characteristics. *Journal Communication Spectrum*, *2*(2).

Anggrawan, D. S., & Tedjaatmadja, H. M. (2013). Address terms used by online shop sellers to their female teenage customers and young mother customers in Facebook. *K@ ta Kita, 1*(1), 122-129.

Anwar, M., & Johanson, G. (2014). Mobile Phones and religion: The Case of women Micro-Entrepreneurs in a religious Community in Indonesia. *Islam and Development: Exploring the Invisible Aid Economy*, 135.

Ardi, R., & Maison, D. (2014). How do Polish and Indonesian disclose in Facebook? *Journal of Information. Communication and Ethics in Society*, *12*(3), 195–218. doi:10.1108/JICES-01-2014-0006

Banerjee, A. V., & Duflo, E. (2008). What is middle class about the middle classes around the world? *The journal of economic perspectives: a journal of the American Economic Association, 22*(2), 3.

Brenner, S. (1995). Why women rule the roost: rethinking Javanese ideologies of gender and self-control. In A. Ong & M. G. Peletz (Eds.), *Bewitching women, pious men: Gender and body politics in Southeast Asia* (pp. 19–50). Berkeley: University of California Press.

Coleman, J. S. (1988). Social capital in the creation of human capital. *American Journal of Sociology*, *94*, S95–S120. doi:10.1086/228943

Djamal, C. (2000). Women in the informal sector, a 'forgotten' workforce. In M.-O. Gardiner & C. Bianpoen (Eds.), *Indonesian women: The journey continues* (pp. 172–188). Canberra: RSPAS Publishing, ANU.

Ellison, N. B., Steinfield, C., & Lampe, C. (2007). The Benefits of Facebook "Friends:" Social Capital and College Students' Use of Online Social Network Sites. *Journal of Computer-Mediated Communication*, *12*(4), 1143–1168. doi:10.1111/j.1083-6101.2007.00367.x

Gallaway, J. H., & Bernasek, A. (2002). Gender and informal sector employment in Indonesia. *Journal of Economic Issues*, *36*(2), 313–321. doi:10.1080/00213624.2002.11506473

Garcia-Gavilanes, R., Quercia, D., & Jaimes, A. (2013). Cultural dimensions in Twitter: Time, individualism and power. Proceedings of AAAI ICWSM.

Gerke, S. (2000). Global lifestyles under local conditions: The new Indonesian middle class. In B.-H. Chua (Ed.), *Consumption in Asia: Lifestyles and identities* (pp. 135–158). London: Routledge.

Goodwin, R., & Giles, S. (2003). Social Support Provision and Cultural Values In Indonesia And Britain. *Journal of Cross-Cultural Psychology*, *34*(2), 240–245. doi:10.1177/0022022102250227

Hargittai, E., & Shafer, S. (2006). Differences in Actual and Perceived Online Skills: The Role of Gender. *Social Science Quarterly*, *87*(2), 432–448. doi:10.1111/j.1540-6237.2006.00389.x

Hofstede, G. (1983). National Cultures in Four Dimensions: A Research-Based Theory of Cultural Differences among Nations. *International Studies of Management & Organization*, *13*(1/2), 46–74. doi:10.2307/40396953

Hospes, O. (1992). les gens qui comptent: Les faces oubliees des associations rotatoires d'epargne et de credit en indonesie [People that count: The forgotten faces of rotating savings and credit associations in Indonesia]. In *Savings and Development* (pp. 371-401).

Hoy, M. G., & Milne, G. (2010). Gender Differences in Privacy-Related Measures for Young Adult Facebook Users. *Journal of Interactive Advertising*, *10*(2), 28–45. doi:10.1080/15252019.2010.10722168

Indonesia's middle class: missing BRIC in the wall (2011, July 21). *The Economist*. Retrieved from http://www.economist.com/node/18989153

Khatri, Y., Ie, W., & Newton, A. (2011, June 13-16). Indonesia: Building Momentum. *Proceedings of the Nomura Asia Equity Forum*, Singapore. Retrieved from http://www.nomura.com/europe/resources/upload/Millenia_6_Day_1_1500_Indonesia_Building_Momentum_Mr_Yougesh_Khatri.pdf

Kobayashi, T., Ikeda, K. i., & Miyata, K. (2006). Social capital online: Collective use of the Internet and reciprocity as lubricants of democracy. *Information Communication and Society*, *9*(5), 582–611. doi:10.1080/13691180600965575

Kosaka, T., & Dananjaya, R. M. (2012). A Cross-Cultural Study of the Feasibility of Vendor Relationship Management in Indonesia and Japan. Retrieved from http://www.ms.kuki.tus.ac.jp/KMSLab/kosaka/papers/IICC201212.pdf

Lim, M. (2013). Many Clicks but Little Sticks: Social Media Activism in Indonesia. *Journal of Contemporary Asia*, *43*(4), 636–657. doi:10.1080/00472336.2013.769386

Manns, H. (2010). Indonesian slang in Internet Chatting. In S. Babatunde, A. Odebunmi, A. Adetunji, & M. Adedimeji (Eds.), *Studies in Slang and Slogans* (pp. 71–99). Munich: Lincom.

Masna, A. (2001). Why is Facebook so popular in Indonesia? *Quora.com*. Retrieved from http://www.quora.com/Aulia-Masna/answers/Indonesia

Masna, A. (2013). Why is Path so Popular in Indonesia. Retrieved from https://en.dailysocial.net/post/why-is-path-so-popular-in-indonesia

Mayoux, L. (2001). Tackling the Down Side: Social Capital, Women's Empowerment and Micro-Finance in Cameroon. *Development and Change*, *32*(3), 435–464. doi:10.1111/1467-7660.00212

McAndrew, F. T., & Jeong, H. S. (2012). Who does what on Facebook? Age, sex, and relationship status as predictors of Facebook use. *Computers in Human Behavior*, *28*(6), 2359–2365. doi:10.1016/j.chb.2012.07.007

Mehdizadeh, S. (2010). Self-presentation 2.0: Narcissism and self-esteem on Facebook. *Cyberpsychology, Behavior, and Social Networking*, *13*(4), 357–364. doi:10.1089/cyber.2009.0257 PMID:20712493

Melissa, E., Hamidati, A., Saraswati, M. S., & Flor, A. G. (2013). Investigating the potentials of social media to support women entrepreneurship in Indonesian urban areas. *Paper presented at the Proceedings of the Sixth International Conference on Information and Communications Technologies and Development* (Vol. 2). doi:10.1145/2517899.2517921

Molyneux, M. (2002). Gender and the Silences of Social Capital: Lessons from Latin America. *Development and Change, 33*(2), 167–188. doi:10.1111/1467-7660.00246

Mysore, S. (2008). Facebook Indonesia Outpaces Southeast Asian Counterparts in 2008. Retrieved from http://www.insidefacebook.com/2008/12/31/facebook-indonesia-outpaces-southeast-asian-counterparts-in-2008/

Na, J., Kosinski, M., & Stillwell, D. J. (2015). When a New Tool Is Introduced in Different Cultural Contexts Individualism–Collectivism and Social Network on Facebook. *Journal of Cross-Cultural Psychology, 46*(3), 355–370. doi:10.1177/0022022114563932

Ng, C., & Mitter, S. (2005). Gender and the digital economy: Perspectives from the developing world. *Sage (Atlanta, Ga.)*.

Papanek, H., & Schwede, L. (1988). Women are good with money: Earning and managing in an Indonesian city. *Economic and Political Weekly*, 1988, WS73–WS84.

Pasek, J., More, E., & Romer, D. (2009). Realizing the Social Internet? Online Social Networking Meets Offline Civic Engagement. *Journal of Information Technology & Politics, 6*(3-4), 197–215. doi:10.1080/19331680902996403

Pisani, E. (2014). *Etc.: Exploring the Improbable Nation*. Indonesia: WW Norton & Company.

Purnell, N. (2014). Facebook Users in Indonesia Rise to 69 Million. *Wall Street Journal*. Retrieved from http://blogs.wsj.com/digits/2014/06/27/facebook-users-in-indonesia-rise-to-69-million/

Putnam, R. (2001). Social capital: Measurement and consequences. *Canadian Journal of Policy Research, 2*(1), 41–51.

Putra, J. S. (2011). Why Facebook is So Popular in Indonesia? *Olson.com*. Retrieved from http://www.penn-olson.com/2011/03/07/why-facebook-is-so-popular-in-indonesia/

Rammohan, A., & Johar, M. (2009). The Determinants of Married Women's Autonomy in Indonesia. *Feminist Economics, 15*(4), 31–55. doi:10.1080/13545700903153989

Rankin, K. N. (2002). Social Capital, Microfinance, and the Politics of Development. *Feminist Economics, 8*(1), 1–24. doi:10.1080/13545700210125167

Royal, C. (2008). Framing the Internet: A Comparison of Gendered Spaces. *Social Science Computer Review, 26*(2), 152–169. doi:10.1177/0894439307307366

Safitri, D. (2011). Why is Indonesia so in love with the Blackberry? *BBC Indonesia Service*. Retrieved from http://news.bbc.co.uk/2/hi/programmes/direct/indonesia/9508138.stm

Sari, E., & Tedjasaputra, A. (2013). Engaging stakeholders through Facebook for teacher professional development in Indonesia. *Proceedings of the 25th Australian Computer-Human Interaction Conference: Augmentation, Application, Innovation, Collaboration* (pp. 201-204). ACM. doi:10.1145/2541016.2541056

Silvey, R., & Elmhirst, R. (2003). Engendering Social Capital: Women Workers and Rural–Urban Networks in Indonesia's Crisis. *World Development, 31*(5), 865–879. doi:10.1016/S0305-750X(03)00013-5

Simandjuntak, D. (2011). We Can't Be Seen As Cheap. *Inside Indonesia*, 2011, 104.

Statistics Indonesia. (2010). Results of the 2010 Population Census. from www.sp2010.bps.go.id

Statistics Indonesia. (2011b). Results of the 2010 Population Census. Sensus Penduduk 2010: Penduduk Berumur 5 Tahun Keatas Menurut Kelompok Umur dan Kemampuan Berbahasa Indonesia [Population Census 2010: Population aged 5 years and over by age groups and Indonesian Language Ability]. Retrieved from www.sp2010.bps.go.id

Triandis, H. C., Bontempo, R., Betancourt, H., Bond, M., Leung, K., Brenes, A., & Montmollin, G. et al. (1986). The measurement of the etic aspects of individualism and collectivism across cultures. *Australian Journal of Psychology*, *38*(3), 257–267. doi:10.1080/00049538608259013

Utomo, A. (2012). Women as secondary earners: Gendered preferences on marriage and employment of university students in modern Indonesia. *Asian Population Studies*, *8*(1), 65–85. doi:10.1080/17441730.2012.646841

Utomo, A., Reimondos, A., Utomo, I., McDonald, P., & Hull, T. H. (2013). Digital inequalities and young adults in Greater Jakarta: A socio-demographic perspective. *International Journal of Indonesian Studies*, *1*(1).

Valenzuela, S., Park, N., & Kee, K. F. (2009). Is There Social Capital in a Social Network Site?: Facebook Use and College Students' Life Satisfaction, Trust, and Participation. *Journal of Computer-Mediated Communication*, *14*(4), 875–901. doi:10.1111/j.1083-6101.2009.01474.x

Vaswani, K. (2012). Indonesia's love affair with social media. *BBC News Asia*. Retrieved from http://www.bbc.co.uk/news/world-asia-17054056

Wasko, M. M., & Faraj, S. (2005). Why Should I Share? Examining Social Capital and Knowledge Contribution in Electronic Networks of Practice. *Management Information Systems Quarterly*, *29*(1), 35–57. doi:10.2307/25148667

Wheeler, D. (2001). New Technologies, Old Culture: A Look at Women, Gender. *Culture, technology, communication: Towards an intercultural global village* (pp. 187-212).

ENDNOTES

1. Decades of educational expansion is strongly reflected in the age group differentials of highest educational attainment. In 2010, less than 13 percent of populations aged 60-64 have at least high school or equivalent qualifications. The corresponding figure for populations aged 25-29 is 43.6 per cent.
2. Citing commentaries on social media in Indonesia (Masna, 2001; Putra, 2011; Safitri, 2011).
3. For studies on collectivism as the dominant modes of organisation in Indonesia, see for example: Goodwin and Giles (2003); Hofstede (1983); and Triandis et al. (1986).

4 Network density measures the number of actual connections within networks. A high density network implies that actors in the networks know and interact with each other. On the opposite end, in low density networks, actors have many connections but may not interact with one another, hence the network is characterised as having many *potential*, as opposed to, *actual* connections. For low density nature of cyber networks in Indonesia see Manns (2010).

5 I joined Facebook in 2008, and my networks of 'Indonesian' friends then included those who were residing in Indonesia as well as overseas. These Facebook connections were largely made up of families, relatives, school friends (from Primary and Junior High), people I met through studying and working at my current university which include students, graduate researchers, and their spouse, and overseas Indonesian networks.

6 I initially tried emailing respondents, and attaching a questionnaire in a word file. This did not work, because the majority of the respondents used their mobile phones with FB application to access the Internet. Some requested to be interviewed via Black Berry Messaging which I had none at the time. In addition to the interviews, I observed online interactions on each seller's Facebook wall. I could read conversations between sellers and their potential customers, checked the pictures of goods being sold, and further observed whether they have been successfully sold or not.

7 Another common mode of Facebook-mediated trade in Jakarta is the practice of drop shipping. Vendors would upload pictures of goods and market them to their networks. They would then place orders, on behalf of the customers, to producers, who would send the goods directly to the customers. None of the interviewed vendors adopted this business model at the initial interviews in 2010.

Related References

To continue our tradition of advancing information science and technology research, we have compiled a list of recommended IGI Global readings. These references will provide additional information and guidance to further enrich your knowledge and assist you with your own research and future publications.

Abrams, S. S. (2010). The dynamics of video gaming: Influences affecting game play and learning. In P. Zemliansky & D. Wilcox (Eds.), *Design and implementation of educational games: Theoretical and practical perspectives* (pp. 78–91). Hershey, PA: Information Science Reference; doi:10.4018/978-1-61520-781-7.ch006

Achtenhagen, L., & Johannisson, B. (2013). Games in entrepreneurship education to support the crafting of an entrepreneurial mindset. In S. de Freitas, M. Ott, M. Popescu, & I. Stanescu (Eds.), *New pedagogical approaches in game enhanced learning: Curriculum integration* (pp. 20–37). Hershey, PA: Information Science Reference; doi:10.4018/978-1-4666-3950-8.ch002

Akcaoglu, M. (2013). Using MMORPGs in classrooms: Stories vs. teachers as sources of motivation. In Y. Baek & N. Whitton (Eds.), *Cases on digital game-based learning: Methods, models, and strategies* (pp. 15–24). Hershey, PA: Information Science Reference; doi:10.4018/978-1-4666-2848-9.ch002

Al-Jenaibi, B. (2011). Gender issues in the diversity and practice of public relations in the UAE case study of P.R. male managers and female P.R. practitioners. *International Journal of E-Politics*, *2*(3), 35–56. doi:10.4018/jep.2011070104

Albert, L. J., Hill, T. R., & Venkatsubramanyan, S. (2011). Effects of perceiver / target gender and social networking presence on web-based impression formation. *International Journal of E-Politics*, *2*(2), 55–73. doi:10.4018/jep.2011040104

Albert, L. J., Hill, T. R., & Venkatsubramanyan, S. (2012). Gender differences in social networking presence effects on web-based impression formation. In C. Romm Livermore (Ed.), *Gender and social computing: Interactions, differences and relationships* (pp. 200–220). Hershey, PA: Information Science Publishing; doi:10.4018/978-1-60960-759-3.ch012

Albuquerque, O., & Moreira, G. G. (2011). The contribution of videogames to anti-social attitudes and behaviours amongst youngsters. In M. Cruz-Cunha, V. Varvalho, & P. Tavares (Eds.), *Business, technological, and social dimensions of computer games: Multidisciplinary developments* (pp. 237–251). Hershey, PA: Information Science Reference; doi:10.4018/978-1-60960-567-4.ch015

Aldrich, C., & DiPietro, J. C. (2011). An overview of gaming terminology: Chapters I – LXXVI. In Gaming and simulations: Concepts, methodologies, tools and applications (pp. 24-44). Hershey, PA: Information Science Reference. doi:10.4018/978-1-60960-195-9.ch102

Alkhattabi, M., Neagu, D., & Cullen, A. (2012). User perceptions of information quality in e-learning systems: A gender and cultural perspective. In R. Pande & T. Van der Weide (Eds.), *Globalization, technology diffusion and gender disparity: Social impacts of ICTs* (pp. 138–145). Hershey, PA: Information Science Reference; doi:10.4018/978-1-4666-0020-1.ch012

Anagnostou, K. (2011). How has the internet evolved the videogame medium? In M. Cruz-Cunha, V. Varvalho, & P. Tavares (Eds.), *Business, technological, and social dimensions of computer games: Multidisciplinary developments* (pp. 448–462). Hershey, PA: Information Science Reference; doi:10.4018/978-1-60960-567-4.ch027

Anderson, B. (2010). MMORPGs in support of learning: Current trends and future uses. In R. Van Eck (Ed.), *Gaming and cognition: Theories and practice from the learning sciences* (pp. 55–81). Hershey, PA: Information Science Reference; doi:10.4018/978-1-61520-717-6.ch003

Appiah, O., & Elias, T. (2011). Race-specific advertising on commercial websites: Effects of ethnically ambiguous computer generated characters in a digital world. In M. Eastin, T. Daugherty, & N. Burns (Eds.), *Handbook of research on digital media and advertising: User generated content consumption* (pp. 161–179). Hershey, PA: Information Science Reference; doi:10.4018/978-1-61692-020-3.ch007

Arroyo-Palacios, J., & Romano, D. M. (2010). Bio-affective computer interface for game interaction. *International Journal of Gaming and Computer-Mediated Simulations*, *2*(4), 16–32. doi:10.4018/jgcms.2010100102

Asbell-Clarke, J., Edwards, T., Rowe, E., Larsen, J., Sylvan, E., & Hewitt, J. (2012). Martian boneyards: Scientific inquiry in an MMO game. *International Journal of Game-Based Learning*, *2*(1), 52–76. doi:10.4018/ijgbl.2012010104

Bachvarova, Y., & Bocconi, S. (2014). Games and social networks. In T. Connolly, T. Hainey, E. Boyle, G. Baxter, & P. Moreno-Ger (Eds.), *Psychology, pedagogy, and assessment in serious games* (pp. 204–219). Hershey, PA: Information Science Reference; doi:10.4018/978-1-4666-4773-2.ch010

Balachandar, A., & Gurusamy, R. (2012). Conflict segments of women employees of IT sector in India: Its relevance with the demographic profile. *International Journal of Human Capital and Information Technology Professionals*, *3*(1), 42–53. doi:10.4018/jhcitp.2012010104

Balzac, S. R. (2010). Reality from fantasy: Using predictive scenarios to explore ethical dilemmas. In K. Schrier & D. Gibson (Eds.), *Ethics and game design: Teaching values through play* (pp. 291–310). Hershey, PA: Information Science Reference; doi:10.4018/978-1-61520-845-6.ch018

Baranowski, T., O'Connor, T., Hughes, S., Beltran, A., Baranowski, J., & Nicklas, T. … Buday, R. (2013). Smart phone video game simulation of parent-child interaction: learning skills for effective vegetable parenting. In S. Arnab, I. Dunwell, & K. Debattista (Eds.), Serious games for healthcare: Applications and implications (pp. 247-264). Hershey, PA: Medical Information Science Reference. doi:10.4018/978-1-4666-1903-6.ch012

Barlow, M. (2011). Game led HCI improvements. In M. Cruz-Cunha, V. Varvalho, & P. Tavares (Eds.), *Business, technological, and social dimensions of computer games: Multidisciplinary developments* (pp. 126–145). Hershey, PA: Information Science Reference; doi:10.4018/978-1-60960-567-4.ch009

Bates, M. (2013). The ur-real sonorous envelope: Bridge between the corporeal and the online techno-self. In R. Luppicini (Ed.), *Handbook of research on technoself: Identity in a technological society* (pp. 272–292). Hershey, PA: Information Science Reference; doi:10.4018/978-1-4666-2211-1.ch015

Belfo, F. (2011). Business process management in the computer games industry. In M. Cruz-Cunha, V. Varvalho, & P. Tavares (Eds.), *Business, technological, and social dimensions of computer games: Multidisciplinary developments* (pp. 383–400). Hershey, PA: Information Science Reference; doi:10.4018/978-1-60960-567-4.ch023

Ben, E. R. (2012). Gendering professionalism in the internationalization of information work. In R. Pande & T. Van der Weide (Eds.), *Globalization, technology diffusion and gender disparity: Social impacts of ICTs* (pp. 51–69). Hershey, PA: Information Science Reference; doi:10.4018/978-1-4666-0020-1.ch005

Berzsenyi, C. (2014). Writing to meet your match: Rhetoric and self-presentation for four online daters. In H. Lim & F. Sudweeks (Eds.), *Innovative methods and technologies for electronic discourse analysis* (pp. 210–234). Hershey, PA: Information Science Reference; doi:10.4018/978-1-4666-4426-7.ch010

Bevc, T. (2010). Models of politics and society in video games. In P. Zemliansky & D. Wilcox (Eds.), *Design and implementation of educational games: Theoretical and practical perspectives* (pp. 47–64). Hershey, PA: Information Science Reference; doi:10.4018/978-1-61520-781-7.ch004

Bhatnagar, K. (2013). Supply chain management and the other half. In *Supply chain management: Concepts, methodologies, tools, and applications* (pp. 106–120). Hershey, PA: Business Science Reference; doi:10.4018/978-1-4666-2625-6.ch007

Bishop, J. (2010). Increasing capital revenue in social networking communities: Building social and economic relationships through avatars and characters. In S. Dasgupta (Ed.), *Social computing: Concepts, methodologies, tools, and applications* (pp. 1987–2004). Hershey, PA: Information Science Reference; doi:10.4018/978-1-60566-984-7.ch131

Bishop, J. (2011). Increasing capital revenue in social networking communities: Building social and economic relationships through avatars and characters. In *Virtual communities: Concepts, methodologies, tools and applications* (pp. 1720–1737). Hershey, PA: Information Science Reference; doi:10.4018/978-1-60960-100-3.ch509

Bishop, J. (2013). The psychology of trolling and lurking: The role of defriending and gamification for increasing participation in online communities using seductive narratives. In J. Bishop (Ed.), *Examining the concepts, issues, and implications of internet trolling* (pp. 106–123). Hershey, PA: Information Science Reference; doi:10.4018/978-1-4666-2803-8.ch009

Black, E. W., Ferdig, R. E., DiPietro, J. C., Liu, F., & Whalen, B. (2011). Visual analyses of the creation of avatars. In R. Ferdig (Ed.), *Discoveries in gaming and computer-mediated simulations: New interdisciplinary applications* (pp. 284–300). Hershey, PA: Information Science Reference; doi:10.4018/978-1-60960-565-0.ch016

Blasko, D. G., Lum, H. C., White, M. M., & Drabik, H. B. (2014). Individual differences in the enjoyment and effectiveness of serious games. In T. Connolly, T. Hainey, E. Boyle, G. Baxter, & P. Moreno-Ger (Eds.), *Psychology, pedagogy, and assessment in serious games* (pp. 153–174). Hershey, PA: Information Science Reference; doi:10.4018/978-1-4666-4773-2.ch008

Blomqvist, M. (2010). Absent women: Research on gender relations in IT education mediated by Swedish newspapers. In S. Booth, S. Goodman, & G. Kirkup (Eds.), *Gender issues in learning and working with information technology: Social constructs and cultural contexts* (pp. 133–149). Hershey, PA: Information Science Reference; doi:10.4018/978-1-61520-813-5.ch008

Boa-Ventura, A. (2012). Virtual worlds and behavioral change: Overcoming time/ space constraints and exploring anonymity to overcome social stigma in the case of substance abuse. In N. Zagalo, L. Morgado, & A. Boa-Ventura (Eds.), *Virtual worlds and metaverse platforms: New communication and identity paradigms* (pp. 271–286). Hershey, PA: Information Science Reference; doi:10.4018/978-1-60960-854-5.ch018

Boivie, I. (2010). Women, men and programming: Knowledge, metaphors and masculinity. In S. Booth, S. Goodman, & G. Kirkup (Eds.), *Gender issues in learning and working with information technology: Social constructs and cultural contexts* (pp. 1–24). Hershey, PA: Information Science Reference; doi:10.4018/978-1-61520-813-5.ch001

Booth, S., & Wigforss, E. (2010). Approaching higher education: A life-world story of home-places, work-places and learn-places. In S. Booth, S. Goodman, & G. Kirkup (Eds.), *Gender issues in learning and working with information technology: Social constructs and cultural contexts* (pp. 173–191). Hershey, PA: Information Science Reference; doi:10.4018/978-1-61520-813-5.ch010

Braun, P. (2011). Advancing women in the digital economy: eLearning opportunities for meta-competency skilling. In *Global business: Concepts, methodologies, tools and applications* (pp. 1978–1990). Hershey, PA: Business Science Reference; doi:10.4018/978-1-60960-587-2.ch708

Bryant, J. A., & Drell, J. (2010). Family fun and fostering values. In K. Schrier & D. Gibson (Eds.), *Ethics and game design: Teaching values through play* (pp. 167–180). Hershey, PA: Information Science Reference; doi:10.4018/978-1-61520-845-6.ch011

Buraphadeja, V., & Dawson, K. (2011). Exploring personal myths from the Sims. In *Gaming and simulations: Concepts, methodologies, tools and applications* (pp. 1750–1762). Hershey, PA: Information Science Reference; doi:10.4018/978-1-60960-195-9.ch705

Byrd, M. Y. (2012). Critical race theory: A framework for examining social identity diversity of Black women in positions of leadership. In C. Scott & M. Byrd (Eds.), *Handbook of research on workforce diversity in a global society: Technologies and concepts* (pp. 426–439). Hershey, PA: Business Science Reference; doi:10.4018/978-1-4666-1812-1.ch025

Carneiro, M. G. (2011). Artificial intelligence in games evolution. In M. Cruz-Cunha, V. Varvalho, & P. Tavares (Eds.), *Business, technological, and social dimensions of computer games: Multidisciplinary developments* (pp. 98–114). Hershey, PA: Information Science Reference; doi:10.4018/978-1-60960-567-4.ch007

Chandra, S., Gruber, T., & Lowrie, A. (2012). Service recovery encounters in the classroom: Exploring the attributes of professors desired by male and female students. *International Journal of Technology and Educational Marketing*, *2*(2), 1–19. doi:10.4018/ijtem.2012070101

Chandra, S., Gruber, T., & Lowrie, A. (2013). Service recovery encounters in the classroom: Exploring the attributes of professors desired by male and female students. In P. Tripathi & S. Mukerji (Eds.), *Marketing strategies for higher education institutions: Technological considerations and practices* (pp. 219–239). Hershey, PA: Business Science Reference; doi:10.4018/978-1-4666-4014-6.ch016

Chen, K., Chen, J. V., & Ross, W. H. (2010). Antecedents of online game dependency: The implications of multimedia realism and uses and gratifications theory. *Journal of Database Management*, *21*(2), 69–99. doi:10.4018/jdm.2010040104

Chen, K., Chen, J. V., & Ross, W. H. (2012). Antecedents of online game dependency: The implications of multimedia realism and uses and gratifications theory. In K. Siau (Ed.), *Cross-disciplinary models and applications of database management: Advancing approaches* (pp. 176–208). Hershey, PA: Information Science Reference; doi:10.4018/978-1-61350-471-0.ch008

Chiu, M. (2013). Gaps between valuing and purchasing green-technology products: Product and gender differences. *International Journal of Technology and Human Interaction*, *8*(3), 54–68. doi:10.4018/jthi.2012070106

Cicchirillo, V. (2010). Online gaming: Demographics, motivations, and information processing. In M. Eastin, T. Daugherty, & N. Burns (Eds.), *Handbook of research on digital media and advertising: User generated content consumption* (pp. 456–479). Hershey, PA: Information Science Reference; doi:10.4018/978-1-60566-792-8.ch023

Concha, A. S. (2012). Filipino cyborg sexualities, chatroom masculinities, self-ascribed identities, ephemeral selves. In R. Pande & T. Van der Weide (Eds.), *Globalization, technology diffusion and gender disparity: Social impacts of ICTs* (pp. 211–224). Hershey, PA: Information Science Reference; doi:10.4018/978-1-4666-0020-1.ch018

Conger, S. (2011). Web 2.0, virtual worlds, and real ethical issues. In *Virtual communities: Concepts, methodologies, tools and applications* (pp. 226–238). Hershey, PA: Information Science Reference; doi:10.4018/978-1-60960-100-3.ch117

Costin, Y. (2012). Adopting ICT in the mompreneurs business: A strategy for growth? In C. Romm Livermore (Ed.), *Gender and social computing: Interactions, differences and relationships* (pp. 17–34). Hershey, PA: Information Science Publishing; doi:10.4018/978-1-60960-759-3.ch002

Costin, Y. (2013). Adopting ICT in the mompreneurs business: A strategy for growth? In *Small and medium enterprises: Concepts, methodologies, tools, and applications* (pp. 322–339). Hershey, PA: Business Science Reference; doi:10.4018/978-1-4666-3886-0.ch018

Coverdale, T. S., & Wilbon, A. D. (2013). The impact of in-group membership on e-loyalty of women online shoppers: An application of the social identity approach to website design. *International Journal of E-Adoption*, *5*(1), 17–36. doi:10.4018/jea.2013010102

Cox, A. D., Eno, C. A., & Guadagno, R. E. (2012). Beauty in the background: A content analysis of females in interactive digital games. *International Journal of Interactive Communication Systems and Technologies*, *2*(2), 49–62. doi:10.4018/ijicst.2012070104

Cozza, M. (2010). Gender and technology: Mind the gap! In A. Hallin & T. Karrbom-Gustavsson (Eds.), *Organizational communication and sustainable development: ICTs for mobility* (pp. 256–274). Hershey, PA: Information Science Reference; doi:10.4018/978-1-60566-822-2.ch015

Cramer, J., & Crocco, M. S. (2010). Women and technology, upon reflection: Linking global women's issues to the digital gender divide in urban social studies education. In J. Yamamoto, J. Kush, R. Lombard, & C. Hertzog (Eds.), *Technology implementation and teacher education: Reflective models* (pp. 184–202). Hershey, PA: Information Science Reference; doi:10.4018/978-1-61520-897-5.ch011

Deale, D. F., Key, S. S., Regina, M., & Pastore, R. (2012). Women and gaming. *International Journal of Gaming and Computer-Mediated Simulations*, *4*(1), 86–89. doi:10.4018/jgcms.2012010105

Devyatkov, V., & Alfimtsev, A. (2011). Human-computer interaction in games using computer vision techniques. In M. Cruz-Cunha, V. Varvalho, & P. Tavares (Eds.), *Business, technological, and social dimensions of computer games: Multidisciplinary developments* (pp. 146–167). Hershey, PA: Information Science Reference; doi:10.4018/978-1-60960-567-4.ch010

Dhar-Bhattacharjee, S., & Takruri-Rizk, H. (2011). Gender segregation and ICT: An Indo-British comparison. *International Journal of E-Politics*, *2*(1), 45–67. doi:10.4018/jep.2011010104

Driouchi, A. (2013). Women empowerment and ICTs in developing economies. In *ICTs for health, education, and socioeconomic policies: Regional cases* (pp. 146–164). Hershey, PA: Information Science Reference; doi:10.4018/978-1-4666-3643-9.ch007

Dubbels, B. (2013). Gamification, serious games, ludic simulation, and other contentious categories. *International Journal of Gaming and Computer-Mediated Simulations*, *5*(2), 1–19. doi:10.4018/jgcms.2013040101

Duin, H., Hauge, J. B., Hunecker, F., & Thoben, K. (2011). Application of serious games in industrial contexts. In M. Cruz-Cunha, V. Varvalho, & P. Tavares (Eds.), *Business, technological, and social dimensions of computer games: Multidisciplinary developments* (pp. 331–347). Hershey, PA: Information Science Reference; doi:10.4018/978-1-60960-567-4.ch020

Dunn, R. A. (2013). Identity theories and technology. In R. Luppicini (Ed.), *Handbook of research on technoself: Identity in a technological society* (pp. 26–44). Hershey, PA: Information Science Reference; doi:10.4018/978-1-4666-2211-1.ch002

Durbin, S. (2010). SET women and careers: A case study of senior female scientists in the UK. In A. Cater-Steel & E. Cater (Eds.), *Women in engineering, science and technology: Education and career challenges* (pp. 232–254). Hershey, PA: Engineering Science Reference; doi:10.4018/978-1-61520-657-5.ch011

Ellcessor, E., & Duncan, S. C. (2011). Forming the guild: Star power and rethinking projective identity in affinity spaces. *International Journal of Game-Based Learning*, *1*(2), 82–95. doi:10.4018/ijgbl.2011040106

Elwell, M. G. (2011). Questing for standards: Role playing games in second life. In M. Cruz-Cunha, V. Varvalho, & P. Tavares (Eds.), *Business, technological, and social dimensions of computer games: Multidisciplinary developments* (pp. 81–97). Hershey, PA: Information Science Reference; doi:10.4018/978-1-60960-567-4.ch006

Erdör, M. (2012). Developments in e-entrepreneurship in Turkey and a case study of a startup company founded by a woman entrepreneur. *International Journal of E-Entrepreneurship and Innovation*, *3*(4), 47–52. doi:10.4018/jeei.2012100104

Ertl, B., Helling, K., & Kikis-Papadakis, K. (2012). The impact of gender in ICT usage, education and career: Comparisons between Greece and Germany. In C. Romm Livermore (Ed.), *Gender and social computing: Interactions, differences and relationships* (pp. 98–119). Hershey, PA: Information Science Publishing; doi:10.4018/978-1-60960-759-3.ch007

Essid, J. (2011). Playing in a new key, in a new world: Virtual worlds, millennial writers, and 3D composition. In A. Cheney & R. Sanders (Eds.), *Teaching and learning in 3D immersive worlds: Pedagogical models and constructivist approaches* (pp. 169–184). Hershey, PA: Information Science Reference; doi:10.4018/978-1-60960-517-9.ch010

Eveleth, D. M., & Eveleth, A. B. (2010). Team identification, team performance and leader-member exchange relationships in virtual groups: Findings from massive multi-player online role play games. *International Journal of Virtual Communities and Social Networking*, *2*(1), 52–66. doi:10.4018/jvcsn.2010010104

Falcão, T. (2012). Structures of agency in virtual worlds: Fictional worlds and the shaping of an in-game social conduct. In N. Zagalo, L. Morgado, & A. Boa-Ventura (Eds.), *Virtual worlds and metaverse platforms: New communication and identity paradigms* (pp. 192–205). Hershey, PA: Information Science Reference; doi:10.4018/978-1-60960-854-5.ch013

Farmer, L. S. (2011). Gaming in adult education. In V. Wang (Ed.), *Encyclopedia of information communication technologies and adult education integration* (pp. 687–706). Hershey, PA: Information Science Reference; doi:10.4018/978-1-61692-906-0.ch041

Farmer, L. S. (2011). Gender impact on adult education. In V. Wang (Ed.), *Encyclopedia of information communication technologies and adult education integration* (pp. 377–395). Hershey, PA: Information Science Reference; doi:10.4018/978-1-61692-906-0.ch023

Farmer, L. S., & Murphy, N. G. (2010). eGaming and girls: Optimizing use in school libraries. In R. Van Eck (Ed.), Interdisciplinary models and tools for serious games: Emerging concepts and future directions (pp. 306-332). Hershey, PA: Information Science Reference. doi:10.4018/978-1-61520-719-0.ch013

Fatma, S. (2013). ICT in Arab education: Issues and challenges. In F. Albadri (Ed.), *Information systems applications in the Arab education sector* (pp. 136–147). Hershey, PA: Information Science Reference; doi:10.4018/978-1-4666-1984-5.ch010

Feinberg, J. R., Schewe, A. H., Moore, C. D., & Wood, K. R. (2013). Puttering, tinkering, building, and making: A constructionist approach to online instructional simulation games. In R. Hartshorne, T. Heafner, & T. Petty (Eds.), *Teacher education programs and online learning tools: Innovations in teacher preparation* (pp. 417–436). Hershey, PA: Information Science Reference; doi:10.4018/978-1-4666-1906-7.ch022

Felicia, P., & Pitt, I. (2011). Harnessing the emotional potential of video games. In *Instructional design: Concepts, methodologies, tools and applications* (pp. 1282–1299). Hershey, PA: Information Science Reference; doi:10.4018/978-1-60960-503-2.ch511

Ferri, G. (2013). Rhetorics, simulations and games: The ludic and satirical discourse of molleindustria. *International Journal of Gaming and Computer-Mediated Simulations*, *5*(1), 32–49. doi:10.4018/jgcms.2013010103

Fitz-Walter, Z., Tjondronegoro, D., & Wyeth, P. (2013). Gamifying Everyday activities using mobile sensing. In D. Tjondronegoro (Ed.), *Tools for mobile multimedia programming and development* (pp. 98–114). Hershey, PA: Information Science Reference; doi:10.4018/978-1-4666-4054-2.ch006

Fogel, G. K., & Lewis, L. F. (2012). Target marketing and ethics: Brand advertising and marketing campaigns. In E. Carayannis (Ed.), *Sustainable policy applications for social ecology and development* (pp. 214–231). Hershey, PA: Information Science Reference; doi:10.4018/978-1-4666-1586-1.ch016

Forman, A. E., Baker, P. M., Pater, J., & Smith, K. (2011). Beautiful to me: Identity, disability, and gender in virtual environments. *International Journal of E-Politics*, *2*(2), 1–17. doi:10.4018/jep.2011040101

Forman, A. E., Baker, P. M., Pater, J., & Smith, K. (2012). The not so level playing field: Disability identity and gender representation in second life. In C. Romm Livermore (Ed.), *Gender and social computing: Interactions, differences and relationships* (pp. 144–161). Hershey, PA: Information Science Publishing; doi:10.4018/978-1-60960-759-3.ch009

Fox, J., & Ahn, S. J. (2013). Avatars: Portraying, exploring, and changing online and offline identities. In R. Luppicini (Ed.), *Handbook of research on technoself: Identity in a technological society* (pp. 255–271). Hershey, PA: Information Science Reference; doi:10.4018/978-1-4666-2211-1.ch014

Freier, N. G., & Saulnier, E. T. (2011). The new backyard: Social and moral development in virtual worlds. In K. Schrier & D. Gibson (Eds.), *Designing games for ethics: Models, techniques and frameworks* (pp. 179–192). Hershey, PA: Information Science Reference; doi:10.4018/978-1-60960-120-1.ch012

Friedman, A., Hartshorne, R., & VanFossen, P. (2010). Exploring guild participation in MMORPGs and civic leadership. In Y. Baek (Ed.), *Gaming for classroom-based learning: Digital role playing as a motivator of study* (pp. 176–204). Hershey, PA: Information Science Reference; doi:10.4018/978-1-61520-713-8.ch011

Gabriels, K., Bauwens, J., & Verstrynge, K. (2012). Second life, second morality? In N. Zagalo, L. Morgado, & A. Boa-Ventura (Eds.), *Virtual worlds and metaverse platforms: New communication and identity paradigms* (pp. 306–320). Hershey, PA: Information Science Reference; doi:10.4018/978-1-60960-854-5.ch020

García-Gómez, A. (2013). Technoself-presentation on social networks: A gender-based approach. In R. Luppicini (Ed.), *Handbook of research on technoself: Identity in a technological society* (pp. 382–398). Hershey, PA: Information Science Reference; doi:10.4018/978-1-4666-2211-1.ch021

Ghosh, A. (2012). Leveraging sexual orientation workforce diversity through identity deployment. In C. Scott & M. Byrd (Eds.), *Handbook of research on workforce diversity in a global society: Technologies and concepts* (pp. 403–424). Hershey, PA: Business Science Reference; doi:10.4018/978-1-4666-1812-1.ch024

Ghuman, D., & Griffiths, M. (2012). A cross-genre study of online gaming: Player demographics, motivation for play, and social interactions among players. *International Journal of Cyber Behavior, Psychology and Learning*, *2*(1), 13–29. doi:10.4018/ijcbpl.2012010102

Gilbert, S. (2010). Ethics at play: Patterns of ethical thinking among young online gamers. In K. Schrier & D. Gibson (Eds.), *Ethics and game design: Teaching values through play* (pp. 151–166). Hershey, PA: Information Science Reference; doi:10.4018/978-1-61520-845-6.ch010

Goeke, R. J., Hogue, M., & Faley, R. H. (2010). The impact of gender and experience on the strength of the relationships between perceived data warehouse flexibility, ease-of-use, and usefulness. *Information Resources Management Journal*, *23*(2), 1–19. doi:10.4018/irmj.2010040101

Gomes, T., & Carvalho, A. A. (2011). The pedagogical potential of MMOG: An exploratory study including four games and their players. In M. Cruz-Cunha, V. Varvalho, & P. Tavares (Eds.), *Computer games as educational and management tools: Uses and approaches* (pp. 103–121). Hershey, PA: Information Science Reference; doi:10.4018/978-1-60960-569-8.ch007

Gómez, M. C., García, A. V., Llorente, A. M., Dávila, P. A., & Sepúlveda, P. Z. (2013). Gender violence experiences of urban adult indigenous women: Case study. In F. García-Peñalvo (Ed.), *Multiculturalism in technology-based education: Case studies on ICT-supported approaches* (pp. 79–99). Hershey, PA: Information Science Reference; doi:10.4018/978-1-4666-2101-5.ch006

Griffiths, M., Hussain, Z., Grüsser, S. M., Thalemann, R., Cole, H., Davies, M. N., & Chappell, D. (2011). Social interactions in online gaming. *International Journal of Game-Based Learning*, *1*(4), 20–36. doi:10.4018/ijgbl.2011100103

Griffiths, M., Hussain, Z., Grüsser, S. M., Thalemann, R., Cole, H., Davies, M. N., & Chappell, D. (2013). Social interactions in online gaming. In P. Felicia (Ed.), *Developments in current game-based learning design and deployment* (pp. 74–90). Hershey, PA: Information Science Reference; doi:10.4018/978-1-4666-1864-0.ch006

Griffiths, M., & Richardson, H. (2010). Against all odds, from all-girls schools to all-boys workplaces: Women's unsuspecting trajectory into the UK ICT sector. In S. Booth, S. Goodman, & G. Kirkup (Eds.), *Gender issues in learning and working with information technology: Social constructs and cultural contexts* (pp. 99–112). Hershey, PA: Information Science Reference; doi:10.4018/978-1-61520-813-5.ch006

Grimes, G., & Bartolacci, M. (2010). Second life: A virtual world platform for profiling online behavior for network and information security education? An initial investigation. *International Journal of Interdisciplinary Telecommunications and Networking*, *2*(4), 60–64. doi:10.4018/jitn.2010100105

Gulz, A., & Haake, M. (2010). Challenging gender stereotypes using virtual pedagogical characters. In S. Booth, S. Goodman, & G. Kirkup (Eds.), *Gender issues in learning and working with information technology: Social constructs and cultural contexts* (pp. 113–132). Hershey, PA: Information Science Reference; doi:10.4018/978-1-61520-813-5.ch007

Gunraj, A., Ruiz, S., & York, A. (2011). Power to the people: Anti-oppressive game design. In K. Schrier & D. Gibson (Eds.), *Designing games for ethics: Models, techniques and frameworks* (pp. 253–274). Hershey, PA: Information Science Reference; doi:10.4018/978-1-60960-120-1.ch016

Gupta, M., Jin, S., Sanders, G. L., Sherman, B. A., & Simha, A. (2012). Getting real about virtual worlds: A review. *International Journal of Virtual Communities and Social Networking*, *4*(3), 1–46. doi:10.4018/jvcsn.2012070101

Guth, J., & Wright, F. (2010). "We don't have the key to the executive washroom": Women's perceptions and experiences of promotion in academia. In A. Cater-Steel & E. Cater (Eds.), *Women in engineering, science and technology: Education and career challenges* (pp. 159–182). Hershey, PA: Engineering Science Reference; doi:10.4018/978-1-61520-657-5.ch008

Guthrie, R. A., Soe, L., & Yakura, E. K. (2011). Support structures for women in information technology careers. *International Journal of E-Politics*, *2*(1), 30–44. doi:10.4018/jep.2011010103

Gwee, S., San Chee, Y., & Tan, E. M. (2011). The role of gender in mobile game-based learning. *International Journal of Mobile and Blended Learning*, *3*(4), 19–37. doi:10.4018/jmbl.2011100102

Gwee, S., San Chee, Y., & Tan, E. M. (2013). The role of gender in mobile game-based learning. In D. Parsons (Ed.), *Innovations in mobile educational technologies and applications* (pp. 254–271). Hershey, PA: Information Science Reference; doi:10.4018/978-1-4666-2139-8.ch016

Hackbarth, G., Dow, K. E., Wang, H., & Johnson, W. R. (2010). Changing attitudes toward women IT managers. *International Journal of Information Systems and Social Change*, *1*(3), 28–44. doi:10.4018/jissc.2010070103

Hackbarth, G., Dow, K. E., Wang, H., & Johnson, W. R. (2012). Changing attitudes toward women IT managers. In J. Wang (Ed.), *Societal impacts on information systems development and applications* (pp. 114–129). Hershey, PA: Information Science Reference; doi:10.4018/978-1-4666-0927-3.ch008

Halder, D., & Jaishankar, K. (2012). Cyber laws for preventing cyber crimes against women in Canada. In *Cyber crime and the victimization of women: Laws, rights and regulations* (pp. 82–94). Hershey, PA: Information Science Reference; doi:10.4018/978-1-60960-830-9.ch006

Halder, D., & Jaishankar, K. (2012). Cyber space regulations for protecting women in UK. In *Cyber crime and the victimization of women: Laws, rights and regulations* (pp. 95–104). Hershey, PA: Information Science Reference; doi:10.4018/978-1-60960-830-9.ch007

Halder, D., & Jaishankar, K. (2012). Definition, typology and patterns of victimization. In *Cyber crime and the victimization of women: Laws, rights and regulations* (pp. 12–39). Hershey, PA: Information Science Reference; doi:10.4018/978-1-60960-830-9.ch002

Halder, D., & Jaishankar, K. (2012). Etiology, motives, and crime hubs. In *Cyber crime and the victimization of women: Laws, rights and regulations* (pp. 40–54). Hershey, PA: Information Science Reference; doi:10.4018/978-1-60960-830-9.ch003

Halder, D., & Jaishankar, K. (2012). Introduction. In *Cyber crime and the victimization of women: Laws, rights and regulations* (pp. 1–11). Hershey, PA: Information Science Reference; doi:10.4018/978-1-60960-830-9.ch001

Halder, D., & Jaishankar, K. (2012). Legal treatment of cyber crimes against women in USA. In *Cyber crime and the victimization of women: Laws, rights and regulations* (pp. 69–81). Hershey, PA: Information Science Reference; doi:10.4018/978-1-60960-830-9.ch005

Halder, D., & Jaishankar, K. (2012). Women's rights in the cyber space and the related duties. In *Cyber crime and the victimization of women: Laws, rights and regulations* (pp. 55–68). Hershey, PA: Information Science Reference; doi:10.4018/978-1-60960-830-9.ch004

Hamari, J., & Järvinen, A. (2011). Building customer relationship through game mechanics in social games. In M. Cruz-Cunha, V. Varvalho, & P. Tavares (Eds.), *Business, technological, and social dimensions of computer games: Multidisciplinary developments* (pp. 348–365). Hershey, PA: Information Science Reference; doi:10.4018/978-1-60960-567-4.ch021

Hartshorne, R., VanFossen, P. J., & Friedman, A. (2012). MMORPG roles, civic participation and leadership among generation Y. *International Journal of Gaming and Computer-Mediated Simulations*, *4*(1), 55–67. doi:10.4018/jgcms.2012010103

Harwood, T. (2012). Emergence of gamified commerce: Turning virtual to real. *Journal of Electronic Commerce in Organizations*, *10*(2), 16–39. doi:10.4018/jeco.2012040102

Heeter, C., Lee, Y., Magerko, B., & Medler, B. (2011). Impacts of forced serious game play on vulnerable subgroups. *International Journal of Gaming and Computer-Mediated Simulations*, *3*(3), 34–53. doi:10.4018/jgcms.2011070103

Heeter, C., Lee, Y., Magerko, B., & Medler, B. (2013). Impacts of forced serious game play on vulnerable subgroups. In R. Ferdig (Ed.), *Design, utilization, and analysis of simulations and game-based educational worlds* (pp. 158–176). Hershey, PA: Information Science Reference; doi:10.4018/978-1-4666-4018-4.ch010

Heeter, C., Magerko, B., Medler, B., & Fitzgerald, J. (2011). Game design and the challenge-avoiding, self-validator player type. In R. Ferdig (Ed.), *Discoveries in gaming and computer-mediated simulations: New interdisciplinary applications* (pp. 49–63). Hershey, PA: Information Science Reference; doi:10.4018/978-1-60960-565-0.ch004

Heeter, C., Sarkar, C. D., Palmer-Scott, B., & Zhang, S. (2012). Engineering sociability: Friendship drive, visibility, and social connection in anonymous co-located local wi-fi multiplayer online gaming. *International Journal of Gaming and Computer-Mediated Simulations*, *4*(2), 1–18. doi:10.4018/jgcms.2012040101

Heider, D., & Massanari, A. L. (2010). Friendship, closeness and disclosure in second life. *International Journal of Gaming and Computer-Mediated Simulations*, *2*(3), 61–74. doi:10.4018/jgcms.2010070104

Heitmann, M., & Tidten, K. (2011). New business models for the computer gaming industry: Selling an adventure. In M. Cruz-Cunha, V. Varvalho, & P. Tavares (Eds.), *Business, technological, and social dimensions of computer games: Multidisciplinary developments* (pp. 401–415). Hershey, PA: Information Science Reference; doi:10.4018/978-1-60960-567-4.ch024

Heo, M., & Spradley-Myrick, L. M. (2012). Girls and computers - Yes we can!: A case study on improving female computer confidence and decreasing gender inequity in computer science with an informal, female learning community. In *Computer engineering: Concepts, methodologies, tools and applications* (pp. 1126–1143). Hershey, PA: Engineering Science Reference; doi:10.4018/978-1-61350-456-7.ch504

Hewahi, N. M., & Baraka, A. M. (2012). Emotion recognition model based on facial expressions, ethnicity and gender using backpropagation neural network. *International Journal of Technology Diffusion*, *3*(1), 33–43. doi:10.4018/jtd.2012010104

Hewett, S. (2011). Using video games to improve literacy levels of males. In *Instructional design: Concepts, methodologies, tools and applications* (pp. 192–206). Hershey, PA: Information Science Reference; doi:10.4018/978-1-60960-503-2.ch115

Hicks, D. (2014). Technology, gender, and professional identity. In *Technology and professional identity of librarians: The making of the cybrarian* (pp. 128–147). Hershey, PA: Information Science Reference; doi:10.4018/978-1-4666-4735-0.ch007

Hobbs, R., & Rowe, J. (2011). Creative remixing and digital learning: Developing an online media literacy learning tool for girls. In *Gaming and simulations: Concepts, methodologies, tools and applications* (pp. 971–978). Hershey, PA: Information Science Reference; doi:10.4018/978-1-60960-195-9.ch405

Hoffman, E. (2010). Sideways into truth: Kierkegaard, Philistines, and why we love sex and violence. In K. Schrier & D. Gibson (Eds.), *Ethics and game design: Teaching values through play* (pp. 109–124). Hershey, PA: Information Science Reference; doi:10.4018/978-1-61520-845-6.ch008

Hoffmann, E. M. (2010). Women in computer science in Afghanistan. In S. Booth, S. Goodman, & G. Kirkup (Eds.), *Gender issues in learning and working with information technology: Social constructs and cultural contexts* (pp. 48–63). Hershey, PA: Information Science Reference; doi:10.4018/978-1-61520-813-5.ch003

Hsu, C. (2010). Exploring the player flow experience in e-game playing. *International Journal of Technology and Human Interaction, 6*(2), 47–64. doi:10.4018/jthi.2010040104

Huang, J., & Aaltio, I. (2010). Social interaction technologies: A case study of Guanxi and women managers' careers in information technology in China. In T. Dumova & R. Fiordo (Eds.), *Handbook of research on social interaction technologies and collaboration software: Concepts and trends* (pp. 257–269). Hershey, PA: Information Science Reference; doi:10.4018/978-1-60566-368-5.ch023

Hughes, G. (2010). Queen bees, workers and drones: Gender performance in virtual learning groups. In S. Booth, S. Goodman, & G. Kirkup (Eds.), *Gender issues in learning and working with information technology: Social constructs and cultural contexts* (pp. 244–254). Hershey, PA: Information Science Reference; doi:10.4018/978-1-61520-813-5.ch014

Igun, S. E. (2010). Gender and national information and communication technology (ICT) policies in Africa. In E. Adomi (Ed.), *Handbook of research on information communication technology policy: Trends, issues and advancements* (pp. 208–221). Hershey, PA: Information Science Reference; doi:10.4018/978-1-61520-847-0.ch013

Igun, S. E. (2013). Gender and national information and communication technology (ICT) policies in Africa. In B. Maumbe & J. Okello (Eds.), *Technology, sustainability, and rural development in Africa* (pp. 284–297). Hershey, PA: Information Science Reference; doi:10.4018/978-1-4666-3607-1.ch018

Ikolo, V. E. (2010). Gender digital divide and national ICT policies in Africa. In E. Adomi (Ed.), *Handbook of research on information communication technology policy: Trends, issues and advancements* (pp. 222–242). Hershey, PA: Information Science Reference; doi:10.4018/978-1-61520-847-0.ch014

Ikolo, V. E. (2013). Gender digital divide and national ICT policies in Africa. In *Digital literacy: Concepts, methodologies, tools, and applications* (pp. 812–832). Hershey, PA: Information Science Reference; doi:10.4018/978-1-4666-1852-7.ch042

Ionescu, A. (2012). ICTs and gender-based rights. *International Journal of Information Communication Technologies and Human Development, 4*(2), 33–49. doi:10.4018/jicthd.2012040103

Ionescu, A. (2013). Cyber identity: Our alter-ego? In R. Luppicini (Ed.), *Handbook of research on technoself: Identity in a technological society* (pp. 189–203). Hershey, PA: Information Science Reference; doi:10.4018/978-1-4666-2211-1.ch011

Ionescu, A. (2013). ICTs and gender-based rights. In J. Lannon & E. Halpin (Eds.), *Human rights and information communication technologies: Trends and consequences of use* (pp. 214–234). Hershey, PA: Information Science Reference; doi:10.4018/978-1-4666-1918-0.ch013

Irving, C. J., & English, L. M. (2011). Women, information and communication technologies, and lifelong learning. In V. Wang (Ed.), *Encyclopedia of information communication technologies and adult education integration* (pp. 360–376). Hershey, PA: Information Science Reference; doi:10.4018/978-1-61692-906-0.ch022

Jarmon, L. (2010). Homo virtualis: Virtual worlds, learning, and an ecology of embodied interaction. *International Journal of Virtual and Personal Learning Environments*, *1*(1), 38–56. doi:10.4018/jvple.2010091704

Jayasingh, S., & Eze, U. C. (2012). Analyzing the intention to use mobile coupon and the moderating effects of price consciousness and gender. *International Journal of E-Business Research*, *8*(1), 54–75. doi:10.4018/jebr.2012010104

Jenson, J., & de, C. S. (2010). Gender and digital gameplay: Theories, oversights, accidents, and surprises. In D. Kaufman & L. Sauvé (Eds.), *Educational gameplay and simulation environments: Case studies and lessons learned* (pp. 96-105). Hershey, PA: Information Science Reference. doi:10.4018/978-1-61520-731-2.ch006

Johnson, R. D. (2011). Gender differences in e-learning: Communication, social presence, and learning outcomes. *Journal of Organizational and End User Computing*, *23*(1), 79–94. doi:10.4018/joeuc.2011010105

Johnson, V. (2012). The gender divide: Attitudinal issues inhibiting access. In R. Pande & T. Van der Weide (Eds.), *Globalization, technology diffusion and gender disparity: Social impacts of ICTs* (pp. 110–119). Hershey, PA: Information Science Reference; doi:10.4018/978-1-4666-0020-1.ch009

Jyothi, P. (2012). Challenges faced by women: BPO sector. In R. Pande & T. Van der Weide (Eds.), *Globalization, technology diffusion and gender disparity: Social impacts of ICTs* (pp. 147–155). Hershey, PA: Information Science Reference; doi:10.4018/978-1-4666-0020-1.ch013

Kafai, Y. B., Fields, D., & Searle, K. A. (2010). Multi-modal investigations of relationship play in virtual worlds. *International Journal of Gaming and Computer-Mediated Simulations*, *2*(1), 40–48. doi:10.4018/jgcms.2010010104

Kallay, J. (2010). Rethinking genre in computer games: How narrative psychology connects game and story. In R. Van Eck (Ed.), *Interdisciplinary models and tools for serious games: Emerging concepts and future directions* (pp. 30–49). Hershey, PA: Information Science Reference; doi:10.4018/978-1-61520-719-0.ch002

Kallergi, A., & Verbeek, F. J. (2014). Playful interfaces for scientific image data: A case for storytelling. In K. Blashki & P. Isaias (Eds.), *Emerging research and trends in interactivity and the human-computer interface* (pp. 471–489). Hershey, PA: Information Science Reference; doi:10.4018/978-1-4666-4623-0.ch024

Karl, K., Peluchette, J., & Schlagel, C. (2010). A cross-cultural examination of student attitudes and gender differences in Facebook profile content. *International Journal of Virtual Communities and Social Networking*, *2*(2), 11–31. doi:10.4018/jvcsn.2010040102

Kaul, A., & Kulkarni, V. (2010). Gender and politeness in Indian emails. In R. Taiwo (Ed.), *Handbook of research on discourse behavior and digital communication: Language structures and social interaction* (pp. 389–410). Hershey, PA: Information Science Reference; doi:10.4018/978-1-61520-773-2.ch025

Ke, F., Yildirim, N., & Enfield, J. (2012). Exploring the design of game enjoyment through the perspectives of novice game developers. *International Journal of Gaming and Computer-Mediated Simulations*, *4*(4), 45–63. doi:10.4018/jgcms.2012100104

King, E. (2013). Possibility spaces: Using the Sims 2 as a sandbox to explore possible selves with at-risk teenage males. In P. Felicia (Ed.), *Developments in current game-based learning design and deployment* (pp. 169–187). Hershey, PA: Information Science Reference; doi:10.4018/978-1-4666-1864-0.ch013

Kirkup, G. (2010). Gendered knowledge production in universities in a web 2.0 world. In S. Booth, S. Goodman, & G. Kirkup (Eds.), *Gender issues in learning and working with information technology: Social constructs and cultural contexts* (pp. 231–243). Hershey, PA: Information Science Reference; doi:10.4018/978-1-61520-813-5.ch013

Kirkup, G., Schmitz, S., Kotkamp, E., Rommes, E., & Hiltunen, A. (2010). Towards a feminist manifesto for e-learning: Principles to inform practices. In S. Booth, S. Goodman, & G. Kirkup (Eds.), *Gender issues in learning and working with information technology: Social constructs and cultural contexts* (pp. 255–274). Hershey, PA: Information Science Reference; doi:10.4018/978-1-61520-813-5.ch015

Koh, E., Liu, N., & Lim, J. (2012). Gender and anonymity in virtual teams: An exploratory study. In C. Romm Livermore (Ed.), *Gender and social computing: Interactions, differences and relationships* (pp. 1–16). Hershey, PA: Information Science Publishing; doi:10.4018/978-1-60960-759-3.ch001

Kongmee, I., Strachan, R., Pickard, A., & Montgomery, C. (2012). A case study of using online communities and virtual environment in massively multiplayer role playing games (MMORPGs) as a learning and teaching tool for second language learners. *International Journal of Virtual and Personal Learning Environments*, *3*(4), 1–15. doi:10.4018/jvple.2012100101

Koo, G., & Seider, S. (2010). Video games for prosocial learning. In K. Schrier & D. Gibson (Eds.), *Ethics and game design: Teaching values through play* (pp. 16–33). Hershey, PA: Information Science Reference; doi:10.4018/978-1-61520-845-6.ch002

Kumari, B. R. (2012). Gender, culture, and ICT use. In R. Pande & T. Van der Weide (Eds.), *Globalization, technology diffusion and gender disparity: Social impacts of ICTs* (pp. 36–50). Hershey, PA: Information Science Reference; doi:10.4018/978-1-4666-0020-1.ch004

Kwok, N. W., & Khoo, A. (2011). Gamers' motivations and problematic gaming: An exploratory study of gamers in World of Warcraft. *International Journal of Cyber Behavior, Psychology and Learning*, *1*(3), 34–49. doi:10.4018/ijcbpl.2011070103

Kwok, N. W., & Khoo, A. (2013). Gamers' motivations and problematic gaming: An exploratory study of gamers in World of Warcraft. In R. Zheng (Ed.), *Evolving psychological and educational perspectives on cyber behavior* (pp. 64–81). Hershey, PA: Information Science Reference; doi:10.4018/978-1-4666-1858-9.ch005

Lamoreaux, K., & Varghese, D. (2012). Deliberate leadership: Women in IT. In *Computer engineering: Concepts, methodologies, tools and applications* (pp. 1381–1402). Hershey, PA: Engineering Science Reference; doi:10.4018/978-1-61350-456-7.ch601

Lankoski, P., Johansson, A., Karlsson, B., Björk, S., & Dell'Acqua, P. (2011). AI design for believable characters via gameplay design patterns. In M. Cruz-Cunha, V. Varvalho, & P. Tavares (Eds.), *Business, technological, and social dimensions of computer games: Multidisciplinary developments* (pp. 15–31). Hershey, PA: Information Science Reference; doi:10.4018/978-1-60960-567-4.ch002

Laosethakul, K., Leingpibul, T., & Coe, T. (2010). Investigation into gender perception toward computing: A comparison between the U.S. and India. *International Journal of Information and Communication Technology Education*, *6*(4), 23–37. doi:10.4018/jicte.2010100103

Laosethakul, K., Leingpibul, T., & Coe, T. (2012). Investigation into gender perception toward computing: A comparison between the U.S. and India. In L. Tomei (Ed.), *Advancing education with information communication technologies: Facilitating new trends* (pp. 305–319). Hershey, PA: Information Science Reference; doi:10.4018/978-1-61350-468-0.ch025

Lawrence, H. R. (2013). Women's roles: Do they exist in a technological workforce? In S. Wang & T. Hartsell (Eds.), *Technology integration and foundations for effective leadership* (pp. 57–69). Hershey, PA: Information Science Reference; doi:10.4018/978-1-4666-2656-0.ch004

Lin, T., Wu, Z., Tang, N., & Wu, S. (2013). Exploring the effects of display characteristics on presence and emotional responses of game players. *International Journal of Technology and Human Interaction*, *9*(1), 50–63. doi:10.4018/jthi.2013010104

Linares, K., Subrahmanyam, K., Cheng, R., & Guan, S. A. (2011). A second life within second life: Are Virtual world users creating new selves and new lives? *International Journal of Cyber Behavior, Psychology and Learning*, *1*(3), 50–71. doi:10.4018/ijcbpl.2011070104

Linares, K., Subrahmanyam, K., Cheng, R., & Guan, S. A. (2013). A second life within second life: Are virtual world users creating new selves and new lives? In R. Zheng (Ed.), *Evolving psychological and educational perspectives on cyber behavior* (pp. 205–228). Hershey, PA: Information Science Reference; doi:10.4018/978-1-4666-1858-9.ch013

Livermore, C. R., & Somers, T. M. (2011). Gender, power, and edating. *International Journal of E-Politics*, *2*(2), 74–88. doi:10.4018/jep.2011040105

Lorentz, P. (2012). Is there a virtual socialization by acting virtual identities? Case study: The Sims. In N. Zagalo, L. Morgado, & A. Boa-Ventura (Eds.), *Virtual worlds and metaverse platforms: New communication and identity paradigms* (pp. 206–218). Hershey, PA: Information Science Reference; doi:10.4018/978-1-60960-854-5.ch014

Losh, S. C. (2013). American digital divides: Generation, education, gender, and ethnicity in American digital divides. In *Digital literacy: Concepts, methodologies, tools, and applications* (pp. 932–958). Hershey, PA: Information Science Reference; doi:10.4018/978-1-4666-1852-7.ch048

Ludi, S. (2012). Educational robotics and broadening participation in STEM for underrepresented student groups. In B. Barker, G. Nugent, N. Grandgenett, & V. Adamchuk (Eds.), *Robots in K-12 education: A new technology for learning* (pp. 343–361). Hershey, PA: Information Science Reference; doi:10.4018/978-1-4666-0182-6.ch017

Lund, K., Lochrie, M., & Coulton, P. (2012). Designing scalable location based games that encourage emergent behaviour. *International Journal of Ambient Computing and Intelligence*, *4*(4), 1–20. doi:10.4018/jaci.2012100101

Ma, M., & Oikonomou, A. (2010). Network architectures and data management for massively multiplayer online games. *International Journal of Grid and High Performance Computing*, *2*(4), 40–50. doi:10.4018/jghpc.2010100104

Macgregor, R., Hyland, P. N., & Harvey, C. (2012). The effect of gender on associations between driving forces to adopt ICT and benefits derived from that adoption in medical practices in Australia. In C. Romm Livermore (Ed.), *Gender and social computing: Interactions, differences and relationships* (pp. 120–142). Hershey, PA: Information Science Publishing; doi:10.4018/978-1-60960-759-3.ch008

Macgregor, R., Hyland, P. N., & Harvey, C. (2013). The effect of gender on associations between driving forces to adopt ICT and benefits derived from that adoption in medical practices in Australia. In *Small and medium enterprises: Concepts, methodologies, tools, and applications* (pp. 1186–1207). Hershey, PA: Business Science Reference; doi:10.4018/978-1-4666-3886-0.ch058

MacGregor, R. C., Hyland, P. N., & Harvie, C. (2011). The effect of gender on perceived benefits of and drivers for ICT adoption in Australian medical practices. *International Journal of E-Politics*, *2*(1), 68–85. doi:10.4018/jep.2011010105

Maguire, K. C. (2011). Is it a boy or a girl? Anonymity and gender in computer-mediated interactions. In *Virtual communities: Concepts, methodologies, tools and applications* (pp. 1590–1610). Hershey, PA: Information Science Reference; doi:10.4018/978-1-60960-100-3.ch501

Mano, R. S. (2013). Gender effects on managerial communication and work performance. *International Journal of Cyber Behavior, Psychology and Learning*, *3*(2), 34–46. doi:10.4018/ijcbpl.2013040103

Manuel, A. (2010). The career challenge of the gendered academic research culture: Can internet technologies make a difference? In A. Cater-Steel & E. Cater (Eds.), *Women in engineering, science and technology: Education and career challenges* (pp. 255–279). Hershey, PA: Engineering Science Reference; doi:10.4018/978-1-61520-657-5.ch012

Marache-Francisco, C., & Brangier, E. (2014). The gamification experience: UXD with a gamification background. In K. Blashki & P. Isaias (Eds.), *Emerging research and trends in interactivity and the human-computer interface* (pp. 205–223). Hershey, PA: Information Science Reference; doi:10.4018/978-1-4666-4623-0.ch010

Marciano, A. (2011). The role of internet newsgroups in the coming-out process of gay male youth: An Israeli case study. In E. Dunkels, G. Franberg, & C. Hallgren (Eds.), *Youth culture and net culture: Online social practices* (pp. 222–241). Hershey, PA: Information Science Reference; doi:10.4018/978-1-60960-209-3.ch013

Maree, D. J., & Maree, M. (2010). Factors contributing to the success of women working in science, engineering and technology (SET) careers. In A. Cater-Steel & E. Cater (Eds.), *Women in engineering, science and technology: Education and career challenges* (pp. 183–210). Hershey, PA: Engineering Science Reference; doi:10.4018/978-1-61520-657-5.ch009

Martin, S. (2012). Exploring identity and citizenship in a virtual world. *International Journal of Virtual and Personal Learning Environments*, *3*(4), 53–70. doi:10.4018/jvple.2012100105

Martins, H. F. (2012). The use of a business simulation game in a management course. In M. Cruz-Cunha (Ed.), *Handbook of research on serious games as educational, business and research tools* (pp. 693–707). Hershey, PA: Information Science Reference; doi:10.4018/978-1-4666-0149-9.ch035

Masrom, M., & Ismail, Z. (2010). Women access to computers and internet: A Malaysian perspective. In A. Cater-Steel & E. Cater (Eds.), *Women in engineering, science and technology: Education and career challenges* (pp. 211–231). Hershey, PA: Engineering Science Reference; doi:10.4018/978-1-61520-657-5.ch010

Mattingly, D. J. (2012). Indian women working in call centers: Sites of resistance? In R. Pande & T. Van der Weide (Eds.), *Globalization, technology diffusion and gender disparity: Social impacts of ICTs* (pp. 156–168). Hershey, PA: Information Science Reference; doi:10.4018/978-1-4666-0020-1.ch014

McDaniel, R., & Fiore, S. M. (2010). Applied ethics game design: Some practical guidelines. In K. Schrier & D. Gibson (Eds.), *Ethics and game design: Teaching values through play* (pp. 236–254). Hershey, PA: Information Science Reference; doi:10.4018/978-1-61520-845-6.ch015

McDonald, J., Loch, B., & Cater-Steel, A. (2010). Go WEST - Supporting women in engineering, science and technology: An Australian higher education case study. In A. Cater-Steel & E. Cater (Eds.), *Women in engineering, science and technology: Education and career challenges* (pp. 118–136). Hershey, PA: Engineering Science Reference; doi:10.4018/978-1-61520-657-5.ch006

McKinnell Jacobson, C. (2011). Virtual worlds and the 3-D internet. In *Virtual communities: Concepts, methodologies, tools and applications* (pp. 1855–1879). Hershey, PA: Information Science Reference; doi:10.4018/978-1-60960-100-3.ch520

McLean, L., & Griffiths, M. D. (2013). Gamers' attitudes towards victims of crime: An interview study using vignettes. *International Journal of Cyber Behavior, Psychology and Learning*, *3*(2), 13–33. doi:10.4018/ijcbpl.2013040102

Mellström, U. (2010). New gender relations in the transforming IT-industry of Malaysia. In S. Booth, S. Goodman, & G. Kirkup (Eds.), *Gender issues in learning and working with information technology: Social constructs and cultural contexts* (pp. 25–47). Hershey, PA: Information Science Reference; doi:10.4018/978-1-61520-813-5.ch002

Mena, R. J. (2014). The quest for a massively multiplayer online game that teaches physics. In T. Connolly, T. Hainey, E. Boyle, G. Baxter, & P. Moreno-Ger (Eds.), *Psychology, pedagogy, and assessment in serious games* (pp. 292–316). Hershey, PA: Information Science Reference; doi:10.4018/978-1-4666-4773-2.ch014

Mendes, R. (2010). Glass ceilings in Portugal? An analysis of the gender wage gap using a quantile regression approach. *International Journal of Human Capital and Information Technology Professionals*, *1*(2), 1–18. doi:10.4018/jhcitp.2010040101

Miller, K. B. (2013). Gaming as a woman: Gender difference issues in video games and learning. In S. D'Agustino (Ed.), *Immersive environments, augmented realities, and virtual worlds: Assessing future trends in education* (pp. 106–122). Hershey, PA: Information Science Reference; doi:10.4018/978-1-4666-2670-6.ch007

Milolidakis, G., Kimble, C., & Grenier, C. (2011). A practice-based analysis of social interaction in a massively multiplayer online gaming environment. In M. Cruz-Cunha, V. Varvalho, & P. Tavares (Eds.), *Business, technological, and social dimensions of computer games: Multidisciplinary developments* (pp. 32–48). Hershey, PA: Information Science Reference; doi:10.4018/978-1-60960-567-4.ch003

Mitgutsch, K. (2011). Playful learning experiences: Meaningful learning patterns in players' biographies. *International Journal of Gaming and Computer-Mediated Simulations*, *3*(3), 54–68. doi:10.4018/jgcms.2011070104

Modesto, F. A. (2012). Virtual worlds innovation with open wonderland. In M. Cruz-Cunha (Ed.), *Handbook of research on serious games as educational, business and research tools* (pp. 250–268). Hershey, PA: Information Science Reference; doi:10.4018/978-1-4666-0149-9.ch013

Mora-García, A. M., & Merelo-Guervós, J. J. (2012). Evolving bots' ai in Unreal. In A. Kumar, J. Etheredge, & A. Boudreaux (Eds.), *Algorithmic and architectural gaming design: Implementation and development* (pp. 134–157). Hershey, PA: Information Science Reference; doi:10.4018/978-1-4666-1634-9.ch007

Moro, M. M., Weber, T., & Freitas, C. M. (2012). Women in Brazilian CS research community: The state-of-the-art. In *Computer engineering: Concepts, methodologies, tools and applications* (pp. 1824–1839). Hershey, PA: Engineering Science Reference; doi:10.4018/978-1-61350-456-7.ch801

Mörtberg, C., & Elovaara, P. (2010). Attaching people and technology: Between E and government. In S. Booth, S. Goodman, & G. Kirkup (Eds.), *Gender issues in learning and working with information technology: Social constructs and cultural contexts* (pp. 83–98). Hershey, PA: Information Science Reference; doi:10.4018/978-1-61520-813-5.ch005

Mosca, I. (2013). From fiction to reality and back: Ontology of ludic simulations. *International Journal of Gaming and Computer-Mediated Simulations*, *5*(1), 13–31. doi:10.4018/jgcms.2013010102

Moseley, A. (2012). An alternate reality for education? Lessons to be learned from online immersive games. *International Journal of Game-Based Learning*, *2*(3), 32–50. doi:10.4018/ijgbl.2012070103

Moseley, A. (2014). A case for integration: Assessment and games. In T. Connolly, T. Hainey, E. Boyle, G. Baxter, & P. Moreno-Ger (Eds.), *Psychology, pedagogy, and assessment in serious games* (pp. 342–356). Hershey, PA: Information Science Reference; doi:10.4018/978-1-4666-4773-2.ch016

Murphy, J., & Zagal, J. (2011). Videogames and the ethics of care. *International Journal of Gaming and Computer-Mediated Simulations*, *3*(3), 69–81. doi:10.4018/jgcms.2011070105

Mutaza, S., & Sami, L. K. (2012). Gender aspects in the use of ICT in information centres. In R. Pande & T. Van der Weide (Eds.), *Globalization, technology diffusion and gender disparity: Social impacts of ICTs* (pp. 129–137). Hershey, PA: Information Science Reference; doi:10.4018/978-1-4666-0020-1.ch011

Nezlek, G., & DeHondt, G. (2011). Gender wage differentials in information systems: 1991 – 2008 a quantitative analysis. *International Journal of Social and Organizational Dynamics in IT*, *1*(1), 13–29. doi:10.4018/ijsodit.2011010102

Nezlek, G., & DeHondt, G. (2013). Gender wage differentials in information systems: 1991 – 2008 a quantitative analysis. In B. Medlin (Ed.), *Integrations of technology utilization and social dynamics in organizations* (pp. 31–47). Hershey, PA: Information Science Reference; doi:10.4018/978-1-4666-1948-7.ch003

Ng, E. M. (2011). Exploring the gender differences of student teachers when using an educational game to learn programming concepts. In P. Felicia (Ed.), *Handbook of research on improving learning and motivation through educational games: Multidisciplinary approaches* (pp. 550–566). Hershey, PA: Information Science Reference; doi:10.4018/978-1-60960-495-0.ch026

Nikolaos, P. (2013). A conceptual "cybernetic" methodology for organizing and managing the e-learning process through [D-] CIVEs: The case of "second life". In P. Renna (Ed.), Production and manufacturing system management: Coordination approaches and multi-site planning (pp. 242-277). Hershey, PA: Engineering Science Reference. doi:10.4018/978-1-4666-2098-8.ch013

Nitsche, M. (2012). The players' dimension: From virtual to physical. In N. Zagalo, L. Morgado, & A. Boa-Ventura (Eds.), *Virtual worlds and metaverse platforms: New communication and identity paradigms* (pp. 181–191). Hershey, PA: Information Science Reference; doi:10.4018/978-1-60960-854-5.ch012

Nordlinger, J. (2010). Virtual ethics: Ethics and massively multiplayer online games. In K. Schrier & D. Gibson (Eds.), *Ethics and game design: Teaching values through play* (pp. 102–108). Hershey, PA: Information Science Reference; doi:10.4018/978-1-61520-845-6.ch007

Nsibirano, R., Kabonesa, C., & Madanda, A. (2012). Gender symbolism and technology uptake: A literature review. In R. Pande & T. Van der Weide (Eds.), *Globalization, technology diffusion and gender disparity: Social impacts of ICTs* (pp. 120–127). Hershey, PA: Information Science Reference; doi:10.4018/978-1-4666-0020-1.ch010

Okafor, C., & Amalu, R. (2012). Motivational patterns and the performance of entrepreneurs: An empirical study of women entrepreneurs in south-west Nigeria. *International Journal of Applied Behavioral Economics*, *1*(1), 29–40. doi:10.4018/ijabe.2012010103

Okdie, B. M., Guadagno, R. E., Petrova, P. K., & Shreves, W. B. (2013). Social influence online: A tale of gender differences in the effectiveness of authority cues. *International Journal of Interactive Communication Systems and Technologies*, *3*(1), 20–31. doi:10.4018/ijicst.2013010102

Ortiz, J. A. (2011). Knowing the game: A review of videogames and entertainment software in the United States - Trends and future research opportunities. In M. Cruz-Cunha, V. Varvalho, & P. Tavares (Eds.), *Business, technological, and social dimensions of computer games: Multidisciplinary developments* (pp. 293–311). Hershey, PA: Information Science Reference; doi:10.4018/978-1-60960-567-4.ch018

Ortiz de Gortari, A. B., Aronsson, K., & Griffiths, M. (2011). Game transfer phenomena in video game playing: A qualitative interview study. *International Journal of Cyber Behavior, Psychology and Learning*, *1*(3), 15–33. doi:10.4018/ijcbpl.2011070102

Orvalho, V. C., & Orvalho, J. (2011). Character animation: Past, present and future. In M. Cruz-Cunha, V. Varvalho, & P. Tavares (Eds.), *Business, technological, and social dimensions of computer games: Multidisciplinary developments* (pp. 49–64). Hershey, PA: Information Science Reference; doi:10.4018/978-1-60960-567-4.ch004

Özdemir, E. (2012). Gender and e-marketing: The role of gender differences in online purchasing behaviors. In C. Romm Livermore (Ed.), *Gender and social computing: Interactions, differences and relationships* (pp. 72–86). Hershey, PA: Information Science Publishing; doi:10.4018/978-1-60960-759-3.ch005

Pande, R. (2012). Gender gaps and information and communication technology: A case study of India. In R. Pande & T. Van der Weide (Eds.), *Globalization, technology diffusion and gender disparity: Social impacts of ICTs* (pp. 277–291). Hershey, PA: Information Science Reference; doi:10.4018/978-1-4666-0020-1.ch022

Pande, R. (2013). Gender gaps and information and communication technology: A case study of India. In *Digital literacy: Concepts, methodologies, tools, and applications* (pp. 1425–1439). Hershey, PA: Information Science Reference; doi:10.4018/978-1-4666-1852-7.ch075

Pannicke, D., Repschläger, J., & Zarnekow, R. (2011). Business opportunities in social virtual worlds. In M. Cruz-Cunha, V. Varvalho, & P. Tavares (Eds.), *Business, technological, and social dimensions of computer games: Multidisciplinary developments* (pp. 432–447). Hershey, PA: Information Science Reference; doi:10.4018/978-1-60960-567-4.ch026

Parker, J. R., & Becker, K. (2013). The simulation-game controversy: What is a ludic simulation? *International Journal of Gaming and Computer-Mediated Simulations*, *5*(1), 1–12. doi:10.4018/jgcms.2013010101

Phelps, D. (2010). What videogames have to teach us about screenworld and the humanistic ethos. In K. Schrier & D. Gibson (Eds.), *Ethics and game design: Teaching values through play* (pp. 125–149). Hershey, PA: Information Science Reference; doi:10.4018/978-1-61520-845-6.ch009

Poggi, A. (2011). Enhancing online games with agents. In M. Cruz-Cunha, V. Varvalho, & P. Tavares (Eds.), *Business, technological, and social dimensions of computer games: Multidisciplinary developments* (pp. 65–80). Hershey, PA: Information Science Reference; doi:10.4018/978-1-60960-567-4.ch005

Pole, A. (2012). Would Elizabeth Cady Stanton blog?: Women bloggers, politics, and political participation. In C. Romm Livermore (Ed.), *Gender and social computing: Interactions, differences and relationships* (pp. 183–199). Hershey, PA: Information Science Publishing; doi:10.4018/978-1-60960-759-3.ch011

Poster, W. R. (2012). The case of the U.S. mother / cyberspy / undercover Iraqi militant: Or, how global women have been incorporated in the technological war on terror. In R. Pande & T. Van der Weide (Eds.), *Globalization, technology diffusion and gender disparity: Social impacts of ICTs* (pp. 247–260). Hershey, PA: Information Science Reference; doi:10.4018/978-1-4666-0020-1.ch020

Pragnell, C., & Gatzidis, C. (2012). Addiction in World of Warcraft: A virtual ethnography study. In H. Yang & S. Yuen (Eds.), *Handbook of research on practices and outcomes in virtual worlds and environments* (pp. 54–74). Hershey, PA: Information Science Publishing; doi:10.4018/978-1-60960-762-3.ch004

Prakash, N. (2012). ICT and women empowerment in a rural setting in India. In R. Pande & T. Van der Weide (Eds.), *Globalization, technology diffusion and gender disparity: Social impacts of ICTs* (pp. 15–24). Hershey, PA: Information Science Reference; doi:10.4018/978-1-4666-0020-1.ch002

Prescott, J., & Bogg, J. (2010). The computer games industry: Women's experiences of work role in a male dominated environment. In A. Cater-Steel & E. Cater (Eds.), *Women in engineering, science and technology: Education and career challenges* (pp. 138–158). Hershey, PA: Engineering Science Reference; doi:10.4018/978-1-61520-657-5.ch007

Prescott, J., & Bogg, J. (2013). Career development, occupational choice, and organizational culture: Societal expectations, constraints, and embedded practices. In *Gendered occupational differences in science, engineering, and technology careers* (pp. 136–165). Hershey, PA: Information Science Reference; doi:10.4018/978-1-4666-2107-7.ch006

Prescott, J., & Bogg, J. (2013). Career promoters: A gender divide. In *Gendered occupational differences in science, engineering, and technology careers* (pp. 216–238). Hershey, PA: Information Science Reference; doi:10.4018/978-1-4666-2107-7.ch009

Prescott, J., & Bogg, J. (2013). Engendered workplace segregation: Work is still essentially a male domain. In *Gendered occupational differences in science, engineering, and technology careers* (pp. 1–25). Hershey, PA: Information Science Reference; doi:10.4018/978-1-4666-2107-7.ch001

Prescott, J., & Bogg, J. (2013). Final thoughts and concluding comments. In *Gendered occupational differences in science, engineering, and technology careers* (pp. 239–263). Hershey, PA: Information Science Reference; doi:10.4018/978-1-4666-2107-7.ch010

Prescott, J., & Bogg, J. (2013). Male dominated industries: Jobs for the boys. In *Gendered occupational differences in science, engineering, and technology careers* (pp. 26–63). Hershey, PA: Information Science Reference; doi:10.4018/978-1-4666-2107-7.ch002

Prescott, J., & Bogg, J. (2013). Progression aspirations and leadership. In *Gendered occupational differences in science, engineering, and technology careers* (pp. 192–215). Hershey, PA: Information Science Reference; doi:10.4018/978-1-4666-2107-7.ch008

Prescott, J., & Bogg, J. (2013). Self, career, and gender issues: A complex interplay of internal/external factors. In *Gendered occupational differences in science, engineering, and technology careers* (pp. 79–111). Hershey, PA: Information Science Reference; doi:10.4018/978-1-4666-2107-7.ch004

Prescott, J., & Bogg, J. (2013). Stereotype, attitudes, and identity: Gendered expectations and behaviors. In *Gendered occupational differences in science, engineering, and technology careers* (pp. 112–135). Hershey, PA: Information Science Reference; doi:10.4018/978-1-4666-2107-7.ch005

Prescott, J., & Bogg, J. (2013). The computer games industry: New industry, same old issues. In *Gendered occupational differences in science, engineering, and technology careers* (pp. 64–77). Hershey, PA: Information Science Reference; doi:10.4018/978-1-4666-2107-7.ch003

Prescott, J., & Bogg, J. (2013). Work life balance issues: The choice, or women's lack of it. In *Gendered occupational differences in science, engineering, and technology careers* (pp. 167–191). Hershey, PA: Information Science Reference; doi:10.4018/978-1-4666-2107-7.ch007

Preston, J. A., Chastine, J., O'Donnell, C., Tseng, T., & MacIntyre, B. (2012). Game jams: Community, motivations, and learning among jammers. *International Journal of Game-Based Learning*, *2*(3), 51–70. doi:10.4018/ijgbl.2012070104

Quan, J. J., Dattero, R., Galup, S. D., & Dhariwal, K. (2011). The determinants of information technology wages. *International Journal of Human Capital and Information Technology Professionals*, *2*(1), 48–65. doi:10.4018/jhcitp.2011010104

Quesenberry, J. L. (2012). Re-examining the career anchor model: An investigation of career values and motivations among women in the information technology profession. In R. Pande & T. Van der Weide (Eds.), *Globalization, technology diffusion and gender disparity: Social impacts of ICTs* (pp. 169–183). Hershey, PA: Information Science Reference; doi:10.4018/978-1-4666-0020-1.ch015

Quick, J. M., Atkinson, R. K., & Lin, L. (2012). Empirical taxonomies of gameplay enjoyment: Personality and video game preference. *International Journal of Game-Based Learning*, *2*(3), 11–31. doi:10.4018/ijgbl.2012070102

Quick, J. M., Atkinson, R. K., & Lin, L. (2012). The gameplay enjoyment model. *International Journal of Gaming and Computer-Mediated Simulations*, *4*(4), 64–80. doi:10.4018/jgcms.2012100105

Raditloaneng, W. (2012). Gender equality as a development factor in the application of ICT for agroforestry. In R. Lekoko & L. Semali (Eds.), *Cases on developing countries and ICT integration: Rural community development* (pp. 123–133). Hershey, PA: Information Science Reference; doi:10.4018/978-1-60960-117-1.ch012

Rafi, M. S. (2010). The sociolinguistics of SMS ways to identify gender boundaries. In R. Taiwo (Ed.), *Handbook of research on discourse behavior and digital communication: Language structures and social interaction* (pp. 104–111). Hershey, PA: Information Science Reference; doi:10.4018/978-1-61520-773-2.ch006

Rajesh, M. N. (2012). Virtual tourism as a new form of oppression against women. In R. Pande & T. Van der Weide (Eds.), *Globalization, technology diffusion and gender disparity: Social impacts of ICTs* (pp. 200–209). Hershey, PA: Information Science Reference; doi:10.4018/978-1-4666-0020-1.ch017

Rambo, K., & Liu, K. (2011). Culture-sensitive virtual e-commerce design with reference to female consumers in Saudi Arabia. In B. Ciaramitaro (Ed.), *Virtual worlds and e-commerce: Technologies and applications for building customer relationships* (pp. 267–289). Hershey, PA: Business Science Reference; doi:10.4018/978-1-61692-808-7.ch016

Ratan, R. (2013). Self-presence, explicated: Body, emotion, and identity extension into the virtual self. In R. Luppicini (Ed.), *Handbook of research on technoself: Identity in a technological society* (pp. 322–336). Hershey, PA: Information Science Reference; doi:10.4018/978-1-4666-2211-1.ch018

Reimann, D. (2012). Shaping interactive media with the sewing machine: Smart textile as an artistic context to engage girls in technology and engineering education. In *Computer engineering: Concepts, methodologies, tools and applications* (pp. 1342–1351). Hershey, PA: Engineering Science Reference; doi:10.4018/978-1-61350-456-7.ch517

Reiners, T., & Wood, L. C. (2013). Immersive virtual environments to facilitate authentic education in logistics and supply chain management. In Y. Kats (Ed.), *Learning management systems and instructional design: Best practices in online education* (pp. 323–343). Hershey, PA: Information Science Reference; doi:10.4018/978-1-4666-3930-0.ch017

Rensfeldt, A. B., & Riomar, S. (2010). Gendered distance education spaces: "Keeping women in place"? In S. Booth, S. Goodman, & G. Kirkup (Eds.), *Gender issues in learning and working with information technology: Social constructs and cultural contexts* (pp. 192–208). Hershey, PA: Information Science Reference; doi:10.4018/978-1-61520-813-5.ch011

Resmi, A. T., & Kamalanabhan, T. J. (2013). Confirmatory factor analysis and alternate test models for impression management in SMEs: A gender based study. *International Journal of Information Systems and Supply Chain Management*, *6*(2), 72–87. doi:10.4018/jisscm.2013040106

Rhima, T. E. (2010). Gender and ICT policy. In E. Adomi (Ed.), *Frameworks for ICT policy: Government, social and legal issues* (pp. 164–181). Hershey, PA: Information Science Reference; doi:10.4018/978-1-61692-012-8.ch011

Rodrigues, R. G., Pinheiro, P. G., & Barbosa, J. (2012). Online playability: The social dimension to the virtual world. In M. Cruz-Cunha (Ed.), *Handbook of research on serious games as educational, business and research tools* (pp. 391–421). Hershey, PA: Information Science Reference; doi:10.4018/978-1-4666-0149-9.ch021

Romm-Livermore, C., Somers, T. M., Setzekorn, K., & King, A. L. (2012). How e-daters behave online: Theory and empirical observations. In C. Romm Livermore (Ed.), *Gender and social computing: Interactions, differences and relationships* (pp. 236–256). Hershey, PA: Information Science Publishing; doi:10.4018/978-1-60960-759-3.ch014

Rommes, E. (2010). Heteronormativity revisited: Adolescents' educational choices, sexuality and soaps. In S. Booth, S. Goodman, & G. Kirkup (Eds.), *Gender issues in learning and working with information technology: Social constructs and cultural contexts* (pp. 150–172). Hershey, PA: Information Science Reference; doi:10.4018/978-1-61520-813-5.ch009

Rosas, O. V., & Dhen, G. (2012). One self to rule them all: A critical discourse analysis of French-speaking players' identity construction in World of Warcraft. In N. Zagalo, L. Morgado, & A. Boa-Ventura (Eds.), *Virtual worlds and metaverse platforms: New communication and identity paradigms* (pp. 337–366). Hershey, PA: Information Science Reference; doi:10.4018/978-1-60960-854-5.ch022

Rose, L. (2012). Social networks, online technologies, and virtual learning: (Re)structuring oppression and hierarchies in academia. In N. Ekekwe & N. Islam (Eds.), *Disruptive technologies, innovation and global redesign: Emerging implications* (pp. 266–279). Hershey, PA: Information Science Reference; doi:10.4018/978-1-4666-0134-5.ch014

Rowan, L., & Bigum, C. (2011). Reassembling the problem of the under-representation of girls in IT courses. In A. Tatnall (Ed.), *Actor-network theory and technology innovation: Advancements and new concepts* (pp. 208–222). Hershey, PA: Information Science Reference; doi:10.4018/978-1-60960-197-3.ch014

Russo, M. R., & Bryan, V. C. (2013). Technology, the 21st century workforce, and the construct of social justice. In V. Wang (Ed.), *Handbook of research on technologies for improving the 21st century workforce: Tools for lifelong learning* (pp. 56–75). Hershey, PA: Information Science Publishing; doi:10.4018/978-1-4666-2181-7.ch005

Saadé, R. G., Kira, D., & Otrakji, C. A. (2012). Gender differences in interface type task analysis. *International Journal of Information Systems and Social Change, 3*(2), 1–23. doi:10.4018/jissc.2012040101

Sadowska, N. M. (2010). Commerce and gender: Generating interactive spaces for female online user. In T. Dumova & R. Fiordo (Eds.), *Handbook of research on social interaction technologies and collaboration software: Concepts and trends* (pp. 245–256). Hershey, PA: Information Science Reference; doi:10.4018/978-1-60566-368-5.ch022

Salminen-Karlsson, M. (2010). Computer courses in adult education in a gender perspective. In S. Booth, S. Goodman, & G. Kirkup (Eds.), *Gender issues in learning and working with information technology: Social constructs and cultural contexts* (pp. 209–230). Hershey, PA: Information Science Reference; doi:10.4018/978-1-61520-813-5.ch012

San Chee, Y., Gwee, S., & Tan, E. M. (2011). Learning to become citizens by enacting governorship in the statecraft curriculum: An evaluation of learning outcomes. *International Journal of Gaming and Computer-Mediated Simulations, 3*(2), 1–27. doi:10.4018/jgcms.2011040101

Sánchez-Apellániz, M., Núñez, M., & Charlo-Molina, M. J. (2012). Women and globalization. In C. Wankel & S. Malleck (Eds.), *Ethical models and applications of globalization: Cultural, socio-political and economic perspectives* (pp. 119–140). Hershey, PA: Business Science Reference; doi:10.4018/978-1-61350-332-4.ch009

Sappleton, N. (2011). Overcoming the segregation/stereotyping dilemma: Computer mediated communication for business women and professionals. *International Journal of E-Politics*, *2*(2), 18–36. doi:10.4018/jep.2011040102

Sappleton, N. (2012). Overcoming the segregation/stereotyping dilemma: Computer mediated communication for business women and professionals. In C. Romm Livermore (Ed.), *Gender and social computing: Interactions, differences and relationships* (pp. 162–182). Hershey, PA: Information Science Publishing; doi:10.4018/978-1-60960-759-3.ch010

Sauvé, L., Villardier, L., & Probst, W. (2010). Online multiplayer games: A powerful tool for learning communication and teamwork. In D. Kaufman & L. Sauvé (Eds.), *Educational gameplay and simulation environments: Case studies and lessons learned* (pp. 175–194). Hershey, PA: Information Science Reference; doi:10.4018/978-1-61520-731-2.ch012

Sawyer, B. (2011). Research essay: What will serious games of the future look like? *International Journal of Gaming and Computer-Mediated Simulations*, *3*(3), 82–90. doi:10.4018/jgcms.2011070106

Schulz, H. M., & Eastin, M. S. (2010). An opportunity for in-game ad placement: The history of the video game industry interpreted through the meaning lifecycle. In M. Eastin, T. Daugherty, & N. Burns (Eds.), *Handbook of research on digital media and advertising: User generated content consumption* (pp. 480–490). Hershey, PA: Information Science Reference; doi:10.4018/978-1-60566-792-8.ch024

Sedehi, H., & Baleani, F. (2012). Business interactive game business interactive game (BIG): An innovative game to support enterprise management training. In M. Cruz-Cunha (Ed.), *Handbook of research on serious games as educational, business and research tools* (pp. 859–872). Hershey, PA: Information Science Reference; doi:10.4018/978-1-4666-0149-9.ch044

Sefyrin, J. (2010). "For me it doesn't matter where I put my information": Enactments of agency, mutual learning, and gender in IT design. In S. Booth, S. Goodman, & G. Kirkup (Eds.), *Gender issues in learning and working with information technology: Social constructs and cultural contexts* (pp. 65–82). Hershey, PA: Information Science Reference; doi:10.4018/978-1-61520-813-5.ch004

Sell, A., de Reuver, M., Walden, P., & Carlsson, C. (2012). Context, gender and intended use of mobile messaging, entertainment and social media services. *International Journal of Systems and Service-Oriented Engineering*, *3*(1), 1–15. doi:10.4018/jssoe.2012010101

Seth, N., & Patnayakuni, R. (2012). Online matrimonial sites and the transformation of arranged marriage in India. In C. Romm Livermore (Ed.), *Gender and social computing: Interactions, differences and relationships* (pp. 272–295). Hershey, PA: Information Science Publishing; doi:10.4018/978-1-60960-759-3.ch016

Sevo, R., & Chubin, D. E. (2010). Bias literacy: A review of concepts in research on gender discrimination and the U.S. context. In A. Cater-Steel & E. Cater (Eds.), *Women in engineering, science and technology: Education and career challenges* (pp. 21–54). Hershey, PA: Engineering Science Reference; doi:10.4018/978-1-61520-657-5.ch002

Shaw, A. (2011). Toward an ethic of representation: Ethics and the representation of marginalized groups in videogames. In K. Schrier & D. Gibson (Eds.), *Designing games for ethics: Models, techniques and frameworks* (pp. 159–177). Hershey, PA: Information Science Reference; doi:10.4018/978-1-60960-120-1.ch011

Shin, N., Norris, C., & Soloway, E. (2011). Mobile gaming environment: Learning and motivational effects. In P. Felicia (Ed.), *Handbook of research on improving learning and motivation through educational games: Multidisciplinary approaches* (pp. 467–481). Hershey, PA: Information Science Reference; doi:10.4018/978-1-60960-495-0.ch022

Shirk, S., Arreola, V., Wobig, C., & Russell, K. (2012). Girls' e-mentoring in science, engineering, and technology based at the University of Illinois at Chicago women in science and engineering (WISE) program. In Computer engineering: concepts, methodologies, tools and applications (pp. 1144-1163). Hershey, PA: Engineering Science Reference. doi:10.4018/978-1-61350-456-7.ch505

Sicart, M. (2010). Values between systems: Designing ethical gameplay. In K. Schrier & D. Gibson (Eds.), *Ethics and game design: Teaching values through play* (pp. 1–15). Hershey, PA: Information Science Reference; doi:10.4018/978-1-61520-845-6.ch001

Simão de Vasconcellos, M., & Soares de Araújo, I. (2013). Massively multiplayer online role playing games for health communication in Brazil. In K. Bredl & W. Bösche (Eds.), *Serious games and virtual worlds in education, professional development, and healthcare* (pp. 294–312). Hershey, PA: Information Science Reference; doi:10.4018/978-1-4666-3673-6.ch018

Simkins, D. (2010). Playing with ethics: Experiencing new ways of being in RPGs. In K. Schrier & D. Gibson (Eds.), *Ethics and game design: Teaching values through play* (pp. 69–84). Hershey, PA: Information Science Reference; doi:10.4018/978-1-61520-845-6.ch005

Stacey, P., & Nandhakumar, J. (2011). Emotional journeys in game design teams. In M. Cruz-Cunha, V. Varvalho, & P. Tavares (Eds.), *Business, technological, and social dimensions of computer games: Multidisciplinary developments* (pp. 220–236). Hershey, PA: Information Science Reference; doi:10.4018/978-1-60960-567-4.ch014

Staines, D. (2010). Videogames and moral pedagogy: A neo-Kohlbergian approach. In K. Schrier & D. Gibson (Eds.), *Ethics and game design: Teaching values through play* (pp. 35–51). Hershey, PA: Information Science Reference; doi:10.4018/978-1-61520-845-6.ch003

Starosky, P., & Pereira, M. D. (2013). Role-playing game as a pedagogical proposition for story co-construction: A Brazilian experience with deaf individuals in an educational context. In C. Gonzalez (Ed.), *Student usability in educational software and games: Improving experiences* (pp. 274–292). Hershey, PA: Information Science Reference; doi:10.4018/978-1-4666-1987-6.ch013

Steinkuehler, C., & Johnson, B. Z. (2011). Computational literacy in online games: The social life of mods. In R. Ferdig (Ed.), *Discoveries in gaming and computer-mediated simulations: New interdisciplinary applications* (pp. 218–231). Hershey, PA: Information Science Reference; doi:10.4018/978-1-60960-565-0.ch012

Surgevil, O., & Özbilgin, M. F. (2012). Women in information communication technologies. In C. Romm Livermore (Ed.), *Gender and social computing: Interactions, differences and relationships* (pp. 87–97). Hershey, PA: Information Science Publishing; doi:10.4018/978-1-60960-759-3.ch006

Švelch, J. (2010). The good, the bad, and the player: The challenges to moral engagement in single-player avatar-based video games. In K. Schrier & D. Gibson (Eds.), *Ethics and game design: Teaching values through play* (pp. 52–68). Hershey, PA: Information Science Reference; doi:10.4018/978-1-61520-845-6.ch004

Swain, C. (2011). Culturally responsive games and simulations. In *Gaming and simulations: Concepts, methodologies, tools and applications* (pp. 1298–1312). Hershey, PA: Information Science Reference; doi:10.4018/978-1-60960-195-9.ch504

Swim, J., & Barker, L. (2012). Pathways into a gendered occupation: Brazilian women in IT. *International Journal of Social and Organizational Dynamics in IT*, *2*(4), 34–51. doi:10.4018/ijsodit.2012100103

Takruri-Rizk, H., Sappleton, N., & Dhar-Bhattacharjee, S. (2010). Progression of UK women engineers: Aids and hurdles. In A. Cater-Steel & E. Cater (Eds.), *Women in engineering, science and technology: Education and career challenges* (pp. 280–300). Hershey, PA: Engineering Science Reference; doi:10.4018/978-1-61520-657-5.ch013

Tan, S., Baxa, J., & Spackman, M. P. (2010). Effects of built-in audio versus unrelated background music on performance in an adventure role-playing game. *International Journal of Gaming and Computer-Mediated Simulations*, *2*(3), 1–23. doi:10.4018/jgcms.2010070101

Tara, S., & Ilavarasan, P. V. (2012). Western work worlds and altering approaches to marriage: An empirical study of women employees of call centers in India. In R. Pande & T. Van der Weide (Eds.), *Globalization, technology diffusion and gender disparity: Social impacts of ICTs* (pp. 262–276). Hershey, PA: Information Science Reference; doi:10.4018/978-1-4666-0020-1.ch021

Teixeira, P. M., Félix, M. J., & Tavares, P. (2012). Playing with design: The universality of design in game development. In M. Cruz-Cunha (Ed.), *Handbook of research on serious games as educational, business and research tools* (pp. 217–231). Hershey, PA: Information Science Reference; doi:10.4018/978-1-4666-0149-9.ch011

Teng, C., Jeng, S., Chang, H. K., & Wu, S. (2012). Who plays games online? The relationship between gamer personality and online game use. *International Journal of E-Business Research*, *8*(4), 1–14. doi:10.4018/jebr.2012100101

Terry, A., & Gomez, R. (2012). Gender and public access ICT. In R. Gomez (Ed.), *Libraries, telecentres, cybercafes and public access to ICT: International comparisons* (pp. 51–64). Hershey, PA: Information Science Publishing; doi:10.4018/978-1-60960-771-5.ch006

Thacker, S., & Griffiths, M. D. (2012). An exploratory study of trolling in online video gaming. *International Journal of Cyber Behavior, Psychology and Learning*, *2*(4), 17–33. doi:10.4018/ijcbpl.2012100102

Thomas, D. I., & Vlacic, L. B. (2011). Human and virtual beings as equal collaborative partners in computer games. In M. Cruz-Cunha, V. Varvalho, & P. Tavares (Eds.), *Computer games as educational and management tools: Uses and approaches* (pp. 23–51). Hershey, PA: Information Science Reference; doi:10.4018/978-1-60960-569-8.ch003

Toprac, P., & Abdel-Meguid, A. (2011). Causing fear, suspense, and anxiety using sound design in computer games. In M. Grimshaw (Ed.), *Game sound technology and player interaction: Concepts and developments* (pp. 176–191). Hershey, PA: Information Science Reference; doi:10.4018/978-1-61692-828-5.ch009

Tran, B. (2012). Gendered technology-based organizations: A view of the glass cliff through the window of the glass ceiling. In D. Jemielniak & A. Marks (Eds.), *Managing dynamic technology-oriented businesses: High-tech organizations and workplaces* (pp. 253–272). Hershey, PA: Business Science Reference; doi:10.4018/978-1-4666-1836-7.ch015

Tran, B. (2014). Rhetoric of play: Utilizing the gamer factor in selecting and training employees. In T. Connolly, T. Hainey, E. Boyle, G. Baxter, & P. Moreno-Ger (Eds.), *Psychology, pedagogy, and assessment in serious games* (pp. 175–203). Hershey, PA: Information Science Reference; doi:10.4018/978-1-4666-4773-2.ch009

Trauth, E. M., Quesenberry, J. L., & Huang, H. (2010). Factors influencing career choice for women in the global information technology workforce. In M. Hunter & F. Tan (Eds.), *Technological advancement in developed and developing countries: Discoveries in global information management* (pp. 23–48). Hershey, PA: Information Science Reference; doi:10.4018/978-1-60566-920-5.ch002

Trepte, S., Reinecke, L., & Behr, K. (2011). Playing myself or playing to win? Gamers' strategies of avatar creation in terms of gender and sex. In R. Ferdig (Ed.), *Discoveries in gaming and computer-mediated simulations: New interdisciplinary applications* (pp. 329–352). Hershey, PA: Information Science Reference; doi:10.4018/978-1-60960-565-0.ch019

Tu, C., Yen, C., & Blocher, M. (2011). A study of the relationship between gender and online social presence. *International Journal of Online Pedagogy and Course Design*, *1*(3), 33–49. doi:10.4018/ijopcd.2011070103

Tyagi, A. (2011). Virtual reality and identity crisis—: Implications for individuals and organizations. In K. Malik & P. Choudhary (Eds.), *Business organizations and collaborative web: Practices, strategies and patterns* (pp. 202–218). Hershey, PA: Information Science Reference; doi:10.4018/978-1-60960-581-0.ch013

Umarov, I., & Mozgovoy, M. (2012). Believable and effective AI agents in virtual worlds: Current state and future perspectives. *International Journal of Gaming and Computer-Mediated Simulations*, *4*(2), 37–59. doi:10.4018/jgcms.2012040103

Ursyn, A. (2014). Challenges in game design. In *Computational solutions for knowledge, art, and entertainment: Information exchange beyond text* (pp. 413–428). Hershey, PA: Information Science Reference; doi:10.4018/978-1-4666-4627-8.ch021

Uzun, L., Ekin, M. T., & Kartal, E. (2013). The opinions and attitudes of the foreign language learners and teachers related to the traditional and digital games: Age and gender differences. *International Journal of Game-Based Learning*, *3*(2), 91–111. doi:10.4018/ijgbl.2013040106

van de Laar, B., Reuderink, B., Bos, D. P., & Heylen, D. (2010). Evaluating user experience of actual and imagined movement in BCI gaming. *International Journal of Gaming and Computer-Mediated Simulations*, *2*(4), 33–47. doi:10.4018/jgcms.2010100103

van der Weide, T. (2012). A digital (r)evolution to the information age. In R. Pande & T. Van der Weide (Eds.), *Globalization, technology diffusion and gender disparity: Social impacts of ICTs* (pp. 1–14). Hershey, PA: Information Science Reference; doi:10.4018/978-1-4666-0020-1.ch001

Velazquez, M. (2013). "Come fly with us": Playing with girlhood in the world of pixie hollow. In Y. Baek & N. Whitton (Eds.), *Cases on digital game-based learning: Methods, models, and strategies* (pp. 1–14). Hershey, PA: Information Science Reference; doi:10.4018/978-1-4666-2848-9.ch001

Veltri, N. F., Webb, H. W., & Papp, R. (2010). GETSMART: An academic-industry partnership to encourage female participation in science, technology, engineering and math careers. In A. Cater-Steel & E. Cater (Eds.), *Women in engineering, science and technology: Education and career challenges* (pp. 56–77). Hershey, PA: Engineering Science Reference; doi:10.4018/978-1-61520-657-5.ch003

Vikaros, L., & Degand, D. (2010). Moral development through social narratives and game design. In K. Schrier & D. Gibson (Eds.), *Ethics and game design: Teaching values through play* (pp. 197–215). Hershey, PA: Information Science Reference; doi:10.4018/978-1-61520-845-6.ch013

Voulgari, I., & Komis, V. (2011). Collaborative learning in massively multiplayer online games: A review of social, cognitive and motivational perspectives. In P. Felicia (Ed.), *Handbook of research on improving learning and motivation through educational games: Multidisciplinary approaches* (pp. 370–394). Hershey, PA: Information Science Reference; doi:10.4018/978-1-60960-495-0.ch018

Wakunuma-Zojer, K. J. (2012). Gender and ICT policy for development and empowerment: A critique of a national ICT policy. In *Regional development: Concepts, methodologies, tools, and applications* (pp. 1005–1027). Hershey, PA: Information Science Reference; doi:10.4018/978-1-4666-0882-5.ch510

Wallgren, L. G., Leijon, S., & Andersson, K. M. (2013). IT managers' narratives on subordinates' motivation at work: A case study. In A. Mesquita (Ed.), *User perception and influencing factors of technology in everyday life* (pp. 282–297). Hershey, PA: Information Science Reference; doi:10.4018/978-1-4666-1954-8.ch019

Weber, R., & Shaw, P. (2009). Player types and quality perceptions: A social cognitive theory based model to predict video game playing. *International Journal of Gaming and Computer-Mediated Simulations*, *1*(1), 66–89. doi:10.4018/jgcms.2009010105

Wei, Z., & Kramarae, C. (2012). Women, big ideas, and social networking technologies: Hidden assumptions. In R. Pande & T. Van der Weide (Eds.), *Globalization, technology diffusion and gender disparity: Social impacts of ICTs* (pp. 70–82). Hershey, PA: Information Science Reference; doi:10.4018/978-1-4666-0020-1.ch006

Weiss, A., & Tettegah, S. (2012). World of race war: Race and learning in World of Warcraft. *International Journal of Gaming and Computer-Mediated Simulations*, *4*(4), 33–44. doi:10.4018/jgcms.2012100103

White, G. (2010). Increasing the numbers of women in science. In A. Cater-Steel & E. Cater (Eds.), *Women in engineering, science and technology: Education and career challenges* (pp. 78–95). Hershey, PA: Engineering Science Reference; doi:10.4018/978-1-61520-657-5.ch004

White, M. M. (2012). Designing tutorial modalities and strategies for digital games: Lessons from education. *International Journal of Game-Based Learning*, *2*(2), 13–34. doi:10.4018/ijgbl.2012040102

Winter, A. (2010). The smart women – Smart state strategy: A policy on women's participation in science, engineering and technology in Queensland, Australia. In A. Cater-Steel & E. Cater (Eds.), *Women in engineering, science and technology: Education and career challenges* (pp. 1–20). Hershey, PA: Engineering Science Reference; doi:10.4018/978-1-61520-657-5.ch001

Wolfenstein, M. (2013). Digital structures and the future of online leadership. In S. D'Agustino (Ed.), *Immersive environments, augmented realities, and virtual worlds: Assessing future trends in education* (pp. 257–279). Hershey, PA: Information Science Reference; doi:10.4018/978-1-4666-2670-6.ch015

Woodfield, R. (2012). Gender and employability patterns amongst UK ICT graduates: Investigating the leaky pipeline. In R. Pande & T. Van der Weide (Eds.), *Globalization, technology diffusion and gender disparity: Social impacts of ICTs* (pp. 184–199). Hershey, PA: Information Science Reference; doi:10.4018/978-1-4666-0020-1.ch016

Yakura, E. K., Soe, L., & Guthrie, R. (2012). Women in IT careers: Investigating support for women in the information technology workforce. In C. Romm Livermore (Ed.), *Gender and social computing: Interactions, differences and relationships* (pp. 35–49). Hershey, PA: Information Science Publishing; doi:10.4018/978-1-60960-759-3.ch003

York, A. M., & Nordengren, F. R. (2013). E-learning and web 2.0 case study: The role of gender in contemporary models of health care leadership. In H. Yang & S. Wang (Eds.), *Cases on formal and informal e-learning environments: Opportunities and practices* (pp. 292–313). Hershey, PA: Information Science Reference; doi:10.4018/978-1-4666-1930-2.ch016

Yost, E., Handley, D. M., Cotten, S. R., & Winstead, V. (2010). Understanding the links between mentoring and self-efficacy in the new generation of women STEM scholars. In A. Cater-Steel & E. Cater (Eds.), *Women in engineering, science and technology: Education and career challenges* (pp. 97–117). Hershey, PA: Engineering Science Reference; doi:10.4018/978-1-61520-657-5.ch005

Youngs, G. (2012). Globalization, information and communication technologies, and women's lives. In R. Pande & T. Van der Weide (Eds.), *Globalization, technology diffusion and gender disparity: Social impacts of ICTs* (pp. 25–34). Hershey, PA: Information Science Reference; doi:10.4018/978-1-4666-0020-1.ch003

Zhang, S., Jiang, H., & Carroll, J. M. (2010). Social identity in Facebook community life. *International Journal of Virtual Communities and Social Networking*, 2(4), 64–76. doi:10.4018/jvcsn.2010100105

Zhao, Y., Wang, W., & Zhu, Y. (2010). Antecedents of the closeness of human-avatar relationships in a virtual world. *Journal of Database Management*, *21*(2), 41–68. doi:10.4018/jdm.2010040103

Zutshi, A., & Creed, A. (2010). ICT and gender issues in the higher education of entrepreneurs. *International Journal of E-Entrepreneurship and Innovation*, *1*(1), 42–59. doi:10.4018/jeei.2010010103

Compilation of References

Abdullah, N. H., Wahab, E., & Shamsuddin, A. (2013). Exploring the common technology adoption enablers among Malaysian SMES: Qualitative findings. *Journal of Management and Sustainability*, *3*(4), 78–91. doi:10.5539/jms.v3n4p78

Abraham, L.B., Mörn, M.P., & Vollman, A. (2010, June). Women on the Web: How Women are Shaping the Internet. *comScore Inc.*

ACMA (Australian Communication and Media Authority). (2008). *Australian families with children are 'media-rich', research finds.* Retrieved from http://www.acma.gov.au/WEB/STANDARD/pc=PC_310897

Actman, H. (1995). Net Results. *Sporting Goods Business*, *28*(6), 36–38.

Adjei, M., Noble, S., & Noble, C. (2010). The influence of C2C communications in online brand communities on customer purchase behaviour. *Journal of the Academy of Marketing Science*, *38*(5), 634–653. doi:10.1007/s11747-009-0178-5

Adya, M. P. (2008). Women at work: Differences in IT career experiences and perceptions between South Asian and American women. *Human Resource Management*, *47*(3), 601–635. doi:10.1002/hrm.20234

Afshar, H., Aitkin, R., & Franks, M. (2005). Feminisms, Islamophobia and Identities. *Political Studies*, *53*(2), 262–283. doi:10.1111/j.1467-9248.2005.00528.x

Agarwal, R., & Karahanna, E. (2000). Time flies when you're having fun: Cognitive absorption and beliefs about information technology usage. *Management Information Systems Quarterly*, *24*(4), 665–694. doi:10.2307/3250951

Aitken, R., Ballantyne, D., Osborne, P., & Williams, J. (2006). Introduction to the special issue on the Service-Dominant Logic of Marketing: Insights from The Otago Forum. *Marketing Theory*, *6*(3), 275–280. doi:10.1177/1470593106066780

Akar, E., & Topçu, B. (2011). An examination of the factors influencing consumers' attitudes toward social media marketing. *Journal of Internet Commerce*, *10*(1), 35–67. doi:10.1080/15332861.2011.558456

Albert, A., & Hersinta, H. (2013). Shopping on Social Networking Sites: A Study on Facebook Consumers' psychological Characteristics. *Journal Communication Spectrum*, *2*(2).

American Women and Terrorism: A Growing Trend (2010). *Anti-Defamation League.* Retrieved from http://www.adl.org/main_Terrorism/american_women_terrorists.htm

Anderson, J. B. (2012). The future of higher education. Retrieved from http://pewinteret.ore/Reports/2012/Future-of-Higher-Education/Overview.aspx

Anderson, E. D. (2009). The maintenance of masculinity among the stakeholders of sport. *Sport Management Review*, *12*(1), 3–14. doi:10.1016/j.smr.2008.09.003

Anderson, L. F., & Littrell, M. A. (1995). Souvenir-purchase behaviour of women tourists. *Annals of Tourism Research, 22*(2), 328–348. doi:10.1016/0160-7383(94)00080-8

Andreasen, A. R. (1965). Attitudes and Customer Behavior: A Decision Model. In L. E. Preston (Ed.), New Research in Marketing. Berkley, CA, USA.

Anggrawan, D. S., & Tedjaatmadja, H. M. (2013). Address terms used by online shop sellers to their female teenage customers and young mother customers in Facebook. *K@ ta Kita, 1*(1), 122-129.

Anwar, M., & Johanson, G. (2014). Mobile Phones and religion: The Case of women Micro-Entrepreneurs in a religious Community in Indonesia. *Islam and Development: Exploring the Invisible Aid Economy*, 135.

Ardi, R., & Maison, D. (2014). How do Polish and Indonesian disclose in Facebook? *Journal of Information. Communication and Ethics in Society, 12*(3), 195–218. doi:10.1108/JICES-01-2014-0006

Armentor-Cota, J. (2006). In E. Trauth (Ed.), *Gender and Chat Forums. Encyclopedia of Gender and Information Technology* (pp. 361–364). Hershey, PA, USA: IGI Global. doi:10.4018/978-1-59140-815-4.ch056

Australian Bureau of Statistics. (2014a). *Gender indicators, Australia: Life expectancy (Cat. no. 4125.0).* Canberra, Australia: ABS.

Australian Bureau of Statistics. (2014b). *Australian historical population statistics: Life expectancy (Cat. no. 3105.0.65.001).* Canberra, Australia: ABS.

Australian Institute of Health and Welfare. (2008). *Australia's Health: 2008 (Cat. no. 99).* Canberra, Australia: AIHW.

Australian Vaccination-skeptics Network Inc. (2014). *Making an informed choice.* Retrieved from http://avn.org.au/making-an-informed-choice/

Awan, A. N. (2007). Virtual jihadist media. *European Journal of Cultural Studies, 10*(3), 389–408. doi:10.1177/1367549407079713

Baaren, E., van deWijngaert, L., & Huizer, E. (2011). Understanding technology adoption through individual and context characteristics: The case of HDTV. *Journal of Broadcasting & Electronic Media, 55*(1), 72–89. doi:10.1080/08838151.2011.546257

Bae, S., & Lee, T. (2011). Gender differences in consumers' perception of online consumer reviews. *Electronic Commerce Research, 11*(2), 201–214. doi:10.1007/s10660-010-9072-y

Bagozzi, R., & Dholakia, U. (2002, Spring). Intentional Social Action in Virtual Communities, Journal of Interactive Marketing, 16(2).

Ballantyne, D. & Varey, R. (2006) Introducing a dialogical orientation to the Service-Dominant Logic of Marketing. In *The Service-Dominant Logic of Marketing: Dialog, debate, and directions* (pp. 224–235).

Ballantyne, D., & Varey, R. (2008). The service-dominant logic and the future of marketing. *Journal of the Academy of Marketing Science, 36*(1), 11–14. doi:10.1007/s11747-007-0075-8

Ballantyne, D., & Varey, R. J. (2008). The Service-Dominant Logic and the future of Marketing. *Journal of the Academy of Marketing Science. Springer Science & Business Media B., 36*, 11–14.

Bandias, S., & Warne, L. 2009. Women in ICT – Retain and Sustain: An overview of the ACS-W Survey.*Proceedings of the Australasian Conference in Information Systems (ACIS).*

Banerjee, A. V., & Duflo, E. (2008). What is middle class about the middle classes around the world? *The journal of economic perspectives: a journal of the American Economic Association, 22*(2), 3.

Barford, A., Dorling, D., Smith, G. D., & Shaw, M. (2006). Life expectancy: Women now on top everywhere. *British Medical Journal, 332*(7545), 808. doi:10.1136/bmj.332.7545.808 PMID:16601021

Barker, V. (2009). Older adolescents' motivations for social network site use: The influence of gender, group identity, and collective self-esteem. *Cyberpsychology & Behavior: The Impact of the Internet, Multimedia and Virtual Reality On Behavior. Society, 12*(2), 209–213.

Bates, S. (1993). *Battleground: One mother's crusade, the religious right, and the struggle for control of our classrooms.* New York: Poseidon.

Battersby, L. (2015, January 26). Tony Abbott dismisses social media as 'electronic graffiti', again. *The Age.* Retrieved from http://www.theage.com.au/it-pro/government-it/tony-abbott-dismisses-social-media-as-electronic-graffiti-again-20150126-12yg26.html

Beale, A., & Hall, K. (2012). Cyberbullying: What School Administrators (and Parents) Can Do. *School Psychology International, 81*(1), 8–12.

Beavis, C. (2013). Young people, new media and education: Participation and possibilities. *Social Alternatives, 32*(2), 39.

Beck, C. (2012). Home education: The social motivation. *International electronic journal of elementary education.* 3(1). 72-81

Behnke, K. 2012, Ladies of Warcraft: changing perceptions of women and technology through productive play. *Proceedings of the International Conference on the Foundations of Digital Games* (pp. 288 – 289).

Belk, R. W. (1975). Situational Variables and Consumer Behavior. *The Journal of Consumer Research, 2*(3), 157–164. doi:10.1086/208627

Bell, V. (1999). Performativity and belonging: An introduction. In V. Bell (Ed.), *Performativity and belonging.* Thousand Oaks, Calif; London: Sage Publications. doi:10.4135/9781446219607.n1

Benin, A., Wisler-Scher, D., Colson, E., Shapiro, E., & Holmboe, E. (2006). Qualitative Analysis of Mothers' Decision-Making about Vaccines for Infants: The Importance of Trust. Pediatrics. *Official Journal of the American Academy of Pediatrics, 117*(5), 1532–1541. doi:10.1542/peds.2005-1728

Bennet, J. (2014). Behold the Power of Hashtag Feminism. *Time Magazine.* Retrieved from http://time.com/3319081/whyistayed-hashtag-feminism-activism/

Bennett, S. (2014, October 2). Men Are From LinkedIn, Google+ & YouTube, Women Are From Twitter, Instagram & Pinterest. *AdWeek.* Retrieved from http://www.adweek.com/socialtimes/men-women-social-media-study/502009

Benson, V., & Morgan, S. (2013). *Social Higher Education: How Effective is it?* Kingston University.

Benwell, B., & Stokoe, E. (2006). *Discourse and identity.* Edinburgh, UK: Edinburgh University Press.

Berard, T. J. (2005). Rethinking practices and structures. *Philosophy of the Social Sciences, 35*(2), 196–230. doi:10.1177/0048393105275290

Berger, P., & Luckmann, T. (1966). *The Social Construction of Reality.* New York: Doubleday.

Bernstein, B. (1990). *Class, Codes and Control* (Vol. 4). London: RKP. doi:10.4324/9780203011263

Bhatnagar, A., & Ghose, S. (2004). Online information search termination patterns across product categories and consumer demographics. *Journal of Retailing*, *80*(3), 221–228. doi:10.1016/j.jretai.2003.10.001

Blalock, H. M. (1969). *Theory Construction - From Verbal to Mathematical Formulations* (p. 180). Englewood Cliffs, NJ: Prentice-Hall Inc.

Blanchet, K. B. (2011). Moustaches promote men's health. *British Journal of Urology International*, *108*(10), ii–vii. PMID:22032206

Blankenship, M. (2011). How Social Media Can and should Impact Higher Education. *Education Digest*, *76*(7), 39–42.

Blichfeldt, B. S., Pedersen, B. M., Johansen, A., & Hansen, L. (2010). Tween Tourists: Children and Decision-Making. *Journal of Tourism Consumption and Practice*, *2*(1), 1–24.

Bohr, M., Murray, K., Anderson, R., Henson, L., Murphy, M., & Amr, F. (2013, October). Bullying, cyberbullying and female to female aggression: Empowering students to be part of the solution. *Connect*, *303*, 3–8.

Bourdieu, P., & Passeron, J. C. (1979). *The inheritors: French students and their relations to culture*. Chicago, IL: University of Chicago Press.

Bourdieu, P., & Wacquant, L. J. D. (1992). *An invitation to reflexive sociology*. Cambridge, UK: Polity Press.

Boyce, C., & Neale, P. (2006, May). Conducting in-depth interviews: A guide for designing and conducting in-depth interviews for evaluation input. *Pathfinder.org*. Retrieved from http://www2.pathfinder.org/site/DocServer/m_e_tool_series_indepth_interviews.pdf

boyd, d. (2004). Friendster and publicly articulated social networking. ACM.

boyd, d. (2011). Social network sites as networked publics: Affordance, dynamics, and implications. In Z. Papacharissi (Ed.), *A networked self: Identity, community and culture on social network sites* (pp. 39-58). New York: Routledge.

Boyd, D. M., & Ellison, N. B. (2007). Social network sites: Definition, history, and scholarship. *Journal of Computer-Mediated Communication*, *13*(1), 210–230. doi:10.1111/j.1083-6101.2007.00393.x

Brenner, S. (1995). Why women rule the roost: rethinking Javanese ideologies of gender and self-control. In A. Ong & M. G. Peletz (Eds.), *Bewitching women, pious men: Gender and body politics in Southeast Asia* (pp. 19–50). Berkeley: University of California Press.

Briones, R. L., Kuch, B., Liu, B. F., & Jin, Y. (2011). Keeping up with the digital age: How the American Red Cross uses social media to build relationships. *Public Relations Review*, *37*(1), 37–43. doi:10.1016/j.pubrev.2010.12.006

Brodie, R., Ilic, A., Juric, B., & Hollebeek, L. (2013) Customer engagement in a virtual brand community: an exploratory analysis, 66, 2013, 105 – 114

Brodie, R. J., Hollebeek, L. D., Jurić, B., & Ilić, A. (2011). Customer engagement: Conceptual domain, fundamental propositions, and implications for research. *Journal of Service Research*, *14*(3), 252–271. doi:10.1177/1094670511411703

Brodie, R. J., Ilić, A., Jurić, B., & Hollebeek, I. (2013). Consumer engagement in a virtual brand community: An exploratory analysis. *Journal of Business Research*, *66*(1), 105–114. doi:10.1016/j.jbusres.2011.07.029

Bronstein, J. (2013). Personal blogs as online presences on the internet: Exploring self-presentation and self-disclosure in blogging. *Aslib Proceedings*, *65*(2), 161–181. doi:10.1108/00012531311313989

Brown, M. T. (2012). *Enlisting masculinity: The construction of gender in US military recruiting advertising during the all-volunteer force*. Oxford Scholarship University Press Online; doi:10.1093/acprof:oso/9780199842827.001.0001

Bruns, A. (2006). Introduction. In A. Bruns & J. Jacobs (Eds.), *Uses of Blogs* (pp. 1–9). New York: Peter Lang Publishing.

Buckingham, D., & Martínez-Rodríguez, J. B. (2013). Interactive youth: New citizenship between social networks and school settings. *Comunicar, 20*(40), 10.

Burgess, J. (2007). *Vernacular Creativity and New Media* [PhD dissertation]. Queensland University of Technology.

Burgess, J., & Banks, J. (2010). In S. Cunningham & G. Turner (Eds.), *User-Created Content and Online Social Networks* (3rd ed., pp. 295–307). NSW: Allen and Unwin.

Butler, J. (2011a). Bodies That Matter. New York: Taylor and Francis.

Butler, J. (2011b). Gender trouble. New York: Taylor and Francis.

Butler, J. (1988). Performative acts and gender constitution: An essay in phenomenology and feminist theory. *Theatre Journal, 40*(4), 519–531. http://www.flimmer.nu/sites/default/files/butlerPerformance.pdf doi:10.2307/3207893

Byrnes, J. P., Miller, D. C., & Schafer, W. D. (1999). Gender differences in risk taking: A meta-analysis. *Psychological Bulletin, 125*(3), 367–383. doi:10.1037/0033-2909.125.3.367

Calder, B. J., & Malthouse, E. C. (2008). Media engagement and advertising effectiveness. In B. J. Calder (Ed.), *Kellogg on advertising and media* (pp. 1–36). Hoboken, NJ: Wiley.

Caldwell, G.A., Osborne, L., Mewburn, I., & Crowther, P. (2013). Guerrillas in the [urban] midst: developing and using creative research methods – guerrilla research tactics. *Journal of Urban Technology* (Special issue on urban acupuncture: revitalising cities with ambient media and networked technologies).

Campbell, D. (2008). Reaching Students Where They Live. *BizED., 7*, 60–61.

Carper, J. (2000). Pluralism to Establishment to Dissent: The Religious and Educational Context of Home Schooling. *Peabody Journal of Education, 75*(1-2), 8–19. doi:10.1080/0161956X.2000.9681932

Carr, N. (Ed.). (2011). *Children's and Families' Holiday Experiences* (p. 201). London, New York: Routledge.

Chad, P. (2013). Implementing marketing orientation in charities: A necessity for survival. *Marketing Theory, 13*(3), 303–322. doi:10.1177/1470593113484921

Chad, P., Kyriazis, E., & Motion, J. (2013). Development of a market orientation research agenda for the non-profit sector. *Journal of Nonprofit & Public Sector Marketing, 25*(1), 1–27. doi:10.1080/10495142.2013.759814

Chang, C. (2006). Cultural masculinity/femininity influences in advertising appeals. *Journal of Advertising Research, 46*(3), 315–323. doi:10.2501/S0021849906060296

Chelly, M., & Mataillet, H. (2012, September). Social Media and the impact on education: Social media and home education. Proceedings of the 2012 International Conference on e-Learning and e-Technologies in Education (ICEEE) (pp. 24-26).

Chi, H.-H. (2011). Interactive digital advertising vs. Virtual brand community: Exploratory study of user motivation and social media marketing responses in Taiwan. *Journal of Interactive Advertising, 12*(1), 44–61. doi:10.1080/15252019.2011.10722190

Choi, H., & Burnes, B. (n. d.). The internet and value co-creation: the case of the popular music industry. *Promethus: Critical Studies in Innovation*, 31(1), 35 – 53.

Clark, R., & Gieve, S. N. (2006). On the discursive construction of 'the Chinese learner'. *Language, Culture and Curriculum*, *19*(1), 54–73. doi:10.1080/07908310608668754

Clifford, C. (2014). Women dominate every social media network – except one (Infographic). Retrieved from http://www.entrepreneur.com/article/231970

Cockburn, C. (1992). In R. Silverstone & E. Hirsch (Eds.), *The circuit of technology: Gender, identity and power. Consuming Technologies* (pp. 33–47). London: Routledge.

Coetsee, R. (2012, August 11). School Bans Social Media in Student Campaigns: Heritage High makes candidates use fliers, posters. *Contra Costa Times, p B.4.*

Coleman, J. S. (1988). Social capital in the creation of human capital. *American Journal of Sociology*, *94*, S95–S120. doi:10.1086/228943

Colman, G. (2014). *Cyberbullying and Internet Safety*. Waterbury, CT.

Connell, R. W. (1987). *Gender and Power: Society, the Person and Sexual Politics*. Stanford, CA: Stanford University Press.

Constantinides, E., & Zinck Stagno, M. (2011). Potential of the social media as instruments of higher education marketing: A segmentation study. *Journal of Marketing for Higher Education*, *21*(1), 7–24. doi:10.1080/08841241.2011.573593

Conway, M. (2006). Terrorism and the Internet: New Media—New Threat? *Parliamentary Affairs*, *59*(2), 283–298. doi:10.1093/pa/gsl009

Cook, K. E. (2008). In-depth interview. In L. M. Given (Ed.), *The Sage encyclopedia of qualitative research methods* (pp. 423–424). Thousand Oaks: Sage Publications, Ltd. doi:10.4135/9781412963909.n209

Cook, S. (2012). Women Lead in Adopting New Technologies. *Women in Higher Education*, *21*(2), 24–25. doi:10.1002/whe.10296

Cornell, K. (2012). 'The Mommy Blogger Market: Social Media's Effect on Motherhood (pp. 1–9). East Carolina University. Retrieved from http://www.katiecornelldesigns.com/ECUCourseWork/ICTN6855/The%20Mommy%20Blogger%20Market.pdf

Correa, T., Hinsley, A., & de Zúñiga, H. (2010, March). Who interacts on the Web?: The intersection of users' personality and social media use. *Computers in Human Behavior*, *26*(2), 247–253. doi:10.1016/j.chb.2009.09.003

Cosenza, R. M., & Davis, D. L. (1981). Family Vacation Decision Making Over the Family Life Cycle: A Decision and Influence Structure Analysis. *Journal of Travel Research*, *20*(2), 17–23. doi:10.1177/004728758102000203

Cox, D., & McLeod, S. (2014). Social media strategies for school principals. National Association of Secondary School Principals. *NASSP Bulletin*, *98*(1), 5–25. doi:10.1177/0192636513510596

Curran, K., Graham, S., & Temple, C. (2011). Advertising on Facebook. *International Journal of E-Business Development*, *1*(1), 26–33.

Cyr, D., & Bonanni, C. (2005). Gender and website design in e-business. *International Journal of Electronic Business*, *3*(6), 565–582. doi:10.1504/IJEB.2005.008536

Dale, N. F. (2013). *Destination choice by school excursions groups in Australia: Understanding the factors that influence preference* (Unpublished PhD thesis). University of Canberra

Daniel, A., Salmon, D., Moulton, L., Omer, S., deHart, M., Stokley, S., & Halsey, N. (2005). Factors Associated with Refusal of Childhood Vaccines Among Parents of School-aged Children: A Case-Control study. *JAMA Pediatrics* 59(5), 470-476. DOI . Retrieved from http://archpedi.jamanetwork.com/article.aspx?articleid=486011IJune 201510.1001/archpedi.159.5.470

Darley, W.K., & Jeen-Su Lim (1986). Family Decision Making in Leisure-Time Activities: an Exploratory Investigation of the Impact of Locus of Control, Child Age Influence Factor and Parental Type on Perceived Child Influence. *Advances in Consumer Research,13*(1), 370-374.

Davis, C. H. F., III, Deil-Amen, R., Rios-Aguilar, C., & González Canché, M. S. (2012). Social media and higher education: A literature review and research directions. *Immunising your children. University of Arizona and Claremont Graduate University Department of Human Services.* Retrieved from http://www.humanservices.gov.au/customer/subjects/immunising-your-children

Davis, J. (2006). Women and Terrorism in Radical Islam: Planners, perpetrators, patrons? *Centre for Foreign Policy Studies.* Retrieved from http://centreforforeignpolicystudies.dal.ca/pdf/gradsymp06/Davis.pdf

Davis, F. D. (1989). Perceived usefulness, perceived ease of use, and user acceptance of information technologies. *Management Information Systems Quarterly, 13*(3), 319–340. doi:10.2307/249008

de Valck, K., van Bruggen, G. H., & Wierenga, B. (2009). Virtual communities: A marketing perspective. *Decision Support Systems, 47*(3), 185–203. doi:10.1016/j.dss.2009.02.008

Decrop, A. (Ed.), (2006). *Vacation Decision Making.* UK: CABI Publishing. doi:10.1079/9781845930400.0000

Decrop, A., & Kozak, M. (2009). Decision Strategies in Tourism Evaluation. In M. Kozak & A. Decrop (Eds.), *Handbook of Tourist Behavior - Theory & Practice* (pp. 67–82). New York: Routledge.

Decrop, A., & Snelders, D. (2004). Planning the Summer Vacation - An Adaptable Process. *Annals of Tourism Research, 31*(4), 1008–1030. doi:10.1016/j.annals.2004.03.004

Deloitte. (2014). Media consumer survey. *Australian Media and Digital Preferences* (3rd ed.).

Department of Health and Ageing. (2010). *National male health policy: Building on the strengths of Australian males.* Retrieved from www.health.gov.au/internet/main/publishing.nsf/Content/male-policy

Derlega, V. J., & Chaikin, A. L. (1977). Privacy and self-disclosure in social relationships. *The Journal of Social Issues, 33*(3), 102–115. doi:10.1111/j.1540-4560.1977.tb01885.x

Deviney, D.E., Crawford, J., & Elder, K.L. (2012). Classroom antics: Fun with a purpose. *SOBIE: Proceedings of Annual Meetings.*

Dezuanni, M. (2006). Prince Charming has perfect white teeth: Performativity and media education. *Media International Australia, 120*(120), 156-167. Retrieved from http://eprints.qut.edu.au/5337/1/5337.pdf

Dezuanni, M. (2009). *Young people and participatory culture: Reconceptualising Australian media education for 21st century citizenship* (pp. 31–50). Dordrecht: Springer Netherlands.

Dickson, C. (2011). Al Qaeda's New Women's Magazine. *The Atlantic Wire.* Retrieved from http://www.theatlanticwire.com/global/2011/03/al-qaedas-new-womens-magazine/35808/

Digital, social and mobile in 2015 report. (2015). *We Are Social*. Retrieved from http://wearesocial.sg/blog/2015/01/digital-social-mobile-2015/

Diriker, E. (2004). *De-/re-contextualizing conference interpreting: Interpreters in the ivory tower?* Amsterdam, The Netherlands: John Benjamins Publishing Company. doi:10.1075/btl.53

Djamal, C. (2000). Women in the informal sector, a 'forgotten' workforce. In M.-O. Gardiner & C. Bianpoen (Eds.), *Indonesian women: The journey continues* (pp. 172–188). Canberra: RSPAS Publishing, ANU.

Doane, A. N., Kelley, M. L., & Pearson, M. R. (2015). Reducing cyberbullying: A theory of reasoned action-based video prevention program for college students. *Aggressive Behavior*. doi:10.1002/ab.21610 PMID:26349445

Domenico, D., & Johes, K. (2007). Career Aspirations of Women in the 20th Century. *Journal of Career and Technical Education*, *22*(2).

Donath, J. (2007). Signals in social supernets. *Journal of Computer-Mediated Communication*, *13*(1), 231–251. doi:10.1111/j.1083-6101.2007.00394.x

Donthu, N., & Gilliland, D. (1996). Observations: The infomercial shopper. *Journal of Advertising Research*, *36*(2), 69–77.

Dredger, K., Woods, D., Beach, C., & Sagstetter, V. (2010). Engage me: Using new literacies to create third space classrooms that engage student writers. *The National Association for Media Literacy Education's Journal of Media Literacy Education*, *2*(2), 85–101.

Drell, L. (2014). Getting hairy for charity. *Marketing Health Services*, *34*(1), 6–7. PMID:24741759

Driver, M. J., Brousseau, K. E., & Hunsaker, P. L. (1990). *The Dynamic Decision-maker*. New York: Harper.

Duggan, M. (2013). It's a Woman's (Social Media) World. *Pew Research Centre*. Retrieved http://www.pewresearch.org/fact-tank/2013/09/12/its-a-womans-social-media-world/

Duggan, M. (2013). It's a woman's (social media) world. Retrieved from www.pewresearch.org/fact-tank/2013/09/12/its-a-womans-social-media-world/

Duggan, M., & Smith, A. (2013). Social media update 2013: PEW Research Center's Internet & American Life Project. Retrieved from www.pewinternet.org/2013/12/30/social-media-update-2013/

Dupagne, M., & Salwen, M. B. (2005). Communication technology adoption and ethnicity. *The Howard Journal of Communications*, *16*(1), 21–32. doi:10.1080/10646170590915826

Edvardsson, B., Tronvoll, B., & Gruber, T. (2011). Expanding understanding of service exchange and value co-creation: a social construction approach. *Journal for the Academy of Marketing Science*, 39, 327-339.

Eight British school girls travel to Syria to become IS brides. (2015). *The Tribune*. Retrieved from http://tribune.com.pk/story/843348/eight-british-school-girls-travel-to-syria-to-become-is-brides/

Ellison, N. B., Steinfield, C., & Lampe, C. (2007). The Benefits of Facebook "Friends:" Social Capital and College Students' Use of Online Social Network Sites. *Journal of Computer-Mediated Communication*, *12*(4), 1143–1168. doi:10.1111/j.1083-6101.2007.00367.x

El-Nawawy. M., & Khamis, S. (2013). Blogging on Violations of Human Rights and Limitations on Freedom. In Egyptian Revolution 2.0: Political Blogging, Civic Engagement and Citizen Journalism. New York: Palgrave Macmillan.

Engel, J. F., Blackwell, R. D., & Miniard, P. W. (1990). *Consumer Behavior* (6th ed.). USA: The Dryden Press.

English, R. (2013). The most private private education: Home education in Australia. *Homeschool Researcher*, *29*(4), 1–7.

English, R. (2015a). Use your freedom of choice: Reasons for choosing homeschool in Australia. *Journal of Unschooling and Alternative Learning*, *9*(17).

English, R. (2015b). Too cool for homeschool? Accessing underground unschoolers with Web 2.0. In K. Trimmer, A. Black, & S. Riddle (Eds.), *Mainstreams, Margins and the Spaces In-between New possibilities for education research*(pp. 112–124). New York: Routledge.

Ennion, J. (2012). How Girl's Guide to Homelessness blogger Brianna Karp's life has changed. *News.com.au*. Retrieved from http://www.news.com.au/technology/how-girls-guide-to-homelessness-blogger-brianna-karps-life-has-changed/story-e6frfro0-1226235960256

Enrolment Categories. (2015). The State of Queensland: Department of Education and Training. Retrieved from https://brisbanesde.eq.edu.au/Enrolments/enrolmentcategories/Pages/enrolment-categories.aspx

Eysenbach, G. (2008). Medicine 2.0: Social networking, collaboration, participation, apomediation, and openness. *Journal of Medical Internet Research*, *10*(3), e22. doi:10.2196/jmir.1030 PMID:18725354

Ezzedeen, S., Budworth, M., & Baker, S. (2015). The Glass Ceiling and Executive Careers: Still an issue for pre-career women. *Journal of Career Development*, January 7, 1–15.

Fairclough, N. (1992). *Discourse and social change*. Cambridge, UK: Polity Press.

Fairclough, N. (1995). *Critical discourse analysis*. Boston, MA: Addison Wesley.

Fairclough, N. (2000). *New Labour, new language?* London, UK: Routledge.

Fairclough, N. (2001). The discourse of New Labour: Critical discourse analysis. In M. Wetherell, S. Taylor, & S. Yates (Eds.), *Discourse as data: A guide for analysis* (pp. 221–260). London, UK: Sage.

Fairclough, N. (2003). *Analyzing discourse: Textual analysis for social research*. London, UK: Routledge.

Fairclough, N., & Wodak, R. (1997). Critical discourse analysis. In T. van Dijk (Ed.), *Discourse as social interaction* (pp. 258–284). Thousand Oaks, CA: Sage.

Fallis, D. (2008). Toward an epistemology of Wikipedia. *Journal of the American Society for Information Science and Technology*, *59*(10), 1662–1674. doi:10.1002/asi.20870

Fan, J. (2015). Patient value co-creation in online health communities: Social identity effects on customer knowledge contribution and membership continuance intentions in online health communities. *Journal of Service Management*, *26*(1).

Fan, Y., & Miao, Y. (2012). Effect of Electronic word-of-mouth on consumer purchase intention: The perspective of gender differences. *International Journal of Electronic Business Management*, *10*(3), 175–181.

Felsted, A. (2014, November 12). Apps bring web shopping to life, *Financial Times*.

Fenner, Y., Garland, S. M., Moore, E. E., Jayasinghe, Y., Fletcher, A., Tabrizi, S. N., & Wark, J. D. et al. (2012). Web-based recruiting for health research using a social networking site: An exploratory study. *Journal of Medical Internet Research*, *14*(1), 20.

Fishbein, M., & Ajzen, I. (1975). *Beliefs, attitudes, intention, and behavior: An introduction of Theory and Research.* Reading, MA: Addison-Wesley.

Fisher, J., Lang, C., & Craig, A. (2013). Women in the IT Workplace: Learnings for Managers.*Proceedings of the European Conference on Information Systems (ECIS)*, Utrecht, NL.

Fleisher, L. (2012, May 2). City lays out digital rules for teachers. *The Wall Street Journal.* Retrieved from http://www.wsj.com/articles/SB10001424052702303916904577376541510305510

Fleming, P. J., Lee, J. G. L., & Dworkin, S. L. (2014). "Real men don't": Constructions of masculinity and inadvertent harm in public health interventions. *American Journal of Public Health*, *104*(6), 1029–1035. doi:10.2105/AJPH.2013.301820 PMID:24825202

Flyvbjerg, B. (2013). Case study. In N. K. Denzin & Y. S. Lincoln (Eds.), *Strategies of qualitative inquiry* (5th ed.). Thousand Oaks, CA: Sage Publications.

Foley, S. (2010). Second US woman swept up in Jihad Jane murder claims. *The Independent.* Retrieved from http://www.independent.co.uk/news/world/americas/second-us-woman-swept-up-in-jihad-jane-murder-claims-1921435.html

Foucault, M. (1988). The political technology of individuals.

Foucault, M. (1975). *Discipline & Punish: The Birth of the Prison.* New York: Vintage Books.

Foucault, M. (2006). Lectures at the College de France 1973-1974. In J. LaGrange (Ed.), *Michel Foucault: Psychiatric Power* (G. Burchell, Trans.). New York: Palgrave MacMillan.

Fountain, J. (2000). Constructing the information society: Women, information technology and design. *Technology in Society*, *22*(1), 45–62. doi:10.1016/S0160-791X(99)00036-6

Fridan, B. (1963). *The Feminine Mystique* (Contemporary Introduction). New York: WW Norton.

Füller, J., Mühlbacher, H., Matzler, K., & Jawecki, G. (2009). Consumer empowerment through Internet-based co-creation. *Journal of Management Information Systems*, *26*(3), 71–102. doi:10.2753/MIS0742-1222260303

Furse, D. H., Punj, G. N., & Stewart, D. W. (1984). A typology of individual search strategies among purchasers of new automobiles. *The Journal of Consumer Research*, *10*(4), 417–431. doi:10.1086/208980

Gallaway, J. H., & Bernasek, A. (2002). Gender and informal sector employment in Indonesia. *Journal of Economic Issues*, *36*(2), 313–321. doi:10.1080/00213624.2002.11506473

Galvagno, M., & Dalli, D. (2014). Theory of value co-creation: A systematic literature review. *Managing Service Quality: An International Journal*, *24*(6), 643–683. doi:10.1108/MSQ-09-2013-0187

Gambetti, R. C., & Graffigna, G. (2010). The concept of engagement a systematic analysis of the ongoing marketing debate. *International Journal of Market Research*, *52*(6), 801–826. doi:10.2501/S147078531020166

Garcia-Gavilanes, R., Quercia, D., & Jaimes, A. (2013). Cultural dimensions in Twitter: Time, individualism and power. Proceedings ofAAAI ICWSM.

Gefen, D., & Ridings, C. (2005). If you spoke as she does, Sir, instead of the way you do: a sociolinguistics perspective of gender differences in virtual communities. *The data base for advances in information systems*, 36(2).

Gefen, D., & Ridings, C. (2005). If you spoke as she does, Sir, instead of the way you do: a sociolinguistics perspective of gender differences in virtual communities. *The database for advances in information systems*, 36(2).

Gefen, D., & Ridings, C. M. (2005). If you spoke as she does, sir, instead of the way you do: A sociolinguistics perspective of gender differences in virtual communities. *SIGMIS Database*, *36*(2), 78–92. doi:10.1145/1066149.1066156

Gefen, D., & Straub, D. W. (1997). Gender differences in the perception and use of e-mail: An extension to the technology acceptance model. *Management Information Systems Quarterly*, *21*(4), 389–400. doi:10.2307/249720

Gerke, S. (2000). Global lifestyles under local conditions: The new Indonesian middle class. In B.-H. Chua (Ed.), *Consumption in Asia: Lifestyles and identities* (pp. 135–158). London: Routledge.

Gilbert, D. C. (1991). An examination of the consumer behaviour process related to tourism. In C. P. Cooper (Ed.), *Progress in tourism, recreation and hospitality management* (pp. 78–105). Lymington, UK: Belhaven Press.

Gitelson, R., & Kerstetter, D. L. (1995). The Influence of Friends and Relatives in Travel Decision-Making. *Journal of Travel & Tourism Marketing*, *3*(3), 59–68. doi:10.1300/J073v03n03_04

Global mobile media consumption reaching millennials. (2013, February). *InMobi*.

Goldsmith, R. E., & Hofacker, C. F. (1991). Measuring consumer innovativeness. *Journal of the Academy of Marketing Science*, *19*(3), 209–221. doi:10.1007/BF02726497

Goodall, B. (1991). Understanding Holiday Choice. In C. Cooper & A. Lockwood (Eds.), *Progress in Tourism, Recreation and Hospitality Management* (pp. 58–77). Belhaven Press.

Goodwin, R., & Giles, S. (2003). Social Support Provision and Cultural Values In Indonesia And Britain. *Journal of Cross-Cultural Psychology*, *34*(2), 240–245. doi:10.1177/0022022102250227

Gram, M. (2005). Family Holidays. A qualitative analysis of family holiday experiences. *Scandinavian Journal of Hospitality and Tourism*, *5*(1), 2–22. doi:10.1080/15022250510014255

Gram, M. (2007). Children as co-decision makers in the family? The case of family holidays. *Young Consumers*, *8*(1), 19–28. doi:10.1108/17473610710733749

Gray, P. (n. d.). Freedom to Learn: The roles of play and curiosity as foundations for learning. Retrieved from https://www.psychologytoday.com/blog/freedom-learn

Gray, P., & Riley, G. (2013). The challenges and benefits of unschooling, according to 232 families who have chosen that route. *Journal of Unschooling and Alternative Learning*, *7*(14), 1–27.

Griffith, A., & Smith, D. (2005). Mothering for Schooling. New York: Routledge.

Griffiths, K. M., & Christensen, H. (2006). Review of randomised controlled trials of Internet interventions for mental disorders and related conditions. *Clinical Psychologist*, *10*(1), 16–29. doi:10.1080/13284200500378696

Grimmelmann, J. (2009). Facebook and the social dynamics of privacy. *Iowa Law Review*, *95*(4), 1–52. Retrieved from http://www.ciberdemocracia.es/recursos/textosrelevantes/facebook.pdf

Grönroos, C. (2008). Service logic revisited: Who creates value? And who co-creates? *European Business Review*, *20*(4), 298–314. doi:10.1108/09555340810886585

Grönroos, C. (2011). Value co-creation in service logic: A critical analysis. *Marketing Theory*, *11*(3), 279–301. doi:10.1177/1470593111408177

Grönroos, C. (2012). Conceptualising value co-creation: A journey to the 1970s and back to the future. *Journal of Marketing Management*, *28*(13), 1520–1534. doi:10.1080/0267257X.2012.737357

Grönroos, C., & Gummerus, J. (2014). The service revolution and its marketing implications: Service logic vs service-dominant logic. *Managing Service Quality: An International Journal, 24*(3), 206–229. doi:10.1108/MSQ-03-2014-0042

Grönroos, C., & Ravald, A. (2011). Service as business logic: Implications for value creation and marketing. *Journal of Service Management, 22*(1), 5–22. doi:10.1108/09564231111106893

Grönroos, C., & Voima, P. (2013). Critical service logic: Making sense of value creation and co-creation. *Journal of the Academy of Marketing Science, 41*(2), 133–150. doi:10.1007/s11747-012-0308-3

Guadagno, R. E., Eno, C. A., & Okdie, B. M. (2010). Personal Blogging: Individual Differences and Motivations. In Handbook of Research on Social Interaction Technologies and Collaboration Software: Concepts and Trends (pp. 292-301).

Guiry, M., Mägi, A. W., & Lutz, R. J. (2006). Defining and measuring recreational shopper identity. *Journal of the Academy of Marketing Science, 34*(1), 74–83. doi:10.1177/0092070305282042

Gummesson, E. (1991). *Qualitative methods in management research.* Newbury Park, CA: Sage Publications.

Gummesson, E., & Grönroos, C. (2012). The emergence of the new service marketing: Nordic School perspectives. *Journal of Service Management, 23*(4), 479–497. doi:10.1108/09564231211260387

Gurak, L., Antonijevic, S., Johnson, L., Ratliff, C., & Reyman, J. (2005). Introduction: Weblogs, Rhetoric, Community and Culture. In Gurak, L., Antonijevic, S., Johnson, L., Ratliff, C., & Reyman, J. (Eds.), Into the Blogosphere: Rhetoric, Community and Culture of Weblogs. University of Minnesota.

Hagel, J., & Armstrong, A. (1997). *Net gain: expanding markets through virtual communities.* Boston: Harvard Business School Press.

Hannah, M. (2010). Cyberbullying education for parents: A guide for clinicians. *Journal of Social Sciences,* 6(4), 532.

Harden, A. (2005, August 2). *Key website research highlights gender bias.* University of Glamorgan, UK.

Harding, S. (1986). *The Science Question in Feminism.* Ithaca, USA: Cornell University Press.

Harding, T., & Farrell, A. (2003). Home Schooling and Legislated Education. *The Journal of the Australian and New Zealand Educational Law Association, 8*(1&2), 125–133.

Hargittai, E., & Shafer, S. (2006). Differences in Actual and Perceived Online Skills: The Role of Gender. *Social Science Quarterly, 87*(2), 432–448. doi:10.1111/j.1540-6237.2006.00389.x

Hartshorn, S. (2010). Five Differences between Social Media and Social Networking. *Social Media Today.* Retrieved from http://www.socialmediatoday.com/content/5-differences-between-social-media-and-social-networking

Hausman, A. (2000). A multi-method investigation of consumer motivations in impulse buying behavior. *Journal of Consumer Marketing, 17*(5), 403–426. doi:10.1108/07363760010341045

Hay, R., & Pearce, P. (2014). Technology adoption by rural women in Queensland, Australia: Women driving technology from the homestead for the paddock. *Journal of Rural Studies, 36,* 318–327. doi:10.1016/j.jrurstud.2014.10.002

Henderson, A. (1987). *The evidence continues to grow: Parents' involvement improves student achievement.* Columbia, MD: National Committee for Citizens in Education.

Hendricks, L., Lumadue, R., & Rusty Waller, L. (2012). The evolution of bullying to cyber bullying: an overview of the best methods for implementing a cyber bullying preventive program. *National Forum Journal of Counseling and Addiction,* 1(1).

Hickie, I. B., Fogarty, A. S., Davenport, T. A., Luscombe, G. M., & Burns, J. (2007). Responding to experiences of young people with common mental health problems attending Australian general practice. *The Medical Journal of Australia*, *187*(7), S47–S52. PMID:17908026

Hinduja, S., & Patchin, J. W. (2010). Bullying, cyberbullying and suicide. *Archives of Suicide Research*, *14*(3), 206–221. doi:10.1080/13811118.2010.494133 PMID:20658375

Hirshfield, L. (2014). 'She's not good with crying': The effect of gender expectations on graduate students' assessments of their principal investigators. *Gender and Education*, *26*(6), 601–617. doi:10.1080/09540253.2014.940036

Hispanic women connect with friends, brands and news via social. (2014, February 11). *eMarketer.* Retrieved from http://www.emarketer.com/Article/Hispanic-Women-Connect-with-Friends-Brands-News-via-Social/1010597#sthash.ELe3Zmtb.dpuf

Hofstede, G. (1983). National Cultures in Four Dimensions: A Research-Based Theory of Cultural Differences among Nations. *International Studies of Management & Organization*, *13*(1/2), 46–74. doi:10.2307/40396953

Holfeld, B., & Grabe, M. (2012). Middle school students perceptions of and response to cyber bullying. *Journal of Educational Computing Research*, *46*(4), 395–413. doi:10.2190/EC.46.4.e

Holt, J., & Farenga, P. (2003). *Teach Your Own: The John Holt book of Home Schooling*. New York: Perseus Publishing.

Hospes, O. (1992). les gens qui comptent: Les faces oubliees des associations rotatoires d'epargne et de credit en indonesie [People that count: The forgotten faces of rotating savings and credit associations in Indonesia]. In *Savings and Development* (pp. 371-401).

Houseman, D. C. (2011). 'Nerdy know it alls' and 'paranoid parents': Images of alternative learning in film and television programs. *The Journal of Unschooling and Alternative Learning*, *5*(9), 1–17.

Howard, J. (1963). *Marketing Management - Analysis and Planning* (Revised ed.). Illinois, USA: Richard D Irwin Inc.

Howard, J., & Sheth, J. (1969). *The Theory of Buyer Behavior*. United States: John Wiley & Sons Inc.

Howard, P. (2010). *Information Technology and Democratic Islam. In The Digital Origins of Dictatorship and Democracy: Information Technology and Political Islam* (pp. 180–203). New York: Oxford University Press. doi:10.1093/acprof:oso/9780199736416.003.0009

Howcroft, D., & Trauth, E. M. (2008). The implications of a critical agenda in gender and IS research. *Information Systems Journal* [Special issue: exploring the critical agenda in IS research.], *18*(2), 185–202. doi:10.1111/j.1365-2575.2008.00294.x

Hoy, M. G., & Milne, G. (2010). Gender Differences in Privacy-Related Measures for Young Adult Facebook Users. *Journal of Interactive Advertising*, *10*(2), 28–45. doi:10.1080/15252019.2010.10722168

Hrabowski, F. A., Maton, K. I., & Greif, G. L. (1998). *Beating the Odds: Raising Academically Successful African American Males*. New York, New York: Oxford University Press.

Hudson, S. (2000). Consumer Behaviour Related to Tourism. In A. Pizam & Y. Mansfeld (Eds.), *Consumer Behaviour in Travel and Tourism* (pp. 7–30). NY: The Haworth Hospitality Press.

Hughes, D. J., Rowe, M., Batey, M., & Lee, A. (2012). A tale of two sites: Twitter vs. Facebook and the personality predictors of social media usage. *Computers in Human Behavior*, *28*(2), 561–569. doi:10.1016/j.chb.2011.11.001

Hull, B., Dey, A., Mahajan, B., Menzies, R., & McIntyre, P. (2009) Immunisation coverage annual report. Report for the National Centre for Immunisation Research and Surveillance of Vaccine Preventable Diseases (NCIRS). Canberra: Department of Health: Commonwealth of Australia

Hunt, R. G., Krzystofiak, F. J., Meindl, J. R., & Yousry, A. M. (1989). Cognitive Style and Decision Making. *Organizational Behavior and Human Decision Processes*, *44*(3), 436–453. doi:10.1016/0749-5978(89)90018-6

Hwang, Y., Gretzel, U., Xiang, Z., & Fesenmaier, D. R. (2006). Travel Destination Choice Models. In D. R. Fesenmaier, K. W. Wober, & H. Werthner (Eds.), *Destination Recommendation Systems: Behavioural Foundations and Applications* (pp. 17–29). UK: CABI. doi:10.1079/9780851990231.0017

Ind, N., Iglesias, O., & Schultz, M. (2013). Building brands together: Emergence and outcomes of co-creation. *California Management Review*, *55*(3), 5–26. doi:10.1525/cmr.2013.55.3.5

Indonesia's middle class: missing BRIC in the wall (2011, July 21). *The Economist*. Retrieved from http://www.economist.com/node/18989153

Jackson, L. A., Ervin, K. S., Gardner, P. D., & Schmitt, N. (2001). Gender and the internet: Women communicating and men searching. *Sex Roles*, *44*(5-6), 363–379. doi:10.1023/A:1010937901821

Jacobsen, J. K. S., & Munar, A. M. (2012). Tourist information search and destination choice in a digital age. *Tourism Management Perspectives*, *1*, 39–47. doi:10.1016/j.tmp.2011.12.005

Jacobson, J. L. (2010). *Mustachioed men and marathon moms: The marketing of cancer philanthropy* (Masters thesis). Wilfrid Laurier University, Canada. Retrieved from http://scholars.wlu.ca/etd/1002/(1002)

Janda, S. (2008). Does Gender Moderate the Effect of Online Concerns on Purchase Likelihood? *Journal of Internet Commerce*, *7*(3), 339–358. doi:10.1080/15332860802250401

Jeffcott, M., Cagiannos, I., & Zorn, K. C. (2012). Movember update: The Canadian perspective. *Canadian Urological Association Journal*, *6*(3), E111–E114. doi:10.5489/cuaj.12037 PMID:22709880

Jenkins, B. M. (2010). The al Qaeda-Inspired Terrorist Threat: An Appreciation of the Current Situation Retrieved from http://www.rand.org/content/dam/rand/pubs/testimonies/2010/RAND_CT353.pdf

Jenkins, R. L. (1978). Family Vacation Decision-Making. *Journal of Travel Research*, *16*(4), 2–7. doi:10.1177/004728757801600401

Jetnikoff, A. (2009). Using media technologies in English. In S. Gannon, M. Howie, & W. Sawyer (Eds.), *Charged with meaning: re-viewing English* (pp. 307–313). Melbourne: Phoenix Education.

Johns, R. (1997). Sports Promotion and the Internet. *The Cyber Journal of Sports Marketing*. Retrieved from www.ausport.gov.au

Johns, R., & English, R. (2014). Mothers influencing mothers: the use of virtual discussion boards and their influence on consumption. *International Journal of Web Based Communities*.

Johns, N., & Gyimothy, S. (2002). Mythologies of a theme park: An icon of modern family life. *Journal of Vacation Marketing*, *8*(4), 320–331. doi:10.1177/135676670200800403

Johnson, P. E. (1995). *Reason on the balance: The case against naturalism in science, law, and education*. Downers Grove, IL: Intraversity.

Johns, R. (2012). Relationship Marketing in a self-service context – no longer applicable? *Journal of Relationship Marketing*.

Johns, R., & English, R. (2014). Mothers influencing mothers: The use of virtual discussion boards and their influence on consumption. *International Journal of Web Based Communities*, *10*(3), 319–338. doi:10.1504/IJWBC.2014.062945

Johns, R., & McNamara, J. (2014). Career development in higher education through group mentoring: A case study of desirable attributes and perceptions of a current programme. *Australian Journal of Career Development*, *23*(2), 79–87. doi:10.1177/1038416214528883

Joo, J., & Sang, Y. (2013). Exploring Koreans' smartphone usage: An integrated model of the technology acceptance model and uses and gratifications theory. *Telematics and Informatics*, *29*, 2512–2518.

Jordan-Zachery, J. S. (2012). *Blogging at the Intersections: Black Women, Identity, and Lesbianism. In Politics and Gender* (pp. 405–414). United Kingdom: Cambridge University Press.

Juntunen, M., Juntunen, J., & Autere, V. (2013). Co-creating nonprofit brand equity. *International Journal of Nonprofit and Voluntary Sector Marketing*, *18*(2), 122–132. doi:10.1002/nvsm.1453

Kabadayi, S., & Price, K. (2014). Consumer–brand engagement on Facebook: Liking and commenting behaviors. *Journal of Research in Interactive Marketing*, *8*(3), 203–223. doi:10.1108/JRIM-12-2013-0081

Kannan, P. K., Chang, A.-M., & Whinston, A. B. (2000). Electronic communities in e-business: Their role and issues. *Information Systems Frontiers*, *1*(4), 415–426.

Kaplan, A. M., & Haenlein, M. (2010). Users of the world, unite! The challenges and opportunities of social media. *Business Horizons*, *53*(1), 59–68. doi:10.1016/j.bushor.2009.09.003

Kapp, J. M., Peters, C., & Oliver, D. P. (2013). Research recruitment using Facebook advertising: Big potential, big challenges. *Journal of Cancer Education*, *28*(1), 134–137. doi:10.1007/s13187-012-0443-z PMID:23292877

Karl, M., Reintinger, C., & Schmude, J. (2015). Reject or select: Mapping destination choice. *Annals of Tourism Research*, *54*, 48–64. doi:10.1016/j.annals.2015.06.003

Karpen, I. O., Bove, L. L., Lukas, B. A., & Zyphur, M. J. (2015). Service-dominant orientation: Measurement and impact on performance outcomes. *Journal of Retailing*, *91*(1), 89–108.

Katz, E., Blumler, J. G., & Gurevitch, M. (1974). Utilization of mass communication by the individual. In J. G. Blumler & E. Katz (Eds.), *The uses of mass communications: Current perspectives on gratifications research* (Vol. III, pp. 19–32). Beverly Hills, CA: Sage.

Katz, E., Haas, H., & Gurevitch, M. (1973). On the use of the mass media for important things. *American Sociological Review*, *38*(2), 164–181. doi:10.2307/2094393

Kaye, J. (2014). Home schooled children taught 10k year old earth as science. Retrieved from http://www.johnkaye.org.au/home-schooled-children-taught-10k-year-old-earth-as-science/

Khatri, Y., Ie, W., & Newton, A. (2011, June 13-16). Indonesia: Building Momentum. *Proceedings of the Nomura Asia Equity Forum*, Singapore. Retrieved from http://www.nomura.com/europe/resources/upload/Millenia_6_Day_1_1500_Indonesia_Building_Momentum_Mr_Yougesh_Khatri.pdf

Khim-Yong, G., Cheng-Suang, H., & Zhijie, L. (2013). Social media brand community and consumer behavior: Quantifying the relative impact of user- and marketer-generated content. *Information Systems Research*, *24*(1), 88–107. doi:10.1287/isre.1120.0469

Kiesling, S. (2007). Men, masculinities and language. *Language and Linguistics Compass*, *1*(6), 653–673. doi:10.1111/j.1749-818X.2007.00035.x

Kietzmann, J. H., Hermkens, K., McCarthy, I. P., & Silvestre, B. S. (2011). Social media? Get serious! Understanding the functional building blocks of social media. *Business Horizons*, *54*(3), 241–251. doi:10.1016/j.bushor.2011.01.005

Kimbrough, A., Guadagno, R. E., Muscanell, N. L., & Dill, J. (2013). Gender differences in technology use: Women connect more than men. *Computers in Human Behavior*, *29*(3), 896–900. doi:10.1016/j.chb.2012.12.005

Kim, D.-Y., Lehto, X. Y., & Morrison, A. M. (2007). Gender differences in online travel information search: Implications for marketing communications on the internet. *Tourism Management*, *28*(2), 423–433. doi:10.1016/j.tourman.2006.04.001

Kim, Y., Sohn, D., & Choi, S. M. (2011). Cultural difference in motivations for using social network sites: A comparative study of American and Korean college students. *Computers in Human Behavior*, *27*(1), 365–372. doi:10.1016/j.chb.2010.08.015

Kindberg, T., Spasojevic, M., Fleck, R., & Sellen, A. (2005, April-June). The ubiquitous camera: An in-depth study of camera phone use. *Pervasive Computing*, *4*(2), 42–50. doi:10.1109/MPRV.2005.42

Kissell, M. (2011, August 31). Teachers banned from 'friending' students: Schools react to effect, growth and social media. *Dayton Daily News, p A.1.*

Knox, S., & Guar, C. (2007). The application of stakeholder theory to relationship marketing strategy development in a non-profit organisation. *Journal of Business Ethics*, *75*(2), 115–135. doi:10.1007/s10551-006-9258-3

Kobayashi, T., Ikeda, K. i., & Miyata, K. (2006). Social capital online: Collective use of the Internet and reciprocity as lubricants of democracy. *Information Communication and Society*, *9*(5), 582–611. doi:10.1080/13691180600965575

Ko, H.-C., & Kuo, F.-Y.Hsiu-Chia. (2009). Can Blogging Enhance Subjective Well-Being through Self-Disclosure? *CyberPhyschology and Behaviour*, *12*(1), 75–79. doi:10.1089/cpb.2008.016 PMID:19132911

Koh, J., & Kim, Y.-G. (2004). Knowledge sharing in virtual communities: An e-business perspective. *Expert Systems with Applications*, *26*(2), 155–166. doi:10.1016/S0957-4174(03)00116-7

Kohler, T., Füller, J., Stiger, D., & Matzler, K. (2011). Avatar-based innovation: Consequences of the virtual co-creation experience. *Computers in Human Behavior*, *27*(1), 160–168. doi:10.1016/j.chb.2010.07.019

Korda, H., & Itani, Z. (2013). Harnessing social media for health promotion and behaviour change. *Health Promotion Practice*, *14*(1), 15–23. doi:10.1177/1524839911405850 PMID:21558472

Kosaka, T., & Dananjaya, R. M. (2012). A Cross-Cultural Study of the Feasibility of Vendor Relationship Management in Indonesia and Japan. Retrieved from http://www.ms.kuki.tus.ac.jp/KMSLab/kosaka/papers/IICC201212.pdf

Kotzé, T., North, E., Stols, M., & Venter, L. (2012). Gender differences in sources of shopping enjoyment. *International Journal of Consumer Studies*, *36*(4), 416–424. doi:10.1111/j.1470-6431.2011.01060.x

Kowalski, R. M., & Limber, S. P. (2007). Electronic bullying among middle school students. *The Journal of Adolescent Health*, *41*(6), S22–S30. doi:10.1016/j.jadohealth.2007.08.017 PMID:18047942

Kozinets, R. (2010). *Netnography: The Marketer's Secret Weapon*. Netbase.

Kvarme, L.G., Monsen, K.A., & Eboh, W.O. (2014). Evidence-Based Solution-Focused Care for School-Age Children Experiencing Cyberbullying: Using the Omaha System to Guide and Document Psychiatric Nursing Interventions. *Journal of Psychosocial Nursing & Mental Health Services,* 52(3), 34.

Lampe, C., Ellison, N. B., & Steinfield, C. (2008). Changes in use and perception of Facebook. *Paper presented at the2008 ACM conference on Computer supported cooperative work*, San Diego, CA, USA. doi:10.1145/1460563.1460675

Lancaster, K. J. (1966). A New Approach to Consumer Theory. *Journal of Political Economy*, *74*(2), 132–157. doi:10.1086/259131

Lankshear, C., & Knobel, M. (2008). Digital literacy and participation in online social networking spaces. In C. Lankshear & M. Knobel (Eds.), *Digital literacies: Concepts, policies and practices* (Vol. 30). New York: Peter Lang.

Lapointe, L., Ramaprasad, J., & Vedel, I. (2013, January 7-10). Collaborating through social media to create health awareness. *Paper presented at the 2013 46th Hawaii International conference on System Sciences (HICSS).*

Lareau, A. (1994). Parent involvement in schooling: A dissenting view. IN C Fagnano & B. Weber (Eds), School, family and community interaction. Boulder CO: Westview.

Lareau, A. (1987). Social class and family-school relationships: The importance of cultural capital. *Sociology of Education*, *60*(2), 73–85. doi:10.2307/2112583

Lareau, A. (1989). *Home advantage: Social class and parental intervention in elementary education.* London, New York: Falmer Press.

Lareau, A. (2000). Social class and the daily lives of children. *Childhood*, *7*(2), 155–171. doi:10.1177/0907568200007002003

Lareau, A. (2003). *Unequal childhoods: Class, race and family life.* Berkley: University of California Press.

Laroche, M., Saad, G., Cleveland, M., & Browne, E. (2000). Gender differences in information search strategies for a Christmas gift. *Journal of Consumer Marketing*, *17*(6), 500–522. doi:10.1108/07363760010349920

Latina power shift. (2013b). *The Nielsen Company.* Retrieved from http://www.nielsen.com/content/dam/corporate/us/en/reports-downloads/2013%20Reports/Nielsen-Latina-Report-2013.pdf

Latinas are a driving force behind Hispanic purchasing power in the U.S. (2013a, August 1). *The Nielsen Company.* Retrieved from http://www.nielsen.com/us/en/insights/news/2013/latinas-are-a-driving-force-behind-hispanic-purchasing-power-in-.html

Lawson, M. (2013). *Blogging, babies, and business: Mommy blogging as citizen journalism. University Of Colorado.*

Lazar, J., Feng, J. H., & Hochheiser, H. (2010). Research methods in human computer interaction. Chichester, MA: Wiley.

Lee, S. Y. (2014). Examining the factors that influence early adopters' smartphone adoption: The case of college students. *Telematics and Informatics*, *31*(2), 308–318. doi:10.1016/j.tele.2013.06.001

Legris, P., Ingham, J., & Collerette, P. (2003). Why do people use information technology: A critical review of the technology acceptance model. *Information & Management*, *40*(3), 191–204. doi:10.1016/S0378-7206(01)00143-4

Leiken, R. S. (2005). Europe's Angry Muslims. *Foreign Affairs*, *84*(4), 120–135. doi:10.2307/20034425

Leimeister, J., Sidiras, P., & Kremar, H. (2004). Success factors of virtual communities from the perspective of members and operators: an empirical study. *Proceedings of the 37th Hawaii International Conference on System Sciences.* doi:10.1109/HICSS.2004.1265459

Lenhart, A., Purcell, K., Smith, A., & Zickuhr, K. (2010). Social media & mobile internet use among teens and young adults. *PEW Research Center's Internet & American Life Project.*

Levine, S. (2013). Movember: A month of moustaches and social media. *Sysomos blog*. Retrieved from http://blog.sysomos.com/2013/12/03/movember-2013/

Lewis, S., Thomas, S. L., Blood, R. W., Castle, D., Hyde, J., & Komesaroff, P. A. (2011). 'I'm searching for solutions': Why are obese individuals turning to the Internet for help and support with 'being fat'? *Health Expectations*, *14*(4), 339–350. doi:10.1111/j.1369-7625.2010.00644.x PMID:21199200

Li, X., & Zeng, L. (2011, Fall). Technology attributes, perceived value of information, and social utility: Predicting podcast adoption and use. *Southwestern Mass Communication Journal*, 83-69.

Lim, M. (2013). Many Clicks but Little Sticks: Social Media Activism in Indonesia. *Journal of Contemporary Asia*, *43*(4), 636–657. doi:10.1080/00472336.2013.769386

Lin, J. C. C., & Liu, E. S. Y. (2009). The adoption behaviour for mobile video call services. *International Journal of Mobile Communications*, *7*(6), 646–666. doi:10.1504/IJMC.2009.025536

Liu, C.-C., . . . (2014). Enabling a Positive First Year Experience in Higher Education through Social Media and Mobile Technologies. In Liu, C.-C. et al. (Eds.) *Proceedings of the 22nd International Conference on Computers in Education.* Japan: Asia-Pacific Society for Computers in Education.

Li, Y. M., Lee, Y. L., & Lien, N. J. (2012). Online social advertising via influential endorsers. *International Journal of Electronic Commerce*, *16*(3), 119–154. doi:10.2753/JEC1086-4415160305

Locke, B. D., & Mahalik, J. R. (2005). Examining masculinity norms, problem drinking, and athletic involvement as predictors of sexual aggression in college men. *Journal of Counseling Psychology*, *52*(3), 279–283. doi:10.1037/0022-0167.52.3.279

Lopez, M. H., Gonzalez-Barrera, A., & Patten, E. (2013, March 7). *Closing the digital divide: Latinos and technology adoption*. Washington, DC: PEW Research Center. Retrieved from http://www.pewhispanic.org/2013/03/07/closing-the-digital-divide-latinos-and-technology-adoption/

Lukka, V., & James, P. T. J. (2014). Attitudes toward Facebook advertising. *Journal of Management and Marketing Research*, *14*, 1–26.

Lusch, R. F., Vargo, S. L., & Malter, A. J. (2006). Marketing as a service exchange: Taking a leadership role in global marketing management. *Organizational Dynamics*, *35*(3), 264–278. doi:10.1016/j.orgdyn.2006.05.008

Lynch, W. (2013). Men's health in Australia. *Trends in Urology and Men's Health*, *4*(1), 7–10. doi:10.1002/tre.305

MacDonald, S. (2014, April 15). Schools tackle social media use by parents. *Daily Bulletin*, p A.3

Mackrell, D., & Boyle, M. (2010). Not so 'invisible': A Qualitative Case Study Exploring Gender Relations and Farm Management Software. *Australasian Journal of Information Systems*, *16*(2), 2. doi:10.3127/ajis.v16i2.578

Magidson, J. (2005). *SI-CHAID 4.0 User's Guide*. Belmont, Massachusetts: Statistical Innovations Inc.

Mahalik, J. R., Burns, S. M., & Syzdek, M. (2007b). Masculinity ad perceived normative health behaviours as predictors of men's health behaviours. *Social Science & Medicine*, *64*(11), 2201–2209. doi:10.1016/j.socscimed.2007.02.035 PMID:17383784

Mahalik, J. R., Levi-Minzi, M., & Walker, G. (2007a). Masculinity and health behaviours in Australian men. *Psychology of Men & Masculinity*, *8*(4), 240–249. doi:10.1037/1524-9220.8.4.240

Mahzari, A., & Ahmadzadeh, M. A. (2013). Finding Gender Preferences in E-Commerce Website Design by an Experimental Approach. *International Journal of Applied Information Systems*, *5*(2), 35–40.

Mangold, W. G., & Faulds, D. J. (2009). Social media: The new hybrid element of the promotion mix. *Business Horizons*, *52*(4), 357–365. doi:10.1016/j.bushor.2009.03.002

Manns, H. (2010). Indonesian slang in Internet Chatting. In S. Babatunde, A. Odebunmi, A. Adetunji, & M. Adedimeji (Eds.), *Studies in Slang and Slogans* (pp. 71–99). Munich: Lincom.

Marathe, S., & Sundar, S. (2011, 2011). What drives customization? Control or identity? *Proceedings of theSIGCHI Conference on human factors in computing systems* (pp. 781-790). ACM.

Marwick, A. E. (2013). Online identity. In J. Hartley, J. Burgess, & A. Bruns (Eds.), *A Companion to New Media Dynamics* (pp. 355–364). Hoboken: Wiley-Blackwell. doi:10.1002/9781118321607.ch23

Marwick, A. E., & boyd, d. m. (2011). I tweet honestly, I tweet passionately: Twitter users, context collapse, and the imagined audience. *New Media & Society*, *13*(1), 114–133. doi:10.1177/1461444810365313

Masna, A. (2001). Why is Facebook so popular in Indonesia? *Quora.com.* Retrieved from http://www.quora.com/Aulia-Masna/answers/Indonesia

Masna, A. (2013). Why is Path so Popular in Indonesia. Retrieved from https://en.dailysocial.net/post/why-is-path-so-popular-in-indonesia

Mastarom, T. R., & Yasin, N. A. M. (2010). The Internet: Avenue for Women Jihadi "Participation". Retrieved from http://dr.ntu.edu.sg/bitstream/handle/10220/6649/RSIS0882010.pdf?sequence=1

Matouschek, B., Wodak, R., & Januschek, F. (1995). *"Notwendige Maßnahmen gegen Fremde?": Genese und Formen von rassistischen Diskursen der Differenz.* Wien, Austria: Passagen.

Matusitz, J. (2008). Similarities between terrorist networks in antiquity and present-day cyberterrorist networks. *Trends in Organized Crime*, *11*(2), 183–199. doi:10.1007/s12117-008-9034-0

Mayoux, L. (2001). Tackling the Down Side: Social Capital, Women's Empowerment and Micro-Finance in Cameroon. *Development and Change*, *32*(3), 435–464. doi:10.1111/1467-7660.00212

Mbakwe, C., & Cunliffe, D. (2007). Hypermedia Seduction: Further Exploration of the Process of "Seductive" Online User Interactions. In B. Ganor, K. von-Knop, & C. A. M. Duarte (Eds.), *Hypermedia seduction for terrorist recruiting* (pp. 207–230). Amsterdam: IOS Press.

McAndrew, F. T., & Jeong, H. S. (2012). Who does what on Facebook? Age, sex, and relationship status as predictors of Facebook use. *Computers in Human Behavior*, *28*(6), 2359–2365. doi:10.1016/j.chb.2012.07.007

McGrath, S. (2010). *Unschooling: A Lifestyle of Learning.* USA: Createspace Independent Publishing Platform.

McKenna, K. Y. A., & Bargh, J. A. (1998). Coming out in the age of the Internet: Identity de- marginalization' from virtual group participation. *Journal of Personality and Social Psychology*, *74*(3), 681–694. doi:10.1037/0022-3514.75.3.681

McKenna, K. Y. A., & Bargh, J. A. (2000). Plan 9 from cyberspace: The implications of the Internet for personality and social psychology. *Personality and Social Psychology Review*, *4*(1), 57–75. doi:10.1207/S15327957PSPR0401_6

McKinlay, A. (2010). Performativity and the politics of identity: Putting Butler to work. *Critical Perspectives on Accounting*, *21*(3), 232–242. doi:10.1016/j.cpa.2008.01.011

McLean, J., & Maalsen, S. (2013). Destroying the Joint and Dying of Shame? A Geography of Revitalised Feminism in Social Media and Beyond. *Geographical Research*, *51*(3), 243–256. doi:10.1111/1745-5871.12023

McNeal, G. S. (2007). Cyber embargo: countering the internet jihad (in German) (Conference Paper). *Case Western Reserve University School of Law*, 39(3), 789-826.

McNeal, J. (1999). *The kids market - myths and realities*. New York: Paramount Market Publishing.

McWilliam, G. (2000). Building Stronger Brands through Online Communities. *MIT Sloan Management Review*, April, 15.

Mehdizadeh, S. (2010). Self-presentation 2.0: Narcissism and self-esteem on Facebook. *Cyberpsychology, Behavior, and Social Networking*, *13*(4), 357–364. doi:10.1089/cyber.2009.0257 PMID:20712493

Melbourne declaration on educational goals for young Australians. (2008). *Ministerial Council on Education Employment Training and Youth Affairs*. Retrieved from http://www.mceecdya.edu.au/mceecdya/melbourne_declaration,25979.html

Melissa, E., Hamidati, A., Saraswati, M. S., & Flor, A. G. (2013). Investigating the potentials of social media to support women entrepreneurship in Indonesian urban areas. *Paper presented at the Proceedings of the Sixth International Conference on Information and Communications Technologies and Development* (Vol. 2). doi:10.1145/2517899.2517921

Mendez, D. (2008, February 15). Facebook and Terrorism: a love hate relationship. Tech.Blorge. Retrieved from http://tech.blorge.com/Structure:%20/2008/02/15/facebook-and-terrorism-a-love-hate-relationship-2/

Meng, F., & Uysal, M. (2008). Effects of Gender Differences on Perceptions of Destination Attributes, Motivations, and Travel Values: An Examination of a Nature-Based Resort Destination. *Journal of Sustainable Tourism*, *16*(4), 445–466. doi:10.1080/09669580802154231

Michael, G. (2009). Adam Gadahn and Al-Qaeda's Internet Strategy. *Middle East Policy*, *16*(3), 135–152. doi:10.1111/j.1475-4967.2009.00409.x

Middleton, V. T. C. (1994). *Marketing in Travel and Tourism* (2nd ed., p. 393). Oxford: Butterworth-Heinemann Ltd.

Miller, C., & Shepherd, D. (2005). Blogging as Social Action: A Genre Analysis of the Weblog. In Gurak, L., Antonijevic, S., Johnson, L., Ratliff, C., & Reyman, J. (Eds.), Into the Blogosphere: Rhetoric, Community and Culture of Weblogs. University of Minnesota.

Mintz, J. (2004, July 28). Building democratic schools. Radio Free School. *Radio4all*. Retrieved from www.radio4all.net/pub/archive/04.01.05/grassroots@hwcn.org/125-1-20040729-0728rfsc10.mp3

Mishna, F., Schwan, K., Lefebvre, R., Bhole, P., & Johnston, D. (2014, September). Students in distress: Unanticipated findings in a cyberbullying study. *Children and Youth Services Review*, *44*, 341–348. doi:10.1016/j.childyouth.2014.04.010

Misson, R., & Morgan, W. (2006). *Critical literacy and the aesthetic: Transforming the English classroom*. Urbana, IL, USA: National Council of Teachers of English.

Mobile, B. (2014, September 18). Briabe mobile launches mobile-social platform 'Latina glam.' Retrieved from http://www.briabemobile.com/news/briabe-mobile-launches-mobile-social-platform-latina-glam

Möller-Leimkühler, A. M. (2003). The gender gap in suicide and premature death or: Why are men so vulnerable? *European Archives of Psychiatry and Clinical Neuroscience*, *253*(1), 1–8. doi:10.1007/s00406-003-0397-6 PMID:12664306

Molyneux, M. (2002). Gender and the Silences of Social Capital: Lessons from Latin America. *Development and Change*, *33*(2), 167–188. doi:10.1111/1467-7660.00246

Moran, M., Seaman, J., & Tinti-Kane, H. (2011). *Teaching, learning and sharing: How today's higher education faculty use social media*. Boston, MA: Pearson Learning Solutions.

Morton, R. (2012). Home education: Constructions of choice. *International electronic journal of elementary education*, 3(1), 46-56.

Mottiar, Z., & Quinn, D. (2004). Couple dynamics in household tourism decision making: Women as the gatekeepers? *Journal of Vacation Marketing*, *10*(2), 149–160. doi:10.1177/135676670401000205

Mourlam, D. (2013). Social Media and Education: Perceptions and Need for Support. *Journal of Science Education and Technology*, *9*(3), 23–28.

Moutinho, L. (1987). Consumer Behaviour in Tourism. *European Journal of Marketing*, *21*(10), 4–44. doi:10.1108/EUM0000000004718

Movember Foundation. (2014a). *Movember Foundation global annual report: FY2013-2014*. Retrieved from http://au.movember.com/about/annual-report

Movember Foundation. (2014b). *The Movember Foundation awareness and education program: Report Card Australia (global)*. Retrieved from http://au.movember.com/report-cards/view/id/2489/the-movember-foundation-awareness-and-education-program

Movember Foundation. (2015a). About us. *Movember (Australia)*. Retrieved from http://au.movember.com/about

Movember Foundation. (2015b). Media room: Ambassadors. *Movember (Australia)*. Retrieved from http://au.movember.com/media-room/ambassadors

Movember Foundation. (2015c). About us: Financials. *Movember (Australia)*. Retrieved from http://au.movember.com/about/money

Movember Foundation. (2015d). Media room: Movember 101. *Movember (Australia)*. Retrieved from http://au.movember.com/media-room/movember-101

Murphy, D. M., & White, J. F. (2007). Propaganda: Can a Word Decide a War? *Parameters*, *37*(3), 15–27.

Muscanell, N., & Guadagno, R. (2012). Make new friends or keep the old: Gender and personality differences in social networking use. *Computers in Human Behavior*, *28*(1), 107–112. doi:10.1016/j.chb.2011.08.016

Myers-Levy. (1986). 'Gender differences in information processing: A selectivity interpretation. In P. Cafferata & A. M. Tybout (Eds.), *Cognitive and affective responses to advertising* (pp. 219–260). Addison-Wiley Publishing.

Mysore, S. (2008). Facebook Indonesia Outpaces Southeast Asian Counterparts in 2008. Retrieved from http://www.insidefacebook.com/2008/12/31/facebook-indonesia-outpaces-southeast-asian-counterparts-in-2008/

Na, J., Kosinski, M., & Stillwell, D. J. (2015). When a New Tool Is Introduced in Different Cultural Contexts Individualism–Collectivism and Social Network on Facebook. *Journal of Cross-Cultural Psychology*, *46*(3), 355–370. doi:10.1177/0022022114563932

Nambisan, S., & Baron, R. A. (2009). Virtual customer environments: Testing a model of voluntary participation in value co-creation activities. *Journal of Product Innovation Management*, *26*(4), 388–406. doi:10.1111/j.1540-5885.2009.00667.x

Neiger, B. L., Thackeray, R., Van Wagenen, S. A., Hanson, C. L., West, J. H., Barnes, M. D., & Fagen, M. C. (2012). Use of social media in health promotions: Purposes, key performance indicators, and evaluation metrics. *Health Promotion Practice*, *13*(2), 159–164. doi:10.1177/1524839911433467 PMID:22382491

Nelson, C. S., & Watson, J. A. (1990). The computer gender gap: Children's attitudes, performance and socialization. *Journal of Educational Technology Systems*, *19*(4), 345–353. doi:10.2190/51CF-7CHE-DX52-E9F5

Nelson, P., Gabriella, B., Lia, P., & Raymond, P. F. (2014). Understanding value co-creation in complex services with many actors. *Journal of Service Management*, *25*(4), 470–493. doi:10.1108/JOSM-02-2014-0055

Ng, C., & Mitter, S. (2005). Gender and the digital economy: Perspectives from the developing world. *Sage (Atlanta, Ga.)*.

Nicosia, F.M. (1966). Consumer Decision Processes - Marketing and Advertising Implications. Englewood Cliffs, NJ: Prentice Hall Inc.

Norman, C. D., & Skinner, H. A. (2006). eHealth Literacy: Essential Skills for Consumer Health in a Networked World. *Journal of Internet medical research*, 8(2) e9. Retrieved on August 3 2014 from http://www.ncbi.nlm.nih.gov/pmc/articles/PMC1550701/

Norman, C. D. (2012). Social media and health promotion. *Global Health Promotion and Education*, *19*(4), 3–6. doi:10.1177/1757975912464593 PMID:24803437

Nykvist, S. S. (2008). Creating contexts for effective online communities of practice. In N. Yelland, G. A. Neal, & E. Dakich (Eds.), *Rethinking Education with ICT: New directions for effective practices* (pp. 165–180). Rotterdam, The Netherlands: Sense Publishers.

Nykvist, S. S., & Lee, K.-T. (2013). Mixing higher education teaching and learning with mobile devices and social media. *Proceedings of IAC-ETeL 2013*, Prague, Czech Republic.

O'Barr, W. M. (2006). Representations of masculinity and femininity in advertising. *Advertising and Society Review*, *7*(2).

O'Farrell, C. (2007). Key Concepts. *Michel- Foucault.com.* Retrieved from http://www.michel-foucault.com/concepts/

O'Rourke, S. (2007). Virtual Radicalisation: Challenges for Police. *Paper presented at the8th Australian Information Warfare and Security Conference*, Perth.

Odom, S., Jarvis, H., Sandlin, M., & Peek, C. (2013). Social Media Tools in the Leadership Classroom: Students' Perceptions of Use. *Journal of Leadership Education*, *12*(1), 34–53. doi:10.12806/V12/I1/34

Okazaki, S., & Hirose, M. (2009). Does gender affect media choice in travel information search? On the use of mobile internet. *Tourism Management*, *30*(6), 794–804. doi:10.1016/j.tourman.2008.12.012

Online insights: Expanding the conversation - leveraging social media for brand interaction. (2013). *Burst Media.* Retrieved from www.burstmedia.com/pdf/burst_media_online_insights_2013_04.pdf

Orser, B., Riding, A., & Stanley, J. (2012). Perceived career challenges and response strategies of women in the advanced technology sector. *Entrepreneurship and Regional Development*, *24*(1-2), 73–93. doi:10.1080/08985626.2012.637355

Pai, P., & Arnott, D. C. (2013). User adoption of social networking sites: Eliciting uses and gratifications through a means–end approach. *Computers in Human Behavior*, *29*(3), 1039–1053. doi:10.1016/j.chb.2012.06.025

Papacharissi, Z. (2002). The presentation of self in virtual life: Characteristics of personal home pages. *Journalism & Mass Communication Quarterly*, *79*(3), 643–660. doi:10.1177/107769900207900307

Papacharissi, Z. (2007). Audiences as Media Producers: Content Analysis of 260 Blogs. In M. Tremayne (Ed.), *Blogging, Citizenship and the Future of Media* (pp. 21–25). New York: Routledge.

Papacharissi, Z. (2011). Conclusion: A networked self. In Z. Papacharissi (Ed.), *A networked self: identity, community and culture on social network sites* (pp. 304–318). New York: Routledge.

Papacharissi, Z., & Easton, E. (2013). In the habitus of the new: Stucture, agency, and the social media habitus. In J. Hartley, J. Burgess, & A. Bruns (Eds.), *A Companion to New Media Dynamics* (pp. 171–184). Hoboken: Wiley-Blackwell. doi:10.1002/9781118321607.ch9

Papanek, H., & Schwede, L. (1988). Women are good with money: Earning and managing in an Indonesian city. *Economic and Political Weekly*, 1988, WS73–WS84.

Park, M. R. (2010). Social network sites as virtual communities. In Z. Papacharissi (Ed.), *A networked self: Identity, community, and culture on social network sites* (pp. 105–123). Routledge.

Parmelee, J. H. (2013). Political journalists and twitter: Influences on norms and practices. *Journal of Media Practice*, *14*(4), 291–305. doi:10.1386/jmpr.14.4.291_1

Parmelee, J. H. (2014). The agenda-building function of political tweets. *New Media & Society*, *16*(3), 434–450. doi:10.1177/1461444813487955

Pasek, J., More, E., & Romer, D. (2009). Realizing the Social Internet? Online Social Networking Meets Offline Civic Engagement. *Journal of Information Technology & Politics*, *6*(3-4), 197–215. doi:10.1080/19331680902996403

Payne, A., Storbacka, K., & Frow, P. (2008). Managing the co-creation of value. *Journal of the Academy of Marketing Science*, *36*(1), 83–96. doi:10.1007/s11747-007-0070-0

Pearce, P. L. (2005). Studying Tourist Behaviour. In *Tourist Behaviour: Themes and Conceptual Schemes* (pp. 1–17). Clevedon, UK: Channel View Publications.

Pedersen, A., & Hartley, L. K. (2012). Prejudice against Muslim Australians: The role of values, gender and consensus. *Journal of Community & Applied Social Psychology*, *22*(3), 239–255. doi:10.1002/casp.1110

Pedersen, S., & Macafee, C. (2007). Gender Differences in British Blogging. *Journal of Computer-Mediated Communication*, *12*(4), 1472–1492. doi:10.1111/j.1083-6101.2007.00382.x

Pennsylvania Woman Charged for Recruiting Terrorists. (2010). *Newsmixer.net*. Retrieved from http://www.newsmixer.net/politics/pennsylvania-woman-charged-for-recruiting-terrorists/

Pew Internet Research Project. (2014, January). *Mobile technology fact sheet*. Washington, D.C.: Pew.

Pfeil, U., Arjan, R., & Zaphiris, P. (2009). Age differences in online social networking – a study of user profiles and the social capital divide among teenagers and older users in Myspace. *Computers in Human Behavior*, *25*(3), 643–654. doi:10.1016/j.chb.2008.08.015

Phirangee, K. (2013). Beyond the elementary classroom walls: Exploring the ways participation within Web 2.0 spaces are reshaping pedagogy. *Journal of Educational Multimedia and Hypermedia*, *22*(3), 299–316.

Pikas, B., & Sorrentino, G. (2014). The effectiveness of online advertising: Consumer's perceptions of ads on Facebook, Twitter and YouTube. *Journal of Applied Business and Economics*, *16*(4), 70–81.

Pisani, E. (2014). *Etc.: Exploring the Improbable Nation*. Indonesia: WW Norton & Company.

Pongsakornrungsilp, S., & Schroeder, J. (2011). Understanding value co-creation in a co-consuming brand community. *Marketing Theory*, *11*(3), 303–324. doi:10.1177/1470593111408178

Porter, C., Donthu, N., & Baker, A. (2012). Gender differences in trust formation in virtual communities. *Journal of Marketing Theory and Practice*, *20*(1), 39–58. doi:10.2753/MTP1069-6679200103

Portnoy, D. B., Scott-Sheldon, L. A., Johnson, B. T., & Carey, M. P. (2008). Computer-delivered interventions for health promotion and behavioural risk evaluation: A meta-analysis of 75 randomised controlled trials. *Preventive Medicine*, *47*(1), 3–16. doi:10.1016/j.ypmed.2008.02.014 PMID:18403003

Postmes, T., Spears, R., Sakhel, K., & de Groot, D. (2001). Social influence in computer- mediated communication: The effects of anonymity on group behavior. *Personality and Social Psychology Bulletin*, *27*(10), 1243–1254. doi:10.1177/01461672012710001

Prahalad, C. K., & Ramaswamy, V. (2000). Co-opting customer competence. *Harvard Business Review*, *78*(1), 79–87.

Prahalad, C. K., & Ramaswamy, V. (2004). Co-creation experiences: The next practice in value creation. *Journal of Interactive Marketing*, *18*(3), 5–14. doi:10.1002/dir.20015

Preisler, B. (1998). Deconstructing 'feminist linguistics'. *Journal of Sociolinguistics*, *2*(2), 281–295. doi:10.1111/1467-9481.00045

Prensky, M. (2001). Digital natives, digital immigrants part 1. *On the Horizon*, *9*(5), 1–6. doi:10.1108/10748120110424816

Priesnitz, W. (2010). *School Free – The homeschooling handbook*. Toronto, Canada: Life Media.

Profile: 'Jihad Jane' from Main Street. (2010). *BBC News*. Retrieved from http://news.bbc.co.uk/2/hi/8561888.stm

Purnell, N. (2014). Facebook Users in Indonesia Rise to 69 Million. *Wall Street Journal*. Retrieved from http://blogs.wsj.com/digits/2014/06/27/facebook-users-in-indonesia-rise-to-69-million/

Putnam, R. (2001). Social capital: Measurement and consequences. *Canadian Journal of Policy Research*, *2*(1), 41–51.

Putra, J. S. (2011). Why Facebook is So Popular in Indonesia? *Olson.com*. Retrieved from http://www.penn-olson.com/2011/03/07/why-facebook-is-so-popular-in-indonesia/

Putrevu, S. (2001). Exploring the origins and information processing differences between men and women: Implications for advertisers. *Academy of Marketing Science Review*, *10*(1), 1–14.

Rammohan, A., & Johar, M. (2009). The Determinants of Married Women's Autonomy in Indonesia. *Feminist Economics*, *15*(4), 31–55. doi:10.1080/13545700903153989

Rankin, K. N. (2002). Social Capital, Microfinance, and the Politics of Development. *Feminist Economics*, *8*(1), 1–24. doi:10.1080/13545700210125167

Raskauskas, J., & Stoltz, A. D. (2007). Involvement in traditional and electronic bullying among adolescents. *Developmental Psychology*, *43*(3), 564–575. doi:10.1037/0012-1649.43.3.564 PMID:17484571

Rau, P. L. P., Gao, Q., & Ding, Y. (2008). Relationship between the level of intimacy and lurking in online social network services. *Computers in Human Behavior*, *24*(6), 2757–2770. doi:10.1016/j.chb.2008.04.001

Ray, B. D. (2013). Homeschooling Associated with Beneficial Learner and Societal Outcomes but Educators Do Not Promote It. *Peabody Journal of Education*, *88*(3), 324–341. doi:10.1080/0161956X.2013.798508

Reisigl, M., & Wodak, R. (2009). The discourse-historical approach (DHA). In R. Wodak, R. & M. Meyer (Eds.), Methods of critical discourse analysis (2nd ed., pp. 87-121). Thousand Oaks, CA: Sage.

Reuben, R. (2008). The Use of Social Media in Higher Education for Marketing and Communications: A Guide for Professionals in Higher Education.

Ricci, C. (2012). Unschooling and the willed curriculum. *Encounter: Education for Meaning and Social Justice.*

Rich, M. M. (2011). Student research in a Web 2 world: Learning to use new technology to gather primary data. *The Electronic Journal of Business Research Methods*, *9*(1), 78–86.

Ridings, C., Gefen, D., & Arinze, B. (2002). Some antecedents and effects of trust in virtual communities. *The Journal of Strategic Information Systems*, *11*(3-4), 271–295. doi:10.1016/S0963-8687(02)00021-5

Ridley, G., & Young, J. (2012). Theoretical approaches to gender and IT: Examining some Australian evidence. *Information Systems Journal*, *22*(5), 355–373. doi:10.1111/j.1365-2575.2012.00413.x

Ritchie, J. R. B., & Filiatrault, P. (1980). Family Vacation Decision-Making - A Replication and Extension. *Journal of Travel Research*, *18*(4), 3–14. doi:10.1177/004728758001800401

Robinson, M., & Robertson, S. (2014). Health information needs of men. *Health Education Journal*, *73*(2), 150–158. doi:10.1177/0017896912471039

Rochman, B. (2013, April). How Social Networks Influence Parents' Decision to Vaccinate. *Time*. Retrieved from http://healthland.time.com/2013/04/15/how-social-networks-influence-a-parents-decision-to-vaccinate/

Rodriguez, A. (2015, April 6). Retailers duke it out for Hispanic shoppers' dollars. *AdAge.com.* Retrieved from http://adage.com/article/cmo-strategy/retailers-duke-hispanic-shoppers-dollars/297902/?utm_source=daily_email&utm_medium=newsletter&utm_campaign=adage&ttl=1428896238

Rogers, E. M. (1995). *Diffusion of Innovations* (4th ed.). New York: The Free Press.

Rojas, V. (2004). The gender of Latinidad: Latinas speak about Hispanic television. *Communication Review*, *7*(2), 125–153. doi:10.1080/10714420490448688

Roodt, S., & Peier, D. (2013). Using YouTube in the Classroom for the Net Generation of Students.*Proceedings of the Informing Science and Information Technology Education Conference (Vol. 1).*

Rosen, L. D., & Maguire, P. (1990). Myths and realities of computerphobia: A meta-analysis. *Anxiety Research*, *3*(3), 175–191. doi:10.1080/08917779008248751

Roser, T., DeFillippi, R., & Samson, A. (2013). Managing your co-creation mix: Co-creation ventures in distinctive contexts. *European Business Review*, *25*(1), 20–41. doi:10.1108/09555341311287727

Ross, C., Orr, E., Sisic, M., Arseneault, J., Simmering, M., & Orr, R.R. (2009, March). R. Personality and motivations associated with Facebook use. *Computers in Human Behavior*, *25*(2), 578–586. doi:10.1016/j.chb.2008.12.024

Royal, C. (2008). Framing the Internet: A Comparison of Gendered Spaces. *Social Science Computer Review*, *26*(2), 152–169. doi:10.1177/0894439307307366

Ryan, M., Henley, N., & Soutar, G. (1998). Gender Differences in Tourism Destination Choice: Implications for Tourism Marketers. *Proceedings of theAustralia and New Zealand Marketing Conference*, Dunedin, New Zealand.

Safitri, D. (2011). Why is Indonesia so in love with the Blackberry? *BBC Indonesia Service*. Retrieved from http://news.bbc.co.uk/2/hi/programmes/direct/indonesia/9508138.stm

Sarasohn-Kah, J. (2008). *The wisdom of patients: Health care meets online social media. Report for the California Healthcare Foundation*. California: California Healthcare Foundation.

Sari, E., & Tedjasaputra, A. (2013). Engaging stakeholders through Facebook for teacher professional development in Indonesia.*Proceedings of the 25th Australian Computer-Human Interaction Conference: Augmentation, Application, Innovation, Collaboration* (pp. 201-204). ACM. doi:10.1145/2541016.2541056

Saunders, M., & Peerson, A. (2009). Australia's national men's policy: Masculinity matters. *Health Promotion Journal of Australia*, *20*(2), 92–97. PMID:19642955

Scanlon, A. (2014). It's all about the moustache. *Brandwatch blog*. Retrieved from http://www.brandwatch.com/2014/11/moustache/

Schertler, W., Schmid, B., Tjoa, A. M., & Werthner, H. (1995). *Information and communication technologies in tourism*. Wien: Springer. doi:10.1007/978-3-7091-7596-5

Schmoll, G. A. (1977). *Tourism Promotion*. London: Tourism International Press.

Schneider, B. (2012). Blogging Homelessness: Technology of the Self or Practice of Freedom? *Canadian Journal of Communication*, 2012, 405–419.

Schuster, J. (2014). *Invisible feminists? Social media and young women's political participation. In Political Science* (pp. 8–24). New Zealand: Sage.

Seock, Y. K., & Bailey, L. R. (2008). The influence of college students' shopping orientations and gender differences on online information searches and purchase behaviours. *International Journal of Consumer Studies*, *32*(2), 113–121. doi:10.1111/j.1470-6431.2007.00647.x

Shade, L. (2002). *Introduction. In Gender & Community in the Social Construction of the Internet* (pp. 1–15). New York: Peter Lang.

Shirky, C. (2003). *Power Laws, Weblogs and Inequality. In The Internet: Economics and Culture* (pp. 46–52). Media and Community.

Siemens, D. R. (2012). Connecting with prostate cancer survivors. *Canadian Urological Association Journal*, *6*(5), 349. doi:10.5489/cuaj.12268 PMID:23093623

Silogeriene, J., & Oleskeviciene, G. (2014). Confronting Social Media in Higher Education. *Social Studies*, *6*(2), 390–402. doi:10.13165/SMS-14-6-2-10

Silvey, R., & Elmhirst, R. (2003). Engendering Social Capital: Women Workers and Rural–Urban Networks in Indonesia's Crisis. *World Development*, *31*(5), 865–879. doi:10.1016/S0305-750X(03)00013-5

Simandjuntak, D. (2011). We Can't Be Seen As Cheap. *Inside Indonesia*, 2011, 104.

Simon, S. J. (2001). The impact of culture and gender on web sites: An empirical study. *The Data Base for Advances in Information Systems*, *32*(1), 18–37. doi:10.1145/506740.506744

Sirakaya, E., & Woodside, A. G. (2005). Building and testing theories of decision making by travellers. *Tourism Management*, *26*(6), 815–832. doi:10.1016/j.tourman.2004.05.004

Skolnick, A., Bascom, K., & Wilson, D. (2013). Gender role expectations of disgust: Men are low and women are high. *Sex Roles*, *69*(1-2), 72–88. doi:10.1007/s11199-013-0279-y

Social media in education. (2012, 05). Digital Learning, Retrieved from http://search.proquest.com/docview/1018538253?accountid=13380

Spaulding, T. (2010). How can virtual communities create value for business? *Electronic Commerce Research and Applications*, *9*(1), 38–49. doi:10.1016/j.elerap.2009.07.004

Spender, D. (1995). *Nattering on the Net: Women, Power and Cyberspace*. North Melbourne, Vic: Spinifex.

Statista. (2014). *Number of monthly active Facebook users worldwide from 3rd quarter 2008 to 3rd quarter 2014 (in millions)*. Retrieved 24 November 2014, from http://www.statista.com/statistics/264810/number-of-monthly-active-facebook-users-worldwide/

Statistics Indonesia. (2010). Results of the 2010 Population Census. from www.sp2010.bps.go.id

Statistics Indonesia. (2011b). Results of the 2010 Population Census. Sensus Penduduk 2010: Penduduk Berumur 5 Tahun Keatas Menurut Kelompok Umur dan Kemampuan Berbahasa Indonesia [Population Census 2010: Population aged 5 years and over by age groups and Indonesian Language Ability]. Retrieved from www.sp2010.bps.go.id

Stewart, J. (2004). Gender as a Factor in the Uptake and Use of ICTs on Family Farms in Southern Queensland Australia. *Gender, Technology and Development*, *8*(1), 97–117. doi:10.1177/097185240400800106

Stoner, M. (2012) *Social media and advancement: A report on data from 2010 – 2012*. Retrieved from http://www.mstoner.com/blog/,arketing-and-branding/social-media-and-advancement-a-report-on-data-from-2010-2012/

Subrahmanyam, K., & Greenfield, P. (2008). Online Communication and Adolescent Relationships. *The Future of Children*, *18*(1), 119–146. doi:10.1353/foc.0.0006 PMID:21338008

Sullivan, S. G., Komadina, N., Grant, K., Jelley, L., Papadakis, G., & Kelly, H. (2014). Influenza vaccine effectiveness during the 2012 influenza season in Victoria, Australia: Influences of waning immunity and vaccine match. *Journal of Medical Virology*, *86*(6), 1017–1025. doi:10.1002/jmv.23847 PMID:24395730

Sundar, S. S., & Marathe, S. S. (2010). Personalization versus customization: The importance of agency, privacy, and power usage. *Human Communication Research*, *36*(3), 298–322. doi:10.1111/j.1468-2958.2010.01377.x

Sutanonpaiboon, J., & Abuhamdieh, A. (2008). Factors influencing trust in online customer-to-customer (C2C) transactions. *Journal of Internet Commerce*, *7*(2), 203–219. doi:10.1080/15332860802067706

Sutten, M. L. (2009). *The Rising Importance of Women in Terrorism and the Need to Reform Counterterrorism Strategy*. Army Command and General Staff Coll Fort Leavenworth Ks School of Advanced Military Studies.

Taksdal, S. E., Mak, D. B., Joyce, S., Tomlin, S., Carcione, D., Armstrong, P. K., & Effler, P. V. (2013). Predictors of uptake of influenza vaccination – a survey of pregnant women in Western Australia. *Australian Family Physician*, *42*(8), 582–586. PMID:23971070

Tanrıkulu, T., Kınay, H., & Tolga Arıcak, O. (2015). Sensibility development program against cyberbullying. *New Media & Society*, *17*(5), 708–719.

Tan, W.-K., & Chen, T.-H. (2012). The usage of online tourist information sources in tourist information search: An exploratory study. *Service Industries Journal*, *32*(3), 451–476. doi:10.1080/02642069.2010.529130

Teaching Staff (Number). (2013). *Australian Bureau of Statistics*. Retrieved from http://www.abs.gov.au/ausstats/abs@.nsf/Lookup /4221.0main+features502011

Templeton, G. F., Luo, X. R., Giberson, T. R., & Campbell, N. (2012). Leader personal influences on membership decisions in moderated online social networking groups. *Decision Support Systems, 54*, 655–664. doi:10.1016/j.dss.2012.08.011

Thanuskodi, S. (2013). Gender Differences in Internet Usage among College Students: A Comparative Study. *Library Philosophy and Practice* (e-journal).

The Australian curriculum: English v7.0 general capabilities. (2014). Australian Curriculum and Assessment Reporting Authority (ACARA). Retrieved from http://www.australiancurriculum.edu.au/GeneralCapabilities/Overview/General-capabilities-in-the-Australian-Curriculum

The Queensland Studies Authority (QSA). (2012). *Business communication and technologies senior syllabus. The State of Queensland.* QSA.

Thermomix. (2015). *History of Thermomix in Australia.* Retrieved 19 February 2015 from www.thermomix.com.au

Thermomix: From a Polish Kitchen to a thriving business. (2013). *Business View.* Retrieved from http://business.nab.com.au

Thorat, S. B., Kishor, S. B., & Meghe, B. (2013). Social Media Marketing Mix: Applicability Review for Marketing in Education. *IPEDR, 50*(4), 16–20.

Thornton, P. R., Shaw, G., & Williams, A. M. (1997). Tourist group holiday decision-making and behaviour: The influence of children. *Tourism Management, 18*(5), 287–297. doi:10.1016/S0261-5177(97)00017-4

Titscher, S., Meyer, M., Wodak, R., & Vetter, E. (2000). *Methods of Text and Discourse Analysis.* Thousand Oaks, CA: Sage.

To, E., & Ho, K. (2014). Value co-creation and purchase intention in social network sites: The role of electronic Word-of-Mouth and trust – A theoretical analysis. *Computers in Human Behavior, 31*, 182–189.

Trau, R. N. C., Härtel, C. E. J., & Härtel, G. F. (2012). Reaching and hearing the invisible: Organizational research on invisible stigmatized groups via web surveys. *British Journal of Management.* doi:10.1111/j.1467-8551.2012.00826.x

Trauth, E. M., Nielsen, S., & von Hellens, L. (2000). Explaining the IT Gender Gap: Australian Stories. *Proceedings of the 11th Australasian Conference on Information Systems (ACIS)*, Brisbane Qld.

Trauth, E.M. (2006). *Theorising Gender and Information Technology Research. In*E. Trauth (Ed.), *Encyclopedia of Gender and Information Technology* Hershey, PA, USA: Idea Group Inc. doi:10.4018/978-1-59140-815-4

Tremayne, M. (Ed.), (2012). *Blogging, citizenship, and the future of media.* Routledge.

Triandis, H. C., Bontempo, R., Betancourt, H., Bond, M., Leung, K., Brenes, A., & Montmollin, G. et al. (1986). The measurement of the etic aspects of individualism and collectivism across cultures. *Australian Journal of Psychology, 38*(3), 257–267. doi:10.1080/00049538608259013

Tsai, H., & Pai, P. (2013). Explaining members' proactive participation in virtual communities. *International Journal of Human-Computer Studies, 71*(4), 475–491. doi:10.1016/j.ijhcs.2012.12.002

Tsai, H., & Pai, P. (2014). Why do newcomers participate in virtual communities? An integration of self-determination and relationship management theories. *Decision Support Systems, 57*, 178–187. doi:10.1016/j.dss.2013.09.001

Turkle, S. (1984). *The Second Self: Computers and the Human Spirit.* New York: Simon and Schuster.

Tynes, B. M. (2007). Internet safety gone wild? Sacrificing the educational and psychosocial benefits of online social environments. *Journal of Adolescent Research, 22*(6), 575–584. doi:10.1177/0743558407303979

Um, S., & Crompton, J. L. (1990). Attitude Determinants in Tourism Destination Choice. *Annals of Tourism Research, 17*(3), 432–448. doi:10.1016/0160-7383(90)90008-F

Utomo, A. (2012). Women as secondary earners: Gendered preferences on marriage and employment of university students in modern Indonesia. *Asian Population Studies, 8*(1), 65–85. doi:10.1080/17441730.2012.646841

Utomo, A., Reimondos, A., Utomo, I., McDonald, P., & Hull, T. H. (2013). Digital inequalities and young adults in Greater Jakarta: A socio-demographic perspective. *International Journal of Indonesian Studies, 1*(1).

Valenzuela, S., Park, N., & Kee, K. F. (2009). Is There Social Capital in a Social Network Site?: Facebook Use and College Students' Life Satisfaction, Trust, and Participation. *Journal of Computer-Mediated Communication, 14*(4), 875–901. doi:10.1111/j.1083-6101.2009.01474.x

Valkonen, J., & Hänninen, V. (2013). Narratives of masculinity and depression. *Men and Masculinities, 16*(2), 160–180. doi:10.1177/1097184X12464377

Valois, C. (2014). Virtual access: the Ugandan 'anti-gay' movement, lesbian, gay, bisexual and transgender blogging and the public sphere. *Journal of East African Studies.* Doi:10.1080/17531055.2014.987508

van der Heijden, H. (2003). Factors influencing the usage of websites: The case of a generic portal in the Netherlands. *Information & Management, 40*(6), 541–549. doi:10.1016/S0378-7206(02)00079-4

van Dijk, T. A. (2001). Multidisciplinary CDA: A plea for diversity. In R. Wodak, & M. Meyer (Eds.), Methods of critical discourse analysis (pp. 95-120). London, UK: Sage. doi:10.4135/9780857028020.d7

Van Doorn, J., Lemon, K. N., Mittal, V., Nass, S., Pick, D., Pirner, P., & Verhoef, P. C. (2010). Customer engagement behavior: Theoretical foundations and research directions. *Journal of Service Research, 13*(3), 253–266. doi:10.1177/1094670510375599

van Raaij, W. F. (1985). *The Psychological Foundation of Economics: The History of Consumer Theory* (Special Volume).

van Raaij, W. F. (1986). Consumer Research On Tourism - Mental and Behavioral Constructs. *Annals of Tourism Research, 13*(1), 1–9. doi:10.1016/0160-7383(86)90054-X

van Raaij, W. F., & Francken, D. A. (1984). Vacation Decisions, Activities, And Satisfactions. *Annals of Tourism Research, 11*(1), 101–112. doi:10.1016/0160-7383(84)90098-7

Vance, K., Howe, W., & Dellavalle, R. P. (2009, April). Social internet sites as a source of public health information. *Dermatologic Clinics, 27*(2), 133–136. doi:10.1016/j.det.2008.11.010 PMID:19254656

Vannoy, S. A., & Palvia, P. (2010, June). The social influence model of technology adoption. *Communications of the ACM, 53*(6), 149–153. doi:10.1145/1743546.1743585

Vargo, S., & Lusch, R. (2004). Evolving to a new Dominant Logic for Marketing. *Journal of Marketing, 68*(1), 1–17. doi:10.1509/jmkg.68.1.1.24036

Vargo, S., & Lusch, R. (2006). Service-Dominant Logic: What It Is, What It Is Not, What It Might Be. In R. F. Lusch & S. L. Vargo (Eds.), *The Service-Dominant Logic of Marketing: Dialog, Debate, and Directions.* Armonk: M.E. Sharpe.

Vargo, S., & Lusch, R. (2008). Service-Dominant Logic: Continuing the Evolution. *Journal of the Academy of Marketing Science, 36*(1), 1–10. doi:10.1007/s11747-007-0069-6

Vaswani, K. (2012). Indonesia's love affair with social media. *BBC News Asia.* Retrieved from http://www.bbc.co.uk/news/world-asia-17054056

Vázquez, R., Álvarez, L. I., & Santos, M. L. (2002). Market orientation and social services in private non-profit organisations. *European Journal of Marketing*, *36*(9/10), 1022–1046. doi:10.1108/03090560210437316

Venkatesh, V., & Davis, F. D. (2000). A theoretical extension of the technology acceptance model: Four longitudinal field studies. *Management Science*, *46*(2), 186–204.

Venkatesh, V., & Morris, M. G. (2000). Why don't men ever stop to ask for directions? Gender, social influence and their role in technology acceptance and usage behaviour. *MIS Quarterly*, *24*(1), 115–135. doi:10.2307/3250981

Verba, S. et al.. (1987). *The Historical Context of Equality. In Elites and the Idea of Equality: A Comparison of Japan, Sweden and the United States* (pp. 20–58). United States: Harvard College.

Verbick, T. (2001). *Women.* Technology and Gender Bias, Consortium for Computing in Small Colleges.

Verhoef, P. C., Reinartz, W. J., & Krafft, M. (2010). Customer engagement as a new perspective in customer management. *Journal of Service Research*, *13*(3), 247–252. doi:10.1177/1094670510375461

Verkasalo, H., López-Nicolás, C., Molina-Castillo, F. J., & Bouwman, H. (2010). Analysis of users and non-users of smartphone applications. *Telematics and Informatics*, *27*(3), 242–255. doi:10.1016/j.tele.2009.11.001

Villarreal, R., & Peterson, R. A. (2009, Fall). The concept of marketing implications of Hispanicness. *Journal of Marketing Theory and Practice*, *17*(4), 303–316. doi:10.2753/MTP1069-6679170401

Villarrel, R. (2014). Branding implications of the relationship between Hispanic familism and brand related behaviors: A latent variable model approach. *Academy of Marketing Studies Journal*, *18*(2), 103–119.

Vogt, C. A., & Fesenmaier, D. R. (1998). Expanding the functional information search model. *Annals of Tourism Research*, *25*(3), 551–578. doi:10.1016/S0160-7383(98)00010-3

von-Knop, K. (2007). Countering Web-based Islamist Narratives: Conceptualizing an Information War and a Counter-propaganda Campaign. In B. Ganor, K. von-Knop, & C. A. M. Duarte (Eds.), *Hypermedia seduction for terrorist recruiting* (pp. 169–187). Amsterdam: IOS Press.

Wahab, S., Crampon, L. J., & Rothfield, L. M. (1976). *Tourism Marketing.* London: Tourism International Press.

Wahl, S. T., McBride, M. C., & Schrodt, P. (2005). Becoming "point and click" parents: A case study of communication and online adoption. *Journal of Family Communication*, *5*(4), 279–294. doi:10.1207/s15327698jfc0504_3

Wajcman, J. (1991). *Feminism Confronts Technology.* Cambridge, UK: Polity Press.

Wang, A. (2005). The effects of expert and consumer endorsements on audience response. *Journal of Advertising Research*, *45*(4), 402–412. doi:10.1017/S0021849905050452

Warne, L., Bandias, S., & Fuller, D. (2011). The Employment Experiences of Women in the Australian Information Communication Technology Industry. *Journal of Economic and Social Policy*, 14(1-2).

Wasko, M. M., & Faraj, S. (2005). Why Should I Share? Examining Social Capital and Knowledge Contribution in Electronic Networks of Practice. *Management Information Systems Quarterly*, *29*(1), 35–57. doi:10.2307/25148667

Wassersug, R., Oliffe, J., & Han, C. (2014). On manhood and Movember… or why the moustache works. *Global Health Promotion and Education.* doi:10.1177/1757975914536913 PMID:25024274

Webster, J. (1993). Women's skills and word processors: Gender issues in the development of the automated office. In B. Probert & B. W. Wilson (Eds.), *Pink Collar Blues: Work, Gender and Technology* (pp. 41–59). Melbourne, Vic: Melbourne University Press.

Webster, S. (2012). Consumer Kids and Tourists - Creatively Marketing a City to Young Tourists. In H. Schanzel, I. Yeoman, & E. Backer (Eds.), *Family Tourism: Multidisciplinary Perspectives* (pp. 143–155). Bristol, UK: Channel View Publications.

Weimann, G. (2008). The Psychology of Mass-Mediated Terrorism. *The American Behavioral Scientist*, *52*(1), 69–86. doi:10.1177/0002764208321342

Weimann, G. (2010). Terror on Facebook, Twitter, and YouTube. *The Brown Journal of World Affairs*, *16*(2), 45–54.

Weiser, E.B. (2000). Gender Differences in Internet Use Patterns and Internet Application Preferences: A Two-Sample Comparison. *Cyberpsychology & Behavior*, *3*(2), 167–178. doi:10.1089/109493100316012

Welbourne, J., Blanchard, A., & Wadsworth, M. (2013). Motivations in virtual health communities and their relationship to community, connectedness and stress. *Computers in Human Behavior*, *29*(1), 129–139. doi:10.1016/j.chb.2012.07.024

Wellman, B., & Gulia, M. (1999). *Net surfers don't ride alone: Virtual communities as communities. In*P. Kollock, & M. Smith (Eds.), *Communities and Cyberspace.* Routledge New York.

Wellman, B., & Gulia, M. (1999). Net-surfers don't ride alone: virtual communities as communities. In B. Wellman (Ed.), *Networks in the global village*. Boulder: Westview Press.

Werthner, H., & Klein, S. (1999). *Information technology and tourism – A challenging relationship*. Wien: Springer. doi:10.1007/978-3-7091-6363-4

Wheatley, K. (2009). Unschooling: An oasis for development and democracy. *Encounter (Indianapolis)*, *22*(2), 27.

Wheeler, D. (2001). New Technologies, Old Culture: A Look at Women, Gender. *Culture, technology, communication: Towards an intercultural global village* (pp. 187-212).

Wilson, G. (2012, February 9). Al-Qaeda bid for Brit girl bombers. *The Sun*. Retrieved from http://www.thesun.co.uk/sol/homepage/news/politics/4110182/Al-Qaeda-bid-for-Brit-girl-bombers.html

Wodak, R. (2001). The discourse historical approach. In R. Wodak & M. Meyer (Eds.), *Methods of critical discourse analysis* (pp. 63–94). Thousand Oaks, CA: Sage.

Wodak, R. (2004). Critical discourse analysis. In C. Searle, G. Gobo, J. Gubrium, & D. Silverman (Eds.), *Qualitative research practice* (pp. 186–213). London, UK: Sage. doi:10.4135/9781848608191.d17

Woodside, A. G., & Lysonski, S. (1989). A General Model of Traveler Destination Choice. *Journal of Travel Research*, *27*(4), 8–14. doi:10.1177/004728758902700402

Wörsching, M. (2007). Race to the top: Masculinity, sport, and the nature in German magazine advertising. *Men and Masculinities*, *10*(2), 197–221. doi:10.1177/1097184X05284225

Wu, L., Fan, A., & Mattila, A. (2015). Wearable technology in service delivery processes: The gender-moderated technology objectification effect. *International Journal of Hospitality Management*, *51*, 1–7. doi:10.1016/j.ijhm.2015.08.010

Xianga, Z., Magnini, V. P., & Fesenmaier, D. R. (2015). Information technology and consumer behavior in travel and tourism: Insights from travel planning using the internet. *Journal of Retailing and Consumer Services*, *22*, 244–249. doi:10.1016/j.jretconser.2014.08.005

Xiang, Z., & Gretzel, U. (2010). Role of social media in online travel information search. *Tourism Management*, *31*(2), 179–188. doi:10.1016/j.tourman.2009.02.016

Xie, H., Bao, J., & Morais, D. B. (2006).Exploring Gender Differences in Information Search Among Domestic Visitors to Yellow Mountain and Guilin, PRC. *Proceedings of the 2006 Northeastern Recreation Research Symposium* (pp. 120-125).

Yaeger-Dror, M. (1998). Factors influencing the contrast between men's and women's speech. *Women & Language*, *21*(1), 40.

Yang, K. C. C. (2005). Exploring factors affecting the adoption of M-commerce in Singapore. *Telematics and Informatics*, *22*(3), 257–277. doi:10.1016/j.tele.2004.11.003

Yin, R. K. (2014). *Case study research: Design and methods*. Thousand Oaks, CA: Sage.

Zach, F., Gretzel, U., & Xiang, Z. (2010). Innovation in the Web Marketing Programs of American Convention and Visitor Bureaus. *Information Technology & Tourism*, 12(1), 47-63. doi:10.3727/109830510X12747489979628

Zalatan, A. (1998). "Wives" involvement in tourism decision processes. *Annals of Tourism Research*, *25*(4), 890–903. doi:10.1016/S0160-7383(98)00038-3

Zehrer, A., & Grabmuller, A. (2012). Social media marketing in tourism education: Insights into the development and value of a social network site for a higher education institution in tourism. *Journal of Vacation Marketing*, *18*(3), 221–228. doi:10.1177/1356766712449368

Zeng, F., Huang, L., & Dou, W. (2009). Social factors in user perceptions and responses to advertising in online social networking communities. *Journal of Interactive Advertising*, *10*(1), 1–13. doi:10.1080/15252019.2009.10722159

Zettelmeyer, F., Morton, F. S., & Silva-Risso, J. (2006). How the internet lowers prices: Evidence from matched survey and automobile transaction data. *JMR, Journal of Marketing Research*, *43*(2), 168–181. doi:10.1509/jmkr.43.2.168

Zhang, M., & Liu, B. (2015). Technology and gender: A case study on "iron girls" in China (1950s – 1970s). *Technology in Society*, *43*, 86–94. doi:10.1016/j.techsoc.2015.04.005

Zhao, D., & Rosson, M.B. (2009, May). How and why people Twitter: the role that micro-blogging plays in informal communication at work.*Proceedings of the ACM 2009 International Conference on Supporting Group Work* (pp. 243–252). doi:10.1145/1531674.1531710

Zhao, L., Lu, Y., Wang, B., Chau, P., & Zhang, L. (2012). Cultivating the sense of belonging and motivating user participation in virtual communities: A social capital perspective. *International Journal of Information Management*, *32*(6), 574–588. doi:10.1016/j.ijinfomgt.2012.02.006

Zha, X., Zhang, J., Yan, Y., & Xiao, Z. (Forthcoming). Does affinity matter? Slow effects of e-quality on information seeking in virtual communities. *Library and Information Systems Research, 2015*.

Zheng, K., Akhilesh, B., Daponte, B., & Engberg, J. (2006). In E. Trauth (Ed.), *Gender Differences in Internet Usage and Task Preferences. In*E. Trauth (Ed.), *Encyclopedia of Gender and Information Technology* (pp. 557–563). Hershey, PA, USA: Idea Group Inc. doi:10.4018/978-1-59140-815-4.ch086

About the Contributors

Rebecca English is a Lecturer in Education at QUT. Her interests include education, family choices and the way that women make choices about their lives and the lives of their families.

Raechel Johns is an Associate Professor in Marketing and the Head of the School of Management. Her research interests relate to services marketing, including co-creation of value, transformative service and the way technology can be utilised to facilitate and sometimes negatively impact on relationships and customer value.

* * *

Amelia Coleman graduated from the Queensland University of Technology in Australia in 2015 with a Bachelor's degree in Media and Communications and Public Relations. In recent years she has developed knowledge of the cultural impact of all forms of traditional and new media through a mix of media and cultural studies. She has become interested in the theory and practice of distribution of personal and creative content via social media technologies and the audience that has allowed social media content to proliferate. She is currently working on a Masters of Education (Research) at the Queensland University of Technology exploring how marketing materials influence the school choice processes of minority parents. Her chapter "Blogging Their Way Out of Disadvantage: Women, Identity and Agency in the Blogosphere" marries her research interests by offering a review of the recent literature exploring the ways that minority groups are using blogs to tell their story to a wide audience.

Naomi F. Dale is an Assistant Professor of Management and Associate Dean Academic at the University of Canberra. Her research is concerned with Learning and Engagement in Tourism. This incorporates research in the specific areas of educational tourism, policy impacts of curriculum, and visitor research at cultural institutions and national capital attractions. It also captures emerging research interests in the application of social media, and strategies for engagement through e-platforms (in teaching, tourism and events). Other key areas are around consumer behaviour and marketing. She was the recipient of an Australian Post Graduate Award scholarship and recently completed her PhD investigating destination choice by school excursion groups in Australia. Naomi became an Assistant Professor of Management at UC in 2013. She has been an Executive member of the National Capital Attractions Association since 2012.

Kristyn A. Jackson is a member of the faculty of Business, Law and Government, University of Canberra.

Anita Jetnikoff is a Senior lecturer in English Curriculum, Language and Literature at Queensland University of Technology. She is a passionate educator, a poet and is interested in the areas of creative pedagogy and teaching, digital media and literature and teacher professional identity. Anita is a documentary film maker and has taught and written about video production as well as produced many student video productions and vodcasts. Anita's research and publication interests include creative learning and creative pedagogies, adolescent and youth culture identity and cross cultural and gender representations in the media and in literature, along with deploying digital media in the curriculum, documentary video production and digital storytelling and vodcasting. Recent projects include researching creative teaching and learning and what teachers want from professional development, as well as media and literature approaches relevant to the new Australian curriculum: English.

Yowei Kang (Ph.D. in Rhetoric and Composition Studies, UT-El Paso) studied the impacts of emerging media platforms on rhetorical and composition theories. His main research interests focus on digital games and experiential rhetoric.

Melissa Kelly is an English and Business Technologies teacher at Kelvin Grove State College, Queensland. She completed a dissertation into pre-service English teachers' perceptions of their preparedness to mentor positive digital conduct as part of her Bachelor of Education at Queensland University of Technology. Melissa worked in print and digital media for nearly two decades.

Dale MacKrell is an Assistant Professor in Information Systems at the University of Canberra in Australia. Her research interests include business intelligence systems and gender relations, in particular, the adoption and use of farm management systems in rural and community organisations. More recent work is a student work-integrated learning project for a not-for-profit organisation operating in the homelessness sector using action design research. Dale has published in Information Systems Journal, Decision Support Systems journal and the Australasian Journal of Information Systems as well as numerous Australian and international conferences.

Valeria Noguti is a Lecturer at the University of Technology Sydney. She received her PhD in Decision Sciences from INSEAD France in 2006. Valeria's publications focus on social media, advertising, consumer psychology, and consumer behaviour. Prior to joining the PhD program at INSEAD, Valeria has worked in São Paulo for General Electric Plastics South America, Editora Abril (magazine publisher), and Banco Frances e Brasileiro (subsidiary of Credit Lyonnais in Brazil).

Matthew Reeves received his Bachelors in Education (Honours) from Queensland University and Technology (QUT) in 2013. Since then, he has worked in both Secondary and Tertiary Education fields. Matthew writes widely on issues relating to the changes in Education and the notion of choice.

Sonika Singh is a Lecturer at the University of Technology Sydney. She received her PhD in Management Science from the University of Texas at Dallas in 2012. Her research interests are consumer information search and choice, Internet marketing and retail promotions.

Robyn Torok is completing her second PhD in online discourses of radicalisation from Edith Cowan University, Australia. Her research interests include online radicalisation, security, eschatological discourses and social media analysis.

Ariane J. Utomo is a Research Fellow at the Crawford School of Public Policy of the Australian National University. Working in the field of social demography, Ariane's overarching research interest is to examine the relationship between four dimensions of social change in contemporary Indonesia: globalisation, economic development, demographic transition, and democratisation following the political reforms of 1998. Her research and teaching activities are centred on how social change is reflected in attitudes to gender roles, school to work transition, women's employment, changing marriage patterns, and the nature of inequalities and social stratification in Indonesia.

David S. Waller is a Senior Lecturer at the University of Technology Sydney. He has worked in the banking and film industries, and has taught at a number of universities, including University of Newcastle, University of New South Wales and Charles Sturt University-Riverina. David has published over 60 refereed journal articles, including Journal of Advertising; Journal of Advertising Research; European Journal of Marketing, International Journal of Advertising; and Journal of Marketing Communications.

Kenneth C. C. Yang is a Professor at the Department of Communication. His research focuses on new media and advertising, consumer behavior in East Asia, impacts of new media in Asia.

Index